Interface Collection

School Provision for Ethnic Minorities:
The Gypsy Paradigm

The Interface Collection, coordinated and developed by the Gypsy Research Centre at the Université René Descartes, Paris, is published with the support of the European Commission.

Some Collection titles receive Council of Europe support for distribution in Central and Eastern Europe.

The views expressed in this work are the author's, and do not necessarily reflect those of the publisher nor of the Gypsy Research Centre or its research groups (historians, linguists, education specialists and so on).

Original title: *School Provision for Gypsy and Traveller Children*

Cover: Catherine Liégeois
DTP: La 13ème Heure
Editorial assistant: Astrid Thorn Hillig

© Commission of the European Communities, 1987

© 1998 for the new edition

Centre de recherches tsiganes (Gypsy Research Centre) and
University of Hertfordshire Press
University of Hertfordshire
College Lane
Hatfield
Hertfordshire
AL10 9AB - UK

Tel. +44 1707 284654
Fax. +44 1707 284666

ISBN: 0 900458 88 7
Published 1998
Printed by Antony Rowe Ltd, Chippenham, Wiltshire

Jean-Pierre Liégeois

School Provision for Ethnic Minorities: The Gypsy Paradigm

Preface by Domenico Lenarduzzi
Afterword by Arthur Ivatts

Translated from the French by Sinéad ní Shuinéar

Gypsy Research Centre
University of Hertfordshire Press

Jean-Pierre Liégeois

Jean-Pierre Liégeois teaches at the Department of Social Sciences at the Université René Descartes (Paris) and is Director of the Gypsy Research Centre based at the same university. Since the early 1980s he has been working in close collaboration with the European Commission and the Council of Europe on issues of relevance to the Gypsy and Traveller communities.

He is the author of numerous books and articles on these communities. These works have, since their first appearance in 1967, made a major contribution to opening up new perspectives of understanding through their critical examination of policy developments, their analysis of the evolution of Gypsy and Traveller organisations, and by outlining practical proposals for improving a difficult situation.

Contents

Preface, by Domenico Lenarduzzi 9

The Gypsy Paradigm 13
Foreword to the original 'Synthesis Report'

    • State of play 23
    • The study 25

History, politics and culture

    • History 31
            Policies and politics 36
            Exclusion 36
            Containment 38
            Assimilation 40
            Indecision 42
            Images of the Gypsy 45

    • The cultural sphere 48
            A lifestyle 48
            Travelling 52
            Accommodation 56
            Health 57
            Economic activities 60
            Education 64

    • The current situation 68

School provision

    • General data 73
            The state of literacy 73
            The history of school provision 76
            Integration by handicap 83
            Compulsory schooling 88
            Enrolment 92
            Attendance 94
            Different groups 99
            Reception in school 102

- Structures ... 111
    - Mobile classes ... 114
    - On-the-spot provision ... 118
    - Other specialised provision ... 124
    - "Ordinary" classes ... 126
    - Supplementary provision ... 129
    - Preschooling ... 133
    - Secondary schooling ... 135
    - What structures? ... 139

- Teachers ... 147
    - The choice ... 147
    - Administration ... 148
    - Stability ... 150
    - Initial training ... 153
    - In-service training ... 158
    - Information ... 161
    - Liaison ... 165
    - Gypsy teachers ... 172

- Pedagogy ... 175
    - An alien institution ... 175
    - Gypsy education ... 179
    - Two pedagogies ... 183
    - Behaviour in conflict ... 186
    - Towards functional schooling ... 189
    - Convergence? ... 191
    - Teaching content ... 194
    - Gypsy experience at school ... 195
    - Gypsy language in school ... 199
    - The art and method of teaching ... 208
    - Teaching materials ... 211
    - Teamwork ... 214
    - Contact ... 215
    - Towards interculturalism ... 217
    - Gypsy children in school ... 225

- Local authorities ... 230

- Other bodies ... 235

- Vocational training ... 240

- Some complementary considerations ... 248

Summary and recommendations ... 253

Afterword, by Arthur Ivatts ... 279

Bibliography 291

Glossary 301

Annexe 309
The Resolution adopted in May 1989 by the European Council
and the Ministers of Education

Translator's Note

The Danish, Dutch, Greek, Irish and United Kingdom reports for this research were written in English. Where they are quoted in the text, I have simply reproduced them as they appear in the original (French) synthesis report. Extracts from other works – by Gustafsson, Ivatts et al – quoted in English in the original synthesis report, are also reproduced as they appear there. Quotations in French have been translated by me, and page numbers, where given, refer to the French version, but where English versions of these works exist (whether as originals or translations) the bibliography lists them under their English titles and publishing data, preceded by an asterisk. The excerpts from Clark's *Dark Ghetto* and Rosenthal and Jacobson's *Pygmalion in the Classroom* (which appeared in French translation in the original report) have been reproduced directly from their original English sources.

I have retained the author's original usage of **education** and **schooling/school provision** (see Glossary). Their awkwardness is deliberate: as the text makes abundantly clear, his purpose is to jolt the reader out of the cosy (and ethnocentric) assumption that the two are synonymous. Likewise, the "jargon" term, **pedagogy**, is retained in order to draw a clear distinction between the *theory* and *practice* of teaching. The above are described, variously, as inter-, multi-, or pluricultural; again, the author's usages have been retained.

Like Acton/Kenrick in their UK report for this synthesis, I "adhere to the convention of using 'Gypsy' and 'Traveller' indifferently", except in specific historic references; sometimes singly (to avoid stylistic clutter), sometimes in tamdem (to stress the universality of a point). I am acutely aware that this English-language version will be used in countries as dissimilar as Ireland (with its virtually 100% "Traveller" population) and Greece (virtually one hundred percent "Gypsy"). The terminology, as used, will not accurately reflect *any* state's actual situation. This is not, however, to be used as a premise for assuming that text referring to the "wrong" category is not equally applicable to the other.

This report was originally published a decade ago. In the interim we have had ample opportunity to witness the accuracy of the author's observations re. official redefinitions (and concomitant treatment) of Gypsies and Travellers as mere social, rather than bona fide ethnic, categories. Although he explains in detail (see "History") why he has chosen these two particular terms, and spells out precisely what he means by them, there is resistance to accepting that the points he, and the myriad sources he quotes, makes, apply just as much to the flesh and blood people the Gadjo reader encounters, as to some mythical, exotic, "genuine" beings somewhere far away – or recently arrived from such places. In particular: "Traveller" is an ethnonym. It applies to persons born into groups calling themselves by (variations on) this name, whether sedentary or nomadic; it does not apply to Gadjé living a nomadic lifestyle, whether in peripatetic professions such as fairground operators and bargees, or "New Age" recruits to the road. "Traveller" does not means "one who travels"; it does mean "non-Gadjo of (predominantly) indigenous European origin".

Names specific to particular Gypsy/Traveller groups – Manouches, Sinti, Jenische etc. – are reproduced without italics or further explanation.

Rather than complicate the text with tedious "he or she", "his or her" etc. belabouring of the non-gender-specific nature of various points, I have followed the convention of pre-political-correctness days, of using the masculine third person singular as neutral.

Foreign language terms such as names of organisations, titles of publications and the like, have been reproduced in accordance with English conventions regarding capitalisation. They are italicised and, where appropriate, translated in brackets when they first appear.

My profoundest gratitude to Thomas Acton, Donald Kenrick and Patricia McCarthy, all of whom provided invaluable aid, support and direct input to the translation first time round, and thanks again to Professor Acton for his continued cooperation in ironing out the bugs for this second printing. Special thanks to Barry Crowe, head of the English translation division at the Council of Europe, for locating English language data for the bibliography.

Preface

Domenico Lenarduzzi
Director
DG XXII - Education, Training and Youth
European Commission

In 1984 the European Parliament adopted two Resolutions drawing attention to the difficult living conditions of the Gypsy communities. The first of these was the Resolution of 16 March 1984, *On Education for Children whose Parents Have No Fixed Abode*, in which the Parliament urged the European Commission to cooperate with the Member States to develop measures which would ensure that these children receive an appropriate education. The second, on 24 May 1984, focused on the situation of Gypsies in the European Community. In it, the Parliament recommended that the governments of the Member States coordinate their approach and called on the Commission to draw up programmes to be subsidised by Community funds in order to improve the Gypsies' situation without destroying their separate identity.

Grasping the significance of the questions raised by Parliament, the Commission immediately decided to undertake a survey of the current situation in relation to school provision. The Gypsy Research Centre at the Université René Descartes, Paris, was engaged to carry out intensive study over 1984-85. This investigation, involving a coordinated network of experts throughout the states of the Community, entailed synthesising existing work, consulting families, Gypsy organisations and teachers, analysing hundreds of documents and projects. At the outset, Gypsy representatives and experts were invited by the Commission to define what the study should cover and how it should be carried out; afterwards, they met again to discuss their conclusions and recommendations.

In 1986 the Commission decided to disseminate the resulting synthesis report compiled by Jean-Pierre Liégeois. The study itself, testimony from various sources, reflections and analysis all reveal that the situation is grave indeed. In the wake of centuries of policies of negation in various forms and dreadful conditions, rejection remains the dominant tone in relations between Gypsies and their environment. This is reflected in the conditions surrounding school provision: Gypsy children get little schooling and what they get is often poor, yet the future of the Gypsy communities depends to a large degree on the tools with which the schools provide their children.

In 1987, on the basis of this report, the Commission consulted the Ministers of Education and Gypsy experts to formulate concrete recommendations for the Member States and the institutions of the European Community, and to evolve guidelines for an education policy respectful of the Gypsy communities' culture and lifestyle. In 1988, while the Gypsy Research Centre extended the study to cover new Member States Spain and Portugal, the document was referred to the Education Committee comprising senior officials of the Community's various national Ministries of Education, which discussed it at many of its meetings. The Committee devoted in-depth, positive consideration to the report's conclusions. In view of the Community-wide nature of the actions required, a motion for a Resolution was submitted to the Council and the Ministers of Education. Finally, on 22 May 1989, the Council and the Ministers adopted the *Resolution on School Provision for Gypsy and Traveller Children*. As so often noted since, this is indeed an historic text from every point of view, emphasising in its opening lines that Gypsies' and Travellers' language and culture have been part of the Community's cultural and linguistic heritage for over 500 years. It sets out proposals for a series of actions to be carried out by the Member States with a view to improving the conditions of school provision for Gypsy children, and asks the Commission to undertake the necessary promotion, coordination, documentation and assessment. Beginning in 1990 and gaining ground throughout 1991, a whole range of activities was developed, among them pilot projects (involving Gypsy teaching assistants, distance learning, teaching materials, secondary schooling, transition from school to working life), publications, databases, work in history and linguistics, and an information newsletter.

This book is the synthesis report mentioned above. It is important to introduce it with a brief reminder of the history of European Commission action on education issues in relation to the Gypsy communities. This enables us to see the book in context, highlighting the impact it has exerted and continues to exert, and revealing exactly how action carried out by European institutions, took shape.

• This document was the starting point of the European Commission's global, structural (as opposed to piecemeal, short-term) interest in issues of relevance to the Gypsies and Travellers of Europe, undertaken from 1986 and culminating in the adoption of an important text by the Ministers of Education.

• This document is an information source: the data it presents are landmarks offering insights into the situation of the 1980s, by which we can measure how the situation has developed – or stagnated – in the interim.

- It is more than a record of the past: it is also a frequently cited reference document on which much of the reflection and work of recent years is based.

- This document is also very relevant to the current situation: the ideas, concepts, analyses and proposals it presents, like the philosophy behind it, remain valid. Having defined the conditions for the implementation of the Resolution adopted by the Ministers, the working guidelines are as applicable in developing new Community actions in other areas in which the Commission wishes to organise and diversify the support it can offer the Gypsies of Europe, as they are in education: note that the chapter of the Socrates Programme devoted to issues of schooling includes a section on intercultural education in which Gypsies and Travellers are clearly mentioned among priority groups.

- It is relevant for other reasons, too: now that the European Union is intensifying its support to the countries of Central and Eastern Europe, it is clear that the analyses and proposals put forward in this document remain accurate, and useful, throughout Europe.

- It is also relevant because, ten years after its initial publication, so many studies continue to confirm its observations and conclusions. If much has been done to improve the conditions of school provision for Gypsy and Traveller children, much remains to be done, under difficult conditions.

For all these reasons, and after years of use in administrative and political circles, the time has come for this report to become a widely distributed, easily accessible book. Its logical place is in the "Reference Works" series published by the *Interface Collection*, itself launched with the support of the European Commission in the framework of the implementation of the Resolution adopted by the ministers.

Finally, I would like to emphasise that the implementation of the political will expressed by the various European institutions is due to a great extent to the exceptional commitment of the Gypsy Research Centre at the Department of Social Sciences of the Université René Descartes, Paris, under the directorship of Professor Jean-Pierre Liégeois.

[*Editorial note*: Head of Division at the European Commission when work began in 1984, Domenico Lenarduzzi has devoted close attention to, and constant support for, education-related activities developed for Gypsy and Traveller children. He and his colleagues have always insisted on work of the highest quality as the best guarantee of success and coherence despite administrational and political discontinuities. Now a Director, he is in charge of the whole of the Socrates Programme which includes actions relating to higher education (Erasmus), languages (Lingua), adult education, open and distance learning, and exchange on educational systems and policies; but he remains particularly attentive to issues of school provision (the Comenius chapter of the Socrates Programme) and devotes steadfast support to intercultural education in this context, with particular mention of Gypsy and Traveller children.]

The Gypsy Paradigm

A driving force

In 1986 the Commission of the European Communities distributed the findings of a study carried out over the 1984-85 academic year by the Gypsy Research Centre at the Université René Descartes, Paris. This document, *School Provision for Gypsy and Traveller Children*[1], exerted a significant impact in both administrational and institutional circles, as well as inspiring the implementation of new practices. In 1989 the European Council and the Ministers of Education of the European Community adopted an historic text based on this document, recognising Gypsy culture and language and culminating in proposals relating to education[2]. This official text was the end product of a political and administrative process, but, even more significantly, signalled the beginning of a new focus on pedagogical practice for the Gypsy and Traveller communities.

In 1996, ten years after the study was first published, the European Commission circulated a report on the implementation of the measures laid out in the Resolution adopted by the ministers in 1989[3]. This report described the development of Community action as well as activities carried out by the Member States. When it came to drawing up conclusions, their content, priorities and guidelines made explicit reference to the 1986 study, confirming its continued relevance. Yet if the priorities and urgent issues identified a decade ago remain priorities and matters of urgency to this day, this also means that they have not, as yet, been responded to in an adequate manner.

There are many reasons, already noted in the Preface, why this work should be republished now. They are supported by the steady demand for copies from researchers, students, teachers, Gypsy/Traveller organisations, administrative bodies and so on. This text is the original 1986 version, with only the statistics on numbers of Gypsies and Travellers in the different countries updated – made possible by new data and necessary because of rapid demographic growth. We felt it was important to publish the original 1986 text to give today's reader a clear milestone by which to measure the changes that have occurred, and the directions they have taken, as well as to identify those areas in which no movement is apparent. We could have shortened the text, retaining the analyses while deleting the examples on which they were based but, knowing the uses made of it in the past, it is preserved in full. (The change of title reflects the wider relevance of the original report in the 1990s).

There are other important considerations. In 1989, the year in which the ministers adopted the Resolution on school provision for Gypsy and Traveller children, changes in Europe were to have profound consequences for these communities, particularly those in Central and Eastern Europe. Analysis of the situation quickly revealed that the issues arising were – even in the way they were approached and the attempts made to respond to them – similar, even identical, in every part of Europe. Observation also reveals that the extent of difficulties in general, and school-related difficulties in particular, is entirely comparable. Where they do exist, differences can be interpreted more in terms of fluctuations of political emphasis than as presence versus absence of a given phenomenon; this is particularly true in pedagogical practice[4]. The analyses presented here, founded on studies carried out in ten different countries and confirmed in 1986 by further studies carried out in two new Member States, are thus valid, and useful, not only for new members of the European Union, but also for the rest of Europe.

School provision for Gypsy and Traveller children has played a significant trailblazing role in a number of areas, most particularly that of intercultural education but also in relation to the teaching of minority languages, distance learning, the production of teaching materials and teacher training. If Gypsy and Traveller children should be the beneficiaries of multicultural education, they can also provide a model for it because of their unique characteristics, notably the strength of their culture, lived to the full wherever they happen to be, their dispersion among surrounding populations, and the fact that they are present in every state. School provision for Gypsy and Traveller children has played, and continues to play, a driving role in European Union and Council of Europe activities, a mobilising force and a symbol simultaneously.

The Gypsy experience provides a paradigm with much to offer other minorities and indeed all school-related issues[5].

A wider angle on Gypsies and Travellers

The situation has been evolving over the last few years. Change has taken place at institutional level through the adoption of the above-mentioned Resolution and other texts[6], as well as through explicit reference to the Gypsy/Traveller minority in certain major programmes in the field of education, the European Union's Socrates Programme among them. There has been administrational change, too, evident in the proposing and management of certain projects which assume that Gypsy/Traveller-related questions will be taken into account at national level. Finally, there has been practical change in that more and more projects are being developed.

A movement has been launched within the international institutions; it is strongly dominated by education-related issues. These are indeed fundamental but they are insufficient in and of themselves. That is why it is significant to note that, since the early 1990s, a trend towards broadening the focus has been gaining ground. This process is occurring simultaneously on four different fronts:

- *intensified reflection*, accompanied by a will to see thought transformed into action. Where new thinking is evident, it tends to be developed and consolidated. Elsewhere there has been a feeling of ferment – an impulse towards new thinking;

- *diversification* – while education remains a priority, there is increased emphasis on social questions, local authorities' obligations with regard to accommodation, legal issues, human rights etc.;

- a *collaborative approach* – Gypsy/Traveller organisations are increasingly regarded as partners by European institutions; as consultation procedures develop these Gypsy organisations will need to keep firmly in touch with the dynamics of their own communities. There is also increased cooperation between international organisations, each with its own profile and field of interest;

- a *consolidation of knowledge* through technical backup to lend support to research and action-research, assisting in organising and linking actions, disseminating acquired insights in an organised manner and so on.

The education sector has been at the cutting edge; some of the steps it has been recommending are beginning to bear fruit, and other sectors should be able to share in these benefits. By the same token, school-related questions occur within a far broader context and it is essential to establish links between the numerous developments which have been taking shape over the past few years. Such an approach also indicates that meetings, hearings, seminars, publications and so on are not necessarily isolated events leading nowhere, as one may sometimes feel when pessimism gets the upper hand, but are part of a dynamic process on condition they are tied in with what is happening elsewhere in the field.

The Gypsy paradigm appears to be an exceptionally innovative one.

A difficult situation

Some of the fields covered here have undergone positive transformation in the interim: for example, there is more emphasis on preschooling, and in-service teacher training has been developed, as has the training and employment of Gypsy and Traveller mediators. Conditions outside the school gates have, in some cases, improved. It is important, however, to bear in mind that the situation as a whole is no better than it was.

For centuries, policies towards Gypsies and Travellers have been policies of negation: negating their culture, negating their very existence as individuals and as a group. These have taken a variety of forms (from exclusion to assimilation) and entailed dreadful conditions. The situation is a grave one, with rejection the dominant element in relations between Gypsies and their immediate environment: accommodation difficulties, health hazards, evictions, refusal of admission to public places are all commonplace. Tension, always present, can quickly flare up into open antagonism and conflict, particularly during periods characterised by economic difficulties and high unemployment; as a result, Gypsies are frequently mistreated and permanently insecure. This means that any evaluation of school provision is simultaneously an evaluation of general policy, and that interculturalism finds its way into the classroom via interculturalism in the world at large.

We must not lose sight of the fact that the pupil is, first and foremost, a child who is not only part of a family and of a culture which the school must take into account, but also of a global socio-cultural universe. The current upsurge of attitudes and behaviour characterised by rejection, violence and racism places an increased responsibility on the school – on all schools – to actively promulgate understanding geared towards recognition and respect. At the same time, it compels us to consider the big picture: the environment as a whole. The obstacles blocking the implementation of multicultural education projects are not essentially educational, or even cultural, in nature, but often spring from social, political or economic causes.

Given this overall context, and the fact that the school is an institution which is a part of an environment perceived by Gypsies and Travellers as coercive, they may experience it as yet another imposition, and one whose quality leaves much to be desired. Parents may feel that the formative impact the school intends to exert on their children may in fact *de*-form them, that is, alienate them from their own culture. These parental perceptions are entirely justified, in that until recently scholastic practice was inseparable from the policies of negation noted above: indeed, it was merely their scholastic manifestation. Parental resistance, and the very persistence of Gypsy communities in the face of these pressures, are testimony to the strength of their culture, and proof that, generation after generation, parents competently educate their own children.

In consequence, we must not take the *effects* of the overall situation (such as disinterest, absenteeism, outright refusal) as the *causes* of scholastic failure. So long as relations between Gypsy and Traveller communities and surrounding society remain conflictual, parents', and children's, relations with the school will remain largely determined by the negative profile of these broader relations.

We have thus identified a very strong *primary link* between the general situation and that pertaining in the schools. Its *effects* are to be found in statistical form in the following pages, and in the Resolution adopted by the ministers: in the 1980s, only 30–40% of Gypsy and Traveller children attended school with any degree of regularity; over half received no schooling at all; a very small percentage got as far as, or entered into, secondary level; scholastic achievement, particularly as regards the attainment of functional literacy, was not in keeping with the amount of time spent in school.

We cannot say that these facts have changed. Reports issued by local and regional authorities, schools, Gypsy associations and other bodies continue to emphasise the high rate of non-attendance, which may reach a regional average of 50% with localised averages of 90% or more: one of several quantitative indicators revealing the scope of the task in hand. Detailed studies, whether pinpointing a suburb or covering a region, confirm that the 1985 data conveyed in this volume remain valid. While the absolute number of Gypsy children attending school has undoubtedly risen in some countries, the relative number – the percentage – has not. This can be partially explained by the fact that administrators now have a more realistic idea of the number of families, and of children, in this category, but it is also because the number of young people is rising: half the members of the Gypsy and Traveller communities are under sixteen years of age, and demographic growth means that these are predominantly young populations. Taking Europe as a whole, the school-related reflections conveyed here concern approximately four million children of compulsory school age.

We must, therefore, stress that the scholastic situation is one of global stagnation – a conclusion borne out by current study, research and reports. The fact that these considerations are now corroborated by official reports – which they were not, back in the 1980s – denotes a significant change, a willingness to recognise certain weaknesses within the education system and the need to improve the conditions surrounding Gypsy children's access to school. There may even be official recognition that the situation is worsening: "On the whole, scholastic indices are currently undergoing dramatic deterioration"[7]. The same national report goes on to emphasise that "This is a field in which extremely significant long-term results may be achieved through negligible financial input"[8].

The scholastic paradigm remains a hazy one.

Prioritising adaptation

There is *another link*, just as strong as the first, between the general situation and that pertaining in the schools. Gypsies' age-old adaptability is currently being tried to the limits, and established strategies for actively adapting to their environment are becoming inadequate. In consequence, their difficulties in surviving as a minority culture are on the rise. Satisfying the legal requirements surrounding the exercise of the simplest activity – particularly of an economic nature – demands a minimal grasp of the "three Rs" (reading, w/riting, a/rithmetic). Non-literacy no longer provides effective protection from the assaults of other cultures, conveyed by (among others) the school and its teachings, but has become a real handicap in dealing with an environment unavoidably permeated by the written word.

Lack of schooling poses serious problems on the *economic* front, but also has serious *social* and *psychological* repercussions, for example by the fact that it renders the individual dependent on the mediation of the social services – a situation incompatible with the Gypsy's legitimate pride in his ability to manage his own, and his children's, affairs. For Gypsies and Travellers, schooling means *autonomy*, just as it means *savings* for the public purse: the costs of providing appropriate schooling are far below those of welfarism, an option largely rejected by the group itself.

In other words, the future of Gypsy communities depends to a considerable extent upon the manner of their children's schooling – and parents are aware of this. Here we found a *crucial link* between the general situation and the scholastic: transformations in living conditions and the circumstances surrounding economic activities occurring in contemporary societies make basic schooling increasingly essential, and in turn parents show increasing willingness to ensure that their children avail themselves of it. In many instances there is a widening rift between Gypsy/Traveller children and those from surrounding society, and many already bad situations may rapidly degenerate into drastic ones likely to foster various forms of marginality.

Clarifying the scholastic paradigm is an urgent priority.

Education: the positive side

Nonetheless, analysis to date does give grounds for hope:

- measures implemented in connection with projects promoting intercultural education open the way for new practices which recognise the value of the minority's own culture as a matter of course, and take the child's own capabilities and experience as their starting point. Such measures make it possible for the school to adapt itself to Gypsy and Traveller pupils;

- every state has, through a range of experiments and formulas, attempted to respond to Gypsy parents' desire that their children receive schooling. Some aspects of these efforts have been successful, while others have proven dead ends or counterproductive. That is why it is important to identify, analyse and publicise those approaches which have demonstrated their worth, to support genuinely innovative projects and to encourage new ones. This study provided an opportunity for evaluation, which clearly demonstrates that the recommended global, structural approach (involving cooperation, coordination and information) makes a significant contribution to overcoming the major obstacles hampering Gypsy and Traveller children's access to school.

Education must remain a key consideration. Improvements here have positive repercussions in other areas:

- education can increase appreciation of the true value of the Gypsy and Traveller communities, propagating positive counterimages to the predominant negative stereotypes; learning together, learning from and about each other, cultivates the insight and understanding essential to respect;

- education increases personal autonomy, providing the tools for adapting to a changing environment and a means of self-defence from the forces of assimilation; it makes it possible to break out of the passive rut of welfarism to play an active role in cultural and political development;

- in the current sombre climate of intolerance, rejection and problems in connection with a range of issues such as accommodation, work and health, education opens the way for positive reflection and action, and thus for grounded hope; it makes it possible to reason in terms of progress rather than in terms of problems.

The need for evaluation

This study provided a basis for reflection which became a basis for action following the ministers' adoption of a key text, namely the Resolution of 1989. The inclusion of school provision for Gypsy and Traveller children in the framework of the European Union's Socrates Programme on education, Council of Europe initiatives and actions carried out by the states themselves, have all brought about multiple activities. Pieces of a coherent strategy are beginning to fall into place[9] and, by blazing an exploratory trail, school provision for Gypsy and Traveller children is proving a rich source of lessons of relevance to school provision for other minorities and indeed all children.

The time has come to use those elements developed in connection with action strategy, organisation and management, as means for evaluating the work in progress. We have already analysed, in other publications, the diverse risks accompanying the development of a programme of this sort: these include duplication, which entails a waste of time, energy and money; repetitive projects which are "pilot" in name only and have lost their exploratory, driving function; opportunities botched by opportunism as soon as financial support becomes available; expectations that turn into "wait and see" for fear that some decisions might be seen as "politically incorrect"; discontinuity between research and action, so that many activities become mere unchannelled activism, etc.

It is also important to mention the lobbying potential of certain organisations: it is they which are most successful in acquiring support. This trend, in conjunction with the administrative complexity surrounding access to certain programmes and management difficulties within them, effectively bars smaller bodies, whether schools or Gypsy organisations, from participating. This brings us back to the familiar scenario of dependence on middlemen, reminiscent of the way in which families cannot access entitlements without the mediation of social workers. It is the opposite of autonomy, all the more so in that this illustration of inequality occurs within programmes featuring equal opportunity among their priority objectives: only the rich can acquire further funding, and access to resources is confined to those already equipped to obtain them.

The time has thus come to devote serious thought to procedures surrounding the selection, allocation and management of development funding, and to come up with ways of making things simpler and more transparent so that participation can be more broadly based, more open, more balanced

In the absence of precise guidelines for action there is a great risk that activities will splinter, projects fragment and acquired insights be dispersed, thus making it ever more difficult to convey their lessons and reinvest these in new projects[10].

It would be disturbing indeed if all this trail blazing were to lead to a dead end.

At the same time, there are two new courses to explore:

- in the field of education for Gypsies, Travellers and others, projects must forge beyond what has become familiar territory: action supported at European level must form the cutting edge, not perpetuate routines. Consequently, we must branch out, selecting new fields in which to carry out sustained action;

- moreover, what has already been achieved in education should also be undertaken in other fields: we are still waiting for studies along the lines of this one, but focusing for example on cultural development, vocational training, accommodation, economic practices or health issues, etc., the findings of which would provide the relevant ministers with material through which to re-examine, and build upon, existing proposals. This could be a first step towards bringing these topics onto the political agenda and focusing attention on adapting practices, while recognising that the road ahead is a long one and, as we have always stressed in relation to education, demands vigilant monitoring of activities to ensure both their quality and dissemination of the insights they provide.

In many ways Gypsies and Travellers are adapting better to the present, and even to the future, than other groups, through their work flexibility, initiative, geographic mobility, the education of their children, their communal living which places the individual in a reassuring network and gives him a solid sense of identity. Gypsy society is young, with as many children as adults. More books are finding their way into Gypsy homes. Gypsy children are getting more schooling. They will read, and soon they will write, thereby enriching European culture as a whole. Yet many are still waiting for the school gates to open, or to be allowed stay once in, or to be respected as individuals and as representatives of their culture while there.

After six centuries in Europe, Gypsies and Travellers are still waiting for coherent, consistent, respectful policies regarding them. Scholastic policy is part of the package and should be one of its driving forces. This can be achieved by simple, low cost means – as demonstrated in the analyses presented in the following pages. We hope that the reader will find them a source of information and of inspiration.

Jean-Pierre Liégeois

1. *School Provision for Gypsy and Traveller Children. A Synthesis Report.* Jean-Pierre Liégeois, Office for Official Publications of the European Communities, "Documents" series, Luxembourg, 1987. (NB the original French was made available some months earlier.)
2. The Resolution of the Council and the Ministers of Education of 22 May 1989, on *School Provision for Gypsy and Traveller Children* (89/C 153/02) published in the Official Journal of the European Communities of 21 June 1989. Given its historic importance, and the fact that it forms a framework for action and an official referent in activity development, we reproduce it in full at the end of this book. In effect, while the great Socrates Programme on education – and in particular its Comenius chapter – provides a framework for developing activities which may be supported by the European Union, it is this Resolution which provides their content.
3. *School Provision for Gypsy and Traveller Children. Report on the implementation of measures envisaged in the Resolution of the Council and of the Ministers of Education, 22nd May, 1989 (89/C 153/02)*, presented by the Commission. Document COM(96)495 final, Office for Official Publications of the European Communities, Luxembourg, 1996.
4. See, for example, *Roma, Gypsies, Travellers, Socio-Cultural Data, Socio-Political Data*, Jean-Pierre Liégeois, Council of Europe Publications, Strasbourg, 1994.
5. In the field of research proper, it has become blatantly obvious over the course of international conferences and meetings that work in relation to school provision for Gypsy and Traveller children is characterised by enormous originality, and can play a guiding role, a fact which has emerged strongly on many occasions, for example at the European Educational Research Association's 1996 European Conference on Educational Research, Seville.
6. See *On Gypsies: Texts issued by International Institutions,* documents compiled by Marielle Danbakli, Interface Collection, Gypsy Research Centre, CRDP Midi-Pyrénées, 1994, second edition 1998. The very fact that there are so many of these texts is testimony to the attention which international institutions devote to Gypsy/Traveller issues.
7. *Report on the Situation of the Gypsy Community in Hungary,* Executive publisher Dr. Csaba Tabajdi, State Secretary for Minority Affairs at the Office of the Prime Minister, 1996.
8. Idem.
9. One can trace these developments in detail through the pages of *Interface. Gypsies and Travellers, Education, Training, Youth,* a quarterly newsletter published by the Gypsy Research Centre since 1991, with the support of the European Commission and within the framework of implementing the Resolution. The strategic approach is also discussed in the official Commission document referred to in footnote 3, above.
10. The importance, and the implications, of evaluation are explicitly mentioned in *Accomplishing Europe through Education and Training* (Luxembourg, 1997), a report commissioned from an independent expert group by European Commissioner Edith Cresson. Reading through it we note that the course of Gypsy education, and the work and reflection accompanying it, have by and large anticipated what are now identified as general priorities, particularly in connection with innovation and multiculturalism.

Foreword

State of play

The future of Gypsy and Traveller communities depends to a considerable extent upon the manner of their children's schooling. Gypsies and Travellers undertake active adaptation to their social and economic environment through acquiring new skills which enable the group and the individual to analyse a changing reality. In the cultural sphere, these same skills can serve as tools for those who wish to conserve, affirm and develop their own unique identity.

At present, as the Member States begin to appreciate the wealth of their cultural variety, and as international organisations repeat their pleas for respect and development aid for linguistic and cultural minorities (with or without territory of their own), Gypsy populations in each state should take a critical overview of the schooling of their children and consider the ways in which it can and should develop.

This study, undertaken at the initiative of the Commission of the European Communities, presents both the historical background and the present-day situation with regard to school provision for Gypsy and Traveller children within the Member States. It is a critical analysis of the conditions in which this schooling takes place – or does not take place. Global and comparative, and supplemented by a wide variety of data, it presents much food for thought and offers diagnosis as well as proposals of a practical nature.

It is no exaggeration to state that, to date, school provision for Gypsy children has on the whole been a failure for all concerned: for parents who desire schooling for their children, and for those who do not; for the children who have undergone schooling, and for those who have not; for the teachers, administrators and governments involved. This assertion is only superficially paradoxical; in the course of this report we shall try to elucidate the reasons for this shared sense of defeat.

The stakes are high, for the individual and for the culture as a whole. The age-pyramid of Gypsy and Traveller populations has a broad base: about fifty per cent are under sixteen, i.e. of school age and indeed, in the majority of Western Europe, of an age when full-time schooling is legally obligatory. For Gypsies, however, "school" is always somebody else's. And the history of their schooling, inseparable from their history as a whole, has taught them to be wary of such institutions, and cautious before committing their children – which is to say, their future to them.

But times change, and change rapidly. In the final decades of the twentieth century, Gypsies' and Travellers' age-old adaptability – a tradition of change, but change within tradition – is being put to harsh test. Economic transformations, social changes within the broader environment, the influence of television (which, like school, is always "somebody else's" but, unlike school, is unavoidable) and political changes (notably towards social and cultural groups considered "underprivileged", "minorities", "marginal" or even "deviant") oblige Gypsies, if they wish to retain a relative economic and cultural independence, to develop new ways of adapting in order to achieve this. Schooling is seen as a more and more practical (or more and more compulsory, depending on one's point of view) means towards this goal.

Despite general attitudes towards Gypsies and Travellers, as outlined in this study, remaining virtually unchanged, the 1980s have seen certain new developments in schooling, the effects of which have yet to be evaluated. These include parents' increased desire for schooling for their children; the development of the concept of "intercultural pedagogy"; the increasingly important role of Gypsy and Traveller organisations and the accentuation of profound change in these communities. As early as 1980 I wrote that "schooling forms an inseparable part of a totality, and is a fundamental element in the development and transformation of Gypsy and Traveller populations. These are undergoing a critical period in their history. This period will culminate in either a renaissance (through what I have termed a mutation), or disappearance" [Liégeois, 1980b, p.285].

The past few years have shown that the difficulties faced by Gypsies in surviving as a cultural minority are increasing. Family groups to which social and economic flexibility would confer adaptability and independence have, under the pressure of circumstances, rigidified; where once they had flexibility, they are now in danger of snapping. Assimilationist policies, which transform cultural minorities into simple social groups, have not led (as desired and anticipated) to integration, but to the marginalisation of those subjected to them. Closer contact between different communities sharing bad housing conditions and a common background of economic difficulties has not increased understanding, but has brought them into opposition and open conflict. Schooling therefore takes place within a difficult context, and one which is, moreover, heavily laden with historical residue. It is but one factor in a painful process of overall mutation.

There are two reasons why a critical analysis of the conditions surrounding school provision for Gypsy and Traveller children necessarily entails examination of other factors. Firstly, Gypsies are not a "social problem" (singular), nor are they a "problem group". Although their collective experience is particularly revealing, they share the defeats, victories and hopes of other minorities. Secondly, the facts concerning the "school question" are themselves often of a political or economic nature, school and pedagogy being simply elements of relative importance within a greater whole. Taking this into account necessitates a sociological approach, and this is what we have adopted throughout the report. Such an approach is all the more essential since this study is both exploratory and a synthesis: in the majority of Member States, no general research has been undertaken, necessitating the gathering of scattered and disparate data. Correlating this information has made possible the recognition and evaluation of trends which would otherwise have remained invisible. In several Member States, experts have indicated the galvanising effect of this study which may act – in some cases, already has acted – as a stimulus towards more localised and thus perhaps more "pedagogical" studies and reflections now that we have analysed the overall context. To put it another way: in order to examine school, it is first necessary to examine the factors which shape it and its effects on the children concerned (and on their parents). Not to do so may lead to grave and far-reaching misinterpretation. It has become a cliché to point this out, but we still need to consider all the implications, theoretical as well as practical.

However, this report cannot be solely of a "technical" nature. While it is analytical throughout, it is also a reflection on ideologies, particularly political ideologies, and on the policies which they inspire. Its only "agenda" is to improve understanding of the situation it describes and thereby lead to some modification of the philosophy behind the policies which have led to the present situation of almost universal dissatisfaction: "In such a perspective, specialist expertise in the education of migrant children is justified not so much by its intrinsic content of effectiveness, but above all by the extent to which it is brought to bear on the revision of existing practice and the development of new policies" [Wittek, 1983, p.23].

The study

This project was based on the following principles:

- in each Member State experts (alone or in collaboration) coordinated an enquiry within the state and presented an analysis thereof;

- a detailed report was written for each state. When the Commission releases these for general distribution, all of the concerned ministries and other national bodies will have, in addition to this synthesis, a basis for reflection and analysis on their own state;

- Gypsy organisations and families have, in the majority of Member States, been involved with this study in various ways: consultation, direct help in carrying out the study, participation in the formulation of the final report;

- the study is intended to be as exhaustive and comparative as possible. The experts cooperated on the basic document which served both as a workplan throughout the study and as an outline for each individual national report;

- a meeting was held in Brussels half-way through the study period, enabling all the experts, Gypsy/Traveller representatives and representatives of the Commission, to meet. It also made possible, by direct discussion, coordination of both approach and method. The Gypsy representatives offered their advice on the school situation and the ongoing study, and emphasised their own priorities, while the members of the Commission used this opportunity to grasp the dynamics of the research, offer their advice and express their hopes;

- the coordinator visited all the states concerned during the period of the study, meeting and contacting the experts, representatives of Gypsy/Traveller organisations, various associations, families, state services and local groups.

The work was carried out from autumn 1984 to autumn 1985[1] (cf. p. 253). The period of a single year is brief indeed when we consider the breadth of the study, its exploratory character and international scope. All the more so as the budget for the project was limited and if, on the whole, it did cover the expenses of those involved, it did not provide them with any other remuneration. It is thanks to the enthusiasm and self-sacrifice of the experts involved that this study was successfully carried out, and thanks to their competence and experience acquired in this field over a long period (ten to twenty years in most cases) that the results have come up to expectations and are, let us hope, equal to the stakes involved. Their commitment is also the guarantee that, apart from delivering the final report, they will all be concerned that it yields concrete results.

Neither time nor finance permitted undertaking exhaustive new research to achieve this critical evaluation. However, in seeking out and analysing existing documentation, the experts carried out much investigation specifically for this study: visiting homes, schools and families, contacts with administrative services, participation in various meetings, the use of questionnaires with official bodies, teachers and specialist organisations. The result is, at the level of the European Community, a vast comparative analysis of varied elements, as the diversity of situations within each state is considered in addition to the diversity of situations from one state to another. This juxtaposition of such broad ranges of data has proved positive, both because it demonstrates that it is possible to approach "success", or to reproduce failure, in extremely diverse circumstances, and also because this comparative analysis of contrasting factors reveals an experimental situation that has been developing for years in most of the states covered. Pedagogical experiments have been carried out, and continue to be carried out, in ignorance of similar experiments elsewhere. The present study enables comparison and evaluation of their pedagogical results and social consequences.

For populations present throughout Europe, international comparison and reflection are indispensable, and this study examines the results achieved in institutional contexts which differ fundamentally both in the policies which inspire them and in the structures to which they give rise. It will establish a basis for further international exchanges, the usefulness of which is obvious. All stand to benefit from a sharing of information on successes and failures, analyses and the lessons which can be drawn from them. One example directly aided by the Commission itself is a pilot scheme involving Gypsy families in Greece, which has the advantage of drawing upon the experiences of similar pilot schemes in the Netherlands, Ireland and elsewhere.

In evaluating this work the contributing experts from each Member State have all stated that, in addition to the dynamic which it has created and continues to exert, their participation also brought a great deal to them personally. This general feeling is aptly summed up in the following statement from the UK team: "Although two of us have been involved in Traveller education for many years we found that the process of systematic comparative enquiry imposed by participation in a multi-national study challenged our preconceptions and led us on to insights we had not anticipated" [Acton/Kenrick].

The national monographs submitted for this study are as follows:

B-L – Alain Reyniers, *La Scolarisation des Tsiganes et des Voyageurs en Belgique et au Grand-Duché de Luxembourg* (School Provision for Gypsies and Travellers in Belgium and the Grand Duchy of Luxembourg), 175 pp. (the Luxembourg report was unavailable when this synthesis was being written up).

D – Katrin Reemtsma, Sinti Werkstatt Göttingen, *La Scolarisation des Enfants Tsiganes et Nomades en République Fédérale d'Allemagne* (School Provision for Gypsy and Nomad Children in the Federal Republic of Germany), 102 pp.

DK – Bendt Gudmander, Søren Rude, *Report on the Gypsies in Denmark*, 44 pp. + 200 pp. of appendices.

F – Patricia Ferté, *La Scolarisation des Enfants Tsiganes et Nomades en France* (School Provision for Gypsy and Nomad Children in France) (not available – with the exception of a few pages – when this synthesis was being written up).

GR – Evangelos Marselos, Maria Pavli-Korré, *The Education of Gypsy Children in Greece*, 48 pp.

I – Mirella Karpati, Secondo Massano, *La Scolarisation des Enfants Tsiganes et Voyageurs en Italie* (School Provision for Gypsy and Traveller Children in Italy), 110 pp.

IRL – Patricia McCarthy (with the assistance of Mincéir Misli and Sheila Nunan), *The Education of Traveller Children in the Republic of Ireland*, 94 pp.

NL – Pieter Hovens, Ria Timmermans, Marjan van de Zande, *Caravan-dwellers, Gypsies and Education in the Netherlands, an Exploratory Report*, 92 pp.

UK – Thomas A. Acton, Donald S. Kenrick (with the assistance of G. Douglas-Home), *The Education of Gypsy/Traveller Children in Great Britain and Northern Ireland*, 149 pp.

To these national monographs we add a "transversal" report dealing with Gypsy in-family education: Leonardo Piasere, *Connaissance Tsigane et Alphabétisation* (Gypsy Knowledge and Literacy), 36 pp.

Most of the authors of these reports have published other documents to which reference may also be made within the present text. In order to avoid confusion, when citing the report compiled expressly for this project I will mention only the author'(s)' name(s), for example [Piasere], [Acton/Kenrick]. When referring to other publications I will give a dated reference, e.g. [Piasere, 1985], [Acton/Kenrick, 1984] which the reader can then find in the bibliography.

Having drawn attention to the competence and experience of the experts who have participated in this work, I wish also to emphasise that most of them are completely independent, a fact which reinforces the validity and impartiality of their analyses. The same holds true for the coordinator of the study, who also compiled this synthesis: he is neither a school teacher, inspector, administrative civil servant nor in any way involved in social work, and was not elected or mandated to this study by anyone save the Commission. The analyses he puts forward, and for which he alone is responsible, as well as the recommendations he makes, are dictated solely by a concern for clarity and respect for those involved – even though respect for people must often be expressed through severe criticism of institutions.

This report is intended to stand as a self-contained document. For this reason I have begun it with a socio-historical outline which, although brief, enables the reader to understand the present school situation in context. To this I will add a few general socio-cultural facts that must be recognised and taken into account by policy-makers, funding bodies, legislators and all those working directly in the field in whatever capacity (administrators, teachers, social workers etc.). Everything must be included in this text, so that it may be entirely explicit. Ideally, there ought also to be a detailed ethnographical outline, because the school must take account of these realities and their consequences. There ought also to be a summary of contemporary thinking within the science of education. I have, however, had to fit this report within limits which permit it to be specific while remaining of manageable proportions.

My thanks to the experts who compiled the national reports, as well as those who helped them, and also those who were kind enough to participate in the two discussion meetings concerning the study. Among the experts I offer my particular thanks to Thomas Acton, Patricia Ferté, Donald Kenrick and Leonardo Piasere, who kindly helped in proofreading this synthesis to root out any errors or inconsistencies I may have overlooked. Last but not least, I thank Sinéad ní Shuinéar for the quality of her translation, which renders the report accessible to English-speaking readers.

My thanks, too, to all who helped me and who welcomed me during my travels, and who agreed to meet me: experts, Gypsy and Traveller families, representatives of Gypsy/Traveller organisations, teachers, school principals, officials, local representatives, members of various groups and associations from Athens to Dublin and from Rome to Copenhagen. It is thanks to them that I have managed to compile so much data, and with their aid that I have been able to complete this complex and difficult project. I beg all of those whom time did not permit me to meet, to forgive me.

My gratitude is extended, finally, to the officials of the Commission of the European Communities who, by their sustained interest, understanding and patience, have enabled this study to see the light of day in favourable circumstances.

History, politics and culture

History

The first Gypsy groups arrived in Europe, spreading from east to west, mainly in the fourteenth and fifteenth centuries. They had already come a long way, since much later (at the end of the eighteenth century) linguistic science was able to establish that the Gypsies' language is from India, closely related to the Sanskrit from which it is derived. It is probable that the first migrations from India took place between the ninth and fourteenth centuries, in successive waves. Linguistics has also been able, through examination of the vocabulary and grammatical structures of various Gypsy dialects, to give us some idea of the actual routes followed.

Archive materials, vague in the distant past but becoming more and more precise with the march of time, enable us to pinpoint certain key dates. Around 1100 a monk of Mount Athos speaks of a group of *Atsingani*: this may well be a reference to Travellers from India. The name was borrowed from a heretical sect which had existed for several centuries in Greece under the name *Atsinganos* or *Atsinkanos*. Whatever its origins, this name has stuck, in many countries, to Travellers of Indian origin: *Tsiganes* in France, *Zingari* in Italy, *Zigeuner* in Germany, *Ciganos* in Portugal, *Sigøyner* in Norway, etc.

By the fourteenth century, documentation had become more precise. In 1322, near Kandy (Heraklion) in Crete, there is a description of families camping in caves and tents. In 1348, *Cingarije*, already clearly present for some decades, are mentioned in Serbia. In Corfu a Gypsy fiefdom, *feudum Acinganorum*, was created, in which the inhabitants were answerable only to their "baron", excepting in cases demanding the death penalty; this fiefdom survived into the nineteenth century. During this period, many regions frequented by Gypsies seem to have been christened "Little Egypt", perhaps due to their fertility; this is the case in, for example, Epirus in Greece, and is perhaps the reason why Gypsies who subsequently arrived in other European countries became known as *Egyptians*, a name which has stuck to the present day, for example as *Gypsies* in English, *Gitanos* in Spain.

The dispersion of Gypsy groups continued into Wallachia and Bohemia. It was probably in 1417 that Sigismund, Emperor of Germany and King of Bohemia, granted the "chief" of a group of a hundred or so Gypsies a letter of reference and protection. Later this letter travelled out of Bohemia with the group, but the place-name stuck, as *Bohémiens, Bohemianos* and the like. By 1430 men, women and children, with horses and occasionally with carts for their belongings, had spread throughout Western Europe, its northernmost countries excepted: Germany in 1407, France in 1419, the Low Countries in 1420, Italy in 1422, Spain in 1425. The British Isles were first visited slightly later: Scotland by 1505, England by 1514, and Wales by 1579 (dates of first archival references). In 1505 they arrived in Denmark via Scotland. By 1512, a reference exists in Sweden, and by 1584 in Finland. Russian territory was penetrated from the south in 1501. Africa and the Americas were to receive Gypsies, mainly as a result of deportation measures undertaken in the seventeenth century by the Portuguese and Spanish authorities, and a little later by their English and French counterparts. It is possible, even probable, that some families had arrived in the countries in question prior to the dates given, but archive material – at least, that which is known at present – makes no mention of them. [For fuller treatment of these historical aspects, see Vaux de Foletier, 1970.]

Generally speaking, these groups, having arrived, travelled on, and up to the beginning of the sixteenth century there were great displacements of Gypsies all across Europe: paths of migration crisscross and merge. Later, the range and pace of migration slowed down. At the same time it appears that certain groups reduced their travels or even ceased them altogether, primarily for economic reasons, in both rural and urban settings. Here and there this developed into localisation and more or less peaceful coexistence, occasionally even a sort of cultural osmosis (in Andalusia for instance) which might even go as far as mixed marriages and ties of godparentage – for example in Spain, Italy and England.

But Travellers of Indian origin also encountered Travellers of local origin who had developed an identity, social organisation and dialects which differentiated them from their surrounding populations. This is the case in Ireland, where nomads called *Tinklers* or *Tynkers* are noted from the twelfth century; the *Quinquis* appeared in Spain in the sixteenth century, and the *Jenische* in Germany in the seventeenth. Such encounters have sometimes resulted in cultural exchange and even intermarriage. From the sixteenth century to the present day, groups combining strong cultural elements of Indian origin (notably their language: Romani) with cultural elements of local origin, have been differentiating themselves and developing their own unique ethnic and linguistic identities.

We give the example of four groups formed in this way and still present in the United Kingdom [Acton/Kenrick]:

1 North Welsh Kalé, with an inflected dialect of Romani.
2 South Welsh and English Romanichals, with creolised Romani dialects.
3 Irish Pavees or Mincéirs, with Gammon, which mixes Shelta with English and Romani.

4 Scottish Travellers, whose Cant brings together creolised Romani and some Gammon vocabulary.

Situations of exchange, be they due to encounters during travels or occurring within a context of sedentary cohabitation, continue to influence both the persistence of groups which see themselves as similar (or indeed are already linked and thus formally sharing their resemblances), as well as the creation of new groups by a process of amalgamation.

The first wave of immigration of Travellers of Indian origin into Western Europe was ultimately to be followed by other "waves", that is, migrations of significant numbers of persons. The second wave on a European scale occurred during the second half of the nineteenth century, when the Gypsies of Romania, held in slavery for centuries, were emancipated and subsequently emigrated in all directions. The third wave began in Yugoslavia in the 1960s when family groups began emigrating towards the west and north-west – but not, so far, on any large or long-term scale into Spain or the British Isles. Other migrations, often on a considerable scale but involving a smaller number of countries, have also occurred and continue to do so: for example the movement towards Great Britain and the U.S. of many Irish Travellers during the mid-nineteenth century (the Famine period) and more recently since the 1960s (for economic reasons). For similar reasons, there has recently been a considerable movement of Gitanos from Portugal into Spain.

The motivation behind the migrations is diverse. Among the most important factors is the persecution to which Gypsies have been subjected over the centuries: expulsion, various punishments, repressive legislation, compelling them to see if the welcome would be warmer elsewhere. Then there are periods of general difficulty during which Gypsies and Travellers, serving as scapegoats, have been particularly threatened, as well as periods of economic hardship in which they are especially vulnerable. There are also commercial pressures leading them to travel in search of clients, as well as the social necessity of get-togethers for dispersed family groups.

The fact that different groups of Indian origin arrived at different times has resulted in each of them having an historical experience which is partially similar (because of the treatment to which they were subjected), but varying in their contacts with an environment on which different degrees of impact could be made: for some, periods of sedentarism, for others, frequent displacements; encounters with local nomadic groups, etc. All of these factors have created within each state both a stratification and great linguistic and cultural diversity: Gypsies and Travellers in the world today comprise a mosaic of different groups.

The terms used to designate Gypsies and Travellers from "without" usually reflect the very imprecise concepts of those who use them. They may for example refer to a supposed point of origin, reflecting a short-term and fragmentary historical vision. Such is the case with all the terms derived from "Egyptian", such as *Gitans, Gypsies, Gitanos, Giftos* and *Yífti*, not to mention *Bohémiens* in France and *Húngaros* in Spain. Then there are the "amalgamative" terms, giving a blanket, usually derogatory, designation for what are in fact different groups: *Vaganten, Fahrende, Vagabunten, Baraquis* and many others. Names may be descriptive, correctly or incorrectly, of a lifestyle or trade: *Tinkers, Forains, Woonwagenbewoners, Gurbétia, Barakkenvolk*. Furthermore, there are numerous regional terms, sometimes developed into terminologies even more stigmatising than those in general use, despite the already derogatory nature of these. And then there are "administrative" terms, just as arbitrary as the layman's, and frequently simple metaphors or paraphrases: *itinerants, Personnes d'origine nomade* ("persons of nomadic origin"), *HWAO (Häufig Wechselnder Aufenthaltsort* – "persons of frequently changing residence").

Throughout the present report, two terms are used: *Gypsies* and *Travellers*. These terms are relatively unstained by pejorative connotations (save in Germany, where the term *Zigeuner* still resonates with Nazi stigmatisation), perhaps because, to date, they have not been much in common use. Since the Gypsies – that is, Travellers of predominantly Indian origin – subdivided as they are into numerous and diversified groups, have no term of their own for designating themselves as a whole, nor have the Travellers – that is, Travellers of predominantly indigenous European origin – any such term, and since each component group has its own ethnicity, it is convenient to use the terms *Gypsies* and/or *Travellers* to describe the whole of the group, with the additional proviso that distinction between them is not always relevant nor indeed possible. This is due both to the contact (outlined above) between groups of Indian and local origin, and because over the centuries policies for dealing with them have not differentiated between the two. We will use the term *nomadic* to designate those who are travelling at the moment under consideration[2]; these nomads can just as easily be "Gypsies" as "Travellers".

Statistics concerning Gypsies and Travellers are on the whole rather imprecise. The reasons behind this are many: criteria for inclusion (who is a Gypsy? who is a Traveller?) are themselves ambiguous and fluctuating, frequently determined – and manipulated – by political considerations. In most states all terminology relating to ethnicity has disappeared from official administrative vocabulary, and cannot therefore be used on census forms. Moreover, when a census does take place, even if extra "indicators" such as mother tongue are included, it may happen that the majority of Gypsies do not declare themselves or their mother tongue, out of caution learnt over centuries of persecution for the sole fact of being – or being labelled – Gypsy. By the same token, when a specific survey of Traveller families/individuals is undertaken, for example through social workers and in theory with the cooperation of those involved, this collaboration is not always enthusiastic, whence spring the omissions and double counts.

The most "visible" Gypsies and Travellers being those who are nomadic, it is these whose number – often reckoned by a simple caravan count – is best known in most states. But even here we are dealing with indications rather than hard facts, as it is difficult to guess the average number of persons per caravan without taking into account the additional insights which only the Travellers themselves could provide. As for sedentary Travellers, so much less "visible", it would appear that their numbers are in the majority of cases grossly underestimated in official statistics, and that these must be revised (sometimes even doubled) when we consider the estimates put forward by our contributing experts. [The topics touched upon so briefly here in these introductory pages have been developed much more thoroughly in a text prepared for the Council of Europe: Liégeois, 1985a]. The estimated Gypsy and Traveller population of a number of states is given below (NB, these data have been updated for this new edition):

Gypsies and Travellers in Europe : approximate numbers

State	minimum	maximum
- Albania	90,000	100,000
- Austria	20,000	25,000
- Belarus	10,000	15,000
- Belgium	10,000	15,000
- Bosnia-Herzegovina	40,000	50,000
- Bulgaria	700,000	800,000
- Croatia	30,000	40,000
- Cyprus	500	1,000
- Croatia	30,000	40,000
- Czech Republic	250,000	300,000
- Denmark	1,500	2,000
- Estonia	1,000	1,500
- Finland	7,000	9,000
- France	280,000	340,000
- Germany	110,000	130,000
- Greece	160,000	200,000
- Hungary	550,000	600,000
- Ireland	22,000	28,000
- Italy	90,000	110,000
- Latvia	2,000	3,500
- Lithuania	3,000	4,000
- Luxembourg	100	150
- Macedonia	220,000	260,000
- Moldova	20,000	25,000
- the Netherlands	35,000	40,000
- Norway	500	1,000
- Poland	40,000	50,000
- Portugal	40,000	50,000
- Romania	1,800,000	2,500,000
- Russia	220,000	400,000
- Serbia-Montenegro	400,000	450,000
- Slovak Republic	480,000	520,000
- Slovenia	8,000	10,000
- Spain	650,000	800,000
- Sweden	15,000	20,000
- Switzerland	30,000	35,000
- Turkey	300,000	500,000
- the Ukraine	50,000	60,000
- United Kingdom	90,000	120,000
Europe (approximately)	7,000,000	8,500,000

To make sense of these figures, we must bear in mind the *strong demographic growth of the populations in question*, as a result of which data must be frequently updated. Wherever censuses of the Gypsy/Traveller population have been carried out, it is reckoned that *half this population is under sixteen years of age*. In this light, the "schooling question" appears in all its magnitude, and this purely statistical vision takes on a sharper focus still as we analyse the conditions, past and present, associated with it.

Policies and politics

Our present task is to describe and analyse both general and specific policies which have at all times strongly affected Gypsies and Travellers, threatened their very existence as an ethnic group, and provoked responses of adaptation, defence, and survival tactics which will be dealt with later on.

In this simple introduction to the situation we can give only the briefest overview. The interested reader will find more detailed information in the aforementioned Council of Europe publication [Liégeois, 1985a], as well as in another work by the same author, using a similar analytical framework to that employed here [Liégeois, 1983a]. Concrete illustrations are also to be found in the national monographs on which this synthesis is based, although the authors were deliberately brief in describing the evolution of general policies – a topic outside the scope of the present study.

Policies towards Gypsies and Travellers have always constituted, in one form or another, a *negation* of the people and their culture. Policies can be broadly grouped in three categories: *exclusion, containment,* and *assimilation*. These categories are not mutually exclusive: they can occur side by side in different states, or even within a single state, with contradictory policies in simultaneous operation. There is, however, in the historical sense, an evolution from the first category towards the third.

Exclusion

From the time of their arrival in Western Europe in the fourteenth and fifteenth centuries, Gypsies have been considered intruders. Erupting into tight local communities deeply entrenched within closed horizons just as the state was attempting to organise and control the population at large, these "homeless" nomads rapidly inspired mistrust, fear and rejection. Despite their small numbers (generally a couple of thousandths of the overall population of a given country) they nonetheless became an obsession of peasants and princes, of the Church and of the guilds. Each of these groups took measures to keep Gypsies out, and this rejection, localised at first, rapidly became an affair of state with the passing of royal edicts collectively condemning Gypsies and banishing them under pain of corporal punishment. There is usually a very short interval between the arrival of the first families and total rejection. Local populations had no reference point in relation to which they could classify the Gypsies: baffled by their unique clothing, language, lifestyle and the types of contact between the two groups, a negative image quickly formed around them, subsequently inspiring and finally justifying their mistreatment. Popularly conceived as a melange of sorcerer, brigand and general evildoer, the Gypsy was damned for eternity in the eyes of a credulous and easily frightened society.

Examples of exclusion policy are numerous: indeed it is probable that all of the states under consideration have practised it at one time or another. Let us take France as an example. In 1504 Louis XII banished Gypsies altogether; by 1510 the penalty for defying the ban became death by hanging. Later on, any gathering of more than three or four Gypsies was forbidden, and eventually (from 1647, under the Regency) simply being a "Bohemian" was made a crime punishable by the galleys. Turning to Germany we find that, from 1496 onwards, the Reichstag denounces Gypsies as traitors to Christian lands, spies in the pay of the Turks, and carriers of the plague. Accused of brigandry, witchcraft and child abduction, no longer tolerated on German territory, they could be killed with impunity; later, Ferdinand I, as a gesture of clemency, forbade the immediate killing of women and children. Further expulsion orders were passed and repeated; in 1721 the emperor Charles VI once again ordered the extermination of all adult males, while women and children were to have an ear cut off. In 1725, Frederick William I condemned to death by hanging any Gypsy over the age of eighteen caught on Prussian territory – with no distinction as to sex. And let us cite the case of Italy where, between 1506 and 1785, a period of 279 years, a total of 147 anti-Gypsy bans (or one for every 1.9 years) were passed [in fact, the number of known bans seems likely to increase as research continues – Piasere, MS.].

In the Netherlands, rejection was absolute. Painted wooden signposts depicting hanged Gypsies were erected at crossroads so that anyone passing them would know what awaited beyond. In the seventeenth century and at the beginning of the eighteenth, actual Gypsy hunts (*Heidenjachten*: "pagan hunts") were held. The same thing happened in Switzerland and elsewhere: popular hunts took place, sometimes to the sound of the horn, and with orders to shoot if met with resistance; sometimes such hunts were highly organised military affairs with the participation of infantry, cavalry and militia. Bounties for captured Gypsies were instituted, leading to the rise of professional Gypsy-hunters. Similarly, in Venice, a text dated 1692 offers amnesty to galley slaves serving sentences of up to ten years, on condition they take up Gypsy-hunting. Similar policies were pursued in Scandinavia: about fifty years after the arrival of the first Gypsies, Archbishop Laurentius Petri forbade the clergy to marry or bury them. (Indeed, religious authorities almost everywhere rejected the Gypsies. For example, the Council of Trent condemned them for their lifestyle, which made them difficult to control, and forbade priests to marry them without special permission from their bishop; thenceforward, diocesan synods were frequently to order priests to adopt an attitude of rejection towards Gypsies.) A royal ordinance of 1637 – the most severe ever enacted in Swedish legislative history – demands the banishment of all Gypsies, and sanctions the killing of any remaining behind. Similar legislation continued to be formulated; indeed, until 1954, it was illegal for Gypsies to enter Swedish territory (and Sweden has no monopoly on this attitude and its persistence into the twentieth century). In Norway, for many centuries, the law required that Gypsies and Travellers be arrested on sight, their goods confiscated, their leaders executed and the rest deported; if they returned, they were executed. The same situation held in Denmark, though in the eighteenth century the death penalty was commuted to imprisonment.

In this context, no one troubled to find out who the Gypsies were; they are clearly identified, but never defined, in historical documents. The darkly stereotyped image presented in these texts never attempts fairness or accuracy; on the contrary, the negative image is deliberately stressed in order to serve as a basis and justification for repressive measures. For just as no one troubled to define the Gypsy, they were equally unconcerned with their own reasons for reacting to him as they did. The very fact of being Gypsy was seen as sufficient provocation for condemning both the individual and the group. Their difference is automatically interpreted as dissidence, and they are condemned for "living the life of a Bohemian", suspected of the worst even when they had done nothing. As a Strasbourg magistrate wrote at the beginning of the nineteenth century, "I have no evidence of criminal acts committed by these people, but their situation is such that they cannot but be tempted to commit them if the occasion presents itself… They cannot but be dangerous." This type of argument opens the floodgates for all sorts of "preventative" measures, and justifies them in advance.

In the twentieth century, Nazi Germany staged the ultimate anti-Gypsy campaign. The practice of systematic extermination surpassed even the murderous "hunts" of previous centuries in both scope and horror. From the close of the nineteenth century, Gypsies in Germany were subjected to the same sort of registration and surveillance as were practised at the time in neighbouring states. Particularly from 1899, with the creation of the *Zigeuner-Nachrichten-Dienst* (Gypsy Information Bureau) under the direction of the Department of Criminal Investigation, Gypsies became subject to constant police surveillance. These measures were strengthened still further in 1938 with the passing of two circulars: one concerning "asocials", of which Gypsies were a specifically named category, and the other concerning the "fight against the Gypsy menace" (*Bekämpfung der Zigeunerplage*) which stressed that "Experience to date of the fight against the Gypsy menace, and the results of scientific studies, suggest that the Gypsy question be treated as a racial one." At first, they were interned in ghettos; later, from 1939-40, they were deported to Poland. From 1941 onwards, in territories occupied by the German army, many Gypsies were simply shot. In 1942 and 1943 Gypsies and "half-breeds" were interned, mainly in Auschwitz-Birkenau, Dachau and Buchenwald. Their extermination in Nazi-occupied countries was nearly total, and directly affected virtually every Gypsy family in Central Europe [cf. Kenrick/Puxon, 1972].

Containment

The effects of exclusion policies (banishments, various prohibitions, punishments such as branding with hot irons or hanging), terrible as they are for the victims who attempt retreat as a form of resistance, are pointless for the state enacting them. When all states banish Gypsies, where are they to go? They are eternal recidivists, eternally condemned since it is impossible for them to comply with the orders they are given even if they wished to do so. Exclusion policies are of limited effectiveness, and uneconomical: pursuit costs time and money, and deportation deprives the state of potential manpower. The policy of exclusion thus slowly gave way to one of containment, that is, the enforced and generally violent incorporation of Gypsies into surrounding society.

In containment, the goal of making Gypsies "disappear" remains, but instead of pursuing it by pushing them away geographically, it is to take place socially, by enclosing the group, which is then to conform with the rest of the population either through total absorption or by becoming "socially useful". There is no shortage of examples. In this way the death penalty for second offenders was replaced by condemnation to the galleys when these were in need of extra hands, and later by deportation to the colonies, forced labour, and the workhouse. The most extreme example of containment policy is Romania, where from the fourteenth century almost the entire Gypsy population was in slavery to the state, the Church and the nobility. Families were sold at auction, married couples split up, children sold to different masters or simply given away as gifts. Abolition did not take place until 1856.

In Spain too, from the end of the fifteenth century, a policy of containment was pursued. Gypsies were obliged to find a trade and a master; they were forbidden to travel in groups or indeed to go "from place to place" at all. Measures implemented repeatedly over the course of the following centuries demonstrate an unwavering political desire to forcibly assimilate the Gypsies into Spanish society. Banishment figures only as an alternative punishment for those who resist assimilation, and was quickly replaced by the galleys and mercury mines; occasionally roundups of Gypsies were held when the galleys were short-handed. One by one, gatherings of more than three persons, "Gypsy habits and costume", traditional occupations, finally the language and the name Gypsy (*Gitano*) itself, were outlawed. Residence was strictly controlled: limited to forty-one permitted localities in 1717, this was increased to seventy-six in 1746, stipulating a maximum of one Gypsy family per hundred population, and not more than one family per street. Armed troops scoured the countryside seeking any Gypsies living outside the designated areas, "authorised to fire upon them and to deprive them of life".

A gigantic roundup took place in 1749, affecting an enormous number of Spanish Gypsies, yet was a victim of its own success: as facilities, particularly prison space, were totally insufficient for dealing with the numbers concerned, detainees were gradually released up to 1765. Then in 1783 Charles III promoted an extremely detailed (forty-four articles) act of legislation. The text comprises a synthesis of preceding legislation and is a model of the provisions taken by this type of policy. The preamble forms a perfect resumé of assimilationist policies: "We declare that those who are called Gypsies, or who call themselves such, are not so by origin nor by nature, nor do they spring from unwholesome stock. Taking this into account, we order that they, and each one among them, shall cease to practise the language, the costume, and the wandering way of life which they have followed up to the present." And the king gives a ninety days' period of grace "so that all Vagabonds of this sort or that" might settle down "and abandon the costume, language, and habits of the designated Gypsies", on penalty of being branded with hot irons and, for those who persist, "the death penalty will be applied without appeal". The "designated Gypsies" thus had ninety days in which to negate and utterly transform themselves, expected to change language and lifestyle as one would change clothes [cf. Leblon 1985, Liégeois 1980, Sánchez Ortega 1976].

Other examples could be cited at length, particularly the policy implemented in the mid-eighteenth century by Maria Theresa of Austria and continued by her son, Joseph II. Through a series of legal orders nomadism, costume, language and trades were forbidden or regulated, and children were taken from their parents to be brought up by local families. Within the sphere of containment policies, the forcible removal of children from Gypsy parents has often been recommended, and occasionally put into practice, in many countries. One of the most important cases in recent years took place in Switzerland, where from 1926 to 1973 the charitable organisation Pro Juventute's "Children of the Road" division removed Gypsy and Traveller children from their families and confined them in institutions until they could be fostered or adopted – without judicial input. The actions of the organisation were supported by the relevant authorities.

Over the course of time, and despite centuries of enforcement – in Spain for example – the forcible assimilation of Gypsies has universally proved as ineffective as banishing them. This ineffectiveness does not mean that the recommended methods were not enforced: hunts did exist, just as did serfdom, roundups, galley slavery and all the rest, with all the accompanying consequences, individual and collective, for the populations subjected to this treatment. Nor was there any lack of zeal when it came to obeying orders to persecute Gypsies, be it by forcible expulsion, containment, or even extermination; indeed one could even say that practice went beyond official guidelines. It is thus not through lack of application that these measures failed to produce the desired effect, but through lack of realistic understanding of social dynamics, notably Gypsy resistance and the existence of solid social and cultural dynamics in their groups.

It is important to bear in mind that most of the legislation embodying the above-mentioned measures is still on the statute-books. It is rarely indeed that a measure is repealed; quite the contrary, edicts, ordinances and laws pile up on one another with two possible results: either the new legislation is in line with preceding policies, thus adding to the cumulative effect, or the later laws (particularly in the second half of the twentieth century) express a new policy trend (of assimilation, as we shall see). Paradoxically, however, these too have a cumulative negative effect along with that of older legislation, since both sets are still operative and either can be cited to suit the purposes of those applying them. To give but one example: according to operative legislation in most states, local authorities are obliged to provide halting sites for nomads, but are also empowered to expel them by presenting totally arbitrary arguments and subjective evaluations. These cumulative effects mean that nowadays, perhaps even more than during the operation of "exclusion" policies, Travellers are automatically at fault and at risk: measures, even long-forgotten ones, can be reactivated, their sanctions ever dangling over Gypsies' heads.

Assimilation

In the second half of the twentieth century ideas with a humanist slant have come to the fore. They have put a stop to corporal punishment, slavery, the removal of children from their families. At the same time a new, increasingly technological model of society has been adopted. These two tendencies merge in transforming containment policy into one of assimilation, characterised by the goal of absorbing the Gypsy, now redefined as a misfit associated with social and psychological problems.

The implementation of this general policy takes many forms, and we shall examine them briefly here. Firstly, there is *control by means of more and more detailed regulations*, dealing directly with every aspect of Gypsy/Traveller life: travelling, stopping and camping, legal status, the practice of itinerant or artisan trades, scrap collection, etc.

The different elements of such regulations are not always legal or constitutional – particularly those dealing with personal legal status when it is negatively defined or treats Travellers as an undifferentiated group (e.g. when they are subjected to automatic eviction or other discriminatory treatment).

Elements may be mutually contradictory (for example, legislation limiting duration and location of stay in urban areas, versus the legal obligation on children to attend school).

Although these texts, in general, do not apply specifically to Gypsies, it is important to consider the *web* they weave around those who are caught up in them, confronted in their day to day lives by regulations which prevent them from stopping, from moving about according to their wishes and needs, and which limit their possibilities of work. *Gypsies and Travellers form a population for whom these laws are mutually reinforcing in their negative effects.* For example, a person who is forced to move on too quickly, or to stop in bad conditions, loses his sources of income and suffers reduced initiative and adaptability. *Although in theory Gypsies and Travellers are not specifically targeted by this type of legislation, in practice, by reason of their position and lifestyle, they are particularly affected by it.*

It is worth pointing out the *selective manner in which many laws are applied to Gypsies*. For example, legislation controlling the stationing of caravans in built-up areas is enforced differently depending on whether the caravans belong to tourists, workers on a building site, or Gypsies – even if the latter are in fact travelling to exercise a trade (i.e. are workers) or at a given moment are travelling as tourists. In other words, the sole fact of being a Gypsy or Traveller and perceived as such provokes discriminatory treatment which is backed up by law. This also indicates that *anti-Gypsy discrimination is not solely a problem of institutions but also and at root a problem of society at large*. Different chapters in this report will provide ample illustration.

In connection with legislation and in the new spirit of the law, a new approach has developed which, in many states, consists almost exclusively of social welfare. Such policy confers an important executive role on social work and on various official and voluntary bodies formed for, but not by, Gypsies and Travellers. Thus control over Gypsies is made more humane, but at the same time tightened, and, within the overall policy of assimilation, the trend is towards achieving the "normalisation" of persons perceived as marginal or deviant. Such action weighs heavily upon those towards whom it is directed, and *the burgeoning of social welfare frequently acts as a block to genuine aid* which, if administered in accordance with Gypsy socio-cultural realities, could assist them in pro-active adaptation to new situations.

Stereotyped images are employed (consciously or otherwise) to inspire and then to justify attitudes towards and treatment of Gypsies and Travellers. As soon as the will to assimilate becomes predominant, the image which is propagated and on which policy is based cannot allow itself to recognise Gypsies and Travellers as possessing ethnic or cultural identity. The measures in which Gypsies and Travellers find themselves enmeshed must, in order to appear legitimate, be directed towards generalised social groups, since recognising the existence of a genuine and dynamic culture would prevent the implementation of assimilative measures now that forced assimilation is no longer ideologically acceptable.

Thus "official" pictures of Gypsies and Travellers tend to ignore all cultural aspects in order to present a "social problem". Let us give some examples. One possibility is that familiar terms are stripped of all ethnic connotations: for example, in 1967 the High Court in London defined "gypsy" as "a person leading a nomadic life, with no fixed employment and no fixed abode". The following year English magistrates ruled that anyone living in a caravan on an unauthorised site becomes a "gypsy" as a result of his lifestyle. Therefore, a sedentary Gypsy is no longer a "gypsy", but an illegal caravan-dweller is [Acton/Kenrick]. Another possibility, operative in many states, is that the very terms "Gypsy" and "Traveller" are no longer in official use, and are replaced by neologisms or paraphrases bereft of cultural connotations (for example "persons of nomadic origin" in France, "itinerants" in Ireland).

Whatever method is used, Gypsies are effectively stripped of roots and identity to be redefined as a "social problem" requiring "rehabilitation" and "reintegration" into "society". Once perceived as requiring "readaptation" they are, by implication, "maladapted", and this maladaptation is incorporated into the official image – a relationship of cause and effect very difficult to break. Another perverse effect of the development and promotion of such images: since the Traveller is now officially defined in social (rather than ethnic, cultural, or racial) terms, the negative measures directed specifically against him cannot be considered as legally discriminatory. To sum it all up: whatever policy is pursued, *the Gypsy is never defined as he is, but as how he must be in order to suit the purposes of the socio-political order.*

For the state, assimilation has certain advantages over containment; assimilation is still, however, containment in humanist guise. It is more efficient, more radical, and more acceptable. Containment entails persecution, which may provoke dissension. By contrast, the object of assimilation is rewarded for his cooperation; for example, if the nomad settles down, he will be less openly harassed, and if he goes on to conform to certain guidelines he will be entitled to increased social welfare. The present-day situation of Gypsies and Travellers is full of examples of this type, and we shall examine several in connection with schooling.

Indecision

The policy of assimilation, synonymous with absorption, formulated in the 1950s and developed in the '60s, underwent intensive expansion during the '70s when measures for achieving it were set in motion. These measures coincided with a glut of regulations aimed at stopping the remaining loopholes through which anyone attempting to lead an unconventional lifestyle might have slipped. New legislation controlling door to door hawking or the parking of caravans does not affect Gypsies and Travellers alone, but does affect them in a particularly severe way, and doubly so, since it undermines the economic base of a whole lifestyle, and because, in the case of Gypsies and Travellers, it is applied with particular severity.

But in spite of everything, assimilation is not achieved as quickly or easily as planned. New factors enter the picture, notably the necessity for many states to accept the permanent presence within their territory of immigrant workers and their families who until then were tacitly assumed to be a temporary phenomenon, en route back to their homelands. It has thus become necessary to give serious thought to essential transformations in many spheres, to improve coexistence within countries which have become multicultural. As a result, new ideas, such as "intercultural education", have emerged, spread, and are slowly beginning to be put into practice. The '80s seem to be a period of transition, indecision, hesitation, and contradictions too, for better and for worse. And the treatment of Gypsies and Travellers is being affected as well.

With few exceptions, the operative goal in most states is Gypsies' and Travellers' "social integration". But the goal is an ambiguous one, and its realisation fraught with difficulties. Integration, in the sociological sense of the term – is it not the first step towards assimilation? Is it not the putting into practice of a new formulation which presents the political advantage of being fuzzy and thus open to interpretation and manipulation? And between an official goal of integration purportedly based on respect, and its effective realisation, there are a number of obstacles. We will be examining these in further detail when analysing the schooling situation, and have analysed the phenomenon itself in the publications already cited [Liégeois 1983, 1985].

Whatever policy be adopted as regards Gypsies, there will always be two fundamental, inseparable questions: the basic question of taking culture and lifestyle into account, and the formal question of ensuring that the Gypsy and Traveller citizens of a given state receive the full benefit of laws protecting their common group and individual rights. To put it another way: is the existence of culture taken into account? If so, how, and what means are provided for facilitating it, once the talking is over? And, having decided on the means, are they actually implemented? Are they in fact compatible with the criterion of respect? What sort of results do they produce? Within this introduction to the overall political context, we shall briefly examine the content and operation of various national Constitutions, and the gaps between theory, practice, and results.

The great majority of Gypsies and Travellers, being citizens of a given state, are theoretically endowed with the same rights and duties as any other citizens. Constitutions protect citizens, stipulating the equality of all. They frequently also stipulate that aid should be given to those who, for whatever reason (economic hardship, difficulty of access to school, etc.) are deprived of this equality; occasionally minority groups (particularly linguistic minorities) are specifically mentioned in this context. But it is very rare for Gypsies, who have no territory of their own, who moreover have been subjected to coercive measures for centuries, and within the last decade or so redefined as a "deviant" social group, to be included among those minorities officially "recognised" as being entitled to respect and special aid. When it is necessary to clarify Constitutional articles, history weighs heavily indeed on the Gypsies. In Italy, Article 6 of the Constitution guarantees the protection of linguistic minorities – a protection which has been forthcoming only to linguistic minorities in border areas, and that in connection with international treaties. When the parliamentary commission on Constitutional affairs elaborated draft legislation extending the benefits of Article 6 to other linguistic minorities, negotiations were long and difficult; official recognition of Romani was initially blocked by other minorities objecting that their status was lowered by this association with Gypsies [Karpati/Massano].

Even when the state does agree to recognise and support Gypsy languages, this generally has little practical effect (on school policies, for example) not least because of the familiar lack of enthusiasm towards Gypsies but also because of their dispersion (there is usually a stipulated minimum number before legislation becomes operative) and, in the case of nomads, their moving about: virtually all relevant legislation postulates permanent residence.

Turning aside from the linguistic aspects of recognising Gypsies and Travellers as a minority, to consider to what extent their rights as ordinary citizens are respected, we see that a number of everyday – often perfectly "legal" – measures are unconstitutional. Common law, as applied to Travellers, is uncommon in all but name, penalising indiscriminately. *Measures of control, eviction, and many other practices affect the group as a whole, rather than this or that individual in response to concrete allegations.* In this sense, such practices are contrary to the principles of international law guaranteeing freedom of movement, freedom to exercise a trade, freedom to establish domicile, etc., as well as contravening legislation concerning public order and public safety, applicable solely in regard to an individual's personal behaviour. *A generalised attitude towards any human group, backed by official sanctions, as is regularly the case regarding Gypsies, Travellers, and nomads (regardless of what they are called), is not permitted either in the national laws or in Community law under the European Convention.* Moreover, this selective application of common law entails acts contrary to the Constitutions of the states themselves, even though (and this is a classic technique for dealing with Travellers) these are ostensibly aimed at ensuring public order, public health, national security and the like.

To date virtually no state is free of such practices towards Gypsies and Travellers. Legislation backing them is rarely formulated explicitly, but in practice Gypsies and Travellers can be controlled, evicted etc. within the provisions of existing law; some legal justification for surveillance, expulsion and the like can always be found. Again, just one brief example: in Italy, the Ministry of the Interior has repeatedly stressed (through a circular issued in 1973 and reiterated in 1985) that prohibiting halting rights to nomads is unconstitutional. Local authorities have responded by replacing the prohibition on nomads, with a prohibition on their caravans, which neatly transfers the issue into the realm of traffic regulations [Karpati/Massano]. In many countries, in the name of protection of the landscape, or agricultural lands, or public health, or any number of other reasons which are interpreted in a largely subjective manner, the halting of even a single caravan can be prohibited.

Among the new factors mentioned above, which contribute to ongoing changes in the situation, mention must be made, however briefly, of the fact that more and more states are ratifying international conventions, particularly those which provide a legal base for combating discrimination on ethnic or racial grounds (although these do not apply to Gypsies and Travellers insofar as they are defined as a social category). We must also point out that numerous test cases have resulted in decisions in favour of Gypsies and Travellers, all the more important in that they lead to changes in jurisprudence (e.g. decisions by the French Council of State and by the Supreme Court in the Republic of Ireland). Little by little, these are helping to clarify the judicial void surrounding Gypsies and Travellers despite the profusion of regulations affecting them. Finally, let us mention reforms of the penal code, which can have a dual effect: firstly by increasing penalties for those who practise discrimination (particularly public officials), prohibiting forced mass eviction and preventing the hindrance of the group from following its chosen lifestyle without specific reason for so doing (cf. the recent reform of the Spanish penal code, notably articles 18, 137a, 165, 181a). On the other hand such reform can also make a conscious effort to break the longstanding stigmatisation of nomadism, which, traditionally defined in the penal code as vagrancy, was seen as a disturbing phenomenon in and of itself, an aggravating circumstance in case of actual misdemeanour, and a cause for constant suspicion.

A legal guarantee of some minimum degree of security is a fundamental need of Gypsies and Travellers, as much in order that they may follow their trades as for the schooling of their children. No significant modification of existing legislation is required to attain it: in fact *the law as it stands is rather more on the side of Gypsies and Travellers than on the side of those who practise actual or symbolic violence towards them*, be it by rejecting them or by seeking their assimilation. The right to move on, the right to halt, children's right to attend school, the right to practise their chosen trades, the right to develop their culture… *It is the arbitrary interpretation and application of the law, and the proliferation of petty and often contradictory regulations, which must change.* Such practices will be particularly difficult to eradicate, since they spring from deeply-rooted attitudes.

Images of the Gypsy

The stereotyped and prejudiced images surrounding Gypsies and Travellers are of crucial importance: it is these images which to a large extent determine attitudes and behaviour towards them. They are the most important – frequently the only – direct link between these groups and their environment. Such images are numerous indeed. Gypsies and Travellers are not *un*known: everybody has an opinion (frequently categorical) about them, and believes that he understands them. In fact, they are *mis*understood, which is worse again, as reality is largely obscured by the imaginary.

In Western Europe the process began in the fifteenth and sixteenth centuries, when Gypsies began to be described in local chronicles and by legislators in connection with regulations aimed at them. Official imagery developed and rapidly crystallised into stereotypes which over the centuries have built up into a reservoir of images more or less firmly anchored in the collective consciousness, into which anyone can dip at will and find something to back up his argument and justify his policies – be they assimilationist or rejectionist.

These concepts are based on utter incomprehension. From the beginning, the least negative stance has been one of romantic sympathy linked with folklore, or an intellectual curiosity tinged with compassion; otherwise, when chance or necessity (an encounter, a glimpse, a question) arises, it is always the most negative aspects of the image which are reactivated. The pervasiveness of these images is such that popular perception of Gypsies and Travellers can never be "neutral". Objective reality is doubly difficult to grasp: in addition to real cultural differences, in themselves a source of mutual incomprehension, Gypsies and Travellers are perceived through the haze of this legacy of preconceptions and stereotypes..

For example the stereotype of "thieves" springs "… primarily from the suspicion that Gypsy 'riches' – car, caravan, jewellery – cannot be the fruit of honest toil. The working man cannot help comparing, with envy, the restrictions of his own lifestyle with the prodigality of a Gypsy celebration. He cannot realise that security, for a Gypsy, is not based on savings in the bank, but on lavish generosity which he will later receive in return; that the gold jewellery will be sold without hesitation to help out a kinsman; that the car and the caravan are home to a large family" [Karpati/Massano].

Public bodies and administrators form their opinions by the same principle of incomprehension in tandem with the political ideology of the moment, never realising that Gypsies and Travellers do not wish to fall into line in all respects with the general population, having neither the same motivations nor the same priorities. The authorities do, as a general rule, realise that the public at large has an excessively negative image of Gypsies and Travellers, and that a misunderstanding of their true nature lay at the heart of previous policies, or the policies of the opposition. But they do not realise that their own actions are based on equally false images. A good example is the tendency, in connection with assimilationist policies, to neglect cultural aspects in order to classify Gypsies and Travellers as "socially handicapped", "disadvantaged", "underprivileged", etc. – thereby creating for themselves the duty (and thus the right) of active social intervention, all the while postulating that Gypsies' and Travellers' cultural, social and economic dynamics are mere relics of an earlier lifestyle. Such a use of image is, as we have shown elsewhere, "ethnocide by anticipation", insofar as the measures or imagery employed to justify assimilationist policies provide a self-fulfilling prophecy of future reality [Liégeois, 1983a].

Representations are largely propagated by the spoken word, and there is no European language without its share of colloquial terms – all erroneous, mostly negative, though occasionally with an element of folklore [examples can be found in Liégeois, 1985a, in the chapter "The Imaginary Gypsy: Manipulated Images"]. But prejudice and stereotypes are also to be found in dictionaries which, through their function as reference sources, fix, validate, and elaborate upon them [cf. Dégrange, 1974]. Children's first readers introduce and reinforce the stereotypes; these themes are repeated and elaborated at secondary level, so that virtually the entire school-going population is affected [cf. Dégrange, 1980; Kenrick, 1984]. Despite the efforts of some bodies to prevent such texts being included in schoolbooks, they are still all too numerous, as they are in literature for adolescents.

At a later stage, the perpetuation of these images is assured for adolescents and adults in all forms of popular literature ("factual" as well as fiction) and other forms of mass communication, which oscillate between romanticism and alarmism – notably television and, at its most intense, in the pages of the gutter press. There is no place for reality between the alternating dichotomised stereotypes of the "stage Gypsy" (a sunburnt flamenco musician) and the swarthy thief, dirty and threatening. The Gypsy thus has two "doubles": his mythical double, beautiful and artistic, leading a life free of petty constraints, a symbol of liberty; and his wretched, disturbing double who parks his caravan where it will cause maximum inconvenience to the "Settled community" [cf. Dégrange/Liégeois 1971]. The further away the Gypsy is in reality, the better he is perceived to be.

Finally, the question of stereotypes should be examined in the light of what it reveals about the societies which invent and propagate them. It seems that Gypsies and Travellers, despite their small numbers, are troubling, and, like anything indefinable, it is their difference itself which is objectionable and provokes suppression. The image of strangeness, reconstructed in each new era, is a mirror of the preoccupations of the time, evoking the uncertainties and phobias from which society is anxious to distance itself:

"I told you, I don't know what the Gadjo (non-Gypsy) feels about us. Anyway, you can be sure that he recognises the fact that he's facing something very important, an independence, a way of... True enough, he usually says that the women are pretty, they dance well, that the Gypsy is a good musician – that, basically, the Gypsy is grand. Which explains why he pushes us away using only the roughest means, since the Gypsy is also verminous, filthy, refuses to work, the children are wild... In the end, well, it's hard to say, it's hard to explain what the Gadjo means! Basically he's rejecting something which he admires very much, but which is inaccessible to him, and that's why he rejects us. And if he's really nasty, that's because he feels so angry" [Cani, aged twenty, in Belloni, 1981, p. 71].

In fact, *the decision to assimilate has never reduced the desire to exclude – and this is a stumbling-block to assimilationist policies.* The experience of contact is often brutal, just as increased proximity brings increased rejection. *Where assimilation policies have been furthest pursued, it is clear that the result is not integration but marginalisation* in the spheres of employment, schooling, accommodation and so on [cf. Liégeois, 1980b, 1980c, 1983a]. In this context of false and aggravating images, extremist attitudes arise among the population at large as among local authorities, politicians and administrators.

The diffusion of these images creates a circular cause-and-effect phenomenon: official regulations, dictionaries, various books, television, the press, etc. feed on public opinion, pouncing on odd scraps of information which vary with the general mood of the time, then, having exaggerated for good measure, they present these back to the public as universal truths, and the public finds within them a confirmation of its existing opinion. The implementation of new policies clashes with this system of images in a very concrete manner when the Traveller child is rejected at school, when his parents are not allowed to halt if they are nomadic, when, for example, in the Netherlands, a policy of "deconcentration" of ill-suited megasites has been formulated by the authorities only to be blocked by public opinion objecting to the dispersion of Gypsies and Travellers onto smaller ones: no one wants them as neighbours [Hovens et al]. It is simply the fact of being Gypsy which activates the stereotypes; real behaviour does not count. An example: in Denmark it has been noted that Gypsy families are rarely rejected by their neighbours if their Gypsy identity is not known [Gudmander/Rude].

In order that attitudes and policies of respect can be put into practice, it is imperative that we dismantle these age-old stereotypes which block all comprehension and communication between Gypsies and Travellers on the one hand and their human and institutional environment on the other. A difficult task indeed, judging from existing reports on this subject [see the texts already referred to: Binns, Dégrange, Kenrick, Liégeois and many others, for example, Leblon, 1982; Martins-Heuss, 1983. To the best of our knowledge the most complete study, to date, of this topic – unpublished to this day – forms part of a report for the Commission of the European Communities: Dégrange/Liégeois/Michon, 1980]. *It is thus a question of discarding an image of "Gypsyness" founded on imagination or at best on old policies, and formulating in cooperation with those concerned a new understanding of real, living Gypsies.* A study of the genesis of stereotypes and a constant, discerning update of information will doubtless have a role to play if there is real desire to change the present situation.

The cultural sphere

This chapter presents a sketch of Gypsy and Traveller culture – both in order to confirm its very existence and to point out certain aspects of particular relevance to the question of schooling.

A lifestyle

Gypsy reality is enormously varied. The differing historical experience of various groups, their encounters, stopping-places, routes travelled, the diversity of their contacts with constantly changing surroundings, have given rise to a great variety of cultural and social characteristics – and continue to do so. Always immersed in other culture(s), Gypsy life is characterised by continuous adjustment and adaptation. What is more, contact with the wider environment is not "neutral", and Gypsies and Travellers have (as a condition of their survival) developed an extraordinary sensitivity to those aspects of it which affect them directly. Gypsy society is thus characterised, throughout its history, by the invention and development of strategies of adaptation. The result is *a tradition of change and innovation*. Public misunderstanding of Gypsies, and even research concerning them, by seeking to establish constancy and uniformity where in fact there is only change and variety, have contributed to the erroneous image and give rise to analysis based on total misunderstanding – which has a very direct impact on policies affecting the Gypsies themselves. After all, it is argued, Gypsies are changing; they are not what they were in the past, so they are no longer "real Gypsies", i.e. they are no longer themselves, so they need to be helped to "integrate". As we shall see, a different analysis is needed.

Recently, however, more and more attention is being given to the phenomenon of this constant and essential adaptability. As one Finnish Gypsy put it when addressing a conference, "Gypsyness started changing already when it became necessary to start the long trek from India towards Europe, because it was necessary to some extent to fit into the lives of the countries through which they travelled" [Nikkinen, 1976, p.47]; he went on to explain that throughout history Gypsy culture has been undergoing constant remodelling, voluntarily or no, consciously or no. More recently, another Gypsy put it this way: "Is a chameleon betraying his nature by adapting to his surroundings? Quite the contrary – his survival depends on it" [Jean Alciati, Director of the *Centre Culturel Tzigane* (Gypsy Cultural Centre), speaking at a meeting in Brussels, March 1986]. "Part of the 'Gypsy strategy' has always been a certain measure of adjustment" [ABGV, 1984, p.6]. As one young Gypsy put it, "The Gypsy can take on the fashions of the day: he's not afraid of appearances, because his life is elsewhere" [Belloni, 1981, p.60]. The group's identity "is to be, at any given historical moment, just what it is possible to be... to tenaciously practise and modify survival strategies, to have successfully played at mimicry as a principle of existence" [Asséo, 1981, p.13].

The continuity – the very existence – of this lifestyle is encapsulated within a variety of elements which permit and preserve maximum originality while allowing the necessary adaptability. One such element is social organisation.

Gypsies and Travellers form, in the world at large, a mosaic of widely differing groups. This means on the one hand that *they form a whole of related components* in which various links contribute to overall organisation and structure; on the other hand it also means that *each part of the whole possesses its own characteristics* so that, taken in isolation, it appears to be different from all the other components of the mosaic. Yet from the development of differences (of language, occupations, travel habits, rituals, etc.) springs complementarity, and complementarity forms the configuration of the whole.

The names under which individuals group themselves are an obvious sign of diversity; hundreds of names exist, describing hundreds of groups, each of which insists on its own uniqueness. Such groups are usually extended families and *the individual is that which his membership of a given group makes him – he is neither known nor recognised by his personal characteristics but by the ongoing situation within his group which defines his identity* for him (his self-image) and for others (as he sees them, and as they see him). The terms used, for populations which are both scattered and diversified, thus fulfil a function of marking and demarcation, of classification, identification, and finally of mutual adaptation. When an encounter occurs, each side weighs up the other, measures the distance (social and cultural) separating them, and can attempt, through selective emphasis of aspects of their historical and cultural experience, and in accordance with circumstances and inclination, to approach or withdraw.

Language fulfils a similar function. Social position (= group membership) and linguistic behaviour are always strongly linked. When two individuals from different groups make contact, language is manipulated to transcend the difference between dialects, yet at the same time to reaffirm their separateness within this framework of recognised similarity. Any given way of speaking is thus only a part of language-as-a-whole, and actual usage is at least as important as language itself. Language is thus clearly a vehicle of social meaning: speaking is one thing, but the way in which it is done is another. For the Gypsy, language is also an important demarcation between himself and the "alien", the non-Gypsy.

No group can be understood in isolation. Family groups are part of larger social groupings and these in turn are subgroups of larger wholes, forming an extensive network linking more and more elements. It is the *group system* which must be taken into account when attempting a comprehensive and dynamic approach towards Gypsy/Traveller society: groups exist because of, and for, each other, in perpetual cooperation and opposition; it is within this framework that equilibrium is regulated, through marriage alliances as well as economic activity. It is clear, then, that *social organisation is political*. Political life is diffuse, present in all social acts, in all relationships be they of opposition or association.

The interlinking of groups, their acceptance of common values without which there could be no organisation, is maintained by ongoing interaction. Ties are formed from day to day, reinforced, refined, sometimes severed. They do not bind rigidly, but are always subject to modification. Beneath the infinite variety, the diversity of income, dwelling-places, occupations, rites and customs (which form the superficial aspects of culture and lifestyle, and which are constantly evolving in response to changing circumstances) lies the heart. It may seem paradoxical, but this too is infinitely flexible – it consists of the tissue of relationships between social segments which are relatively independent yet linked in an ever-changing configuration. This organisation is flexible but durable, capable of both grasping opportunity and adapting to conditions imposed from without. Groups can intensify their alliances or even merge, others can drift apart, still others can subdivide or even dissolve into individuals assimilated into the larger environment. The whole is capable of accommodating all these phenomena, all the more so as they occur within a framework of rules and prohibitions which limit breaches of the norms and thus guarantee the ongoing cohesion of social structures.

Social control is exercised in a diffuse fashion, all the more effective since the importance of the group outweighs that of the individual. A set of rules regulates various aspects of life, such as food, personal hygiene, behaviour towards others. Many of these rules are based on a dichotomisation into "pure" and "impure": persons, objects, and behaviour will all be classified by this criterion. Taken together, the various categories and rules form a coherent principle of separation and distinction [cf. for example Acton, 1971]. The fundamental distinction is between Gypsy and non-Gypsy – with whom most forms of social interaction are forbidden. A solid barrier is thus posed between the two, since any crossing over of social boundaries is automatically also a crossing over into the realm of the impure, and is thus risky. This barrier of prohibitions reinforces social barriers: non-Gypsies belong to another universe. While each Gypsy/Traveller group emphasises its uniqueness and difference from all other Gypsy/Traveller groups, they are unanimous in their total opposition to non-Gypsies. "Look – for a Frenchman there are the French, the English, the Chinese, the Italians, etc. For us, there's just us, and the Gadjé (non-Gypsies). That's the difference!" [Mona, aged seventeen, quoted in Belloni, 1981, p.77].

Difference is thus an essential component in the construction of identity. Each group strives to maintain its difference from other groups; Gypsies see themselves in diametric opposition to the entire undifferentiated non-Gypsy world, which in turn has always assigned a negative image to the Gypsies as a whole. In this context it is less surprising that assimilationist policies have not had the anticipated success. It also becomes easy to imagine just how Gypsies perceive situations – the school situation in particular – involving prolonged close contact with non-Gypsies. At the same time we see how school, like any other element from the non-Gypsy world, can be made use of, since Gypsy adaptation strategy aims towards using whatever is usable in the non-Gypsy world, without becoming emotionally or socially attached to it. "The different groups have always known how to adapt to new conditions in their environment, to create diversified identities for themselves. What then is 'semi-literacy' (partial use of schooling) if not a traditional approach towards a relatively new phenomenon? It is simply the Nth appropriation of elements of non-Gypsy culture which nonetheless allows children to continue to identify themselves as Gypsy, and to continue to play, with pride, the game of Gypsy life" [Piasere].

Why wouldn't Gypsies and Travellers continue using a strategy which has proved so effective over such a long period? "If culture is an institutionalised response to ambient or latent disorder and an effort to organise and confer sense upon the givens, then the best cultural configuration at any given moment is that which responds best to the actual state of the environment" [Verbunt, 1983, p.138]. Up to the present the individual Gypsy, secure in his family and social groups, finds within them a strong feeling of belonging, both in the elements which constitute his identity and in the support of physical, economic and psychological solidarity, all the stronger and more necessary since the "outside" is so threatening. Travel forms a part of, and support for, this lifestyle: it combines freedom of movement, freedom of occupation, the importance of living the present moment, and many more factors which go to make up a flexibility, an *economic, political, social and psychological system of the ephemeral, a functioning geared to the passing moment, an identity pared down to the essentials; that is to say, a non-material way of being on which the environment can have little hold.*

Travelling

Nomadism, its reality as well as the meaning it carries for those who practise it (and those who observe it) must be considered with sensitivity. The reasons for moving are varied; as mentioned earlier, in the section on "History", persecution, pressure, troubled times – all have played, and continue to play, a role. We will deal with a different set of reasons here, emphasising that *for the Gypsy or Traveller travel is socially and culturally functional: it permits social organisation, authorises flexibility and adaptability, and makes possible the practice of some trades.*

Moving about gives different groups an opportunity for close contact with each other, which can lead to new ties, sometimes even marriages, or on the other hand to mutual opposition within which each group feels its own uniqueness justified and strengthened. Encounters with similar groups reinforce consensus through a communion of shared values; encounters with dissimilar groups serve the same function (reinforcement of identity) by opposite means. Travel makes closer contacts possible, but it also permits separation if conflict arises, as well as providing an escape when the environment proves hostile. Since the Gypsy worldview emphasises the present moment, places are not bonds, but simply stages, by nature temporary.

The economic functions of travel are at least as important as the social side. The exercise of trades characterised by independence often necessitates intensive and long-range market canvassing by the craftsman, tradesman or artist. Economic independence is essential for the Gypsy, and it is often in order to retain it that he takes to the road – regardless of how long or short the break in his travels has been.

An examination of various situations shows that, while nomadism is neither entirely a product of Gypsy and Traveller culture, nor entirely the source of that culture, it is a fundamental component. Apart from this assertion, it is impossible to categorically identify the prime cause of travelling. Like everything else about Gypsies and Travellers, no generalisation is possible, and nomadism with its adaptive function is part of the Gypsy's repertoire for dealing with circumstances as they arise. He can use it, or not, as the situation demands. For example, in *Italy*, "Social cohesion would seem to be the primary motive for travelling today... In the coaches of southern Italy one often meets Gypsies who, too poor to own a car, travel by public transport. In this case, a nomadic lifestyle may become a source of social prestige" [Karpati/ Massano]. Elsewhere, the accent (not the sole motive) may fall, at a given moment, on economic independence: in the *United Kingdom*, "The crucial role which non-Gypsies attribute to nomadism is in fact played by the institution of self-employment. Economic, not geographical freedom is most crucial, but geographical freedom and a willingness to travel are a consequence of economic freedom and a condition of it" [Acton/Kenrick].

In tandem with the diversity of reasons for travelling, there is an equal diversity of practices connected with it, evident in means of transport (from the horse to the aeroplane), the frequency of moves (from daily to almost never), the scope of travel (from a few hundred metres to the whole of Europe), the practical arrangements for setting up camp. And, having observed these various practices, one still cannot generalise about correlations between them: in some cases, it is the most nomadic who is most prosperous, while in others it is he who has the most difficulty in scraping a living.

A few attempts at synthesis may help us to better appreciate the reality and quality of travelling. In the light of the facts considered above, we note that there exists, on the one hand, a *structural nomadism*, due to a certain form of social and economic organisation, and on the other a *reactive nomadism* brought about by outside factors such as eviction, various regulations, family illness, economic opportunity. These combine to determine actual moves. *To Travel, to be "a Travelling person", is an essential identifying symbol for those concerned.* A Traveller is someone who remains detached from his surroundings, who is able to pick up and move whenever it is useful or necessary to do so, when he needs to or simply feels like it. There is an important difference between the objective reality of travelling (the fact of moving from one place to another) and the subjective reality: feeling oneself to be a Traveller. A "Settled person", even when moving about, remains "settled" in spirit. A Traveller – even a "housed" Traveller – is a Traveller still. "A Traveller is a Traveller even if he doesn't travel – and the mark of it is on him" [Cani, in Belloni, 1981, p.70]. *Nomadism is as much a state of mind as a state of fact.* It is therefore, in the majority of cases, more correct or more prudent to speak of those who have halted as being *sedentary,* rather than *settled*. For the Gypsy or Traveller, sedentarism is automatically understood as provisional, so the first word is a more accurate description. The second term implies an irreversibility. In other words, one can be a sedentary Traveller, but the idea of a settled Traveller is anomalous. What is more, in many Gypsy languages the term "Settled" is used – often with condescension – to designate the non-Gypsy population.

These considerations help us to clarify some widespread but erroneous concepts concerning nomadism. The first is that which stipulates "Gypsy = nomad" or "Traveller = nomad" (and, by the same token, that anyone else is not a "real Gypsy"). This may be further limited by additional stipulations – for example, that if travel is not by horse-drawn wagon it is not authentic, nor are those practising it[3]; since this means of transport is on the way out, there is little risk that those posing this criterion will be called upon to accommodate those whose cultural claims they theoretically recognise. The second idea is a sort of inversion of the first: there are no longer any "nomads", only "persons of nomadic origin", who from an official point of view should not be treated much differently from any other settled people. This is an equally grave error, and for two reasons. First, it is based upon the negative effects of sedentarisation policies, without looking into causes. Second, it imposes a notion of permanence on people for whom sedentarism is only a phase while they wait for better days or new opportunities; it is making Travellers into Settled people by wishful thinking, by wilfully ignoring the dynamics of their organisation and adaptability. This is not to underestimate the phenomenon of entirely voluntary sedentarisation, nor the fact that some groups have a tradition of sedentarism, and in such cases the relationship with the environment is generally good; at any rate it is not imposed from without, and withdrawal remains a possibility. But such voluntary practices and their results must never be confused with, or used as a model for, compulsory settlement.

The number of nomads and of caravan-dwellers who are more or less mobile varies from country to country. Estimates concern a fluctuating reality, and one which is notoriously hard to pin down, "for the difficulties of defining who is and who is not a Gypsy amongst those who dwell in houses are ten times those regarding the definitions of those who dwell in caravans. To what degree of assimilation and descent do we count a house-dweller as still a Gypsy? If we go by Government definitions the Gypsy population in England, Wales and Northern Ireland was until recently 100% nomadic and is still 95% nomadic (a few settled Gypsies having been discovered by schools or produced by sedentarisation). Economically successful settled Gypsies, I believe, are excluded from government figures of the Gypsy population in most West European countries" [Acton, personal communication].

In many countries, the number of nomads increases from year to year, if only by reason of the high birth rate: this is the case in Ireland and France. In Belgium and the FRG, on the contrary, the number of nomads tends to remain low. Here are the results of two studies carried out in the *FRG*:

• from a survey based on a nationwide sample of 137 townships [Weiler, 1979, p.308, quoted in Hermans, 1980, p.58. The percentages add up to over 100, but the author does not say why]:

    42.41% of Gypsies live in rented accommodation
    25.39% live in local authority accommodation for the homeless *(Obdachlosenunterkünften)*
    25.05% live on official sites (in caravans or huts)
    12.50% in caravans

• from a questionnaire filled out by local authorities in 339 cities and districts [Freese, Murko, Wurzbacher, 1980, quoted in Hermans, 1980, p.58]:

Travelling patterns of Gypsies and Travellers in the FRG, by percentage:

	do not travel	rarely/irregular distances	regularly in summer	most of the year
Gypsies	15.9	35.4	38.2	3.1
Travellers	12.2	42.3	33.6	11.1

In *Italy*, a survey based on a sample of 13,435 persons was carried out for the present study. It breaks down as follows [Karpati/Massano]:

	nomads		semi-nomads		sedentary		total	
	number	%	number	%	number	%	number	%
North	2,025	44.6	1,650	36.5	860	18.9	4,535	100
Central	2,400	40.0	400	6.6	3,200	53.4	6,000	100
South	-	-	60	2.0	2,840	98.0	2,900	100
ITALY	4,425	32.9	2,110	15.1	6,900	51.4	13,435	100

For the *United Kingdom*, the numbers are as follows [Acton/Kenrick]:
Overall numbers of nomadic and housed Gypsies/Travellers in each country of the UK*
(*Nomadic figures by extrapolation from official sources; housed figures by authors' estimate)

	Nomadic	Housed (estimate)
England	32,000	30,000
Wales	4,000	5,000
Scotland	5,000	12,000
Northern Ireland	1,000	1,000
Isle of Man, Jersey, etc.	0	(50)
Totals	**40,000**	**48,000**

Notes:
1 The total for nomadic Gypsies is less than the sum of the column to allow for up to 2,000 nomads who may appear in the total of more than one country.
2 Among the ethnic groups of Gypsies, it is widely believed that the proportion of Scottish Travellers, Welsh Kalé, Rom, Romungri and Boyash who are housed is much greater, and that of Irish Travellers rather less, than the English Romanichals, who are generally believed to be roughly equally divided between housed and nomadic families.

Certain statistics may give an indication of movement between states. Here is an example from *Belgium* – a "crossroads" country – giving the nationalities of occupants of the "Terrain d'Accueil" site in Brussels, between 1 July 1979 and 1 February 1981 [Reyniers]:

Nationality	No. of individuals
Belgian	22
French	162
German	5
Greek	3
Norwegian	61
Spanish	12
Swiss	2
Yugoslav	162
undetermined	200

To obtain a fuller picture, it would be well to ascertain the movements of each family group of each nationality.

Accommodation

Dwelling places, like types of dwelling, correspond to the variety of situations in which Gypsies and Travellers find themselves, and form part of their repertoire for adapting to changing conditions. At the same time, certain groups have a tradition of travelling and working in rural areas, while others have long urban associations. However, in the twentieth century, economic circumstances have typically led Gypsies and Travellers into suburban concentrations, be it in caravans, houses or huts.

We shall give only one detailed example, particularly striking as an illustration of these new concentrations on the outskirts of national and regional capitals: Dublin, the capital of *Ireland*, where about a third of the country's total Traveller population is now clustered.

Growth in the number of families in County Dublin [*Report of the Travelling People Review Body*, 1983, p.9]:

Dec. 1960	June 1961	Oct. 1974	Oct. 1978	Oct. 1980
85	46	387	387	573

(The low number in June 1961 is doubtless due to the period in which the survey was carried out – many Travellers would have taken to the road for the summer.) If one examines the situation county by county it becomes clear that rural counties are losing their Traveller population, and that the number of Travellers shows its highest growth in the biggest cities.

Other statistics cover the types of dwelling for 2,490 families surveyed in 1980 in the Irish Republic as a whole [ibid. p.12]:

Living in house	957	families
Living on serviced site		
- in chalet	253	families
- in trailer caravan	131	families
Living on the roadside	1,149	families
Total	**2,490**	**families**

The spread of mechanised transport has almost everywhere had the seemingly paradoxical effect of reducing nomadism: numerous halts are no longer necessary when scouting out economic opportunities in an area, nor for visiting relatives even if they are relatively far away. What is more, non-tourist caravans are subject to frequent checks and surveillance, and finding a halting place, even for a brief period, is becoming more and more difficult. All of these factors have contributed towards a tendency for the stabilisation of dwelling place, supplemented as necessary by travel to outlying areas.

There is a huge range of types of dwelling and of transport, from horse-drawn wooden wagons to luxury mobile homes, from the cart to the modern RCV, from the bender-tent to the latest custom-made camping equipment, from the cave to the hotel. Type of dwelling must be seen as both utilitarian and provisional: it is often both precarious and dictated by outside factors. As part of the repertoire for adapting to changing conditions, it almost always reflects a compromise between various social, economic and political factors (such as rejection, local bye-laws, imposition from without). In fact extended families do attempt to live in close proximity, be it in caravans or houses; this enables them to feel united and secure. Given the choice, however, they avoid overcrowding: the huge compulsory official halting sites that proliferated in many countries up to 1980 and beyond, conceived (consciously or not) as a means of confining Travellers, have without exception become ghettos with all that this implies.

Given the choice, both semi-nomadic and sedentary Travellers tend to opt for a "mixed" type of dwelling: often a chalet or other small permanent dwelling with an adjoining space for a caravan or two, or perhaps a large "mobile home" supplemented by a lighter, less cumbersome caravan – with actual sleeping alternating between these. This mixed habitat seems to serve as a dual form of security. The caravan means that, should social or economic necessity arise, the family can take to the roads, while the more stable dwelling is a place of refuge in time of need (for example, hospitalisation of a family member, or loss of transport).

There is much to be learned from these few observations. There is no type of accommodation which is uniquely Traveller, just as there is no particularly Traveller type of vehicle or caravan. As one scholar summarised Gypsy folk tales: "Analysis demonstrates that, while these are not originally Gypsy, there is a characteristic and very marked Gypsy tone, within which the 'Gypsyness' is the manner, the approach, the feel" [Williams, 1981, p.34]. Not, then, a specifically Gypsy dwelling, but a specifically Gypsy use of dwellings, of their layout and space. It follows, therefore, that *there is no problem inherent in Gypsy accommodation as such: instead the problems arise when they are obliged (often arbitrarily) to stop in certain places, or to shift from where they are. The gap between spontaneous Gypsy practices* (e.g. of organisation of space within a halting site, the use of space within a chalet) *and practices imposed by others* (e.g. the way "official" halting sites are organised, the layout of prefab chalets, "resettlement" programmes) *is almost always very great*. Sometimes – and this is serious – a pretext is made of "adapting" dwellings for Gypsies and Travellers, based on erroneous suppositions rather than direct consultation. As a result Gypsies and Travellers continue to be obliged to compromise with imposed conditions. Finally, let us repeat what we have already said in connection with nomadism: travel and sedentarism can alternate. They are only stages, sometimes long and sometimes short, sometimes voluntary, sometimes imposed, in the course of ongoing adaptation. It is well not to repeat the mistake of attaching to either state a greater permanence than it has for those concerned. Social and cultural dynamics – and we shall be coming back to these in detail in connection with schooling – can operate fully only within a context of flexibility.

Health

We have emphasised in many works [notably Liégeois, 1977a] that social workers assigned to help "people with problems" deal mainly with clients answering this description – it is, after all, their job. In so doing, however, they have contributed to propagating an image of Gypsies and Travellers as being generally impoverished and in great difficulty on every count. A similar observation may be made in connection with the more specific issue of health: "Statistics in reports tend to show considerable health problems; but they have often been criticised for exaggeration by Gypsies who have read them; and this criticism has some basis, since the samples are always drawn from poorer Travellers, from among those known to health visitors and social workers, i.e. from among those most likely to suffer high rates of morbidity and mortality" [Acton/Kenrick]. It is therefore well, when interpreting data (statistical and otherwise), to take this methodological bias into account. One must also bear in mind that, from country to country, depending on the institutional and ideological slant used in classifying groups as "underprivileged", studies may concentrate disproportionately on nomadic families (because of their high visibility) or sedentary ones (because of their greater accessibility). This leads to other forms of bias. For example, in the UK it has been suggested that one of the reasons why census results show that there are only a quarter as many Gypsies over the age of sixty-five as there are in the general population, may be due not to death, but to the fact that Gypsies of a certain age tend to settle down, be it in houses or on small private (camping) plots, "away from the eyes of the census-takers" [Acton/Kenrick]. The top of the age pyramid is thus drastically reduced.

Let us indicate tendencies for a few Member States. In *Italy*, statistics based on sample groups were compiled in 1972, 1979 and 1980 [Karpati/Massano]. It appears that the average number of persons per family is 5.5, a low average compared to the birth rate. Two factors remain to be taken into account: children leave their parental family very young – often well below the legal age – to start families of their own; and infant mortality is significant (15% of the families interviewed had lost one or more children). On the other hand, the age pyramid appears to be very flat: in Italy 50% of Gypsies are under fifteen, 75% are under thirty, and only 2% are over sixty.

The most common ailments are directly related to poor living conditions:
respiratory infections, rheumatism, ear/nose/throat infections: 48.9%
gastro-enteritis due to bad food and difficulty of access to clean water supply: 9.3%
hepatitis: 3.5%

We must also mention cardiac ailments (3.8%) and neuroses (9.3%) in connection with which "one should consider the role played by the violent methods employed by the police in the course of evictions" [Karpati/Massano]. Physical and mental handicap account for a further 3.5%, and other pathologies include tumours, burns, alcoholism and drug-related problems. Research carried out for the present report among 162 special teachers (with Gypsy children in their classes) confirms this picture; eighty-seven replies covered the most prevalent forms of illness, distributed as follows:

	number	%
- related to poor accommodation:		
respiratory infections	41	47.1
ear/nose/throat infections	7	8.0
rheumatism	1	1.2
- related to poor hygiene:		
infestations	14	16.0
infectious disease	8	9.2
dermatitis	2	2.3
dental caries	1	1.2
- related to poor nutrition:		
gastro-enteritis	12	13.8
- work-related accidents (collecting scrap)	1	1.2
	87	100.0

(In fact, dental caries is more common, but teachers probably did not consider it to be a disease until the questionnaire drew their attention to it. It must be noted that, in general, nomadic children have the best health, and chalet-dwellers the worst.)

In *Ireland* an official study carried out by the Health Boards in 1980-81 formulated the following list, in order of importance:

- respiratory conditions
- gastro-enteritis and gastric disorders
- alcohol-related conditions
- skin conditions
- infestations
- dental problems [cf. *Report of the Travelling People Review Body*, 1983, p.93].

Infant mortality appears to be three times higher amongst Travellers than the general population. Gastro-enteritis "is virtually endemic in many of the bigger Dublin camp sites as a direct result of living conditions" [McCarthy]. The birth rate in 1981 was 333.3 per 1,000 married women between fifteen and forty-four (in 1979, the figure for the population as a whole was 188.7 per 1,000 married women between fifteen and forty-four). A survey of thirty-eight special teachers carried out for the present report [McCarthy] confirms the preceding findings: "bronchitis, chest infections, gastro-enteritis, tooth decay, low resistance to infections", adding, "speech defects, hearing disabilities, infestations such as head lice and scabies".

Illness due to poor living conditions takes the same forms in all countries. It has also been noted that, where enforced settlement has been carried out (notably in *France*), illnesses specific to house-dwelling have arisen, creating a phenomenon of "sedentarisation-related pathology". In the *FRG* "The rate of emotional and physical illness is very high, and can be explained by the persecution suffered under the Nazis. Persecution-related illness tends to get worse with age and is often the result of a situation of repression. The experience of persecution is psychologically very pervasive and can by one means or another be transmitted even to very small children" [Reemtsma]. In states (such as *Denmark* and the *Netherlands*) where widescale intervention and preventive medicine have been implemented, it seems that the physical health of Gypsies and Travellers is better. Yet other complications may arise: for example in the *Netherlands*, "In 1983 and 1984 there was an overall rise in the incidence of psychosomatic complaints, related by the Gypsies to uncertainty over their legal position and problems in concluding marriages with foreign partners" [Hovens].

One could doubtless also mention a "pathology of acculturation" which shows signs of developing everywhere. It manifests itself in such forms as, for example, overconsumption of medication, which is more a symptom of great unease than a simple result of ignorance as is so often claimed.

Living conditions imposed upon Gypsies and Travellers are, as we have seen through the types of illnesses affecting them, *a determining factor in a significant number of illnesses*: physical conditions, often insalubrious or at best inadequate; social conditions generally characterised by the symptom of rejection be it violent or covert.

Medical conditions themselves are not always favourable: in many countries there are reports of doctors who do not accept Travellers or accept them only reluctantly. Even more frequently, there are difficulties with the health authorities, in the form of overt rejection or petty non-cooperation ("You don't have the right papers"). Bureaucracy makes it difficult to get what, in theory, one is entitled to, and this is particularly true in the case of nomads. The end result is that medical services tend to be used only in case of emergency, omitting preventive medicine and follow-ups. The question of Traveller health is thus largely beyond the scope of medicine as such. "Teachers report that at the time of eviction Traveller children exhibit disturbed or withdrawn behaviour; but whether one should consider this as a medical problem, to be treated by a doctor rather than by political action, seems dubious" [Acton/Kenrick]. It is a fact that, *under actual circumstances, the best preventive medicine would be of a political nature, and would entail the acceptance of Gypsies and Travellers.*

Economic activities

Virtually all trades practised by Gypsies and Travellers consist, in one form or another, of selling goods or services to non-Gypsies. Within this pattern, the Gypsy's economic activities are characterised by *polyvalence,* and *it is by the range of his skills that he will be able to take advantage of fluctuating circumstances.* Thus an individual can practise several compatible economic activities simultaneously. Or, he may concentrate on a single activity for months or even years on end, yet always with the possibility of adding one or more auxiliary activities. Or, he may follow a regular pattern of consecutive activities as dictated by the changing seasons, opportunity, or his travels.

Another, essential characteristic of Gypsy and Traveller work-patterns is *independence*, which permits the individual to be in control of his own time – free to meet his social obligations. *Flexibility of occupation is largely preferred to security*. What is more, independence enables the Traveller to avoid involvement in an alien business world, keeping contact with its members to a necessary minimum. The essential characteristic of an acceptable trade is above all the way in which it can be practised, and the choice of activities is, like choice in other fields, the result of compromise between the necessity of earning a living and the desire to maintain a lifestyle within a changing socio-economic environment.

The basic economic unit is the family group and in principle activities are arranged within this framework, although for bigger projects temporary wider partnerships may be formed. The variety of economic activities practised makes listing them impossible, and their fluidity makes it pointless. There are, however, certain traditions which are also general tendencies: metalwork, the collection and resale of various materials, various forms of entertainment, music, the circus, the fairground, horse-training and dealing, selling door-to-door and at markets, the making and selling of diverse objects, agricultural work, fortune-telling, and supplementary begging. New activities are constantly being developed, often in sectors where Travellers have accurately identified work opportunities well before those who analyse their activities realise the change and adaptation that have taken place. And ancient trades can, despite strong competition, be revived, particularly in the field of handicrafts (basket-making and leather-work, for example) when these come back into fashion in the surrounding population. But there are fashions among Gypsies, too: "There are fashions in trades; at one time everybody wanted to be laying tarmacadam, then it seemed everybody wanted to be mending roofs, then everyone wanted to be exporting antiques" [Acton/Kenrick]. There is also ongoing development of occupations which reconcile the Gypsy/Traveller work ethic with the constraints of the environment: horse-breeding, motor mechanics and lorry-driving are among the more popular choices.

The rare statistics available give only an imprecise indication of economic activities. Let us give illustrations from three countries.

In *Italy*, according to research in Piedmont (1979), Calabria (1979) and Latium (1980), Gypsy economic activities can be categorised as follows [Karpati/Massano]:

type of activity	%
- services	47.2
- commerce	21.3
- agriculture	17.7
- industry and crafts	13.8

In the *Netherlands*, we can see the evolution of trends over a thirty-year period [Teunissen, 1982, p. 28]:

Heads of households as a percentage of the total occupational group

Activities	1947[a]	1960[b]	1970[c]	1977[d]
traditional independent occupations	21	9	5	4
of which : knife grinding	9	5	2	2
chair bottoming	11	3	1	1
hawking	30	32	12	11
dealing in waste and second hand goods	20	44	45	36
other independent occupations	14	–	2	5
paid employment/employment under Sheltered Empl. Act	13	15	15	13
other/unemployed	3	–	21	31
Percentage total	100	100	100	100
Absolute total	**2,109**	**2,072**	**3,580**	**4,736**

a) Source: 1947 Census. Covers the total travelling population as recorded in the Central Population Register, excluding persons working in the fair and circus industry, road construction and agriculture.
b) Source: 1960 Census. The traditional caravan-dwelling population, excluding the building industry and the like.
c) Source: Ministry of Culture, Recreation and Social Welfare, Occupational Structure Survey 1970.
d) Source: Ministry of Culture, Recreation and Social Welfare, Caravan Census 1977.

In the *United Kingdom* the two censuses of the 1960s concerning "nomadic Travellers" took note of their economic activities [quoted by Acton/Kenrick]:

Winter occupations of adult Travellers in Britain in the 1960s, by percentage

Occupations	England and Wales March 1965		Scotland March 1969	
	Males	Females	Males	Females
General/Scrap dealing	52	5	36	2
Hawking	3	8	1	4
Agriculture/Horticulture *	15	7	19	10
Labouring	4	-	6	-
Roadwork/Tarmacadam	4	-	4	-
Building work	3	-	1	-
Timber/Logs	2	-	-	-
Factory work	2	4	-	-
"Traditional" jobs *	1	1	1	-
Other means of livelihood	5	3	2	1
Housewife	-	62	-	61
Retired	2	1	5	2
No occupation/Unemployed	6	11	23	17
School	-	-	-	1
Sick/Not known	1	-	2	1

* A survey carried out in Scotland in August 1969 indicates that the agricultural and "traditional" sector can be up to three times as great in summer. This is probably true in England, too.

Sources: *Gypsies and Other Travellers*, HMSO 1967 (for England and Wales)
Scotland's Travelling People, HMSO 1971

"Showmen, circus and fairground workers of Romani origin were not included in these surveys if they were members of the non-Gypsy-led Showmen's Guild, which has since the 1890s sharply differentiated its members from all other Travellers, and has seen its occupational closure consolidated by many statutory exemptions. Patterns of occupation of house-dwelling Gypsies have not been surveyed, but are probably nearer to those of nomadic Travellers than is often supposed. The house-dwelling Rom tend to specialise in the repair of cookery equipment and of mechanical jacks."

Profound and rapid change, with direct impact on economic activities, has been occurring since the mid-twentieth century. The rural exodus, industrialisation and mass production, the advent of the consumer society, changes in the law (making it difficult to carry on as a small trader), heavy tax burdens (entirely inappropriate to the subsistence scale on which most Travellers practise their trades), administrative red tape, difficulty in finding a place to practise handicrafts, and so on and so forth, have necessitated rapid, often difficult, adaptation.

When the economic and legislative loopholes for "minor trades" and activities considered – often wrongly – to be marginal, are blocked, those directly affected can retain only an illusion of independence, since they must operate within limits set from without rather than freely choosing, in an increasingly constrictive atmosphere; what had been steady work may degenerate into occasional dabbling. On the other hand, many Gypsies and Travellers have successfully adapted by making a virtue of necessity, or by turning to entirely new economic spheres. New contingencies are constantly arising, e.g. the obligation to produce proof of having attended school in order to obtain or renew a trader's, showman's or craftsman's licence. For example in Italy, Law 398 of 1976 requires that, when applying for such licences (authorising the bearer to provide entertainment at fairs, to trade at fairs, or to practise a handicraft, respectively), anyone born before the end of 1951 must produce their primary school certificate, and those born from the beginning of 1952 onwards must produce proof of having completed secondary school. Such requirements cannot be met overnight, and, to avoid breaking the law, or causing economic hardship for many families practising useful and remunerative skills, one must hope that laws of this sort will be enforced very gradually.

Detailed consultation must be undertaken with Gypsies and Travellers about economic questions, particularly in connection with the formulation of legal and social policy. *We can assume that among the various parameters determining the actual situation, many can be easily changed* (if only certain prejudices and ideological slants can be overcome). These are the *practical aspects* (such as the provision of workspace in official halting sites) *which would help Gypsies and Travellers to earn their livelihood within the dynamics of their own economic ethos.* It would also enable costly long-term social welfare to be replaced by short-term practical assistance. Many states offer training or financial aid to those wishing to go into business for themselves – but does a craftsman who is also nomadic, qualify? Is door-to-door retailing as acceptable as retailing from a shop? Social welfare, on the other hand – at any rate as it is practised in some states, usually in the form of intervention by social workers – tends to perpetuate itself and its clientele.

Social welfare is certainly necessary; there are cases of poverty in every country, and some Gypsies are among them. *But it is not a sufficient response, and should certainly not be the only one.* Nor is it always, in all its forms, the best way of helping Gypsies and Travellers. For example, assimilationist policies in many places have given rise to a situation of "handoutism" inducing a state of passive dependence and inertia in many families. Other negative effects can be added to this: there are some states where sedentarisation is a precondition to receiving help of any kind. There are others where the least sign of initiative as regards work, which ought to be encouraged, is instead penalised by automatic withdrawal of aid; thus in *Ireland* "Social welfare regulations also have a demoralising effect because unemployment payments are cut off if Travellers are seen doing scrap work or any other work even though they may be making very little money from it" [McCarthy]. There are other cases, not always foreseeable, where official help has in fact been a factor in progressive deterioration. Thus, in the *Netherlands*, "The loss of traditional sources of income and the provision of state poor relief meant that Dutch Gypsies had much less need to travel, and they settled down in family groups in sites designated by the municipal authorities. These sites were often isolated and lacking in facilities, the result being a process of pauperisation and segregation" [Hovens et al].

While on the subject of social welfare, attention should be drawn to certain other negative effects. In general, what help is theoretically available is unsuited to Gypsies and Travellers in practical terms, and as a result they do not always obtain their entitlements, or get less than do other groups. This is in direct contrast to the popular image, dominant both in the public imagination and in the administrative image itself: Gypsies are seen as a "parasitic" population who do nothing and live off the state.

When analysing Travellers' economic activities, the ongoing and time-honoured error is to once again confuse effects with causes. In fact there is nothing inherently anachronistic or unremunerative about Gypsy and Traveller economic activities, as many examples can be cited to show, but they do tend to become so when prevented from developing naturally. Usually the stumbling-blocks are not even of an economic nature but instead, as usual, spring from the discriminatory treatment to which Gypsies and Travellers are subject. Let us also draw attention to the fact that the Gypsy work ethos, in which freedom to determine one's own schedule is a fundamental value, is being echoed by a new trend in Western societies, in which "quality of life" is invoked, and even those in direct wage-employment express a wish for job-sharing, flexitime, etc.

Education

In this section we shall give a brief outline of the education the Gypsy or Traveller child receives within the bosom of his family, and some reflections on the discrepancies which may arise between this in-family education and the school system. We shall return to this topic in more detail when we come to analyse the different types of school provision.

We begin with three preliminary remarks, the importance of which will be clarified in the text.

- Up to now, *too little attention has been paid to the values and dynamics of education within the Traveller family*. A few ethnographic works on the subject do exist, but it is extremely rare for ethnographical reflection to be combined with reflection of a pedagogical nature. As a result, pedagogical theory and practice are usually opposed to in-family education, instead of being based upon it.

- *The way in which Gypsy and Traveller parents educate their children should not be judged in the light of how the society surrounding them educates theirs.* "It may be said that it is highly improbable that, on the basis of the needs and values of one culture, advice on how to bring up children can be given to members of a culture with other values" [Gustafsson, 1973, p.95]. One could even say that, in many ways, the education given by Traveller parents to their children corresponds to the values which teachers from the wider society would like to impart to their pupils: autonomy, responsibility, a sense of community, etc. [cf. Liégeois 1977a].

- The development of schooling both in intensity and in duration, in European society; the way in which it has taken on more and more of the family's educative role, and correspondingly the degree to which families have relegated this responsibility to the school system, have gradually transformed "schooling" into a synonym for "education". We speak of the "education system" when we mean the school system; we delegate total responsibility to the "Minister for Education" or "Department of Education". If this is the case for many, it is not so for all, and we must emphasise that there are those – including the Gypsies – for whom *schooling is only a part* (and sometimes not even that) *of the education of their children.*

The education of the Gypsy child takes place within an educative *system*: that is, its various elements comprise an organised whole, and are neither haphazard nor gratuitous, as is often claimed. In Gypsy life, everything revolves around the family, the basic social, economic and educative unit. In a world of precariousness and unpredictability, the family is a core of permanence and stability. The individual is never alone and cannot be lonely; he is part of a wide network of intense emotional relationships. Social solidarity is both social and psychological security.

In this context, the child's education is collective. He lives communally, alongside three or four generations, and his socialisation takes place within this context which assures cohesion, coherence, continuity and security. Generations are neither separated nor opposed; children and adults work together, live together, suffer together. Children learn through immersion in the family, through their respect for adults and in being respected for themselves. Experience, exploration, initiative and responsibility are rewarded. But the freedom to initiate does not mean lack of control. There is no plethora of niggly rules that must be observed, but control is holistic – that of the group and its values – and, as regards "the outside world", there are physical (especially for the very young), social and psychological prohibitions. All in all we are dealing with a coherent education towards independence – and not a "laissez faire" – within an educative community which channels behaviour towards the goal of acquiring autonomy in a context of respect for the group and its values.

The affective aspect of learning is important, and the feeling of shame which comes with failure can be much more effectual than physical punishment, which is very little used. The community is seen as a whole, and the individual is brought up to respect others, and the equality of all. No one has a right to control another, or to put himself over another; no one can claim to be superior. If one is successful at one thing or another (for example, in the economic field, which may bring increased social status), it is up to others to acknowledge this, not for the person concerned to make claims. It is difficult to analyse members of the community in isolation from their roles and activities within it: socially and psychologically speaking, the individual exists solely within the context of the network linking him to others. For example, when someone requires hospitalisation, the community does not accept being cut off from one of its members. What happens is that a part of the community accompanies the individual to his hospital ward [frequently setting up a round-the-clock group vigil throughout the hospital stay – Sinead ní Shuinéar]. The same reactions are provoked by the school situation. Separation from the community is all the more violently felt since the child has been brought up to fear and mistrust "the outside world" – an attitude reinforced and justified by the conflictual character of everyday contacts with it. And school is, after all, a part of "the outside world".

Apprenticeship in economic activities occurs within the communal context, as an intrinsic aspect of the holistic education process. As soon as age permits, children participate in their parents' work, thus acquiring long experience, and the parents "may arrange a more varied range of activities for the very purpose of giving their sons and daughters a variety of skills" [Acton/Kenrick]. The work of the very young should be understood as collaboration rather than employment, far less as exploitation (though of course there are, as in any society, cases of abuse): "Quite the contrary it is a means of self-validation. The children derive satisfaction from being active members of a group which appreciates their activities without expecting of them anything beyond their capacities" [Karpati/Massano]. The role of young people as collaborators in family economic activities is important, for both girls and boys.

We shall now quote large excerpts from the study on Gypsy education commissioned for the present report [cf. also for example the approach of Berthier, 1979, and Gustafsson, 1973, notably chapter IV, "Socialisation", pp. 70-83]:

According to available evidence, a powerful and specific *mode of education* operates within the different Gypsy groups. "This mode is based upon particular *educational relationships* which by their very nature preclude the existence of abstract instruction removed from a real-life context – the very foundation of the non-Gypsy concept of 'school' ... What does it mean, then, to 'grow up Gypsy'? It often means that a child has three different categories of educators and at the same time is an educator himself. Grandparents represent the prototype of aged people; from them he learns what old age means and how to accept it. They are also usually the principal direct link with the *mulé*, the dead (whose existence is sometimes conceived as fundamental to the existence of the living), since it is frequently they who have the closest ties of kinship with those *mulé* 'respected' by the whole family. From grandparents one learns above all that in the past, life was different than it is today, and that this is right and proper.

Parents represent the prototype of married people. They are the people to imitate, the people whose behaviour inspires curiosity and a spirit of adventure, persons of authority but rarely authoritarian; they inspire and reward the child's spirit of initiative from his earliest youth... In this way the Gypsy child sometimes finds himself with responsibilities which render him equal to an adult, responsibilities which a non-Gypsy parent would never give to a child. Bearing this in mind, we begin to glimpse the Gypsy community's perception of intergenerational continuity.

The third category of educators consists of other children, of which older brothers or, more often, sisters are the central figures. They play an important mediating role, since they find themselves linked simultaneously with the parental generation and with children of the same age, and are able to pass on to younger siblings both this 'vertical' experience, received from parents and grandparents, and the 'horizontal' experience of persons in their same age group who undergo similar experiences at the same time.

The system permits total integration, since the child is both a subject of education, and an educator: he finds himself transmitting to others concerns, attitudes, advice and reproaches which only a few years previously he was receiving from others and which, with some modifications, he continues to receive while transmitting them. Here, then, is an uninterrupted chain, which fuses together the members of a community; the uninterrupted continuity of transmission; the importance (seen as obsessive by the non-Gypsy) and intensity of interpersonal relations; the means of reproducing a way of thinking by ongoing linkage of each part with all, enabling instant communication of knowledge for coping with life. And everything which we label – mysteriously – as 'resourcefulness', reveals itself as a component of a whole strategy of initiative in which the Gypsy has been systematically educated from his earliest years" [Piasere].

Where does schooling fit into this context?

"The Gypsy perception of public instruction has for centuries followed the same general pattern. Schooling has never been seen as having an educative function, but simply as offering a possibility – which one may exploit or not, to a greater or lesser degree – of mastering a code used by non-Gypsies: writing.

It is said that the Gypsies are a people without writing, but this is not entirely true and perhaps never has been. Forced to live among people who, to a greater or lesser degree, use writing, the Gypsy has always been able to cope with it one way or another. My personal experience has revealed many cases of people, including the elderly, who can read, despite never having gone to school. I can also point out that in any local group I've known, there is always at least one person, man or woman, who is able to write up a simple text.

Non-literacy, accompanied by a small percentage of semi-literacy, still represents today, for many Gypsy communities, a choice along traditional lines which classify literacy as a code proper to non-Gypsies, and thus one's knowledge or otherwise of it functions as an ethnic determinant. There is even a legend among the Xoraxané Romá explaining why the Gypsies possess only part of the non-Gypsy alphabet.

The fact that Gypsies reject an instrument of information-transmission because they consider it to be 'alien' does not mean that they have no instruments of their own, still less that they have no knowledge of their own (observers remark, for example, on an ingenious method of doing multiplication without pencil and paper). The fact is, that Gypsy pedagogic technique differs from the non-Gypsy in one principal aspect, but one which for us is the quintessence of education. For them, it occurs within the context of real-life activity by participation, rather than by verbal instruction out of context, in preparation for future participation. Pedagogic content is also dissimilar: since the problems with which the Gypsy deals in daily life are predominantly connected with personal interaction, abstract generalisations are unknown and useless, replaced instead by concrete and specific symbolism which reflects shared and reciprocal experience. Knowledge is gained, not by asking questions, but by living out responses" [Piasere].

In the wake of these reflections, more detailed consideration should be taken of the wishes and practices of Gypsy/Traveller families in connection with school provision, taking into account the gap between in-family education and school education as it is usually offered.

The current situation

"All are the descendants of rejects, from father to son, and are rejects themselves. They live in the shadow of humanity, be it in France, Europe, or anywhere else in the world. For Gypsies and Travellers, human rights do not exist, or exist only in appearance. Over the years, many have made studies, but only to serve their own interests, for their own fame or fortune. For Gypsies and Travellers there is nothing but persecution, incomprehension, evictions, prohibitions on halting, provocation, defamation, and prison" [Pierre Yung, President of *l'Union des Tsiganes et Voyageurs de France* (The Union of Gypsies and Travellers of France), 1980, p.291].

There is nothing new in this situation; the few historical and socio-political details we have already given make that clear. On the other hand, the fact of cultural persistence in itself proves that, up to now, Traveller survival strategies have been successful. One can observe throughout history periods in which the Gypsies modify the forms of their adaptation: "Relations between Gypsies and non-Gypsies are cyclical in nature. Economic and technological changes break up an older symbiotic relationship; then follows a crisis during which some Gypsies give up their way of life, while the remainder adapt to new circumstances; then there is a new symbiosis" [Acton/Kenrick]. But each period has its own characteristics, and the determining factors in the present situation are not the same as those of earlier periods. In the course of the second half of the twentieth century, important changes have affected the form and nature of contacts between Travellers and surrounding society. Some of these changes are universal, in the sense that they have affected all cultures and societies, while others are specific in that they impact on Gypsies and Travellers in a particular way.

The "universal" changes include the evolution of needs in an ethos of consumption and ostentation linked with far-reaching economic and technological changes. This evolution has two consequences. One is economic in nature: worn goods are no longer repaired, the craftsman is no longer in demand, small-scale entertainment has been swallowed up by "show business". As a result the Gypsy is no longer seen as performing a useful role, and this reinforces the false image of the "parasitic" Gypsy. Even fairground operators – bringing welcome entertainment – find themselves pushed further and further out into the suburbs [cf. Lorenzo, 1985]. One cultural and psychological result: in this new world of consumerism and "modernism", reference values undergo transformation and, particularly through the younger generations, these transformations affect cultures, all the more violently when the culture is in a numerical minority, and distanced from the cultural groups whence the new values spring. At the same time, cultural influences are becoming literally global in nature, through the mass media. This expansion will have important effects. Influences are not disruptive insofar as they are socially localised; on the contrary the group's selective borrowings from such sources enable it to affirm its own unique identity. But *when the influence itself becomes just about the same everywhere, Gypsy populations may become uniform in response to uniform pressures.*

This in turn has many implications for nomads, and for Gypsies and Travellers in particular, which lack of space prevents us from examining in the detail they merit. The quality of life on the road is deteriorating, due to the decrease in rural nomadism and a related increase in suburban nomadism and urban settlement, leading in turn to concentrations of people in poor conditions. At the same time this intensive urbanisation makes halting difficult and increases the motivation for evictions and restrictive legislation. These tendencies are due to rural and urban transformations to which Gypsies have tried to adapt, but their efforts have often proved insufficient when assimilationist policies have stipulated rapid, compulsory settlement. In many European states sedentarisation has been demanded explicitly or implicitly, without any provision being made for Traveller accommodation. Negative effects of a social and a health nature have resulted, as they have in the economic sphere: sedentarisation policies have brought impoverishment, by blocking the functioning of adaptive dynamics. This is when, in political discussion of the subject, sedentarisation becomes described as a means of combating poverty [cf. for example the observations of Hermans, 1980]: a humanist argument which justifies the policy in principle.

The pressure applied to control the movements of people is also brought to bear on their economic activities: the exercise of itinerant trades and crafts has become difficult, and many activities are entangled in a web of incoherent legislation, making them difficult to practise despite the fact that in a period of economic difficulty Gypsies need to be more adaptable than ever. At the same time a social welfare system, as described above, has evolved, overly heavy-handed in certain of its aspects but often rendered necessary by the negative effects of assimilation policies. This social assistance gradually puts those who receive it into a dependence situation which they reject but which they are compelled to accept [as alternative after alternative is closed off – Sinead ní Shuinéar]. The situation is all the more embarrassing in that, in certain states, it affects the Traveller population as a whole; for example, in the *Netherlands*, "Being a Woonwagenbewoner *in itself* qualifies one to receive social welfare" [Hermans, 1980, p.26]. Being placed in this passive role is favourable neither to the development of social and economic strategies which could lead to autonomy, nor to the expression of an identity which could serve as a basis for such development, nor to the use of schooling as a means for achieving independence.

Another worrying aspect of the present situation, for the Gypsies, is that their culture is seen by outsiders as marginal, and contact has always had the effect of activating underlying antagonisms, frequently into full-blown conflict. It is easy to imagine – and one must try to understand – the psychological anguish of those who are constantly subjected to harsh treatment within permanent insecurity. And as soon as politics attempt to trim the margins and bond them to the mainstream, Gypsies and Travellers are particularly affected. The desire is to normalise the marginal in order to integrate him; the cumulative effect of various actions and rules to this end is in fact that the margin becomes rigid, and those on the outside are forced to move even further out to find the flexibility they need to replace the elements which have been made illegal. It is important to bear in mind the Gypsy's relation to the law, situating it within its historical perspective and within his own position (seen by others as marginal). Everything comes together to block an independent existence within the chosen lifestyle – economic activities, mobility, large family groups, all are penalised by current legislation. What is more the variety of laws, the varied and often arbitrary way in which they are enforced, their complexity (which often baffles even the experts), are not conducive to understanding or respect. All of these factors colour the Traveller's subjective experience of his environment.

A youth in *France* described his experience of the coming into effect of the new law of 1969 regulating the legal status of nomads, and which meant that they would no longer require their *carnets anthropométriques*[4]. "The day that I handed in my parents' booklets, I was told, 'Sir, we are also collecting your nomads' cards and your collective booklet (the one with all the family together).' Well they should have given me a new collective booklet at least, in exchange. My father said, 'Sir, I will not give you my collective booklet, because my children are not pigs. I cannot read or write, neither can my wife, neither can my children. How do you propose that I remember all their names, since it's all nicknames with us? I can't! What about the birth dates? I can't remember that either! If you take away my collective card, I won't have anything anymore – I can't agree to it'" [Joseph Robin, in Liégeois, 1980d, p.313].

When dealing with poorly understood populations, legislators have no idea how the law will affect those at whom it is directed; those enforcing it are often equally ignorant. And every form of intervention, even if it is the product of sincere good will and intended to be positive, runs the risk of being perceived as just another coercive measure by those to whom it is applied. The heavy weight of history must be taken into account, and a great demonstration of willingness to respect Gypsies and Travellers will be required if it is to be lightened. For the moment any such willingness, insofar as it has had no practical impact, cannot but be regarded with cynicism by those towards whom it is directed. In the climate of indecision described above, Travellers are kept waiting in a vacuum or a shaky status quo while projects – insufficient, but a step in the right direction – are developed for cultural minorities, be they local or immigrant, with a territorial reference base. For Gypsies and Travellers the essential determinant of the present situation is, as we have seen in connection with each of the themes dealt with so far, the treatment to which they are subjected. For example, "Although there exists a problem of poverty, for most Travellers the problem is not poverty but persecution" [Acton/Kenrick].

At present Gypsies and Travellers, to a greater or lesser degree from place to place and group to group, are experiencing an overall sense of exhaustion, and give an impression of having depleted their adaptive mechanisms [cf. Liégeois, 1967a, 1985a]. "Now, you can see it for yourself – there are Travellers who feel tired, they don't want to travel anymore. They find a spot, set up camp on it, build themselves a sort of a house with a big room so everyone can eat together, and there you are, they don't want to shift." [Mona, aged seventeen, in Belloni, 1981, p.77]. There is a corresponding rise in pauperisation and in crimes of violence as a direct result. And this trend obliges the environment – both population and institutions – to turn its attention to the "problems" of Gypsies and Travellers. It is obvious that while this is the – negative – motivation for interest in a minority culture, concern is once again misdirected, and perception accordingly distorted. Those who are the object of it are deeply affected, as a part of their identity becomes formed by representations of themselves from the surrounding environment. This represented identity, which becomes part of assumed identity, is disturbing, all the more so as one can neither counteract such images, nor avoid being exposed to them – from the mass media and the impersonal agents of surrounding institutions such as the police, administrators, social workers. Let us give a few examples from various Member States, bearing in mind that the list could be long indeed.

"The stereotyped negative image of Travellers in the public perception has a devastating effect on the self-image of many Travellers, especially the younger ones who are more aware of it. It also makes it much easier for the authorities to neglect their obligations towards them and to harass them. This is because there is little public sympathy for their cause. There have been exceptions to this pattern of events where Travellers have been made welcome by local residents and where positive images have been projected in the media but these are very much the exception" [McCarthy, *Ireland*].

"It becomes apparent that even now Gypsies are continuously reminded that they are not welcome, and often 'civilians' (non-Gypsies) are seen to be formally put in the right, in spite of anti-discrimination legislation. Gypsies feel continuously excluded and rejected" [ABGV, 1984, p.4, the *Netherlands*].

"To be a young Gypsy in Italy today means to find oneself in a climate of permanent conflict and crisis of the value of one's own identity; it is to feel alienated in this society and in a situation of frequent dichotomy which, by constantly putting internal values into conflict with those of the 'outside', provokes a situation of incertitude which strains the actual phase of transition between the older and younger generations" [Bruno Morelli, a young Gypsy in *Italy*, in Karpati/Massano].

"They've encountered even stronger rejection when trying to assimilate than they did when they were travelling, completely isolated within the population of cities and villages, and they suffer every kind of injustice at all levels. They pack up and leave, preferring to be rejected in the company of their own kind, than to be rejected from assimilating. The children prefer it too. They're too small to understand why their parents have to suffer the injustice they witness; they feel the consequences. So, when they do leave, they are happy and understand that their parents are too; in this way a sense of complicity is created between them. The children refuse to go to school, the parents understand, the children understand the parents, they've become accomplices... To have the finger pointed at you constantly, insulted, humiliated, defamed, and yet to hold your head up in front of the youngest children! How are they to be taught?" [Pierre Yung, President of *l'Union des Tsiganes et Voyageurs de France*, 1980a, pp. 292-4].

"The marginality of the Sinti is so obvious that it has become, for the majority of Sinti, an integral part of their identity. Many Sinti do not see integration into sedentary society as possible without negating their own identity. As a result, those seeking integration often avoid contact with other Sinti, which means that in a practical sense they cease to live as Sinti. The well-founded fear that professional or economic discrimination would inevitably result if their Sinti identity were known, continues to be very widespread" [Bremer Volkshochschule, 1983, p.6; *FRG*].

"Travellers are dressing more in the fashion. Settled people often say: 'She doesn't look like a Traveller.' I was going for a job and the man asked me where I lived. I said: 'The Watery Road.'

'Oh,' he said, 'down with the itinerants?' 'Yes,' I said, 'I'm one of them.' 'Sorry,' he said, 'you don't look like one.' There is an encouragement for Travellers to pass as Settled. It makes things easier, but it's wrong if you have to feel bad about looking like a Traveller. Why should we feel bad?" [B. McDonagh, *Ireland*, in McCarthy].

There is all the greater risk of identity being disturbed as, confronted by the images that the environment presents him with, the Traveller must develop mechanisms of defence and of compensation. On the one hand, he must behave in accordance with these images, letting others see exactly what they expect to see – it is both prudent and, from a psychological point of view, more economical. It is easier to pretend to conform to others' expectations, than to try to fight; the forces are too unequal, the prejudices too deep-rooted and pervasive. But by pretending, the Traveller reinforces that which he seeks to free himself from, and the image is confirmed each time his behaviour is influenced by it.

It is certain that stereotypes are among the most widespread social phenomena, and the Travellers for their part hold erroneous images of the surrounding population. These two sets of stereotypes often reflect one another as inverted images. Communication between Gypsies and non-Gypsies is rendered particularly difficult by this mutual incomprehension.

In the current situation, and bearing in mind the operative factors we have mentioned, to be realist means to be cautious and sceptical. Gypsies and Travellers are at a critical point in their history. But it is not they alone who are in crisis; apart from the discrimination and coercive measures, it is actually to a large degree the crisis of the surrounding societies, particularly in the economic sphere, and entails difficulties in adapting for their members too. However, there are no grounds for general pessimism. The culture of most Gypsy and Traveller groups is strong, daily life is complete and coherent, and time-honoured adaptive mechanisms are still largely operative. One can also say that, in certain respects, notably in the spheres of economics, mobility, and the education they impart to their children, Gypsies and Travellers are better prepared for life at the close of the twentieth century than are many of those who seek to "help" them [cf. Liégeois, 1977a].

Schooling takes place within this difficult and conflict-ridden context. We shall now examine what effects it has – or does not have – and seek to identify the causes.

School provision

General data

The state of literacy

We have already shown in some detail just how difficult it is to give accurate statistics concerning Gypsies/Travellers and/or nomads. It is thus all the more difficult to give details about the delicate question of how many of them can read and write. What we present here are therefore estimates – sometimes local, sometimes national, sometimes detailed, sometimes general – through which we shall perceive tendencies.

In *Denmark*, "From the experience of the connections to the parents it is the Danish and Yugoslav teachers' impression that the majority of the parent group, and especially the grandparent group, are illiterates. When speaking to the work colleagues in the social welfare system you got the same impression" [Gudmander/Rude].

In the *FRG,* "Hundsalz estimates 36% illiteracy amongst adults. This number does not include those who can read and write with great difficulty, or those who can read but not write. Yet 20% of the illiterates did attend school. According to research on the local school situation carried out by the Rom and Sinti Union of Hamburg in 1981, many Roma and Sinti despite years of schooling are barely able to read and incapable of writing" [Reemtsma].

In *Ireland*, "Almost 90% of adult Travellers are illiterate. There are no statistics to prove this but it is generally accepted as a fact by both Travellers and people working with them" [McCarthy].

In *Greece* a general estimate indicates that 65% of the total Gypsy population is illiterate; 85% amongst semi-nomads, doubtless nearly 100% amongst those over forty and nearly 100% among women over twenty five. No matter what age group is considered, "the percentage of literacy cannot exceed 40%" [Korré/Marselos]. An estimate by age and sex, carried out in three different areas, provides the following data (the percentages given are of illiterates).

For 18-30 year olds	women (%)	men (%)
Ano Liossia	95	78
Kato Ahayia	80	70
Ayia Varvara	75	65
For 6-15 year olds	girls (%)	boys (%)
Ano Liossia	84	75
Kato Ahayia	68	60
Ayia Varvara	45	30

In *Italy* an estimate by age was carried out in many provinces [Karpati/Massano]; the percentages given are of illiterates:

	between 16-30 (%)	over 30 (%)
Bologna	75	90
Padova	80	90
Torino	30	50
Roma	40	80
Catanzaro	80	95
Cosenza	9	90
Foggia	1	70
Reggio Calabria	65	85

In the *United Kingdom* the general situation is varied, both as regards age and group. For the Scottish Travellers, "Even if we exclude all the housed and semi-sedentary Travellers who make up 80% of the community, adult literacy amongst nomadic Scottish Travellers is reckoned to be 50-60%" [Acton/Kenrick]. But it appears that the number of children attending school is showing a tendency to decrease, and it is possible that the literacy rate will drop in years to come: "One community worker echoed this fear, suggesting that among younger adults there was more friction and less social contact with the house-dwelling community." Among other communities, if the number of literates was low up to the 1960s, it has grown considerably since as a result of developments in school provision dating from that period. Thus, if for English and Welsh Travellers the figure of 10% literacy could be given some twenty years ago, "We estimate this has drifted up to around 15% for all adults, but probably double that for adults under thirty years old." In Northern Ireland very few adults can read and write, but it appears that Irish Travellers are much more literate in England – more so, in fact, than are English Travellers themselves. Despite the lack of data, it is also probable that among sedentary Travellers literacy is more important than it is for nomads: "There remains a small minority even of the richest Travellers who possess both houses and caravans who oppose literacy for their children, on the grounds that it is inimical to the development of memory and intelligence – a skill for servants and secretaries, not for businessmen like themselves. Nonetheless, it is likely that three-quarters of the housed Traveller community at least are functionally literate" [Acton/Kenrick]. These estimates are not valid for the small Rom community[5], most of whom are illiterate. The Romungri are certainly literate, as they were when they left Hungary about thirty years ago, whereas the Boyash/Rudari present a similar picture to the English Travellers, with whom they intermarry. These various estimates can be synthesised in the following table:

Adult Literacy Rate, by percentage

Country	England and Wales	Scotland	Northern Ireland
For all Gypsies/Travellers* (1980s)	35-40%	85-95%	25-40%
For nomadic Travellers (a) in the 1960s (b) in the 1980s	5-10% 10-20%	50-60% 50-60%	2-5% 5-10%
For nomadic Travellers aged 16-30 (1980s)	25-35%	45-55%	10-20%

*This estimate refers to the entire ethnic communities, sedentary and nomadic.

In *Belgium* "Illiteracy is the norm among Gypsies (particularly the Rom) and is very extensive amongst Travellers (the Manouches being somewhere in the middle); individuals who have gone beyond the level of primary education are extremely rare" [Reyniers]. For this study, information was collected from the members of sixty families, a total of 323 persons, of whom 211 are over eighteen; this sample is more haphazard than representative [cf. Reyniers]. The study group comprised "23% Manouches and 77% Travellers (to have included the Rom, for the most part illiterate, would have biased the results) established or travelling within the Brussels, Charleroi, Genk, Louvain, Malines, Mons, and Verviers regions. Three levels of literacy and six age-groups were established:

a) *Literacy levels:*
Group I: literate persons (who have mastered reading and writing);
Group II: semi-literate persons (who cannot write and who can read only elementary phrases);
Group III: totally illiterate persons (who have no or almost no elementary understanding of reading and/or writing).

b) *Age-groups:* literacy levels among Manouches and Travellers by age-group, expressed as percentage with the number of individuals concerned indicated in brackets:

Age group	group I	Literacy levels group II	group III
over 60 (7)	14% (1)	0% (0)	86% (6)
51-60 (25)	20% (5)	12% (3)	68% (17)
30-50 (112)	26% (29)	22% (25)	52% (58)
19-29 (67)	31% (21)	13% (9)	56% (37)
12-18 (82)	7% (6)	57% (47)	36% (29)
6-11 (30)	17% (5)	40% (12)	43% (13)
total (323)	21% (67)	30% (96)	49% (160)

This table gives us a great deal of information. It shows that 21% of the sample are literate (Group I) or, to put it another way, "four out of five of the Manouches and Travellers in our survey, were illiterate." We notice too that young adults are the most literate age-group, and in view of these figures it is possible to state that "Within a general state of illiteracy, the mastery of reading and writing is a characteristic of adults" [Reyniers].

At the same time we must be cautious in our analysis of these data, at all times bearing in mind that they cannot be generalised. The various tables are opposed on certain points; for example the findings concerning Scottish Travellers, which echo those for Belgian Manouches and Travellers by indicating a drop in literacy among the younger generations, are opposed to the Greek and Italian data, and indeed to the picture for other Gypsy groups within the same country. Another example from *Italy*: "The rate of illiteracy is highest among adults over thirty, and decreases in the fifteen to thirty age group… a survey in Puglia indicates a 70% illiteracy rate for the over-thirties, but a mere 1% in the fifteen to thirty group" [Karpati/Massano].

The passage of time is not necessarily synonymous with progress as regards school provision or literacy: Scotland and Belgium (and doubtless many other places) show this, although the general tendency is in the opposite direction. This is because *the literacy rate seems to be directly linked to the quality of literacy teaching, that is to say, to the conditions which determine it.* An examination of these conditions will enable us to better understand these observed facts.

The history of school provision

Most of the evidence and analysis indicates that within Traveller groups there have for a very long time existed some literate individuals whose role remains a vital function within the life of the community, notably as regards relations with the surrounding world. For example in the *United Kingdom*, "There has probably always been a small minority of Gypsies who carried out necessary reading and writing for the community" [Acton /Kenrick]. But in almost all cases the learning took place outside the school system, or very intermittently within it. This is to say that, within the small pool of literate persons, most are self-taught (as much evidence testifies). The Gypsy's "primers" are roadsigns, labels, advertisements; television now plays an important role both in acquiring the basic skills and, once these have been mastered, the individual can go on to learn additional languages by watching subtitled foreign films (a widespread phenomenon in countries where foreign films and magazines – notably from the United States – are commonplace). Knowing this offers us an insight into the (non-generalisable) observation above, from Belgium, that literacy is more widespread amongst the adult population. In effect the self-taught individual is usually well past childhood, and is constantly progressing.

The history of school provision is obviously linked to changing policies. There are two basic types of policy, both generally unconscious or hidden. Firstly, there are *the Gypsies' own policies as regards schooling*: their attitudes and behaviour in connection with it, and the ways in which they use it. We will touch only briefly on the subject here, as it is analysed in much greater detail later on. Secondly, there are *non-Gypsy policies as regards schooling*, that is to say the attitudes, behaviour and use of the institution of school on the part of society in general, for children as a whole and for Gypsy/Traveller children in particular.

The fact that Traveller political strategies and the reasons underlying them are not taken into account is obvious, and ignoring this fundamental parameter is a cause of failure of school endeavours. But it is equally common (in practice if not in theory) to fail to consider the direct link between school and non-Gypsy political strategies. While it is self-evident that the school as an institution is immersed in the broad political process, it is much less common to examine the practical implications of this fact, and even rarer that such considerations should have a practical impact. *Up to now official policy has spoken of and acted for Gypsies and Travellers as if their culture and the Gypsy child himself were abstractions within the school, and as if the institution of school could somehow be separated from its socio-political context.*

The school situation of any cultural group must be understood in its long-term historical dimension and in the context of current policies. Attempting to consider it in isolation leads to various pedagogical illusions – and Gypsies and Travellers are a textbook example of this. Thus, the institution of school can accomplish nothing without an overall political context favourable to the initiatives and action which it proposes, particularly as regards minorities. What is more, "It is an irremediable mistake to separate the question of the schooling of the children of immigrant workers, and that of the ongoing relationship of their parents with the host society" [Porcher, 1979, p.7]. When two societies are in a state of conflict, as has been the case for many centuries between Gypsies/Travellers and the surrounding society, this observation becomes particularly pertinent. The child is very sensitive to the division between the two societies, to the differences in what each expects of the other and of him (we shall return to this point), and the resulting social and cultural conflict can easily become personal and psychological.

The history of non-Gypsy schooling policy as regards Gypsies has always been characterised by coercion. School provision has occurred within the framework of containment policies described earlier, notably in Spain and under the Enlightened Despotism of Maria Theresa and Joseph II of Austria at the end of the eighteenth century. In this context schooling is clearly seen as one of a range of disciplinary measures aimed at "training" and "educating" children outside the influence of their own families.

"Maria Theresa tried to be more humane. She wanted to repopulate the Banat region, depopulated as a result of the wars with Turkey. By a decree of 1761 she sent the Bohemians there... but the colonies dispersed... Then came a more severe order: take away the Bohemians' children to be reared by Christian families, towndwellers and peasants... in addition, marriage between two Bohemians was formally banned. As one might have predicted, all these efforts came to nothing. The children ran away from their foster parents and marriages continued to take place. In 1773 an even more severe decree was issued. Children were to be forcibly removed from their parents and placed in boarding schools such as the Theresianeum at Hermannstadt. As with previous efforts the results were nil. Ten years later the Emperor Joseph II issued a general edict... from the earliest age, Gypsy children were obliged to attend church and school. From the age of four, children had to be sent to school in neighbouring parishes, changing schools every two years so as to get a more varied education" [extract from a report by Weitershagen, included in Hohman, 1980, p.149, and quoted by Reemtsma].

But not all states were pursuing containment policies at the time, and in these no central initiative at school provision was made. On the other hand from the beginning of the nineteenth century there was increased concern with Gypsy and Traveller children's schooling on the part of religious missionaries (though even before this time there are many documented cases of Traveller children getting into classes at their own or their families' initiative). It seems that the trend began in England, and the following year similar steps were taken in Prussia:

"The first committee of non-Gypsies to promote the 'general improvement' and education of Gypsies was formed in Southampton on 12 November 1827 by the Rev. J. Crabb. This at first placed Gypsy children in church-run general infant schools, but afterwards made special educational provision... This inspired other similar efforts in Surrey, Dorset and at Kirk Yetholm in Scotland." Later, "The evangelical London City Mission began its outreach to Gypsies in the 1850s and they still have a full-time worker" [Acton/Kenrick].

"In Prussia in 1828 the Union of Evangelical Missions at Friedrichslohra near Naumburg established a Gypsy 'colony'. Families joining it had to promise to lead 'a hardworking, virtuous and Christian life'. In 1831, it had twenty-two school-age children in school. Forced labour and punishment were a part of everyday life. In 1832 the Royal Government of Prussia appealed for financial aid for the project. 'By informing the public of the district of the foundation of the institution to save the Bohemians of Friedrichslohra and by publicising its achievements, we hope to find friends and supporters who will help us to accomplish this act of Christian love for this misguided race, for up to now we have had very little support... the faith shown in undertaking the moral salvation of a group of persons heading for perdition will not be misplaced.' But financial aid was not forthcoming. Schoolmaster Blankenburg was overburdened with responsibility for the 'education' of more than a hundred Gypsies. As soon as government aid was discontinued, the adults were sent to correctional institutions and the children to orphanages. By this time some families had already left Friedrichslohra because its assimilationist policies threatened their social structures, internal legal system, language, culture, and also their economic base, without offering any attainable alternative prospects for them" [Reemtsma, with quotations from Mode/Wölffling, 1968, p. 165, and Hohman, 1981, p.53].

In France, Belgium, and particularly Spain, missionary schools for Gypsy children were spreading. In states where the school system allows for the coexistence of alternative schools, these missions continue to play an important role, sometimes as important as that of the public authorities.

"It is well to emphasise that missionaries have always worked not only towards the achievement of literacy, but were also the first to develop a written version of Gypsy dialects. The first translated excerpts from the Bible were published in 1837. The fact is, that if the missionaries were in general less violent than public bodies in their modest efforts at bringing literacy to the Gypsies, they possibly never realised that the religious instruction which they propagated, just like the alphabet they taught, had a strong ethnic connotation for the Gypsies: the schoolmaster and the priest, the school and the church, the alphabet and the Bible, are phenomena too closely linked with non-Gypsies to be taken on lightly. The history of Gypsy literacy programmes is to a great degree linked with and similar to the history of their evangelisation. Both efforts have been failures, emblematical histories of the struggle of Gypsies for their cultural survival" [Piasere].

In every state, school policy has been coherent with overall policy as regards Gypsies/Travellers. But while general policy has, within a given era, followed very broad lines – containment or assimilation – school policy has, both in action and in results, been extremely varied. There seem to be two main reasons behind this. The first is because the official policy of each state towards Gypsies – particularly as regards centralised interventionism – is formed by, and reflects the same attitudes and mechanisms which characterise, state policy, institutions, etc. in general. On the other hand there are other states in which an official government policy on school provision for Gypsy children has yet to be formulated or where such formulation is very recent. Of course, in this context, the absence of intervention is a political act as surely as repeated intervention is. Absence of intervention has its own institutional and political causes.

The second reason behind the variety of initiatives in school provision is that, as regards Gypsies and Travellers, politicians and administrators are very often completely ignorant. They do not know who the Gypsies and Travellers are, and thus cannot foresee the real consequences of the measures they propose. Policies are implemented and resources allocated on the assumption that they will produce certain desired results. Thus the same type of school may be set up with radically different political objectives. For example, the "special" school (that is, one which accepts only Gypsy and Traveller children) may be promoted as a first step towards "integration" (a term synonymous with assimilation for those who support it) or on the contrary as a place of respect, development and affirmation for a unique culture which could not be adequately catered for in an "ordinary" school. Elsewhere, or at different times, the same premise of respect will condemn the "special" school as a ghetto, claiming that any culture can only thrive in collaboration with others, while the supporters of assimilation continue to extol the "special" school as the most effective means of bringing about fundamental changes in the children's thinking. Every type of school and class is the object of such contradictory claims and counter-allegations, which cross and clash from one moment to the next, from place to place, from one country to another.

A comparative international study of government policies would produce a table ranging from completely white on one side (states which have little or no central or specific policy concerning school provision for Gypsies) to completely black on the other (states in which measures and policies are so complex that it is impossible to make any sense of them). In the middle we would find states where some tendencies have been clearly discernible. It would doubtless be possible, in summarising the measures taken in each state, to place each of them in a continuum. However, such an exercise would be irrelevant to the general reflection we are pursuing here; it is not a question of formulating a "league table" of the countries concerned, by whatever criteria. It is unfortunate when the state is all-intrusive, as this tends to block change and impose uniformity. When the state is absent, this is unfortunate too, as it could be initiating and coordinating. In fact an absence of measures, like a surfeit of them, is neither good nor bad in itself, but in the consequences which result. This is the question to which we must return.

Let us simply give a summary of recent government policy and/or action: this will help us to formulate the next stage of our analysis.

In *Belgium*: "During the entire period between 1899 and the Second World War, private and public initiatives proposed various means of school provision for nomads. The Catholic church was the first of the private bodies to become involved with 'wandering tradesmen' (as it called them). The public sector for its part was involved in the setting up of special classes, special schools, boarding schools, the development of legislation, etc., geared towards 'persons of no fixed abode' (the legal term)... It seems that this schooling was aimed primarily at those itinerants whose profession was socially and administratively recognised. This was the case with travelling showmen, who exerted considerable economic and cultural clout at local level... It was not until after World War II that, very gradually, scattered initiatives began to be forthcoming as regards school provision for Travellers and, much later, for Gypsies. It was not until the end of the 1970s that local and public institutions became involved." But, at present, "In Belgium there are no general policy guidelines specifically dealing with Gypsy and Traveller children. Whether they are Belgian nationals or not, once they are domiciled in Belgium parents are subject to general school legislation; if they persist in an itinerant lifestyle, the law provides that the children of persons of no fixed abode should be placed in institutional 'homes'... Gypsies and Travellers who are officially classed as 'showmen' and 'bargemen' can send their children to special (boarding) schools provided – which is already a blow to families. But those who are classified as 'nomads' are not recognised as having any specific trade and are thus not eligible for state aid towards meeting the fees of their children's (compulsory) boarding schools" [Reyniers]. In this context, provision for Gypsy and Traveller children tends to be haphazard, narrow in scope, and uncoordinated.

In *Denmark* there are no special regulations, and it appears that the whole question of school provision for Gypsy children was only "discovered" in the late 1960s when families from Yugoslavia and Poland arrived in Elsinore and Copenhagen. These townships accordingly set up teaching facilities, as they do for all immigrant children who cannot immediately be accommodated in ordinary classes.

In *France* school provision for children "of no fixed abode" (subsequently rechristened "of nomadic origin", as they are known in official terminology) occurs within the general school system. From 1966 onwards, some circulars have been grafted onto existing regulations concerning those "of no fixed abode" and later those "of nomadic origin". Half of these circulars emanate from the ministry directly concerned (the Ministry of Education), the other half, from the Ministry of the Interior. For a large part they deal with the question of compulsory school attendance, and sanctions to be applied when the requirement is not fulfilled. They also deal with the creation of special "adjustment sections" or "adjustment classes" for children considered "maladjusted". General regulations concerning the teaching of mother tongues, which are dealt with in several circulars, are basically liberal, and could allow for developments in favour of Gypsies and Travellers; but in practice such attempts run aground on stipulations such as "foreign" and "country of origin". What should be done for the Gypsies and Travellers, who are a people without territory of their own, and without the backup of consulate or embassy? And one must not forget to examine schooling policy within the broader context of French policy towards minority groups in general, which (up to the present at any rate) has been one of negation and assimilation [Liégeois 1980e]. In fact there exists in France quite a wide assortment of classes and schools, for example on halting sites, which accept only Gypsy and Traveller children. But, despite administrative centralisation, there is at present no coherent policy towards them, nor are the "special" classes and schools linked into any sort of network – which, as we shall see later, considerably limits their effectiveness and quality.

In *Greece* there are no special measures or structures for Gypsies. Some proposals have recently been formulated but have not as yet been put into effect.

In *Ireland*, "In 1964 the government issued a policy statement with the following reference to education: 'Provision will be made for giving special educational facilities, both primary and vocational, to the children of itinerants and for the erection of special camp schools where necessary.' This was followed in 1970 by a booklet called *The Education of Itinerant Children* which set out the policy of the Department of Education. Their responsibilities were set out as:

a) ensuring that every school throughout the country gives Traveller children the same rights of admission as all other children,
b) employing, where a number of Traveller children with special needs are located in an area, extra teaching staff to cater specifically for their needs,
c) providing teachers for Traveller children of pre-school age where needs have been identified and premises are available, so as to compensate for the deficiencies of their background and prepare them for normal schooling,
d) providing, where premises are available, through the Vocational Education Committees (VECs) special classes for Traveller children between the ages of twelve to fifteen years who cannot attend ordinary classes in vocational or secondary schools,
e) supplying through the VECs the equipment and defraying the cost of teachers and overheads for training centres for young Travellers who are educationally unfitted to attend ordinary classes,
f) providing a pilot teacher service in Dublin and Galway" [McCarthy].

In *Italy* school provision for Gypsy children began in 1959 under private initiative. At first, classes were held in caravans; later they took place in private homes and eventually in school premises. In 1963 they received recognition from the state as special experimental classes. In 1965, the "functioning of special classes was regulated by an agreement between the Minister of Public Instruction and *Opera Nomadi* (Nomads' Action), an association recognised as a responsible body by the state." This act "delegated a portion of responsibility to a voluntary organisation, with no provision for financing the services provided... The eleven recognised classes were state classes, and required to function within ordinary (community) schools, while *Opera Nomadi* was to concern itself with school transport and a campaign of consciousness-raising among Gypsy families, and the Pedagogical Institute of the University of Padua was to organise two-year specialised teacher training courses and investigate the problems specific to the schooling of Gypsies." In an agreement dated 1971, the number of recognised classes had grown to sixty, but it was specified that "They shall have as their aim the preparation of Gypsy and Traveller pupils for entering ordinary classes..." The agreement of 1974 called for "The restructuring of school services for Gypsy and Traveller children with the general aim of their entering ordinary classes. Special classes retain a specific remedial function for Gypsy and Traveller children who are scholastically backward or whose school attendance is very irregular due to nomadism." Finally the agreement of 1982 established that "Gypsy and Traveller children of school age shall be enrolled in ordinary classes". For those pupils who, "due to their belonging to a different culture, encounter learning difficulties, supplementary teachers shall be provided for a collective minimum of six Gypsy and Traveller pupils." *Opera Nomadi* took on the task of organising "information courses for teachers working with Gypsy and Traveller children", and of conducting studies and research in collaboration with the Centro Studi Zingari. But putting Gypsy and Traveller children into ordinary classes has run up against numerous obstacles. Finally, apart from the agreements with *Opera Nomadi*, "It became evident that the state – and the Minister for Public Instruction as well – had never taken direct charge of their responsibility to ensure the right of instruction to these Italian citizens" [Karpati/Massano].

In the *Netherlands* the education system which arose and developed over the nineteenth century was not concerned with Gypsies and Travellers. At the beginning of the twentieth century, with the passing of the "Caravan and House-Boats Act" (1918) school regulations did begin to concern Gypsies and Travellers – as an obligation (living in a mobile dwelling was permitted only if the children attended school). It was not until the 1950s, starting with a Royal Decree in 1951 to be followed by another in 1955, that special schools situated near stopping places were first opened. For some time now the policy has been veering towards the "integration" of the children from these schools into ordinary classes, but the difficulties are great, both because of the general rejection expressed by the other children, and the still substandard scholastic level of Gypsy and Traveller children [cf. Hovens et al].

In the *Federal Republic of Germany* the twentieth century has been marked above all by the genocide of Gypsies under the Nazi regime. The link between this practice and prevailing ideology is all too apparent. A synopsis of Nazi ideas concerning Gypsies is to be found for example in Eva Justin's dissertation, *The Future of Gypsy Children Brought Up in a Manner Foreign to their Kind* (1944): "Is it possible, once they have abandoned their primitive Gypsy lifestyle thanks to education in a German school, to usefully employ Gypsy children (at a level appropriate to their race, of course)? ...Almost all Gypsies and Gypsy half-breeds are a danger because of their greater or lesser weakness of character and their bad nature; they require constant direction and support... The German people need solid and enthusiastic men, not the myriad spawn of these irresponsible primitives." And Dr. Justin emphasises the necessity for sterilisation, in the light of her conclusion that "Destiny, hereditarily determined from birth, cannot be changed by these people, nor by the influence of the environment, nor by education, nor by punishment" [text quoted by Reemtsma].

To this day the central authorities appear to have taken no account of the need for school provision for Gypsy children. "Neither the Federal Minister of Science, nor the Federal Commission of *Länder* (responsible for educational planning), nor the Conference of Education Ministers, nor the Conference of Ministers of Culture (responsible for school provision within their respective *Länder*) have taken any account of the existence of Sinti as a minority group in the schools. In 1982, for the first time, official discussion took place at the Federal Ministry of Education and Sciences, between Sinti representatives, experts, and other scientists" [Reemtsma]. Some interesting conclusions emerged from this discussion, but have not been followed up by any concrete action. Central government left the power of initiative in this field with the regional authorities (*Länder*), and in 1985 it can be said that "Neither the Conference of Ministers of Culture, nor the Commission of the Federation of the *Länder* for Planning and Education, nor the individual Ministers of Culture have, over the last three years, done anything whatsoever towards implementing the measures deemed absolutely necessary by the Sinti in order to ameliorate the scholastic situation of their children" [Reemtsma].

In the *United Kingdom*, "Under the 1974-79 government, national policy, while making some progress on site provision, on education was non-existent. This reached its nadir in 1977 when it was revealed that by a loop-hole in the 1944 Act about 'children not belonging to the area of any authority', Gypsy children did not even have a settled right to go to school" [Acton, 1982].

In the United Kingdom, "There is, almost by definition, no overall state policy on Gypsy education". To summarise the measures that have been taken:

"a) The DES (Department of Education and Science) gave small grants to the National Gypsy Education Council 1971-73 and The Advisory Committee for the Education of Romany and other Travellers 1973-76.
b) There is an official HMI interest in Traveller education... which has, in England only, been instrumental in giving advice leading to extension of educational provision in a great many areas.
c) There were one-week DES in-service training courses for teachers in 1973, '74, '75, '76, '78, '80, '82, and '84.
d) In circular 1/81 of 5th March 1981, applying to England and Wales, explaining the effects of the 1980 Education Act, we find the only statement that exists of explicit written government encouragement for the education of Travellers. Paragraph 5 reads: 'The reference to children 'in the area' of the authority means that each authority's duty extends to all children residing in their area, whether permanently or temporarily. The duty thus embraces in particular travelling children, including gypsies, and, subject to what is said in the annex to this circular, children from overseas.'
The importance of this statement is that it indicated that the government now regarded as illegal actions such as that of Croydon Local Education Authority in 1977 when they refused admittance to nomads without legal sites.
e) In 1983 the DES published an HMI 'discussion paper' (i.e. not a policy document committing the government to anything) entitled *The Education of Travellers' Children*, giving some anonymous case histories of educational practice.
f) The government has not abolished the no-area pool. This is a system under the 1944 Education Act whereby local education authorities pool on a national basis the expenses of education of children deemed not to belong to the area of any one Local Education Authority. In practice this has turned out to mean the children of foreign tourists, members of the armed forces and nomadic Gypsies. Since all authorities have to contribute to the pool whether or not they are claiming for it, this obviously constitutes a strong financial incentive to provide for Gypsy children, although this was not the original intention of the system" [Acton/Kenrick].

Integration by handicap

When pressure began to build up concerning school provision for Gypsy and Traveller children – regardless of whether it came from the state enforcing attendance requirements or from Gypsy parents demanding that their children be admitted – it was practical, from a material, pedagogical and ideological point of view, to fit Gypsy children into existing classes geared towards mentally and/or socially handicapped pupils. Administrative texts testifying to this are numerous and explicit, as are the reports of those involved. For example:

In the *Federal Republic of Germany* the percentage of Gypsy children in school is one of the highest in Europe. But this simple statistic tells us nothing of the difficulties connected with schooling. One detailed local study puts the accent firmly on the placing of the children. It found "that a great number of Sinti children in Bremen attend special classes for the maladjusted, and almost all run the risk of being sent to them. Thus, in 1983, there was not a single Sinti child who had undergone normal schooling; only one was in vocational training; and a total of four – brought up in exceptionally favourable circumstances – attended secondary level classes for a short period. None of the children who had attended the 'special' classes could obtain a certificate of education when they finished their studies, and all are unemployed" [Bremer Volkshochschule, 1983, p.43]. Another study presents a statistical picture of the type of school attended in correlation with the economic situation of the family:

Type of school	Self-employed		Receiving social welfare	
	number	%	number	%
for mentally handicapped	60	20.5	208	37.0
primary school	151	51.7	226	40.1
Hauptschule	75	25.7	123	21.8
secondary school	6	2.1	6	1.1
Total	292	100.0	563	100.0

[Hundsalz, 1982, quoted in Reemtsma].

It is clear that the percentage of children in classes where teaching is geared towards the mentally handicapped, is very significant. Another study [Freese et al, 1980] estimates 50% of Gypsy and nomad children to be in such classes, while the national average is 3%. Thus, "Considering the economic structures operating in the FRG, the chances of a man with a certificate of education from a 'special' school, or not having completed school at all, becoming established in a traditional trade or within the technological sphere amongst the majority population, are practically nil" [Reemtsma].

In the *United Kingdom*, "multi-racial education" is but one of the categories "dealt with by the Educational Disadvantage Unit of the DES. Following on the Warnock Committee *Report on Special Educational Needs* (HMSO, 1978), belonging to an ethnic minority is brought together with poverty and physical and mental handicap in a common category of educational disadvantage. Special schools exist for the handicapped and for those with moderate or severe learning difficulties. There have been complaints that disproportionately many ethnic minority pupils have been placed in special schools" [Acton/Kenrick].

The same tendency exists in the majority of countries. When, in *Italy*, school inspectors (*Provveditori agli Studi*) were asked whether "the working group for the integration of handicapped pupils also covers Gypsy children", 70% (twenty-eight out of forty) answered in the affirmative [Karpati/Massano]. Moreover, from 1971-82, agreements between the Minister of Public Instruction and the body mandated to coordinate scholastic action directed towards Gypsy children (*Opera Nomadi*) stipulate that teachers of Gypsy children must be in possession of a diploma from the *Scuola Magistrale Ortofrenica* (Remedial Teachers' Training College) or a diploma from a "special course on the physiopathology of child psychophysical development" [Piasere, MS.]. In *Ireland* "There are also a number of separate schools for children identified as having special needs: physically handicapped, visually impaired, deaf children, children with reading difficulties, deviant children... Pupils are placed in these classes as a result of some form of assessment, either medical or psychological or both. In the case of Travelling children the classes are set up on the basis of their cultural identity alone. No form of assessment is necessary" [McCarthy]. In the *Netherlands*, when immigrant Gypsy families were recently granted residence permits, "The government decided that the Ministry of Welfare, Health and Cultural Affairs should be responsible for the education familiarisation projects, largely for the reason that the Ministry of Education and Science was not empowered to provide the sort of experimental education deemed necessary in this particular case" [Hovens]. In *France* official policy, practice and structures follow a policy of classifying all "handicaps" together – and these include the fact of having a culture different from that of the "average" Frenchman. A trade union magazine of public sector teachers published the following figures (in: *L'École Libératrice*, no. 17, 1979):

"65% of Gypsy children do not attend school
80% of those attending are in classes for the socially handicapped
75% unjustified absenteeism
71% of the children are 'cases' (that is, have language or behavioural problems)."

(Subjective notions such as "unjustified absenteeism" and "cases" merit closer analysis, and we shall return to them later on.)

For the sake of comparison, and to illustrate that practice with regard to Gypsies and Travellers is the same everywhere, let us present one of many possible examples from a politically different state. In *Hungary* "The situation of Gypsy children has remained unchanged for the past twenty-five years; only a quarter of them complete [compulsory schooling]. Here are some reasons:

- At school entry age, a significant number of Gypsy children obtain a derogation delaying their entry for another year or two, because of scholastic immaturity; this dangerously reduces the length of their schooling;
- In the vicinity of large shanty-towns, there are 'special' schools. This description is a euphemism for provision geared towards pupils with learning disabilities; thus most Gypsy children are classed as retarded, a convenient way of dumping them;
- Classes comprising children above normal age are often all-Gypsy;
- Gypsy children are often authorised to leave school at fourteen;
- Practical difficulties also impede school attendance" (lack of shoes, clothing, copybooks; malnutrition; distance from the school; to this can be added the complication of having a different mother tongue, and the fact that older children need to be working) [Kemény, 1985, p.33].

In this context it becomes essential to carry out a *critical analysis of the use of assessment tests*, which have been used in nearly every country. This practice was largely developed in the 1960s and stabilised in the '70s, before apparently and thankfully decreasing during the '80s. In effect, such tests are rarely if ever adapted for use with Gypsy/Traveller (or for that matter other "minority") children. The consequences are grave indeed, as the results, so precise in appearance (and the annoying tendency towards treating any result which can be expressed in numerical form, as being "rigorous", is universal) are founded on false premises. In fact "The error is equal to the degree of non-adaptation of the test to the tested population" [Liégeois, 1981a, p.4], and finally "the test reveals less about the abilities of Gypsy children than about the ethnocentric assumptions of the testers" [Acton, MS., 1984]. And so it is "established" that these children have "negligible intelligence", "socially inappropriate behaviour", suffer from "a disorganisation of the Self, ranging from emotional disorganisation to mental confusion", etc. [cf. for example the critical analysis by Conquy, 1980, and Liégeois, 1977a]. Apart from questions relating to test calibration, some totally inappropriate forms of assessment have been used: for example in France and Italy Gypsy children have been evaluated on the basis of "the village test" which consists of giving the child an assortment of objects (miniature houses, fences, public buildings, etc.) which he must then put into place. Such a test might indeed have been used as an interesting indicator of *knowledge*, revealing the Gypsy child's vision of the surrounding society, the function of public buildings, etc. But it is used as a projective test on which conclusions concerning the child's *personality structure* are based – information which it clearly cannot convey.

"On the subject of tests, this is what I have to say: they give Gypsy children bricks and ask them to build houses, and when they can't, it's 'These children are crazy.' Listen – some of our kids are even more intelligent than the others. We are quite normal. We have two eyes, two hands, two ears, two feet, just like everybody else" [Matéo Maximoff, Gypsy author, quoted in Liégeois 1980d p.57].

"I think, when I look at some of these studies, that there's no hope for our children; all of us, parents and children, are headed for the asylum" [Pierre Yung, President of *l'Union des Tsiganes et Voyageurs de France*, quoted in Liégeois 1980d p.52].

Placement within "special education", when this is a rather indistinct notion applicable to various sectors of the school-going population, is a troubling question. The temptation is to send to it both those who have "problems", and those who pose a problem; those who do not fulfil, as well as those who fall outside, certain norms. In psychological, social and cultural terms, integration/assimilation through handicap always occurs within bad conditions. What is more, as we have already pointed out, by basing itself on false premises it does not achieve the goals it sets itself, and the end result is "a pedagogy of cross-cultural incomprehension" [Piasere].

We must also draw attention to another negative effect of this situation, observable in many countries: parents themselves accept their children being put into classes for the retarded, because they know they will be better treated, perhaps better protected, than in ordinary classes where they would be subjected to rejection, discrimination and violence. But the children, accommodated in a class which was not made for them, will never make any progress in it nor gain economically viable skills.

The notion of "handicap" as applied to the social and cultural sphere is a by-product of assimilationist policies, and can be traced historically and socially. [We shall mention a few examples taken from Liégeois, 1980b, where they are developed more fully.] Psychiatric and other classifications do not exist in lofty isolation from the changing times. Pointing this out has become a truism, but an often forgotten truism nonetheless. "Instability", "backwardness", "feeblemindedness", "maladjustment" are all useful terms within the vocabulary of those who concern themselves with such questions, but have the consequence that individuals to whom the labels are applied are thenceforward defined and treated accordingly, just as any object is treated according to the value attributed to it or the use that can be made of it [cf.

for example Muel, 1975, Lallemand, 1978, Foucault, 1972]. It is well, then, to exercise prudence when using such terms (which describe relative and ephemeral truths) in theories of education, which are so quickly out of date or even discredited. Let us remember that "One can still hear immigrant communities described as 'disadvantaged environments'. This is a notion typical of paternalist ideology which forms the basis of our teaching practice and which constitutes one of the masks on the politics of integration" [Blot, 1978, p.24]. It is an argument that attributes scholastic failure to "linguistic poverty" and the child's cultural matrix, which constitutes a situation of "deprivation". It is once again to presume the absolute "correctness" of one's own culture, to pronounce ethnocentric judgment which classifies as non-cultural all cultural elements which are alien to itself. A teacher in France proposes a strikingly appropriate image: "No one would dream of classifying as having a 'psychomotor handicap', someone whose table manners are inappropriate because he's unfamiliar with the etiquette required by the situation" [Castanié, 1978, p.34].

Paternalist ideology, like the arguments used to justify assimilationism, has not spared teachers, and illustrations proliferate from their pens:

"The perpetual movements of the nomad lead to a dispersion of his personality: since the nomad is never at home, he is likewise never himself. ...We shall examine how to achieve a rootedness, a precondition for the nomad to solve his problems." [Extract from a book written by a teacher on a halting site, published in France in 1974 – a book often referred to by "special" teachers. These ideas being – or having been? – widespread, it seems pointless (both here and in later references) to stigmatise the authors by giving their names.] What does this mean? That the nomad cannot "be himself" until he settles down, just as "rootedness" is a precondition for him to face his problems? Why does his teacher want to "organise the rooting process"? Binet and Simon, promoters of tests aimed at measuring the "intelligence quotient", define (in their book, *Mentally Defective Children*) "the unstable child" as "a nomad who attends many schools". The phrase is quickly reformulated by the teacher: the nomad who attends many schools, is unstable.

Another author writes that "The gipsy's earliest childhood does not lead to personal autonomy but on the contrary perpetuates group cohesion and the power of the group over the individual. From this fact springs an immaturity, a tendency towards introversion since the child is ignorant and apprehensive of our way of life... In the family environment, the child is loved, but cohabitation in great promiscuity means that he is exposed to violent scenes and sudden uprootings which produce emotional trauma in him. One must add also the fact of physical tiredness due to being on the move, late hours, nutritional deficiency, the effects of inbreeding, and alcoholism – which is omnipresent in this as in every other impoverished society." Here we have summarised in a few lines all the squalid arguments which oppose the concept of multicultural pedagogy: ethnocentrism which cannot concede cultural value to that which is different, incomprehension and criticism of the communal way of life, equal emphasis on "immaturity" and "deficiency". Just two sentences say it all: cohabitation, promiscuity, violent scenes, nomadism, late bedtimes, nutritional deficiency, inbreeding and alcoholism. The author concludes by emphasising "the importance of crèches which will accustom the child to being separated from the group." This text was not written during [the reign of the Tudors or Stuarts], nor during the reign of Maria Theresa, but in 1978, as part of a submission (entitled *Schooling Among the Gipsies*) for promotion in the French civil service.

In other specialised documents we read for example that "Teachers feel their efforts have been in vain once the adolescent returns to his own group"; elsewhere, "To accomplish this transformation the individual must of necessity distance himself from the group, in order to avoid conflict with it." And again, "At the beginning of the school year, children playing with dolls had them living out a Gypsy lifestyle; in June, by contrast, the lifestyle played out was non-Gypsy... It was necessary to prevent the older children from speaking Romani with the younger ones."

These evolutionist and ethnocentric accounts of schooling are, as we have already stressed, linked to overall policy, and within this broader framework initiatives emanating from the schools themselves interact with socio-educative measures from other sources. This relationship must be emphasised, but further investigation is beyond the scope of the present work [the theme of social work has been given broader treatment in another work, Liégeois 1977a, pp.13-136, and other authors have dealt with the same theme in other chapters in the same book; a study of this conjugation of policy and practice is presented in Liégeois 1983a].

What must be done, now, is to "re-culturise" the general analytical frame in order to break out of the rut worn by institutions and their representatives through thinking almost exclusively in terms of deficiency, handicap, or maladjustment. There has been a move in this direction since the beginning of the 1980s, which may augur improvement in future. Thus in many countries where Traveller children had, for schooling purposes, been classed as "maladjusted", they have been reclassified on a par with immigrant children. For example, in France responsibility for school provision for Gypsy and Traveller children has transferred at intra-ministerial level, from "special education" to "education of immigrant children"; in the Netherlands, from the Ministry of Welfare to the Ministry of Education; in England the shift has been at local level, for example within the Inner London Education Authority, etc. But such administrative changes are not always followed up by structural change, and even if the present trend does become established, it will be some time before we will see an appreciable lessening of the disproportionate numbers of Traveller children shunted off into classes for the mentally retarded. Movement seems to be slower still in the realm of ideas.

Compulsory schooling

In almost every state there is a legal obligation for children of school age to attend school, generally backed up by sanctions such as fines or cutting off child benefit (in France for example). In the case of persistent noncompliance, "The responsible bodies may issue a warrant entitling them to forcibly bring the school-age child to school, applying direct constraint as necessary on the child's parent or guardian. If the responsible bodies do not designate their own personnel to execute the warrant, they may ask the police to do so, and to take whatever measures may be necessary in the course of execution" [School Law of Lower Saxony, §153, quoted by Reemtsma].

The question of compulsory schooling, particularly in the case of Gypsy children, requires cautious and sensitive examination. The reasons for this will become apparent within the overall context of the present study, but even now it is possible to emphasise a few points. As we have ascertained, firstly, school attendance has become compulsory for Gypsies in connection with policies of negation (i.e. containment and assimilation). Historically, then, schooling is heavily charged with negative connotations. To make it strictly obligatory without any concessions (as is usually the case, notably for nomads) is to add a further negative connotation: obligation becomes perceived as coercion. Every Gypsy and Traveller group carries its attitudes about surrounding institutions in general, to its perception of school. It cannot be otherwise. School is not only an alien institution; it is the alien institution charged with dispensing cultural norms which the Gypsy does not share (a question we shall discuss at length in connection with Gypsy perceptions of school). When obligation becomes coercion, particularly in the context of the poor overall relationship between the two societies in question, it generates the opposite results to those intended both in the numbers attending school and in the quality of their schooling. Authoritarian assimilation policies, notably in some Eastern European countries, demonstrate clearly that these do not produce better scholastic results than those of states which follow a more liberal policy in this regard. *Compulsory schooling, like integration through the workplace, is a fiasco, due both to its authoritarian character and to rejection by non-Gypsies*, in school as on the factory floor.

By contrast, when school is entered by choice, the result is an increase in both the confidence of the participants and in their numbers. It is important here to take note of the experience of *England and Wales*: "Amazingly, not until 1980 were education authorities legally required to admit nomadic children to schools in England and Wales. The legal requirement on parents to have their children educated is not, and has almost never been, enforced on nomadic Gypsies in England and Wales. Unlike many European countries, therefore, the pressure for education comes more from Gypsies than from the state; education is in practice voluntary, and although this means that in some places unsympathetic teachers and administrators may still, even after 1980, effectively deny educational provision to children, when children do come into school, they do so without the disadvantages of the resentment and indiscipline that a coercive programme brings with it. If Gypsy children quarrel with their teachers, and persuade their parents the quarrel is justified, they just leave" [Acton, MS., 1984]. "As we have seen, the legal obligation to attend school is now only rarely enforced upon nomadic Traveller children in England and Wales, and it was only ever enforced in Scotland in the past. On the whole, then, the rising figures for school attendance among Travellers do indicate increased confidence by Traveller parents in the school system, as well as increased access and provision" [Acton/Kenrick].

The correlation between increased school attendance and decreased pressure to attend is confirmed by observations made in a number of countries. In France for example teachers indicate that even preschooling has been more successful since the presence of children is no longer linked with the teacher's signature on forms attesting to regular school attendance as a prerequisite for the family's receiving child benefit. The paradox is only superficial: the Gypsy, free to choose to send children to school, does so more willingly, even (as in the present case) with toddlers who have not yet reached compulsory school age. But not all teachers agree with this type of analysis [for their different interpretations see the responses to Ferté's questionnaire].

"School is disliked because it is forced upon the families and the children against their wills... On the question of absenteeism, the school should try to woo the Gypsy families rather than force them with threats of the Courts. Court action can only be counter-productive to the building of a better relationship between the school and the Gypsies. Besides, prosecution has little, if any, impact on the attendance levels... Selling education to the Gypsies should be the aim of the school, and this is compatible with progressive educational objectives. One cannot force people to learn" [Ivatts, 1975, p.25, p.36].

In the light of this, we conclude that, in certain cases at any rate, "Since Gypsies do not have the option of rejecting the institution of school as such, they have come to reject its pedagogical content" [Ferté, 1985, p.83].

To conclude our present treatment of this subject, we add a few points for consideration. Firstly, it appears difficult, indeed impossible, to impose strictly compulsory schooling while so many families continue to be so badly rejected by their environment. Moreover, in certain countries, a new trend is gradually but significantly further reinforcing the coercive nature of school attendance, as having a school certificate becomes a prerequisite for obtaining a licence to practise various trades. For example, in Italy, from 1976, the law requires that an applicant for a permit to work as a travelling showman, pedlar, or craftsman, produce a certificate of primary education (if born before the end of 1951) or a certificate of secondary education (if born from 1952 onwards). Analogous preconditions exist in many countries, and are increasingly enforced.

In the past, Travellers have often been hastily accused of not wanting their children to go to school. Here too it is necessary to qualify the statement and, as we shall see, an attitude of refusal is often above all an attitude of understandable caution: absenteeism is one way – often, in practice, the only way – of extracting oneself from a conflict situation. To propagate the view that the rejection is exclusively one-sided, is to provide both teachers and administration with a handy excuse for scholastic failure. It is to shift the blame to the families, pronouncing them guilty of "refusal to integrate", which in turn justifies inaction from public bodies; it is to "assign the reasons for so many Gypsy children's failure, and the ambivalent relation of some families to the school, to a conscious choice by Gypsies and not to the incapacity of the school system to recognise ethnic minorities as integral elements of the school" [Reemtsma]. It has also been written that "Any teacher instructing Gypsy children is an accomplice in their genocide, because he contributes to the loss of Gypsy identity" [a social worker, quoted in Reemtsma]. The text from which that quotation is taken, is presented as "anthropological" in tone, yet attempts to present Gypsy cultural reality as stagnant. The same author goes on to state that "the Gypsies have lost their original cultural identity" and that "integration will be a necessary evil". To adopt such an approach is on the one hand to ignore all the adaptive dynamics of a culture, of its constant situation of contact with others and the changes to which it is subject; on the other, as we have already explained, "To pretend to promote (cultural) diversity and respect for identity, without giving to each – particularly to minorities – the possibility of obtaining the instruments for active adaptation, is hypocrisy" [Liégeois, 1983b, p.5]. And to conclude that "integration will be a necessary evil" is to open the floodgates for authoritarian acts of assimilation, and to justify them.

In a text submitted in 1982 to the Minister of Youth, the Family and Health, the *Zentralrat Deutscher Sinti und Roma* (Federation of German Gypsy Organisations) in the *FRG*, responded to allegations about Gypsy attitudes towards school as follows: "If certain scientists claim today that a conscious rejection of learning to read and write, that is to say a conscious refusal to attend school, is a part of the ethnic identity of the Sinti and Rom, they do so without apparently knowing history since it is not a question of Sinti and Rom not wishing to attend school, but rather of their not being allowed to because of persecution in the past" [quoted by Reemtsma].

In fact, in more and more cases, the willingness of parents to send their children to school is being confirmed; all the more so, we repeat, when schooling is not promoted in a coercive way. In *Greece*, for example, "The very few parents who have attended some classes of school are more and more willing to send their children as well, and try to conform their family way of life so as to facilitate their attendance" [Korré/Marselos]. And let us recall the case of the *United Kingdom*: "The major conclusion that must be drawn from this history as a whole is that there has been substantial demand from Gypsies for education over nearly two centuries. All too often the history has been presented as one of well-meaning non-Gypsies inducing recalcitrant Gypsies to accept schooling. In reality the action by benevolent non-Gypsies has always followed on action by Gypsies themselves, and has probably been outweighed by those non-Gypsies who have prevented Gypsies attending school, or made their school attendance, if they succeeded in going, utterly miserable by discrimination in school" [Acton/Kenrick].

But it must be emphasised that, while the example of the United Kingdom is particularly important when considering the effects of compulsion on the one hand, and the rejection of the Gypsy child by the scholastic institution on the other, it is preferable not to generalise too quickly as regards the willingness of parents to send their children to school. Factors mentioned at the end of the section on "The Cultural Sphere" (under the heading, "Education") remind us to be cautious about drawing conclusions: in Italy, France, Denmark, etc. families hesitate or refuse altogether to send their children to school. Even within the United Kingdom itself [cf. Ivatts, 1975] the desire for schooling is not universal and, according to British experts, it is limited to primary education. There is no contradiction between these two observations, and we shall attempt later on to analyse the reasons behind these different parental attitudes.

It is known that schooling, in colonial situations, was a potent instrument of domination or attempted domination, an important means of active ideological imposition in the name of liberating humanism. It is also known that it was – still is? – an ethnocidal process of cultural disruption. Gypsies are aware of this: "It is not that parents do not want them (the children) in school, or that the children do not want to be there, but that the society we are living in is doing its utmost to make Gypsies extinct" [from the introduction to *The Travelling Man and Other Stories* (NGEC, 1976) by James Hutchinson, a Borders Scottish Gypsy and chairman of the National Gypsy Education Council, quoted by Acton/Kenrick]. *For Gypsy parents and children, the surrounding institutions which are offered to or imposed upon them are, up to the present time, for historic reasons, still the institutions of others; authority is that of others; representatives are there to represent others; the school – and its teachers – is the school of others.* In each of the two societies which up to now have lived side by side with few points of contact other than functional and conflictual, the education of children contributes to maintaining the separateness; their encounter in the school is thus difficult, requiring much time, effort and courage, on both sides, in order to bring the parallel lines closer together or to form some bridge between them.

Enrolment

As already indicated, statistics of every kind – particularly those of a global nature must be approached with caution. In this section, we shall attempt to express and illustrate certain tendencies, based upon the most precise data available in the various national monographs. These statistics have been obtained either through specific surveys or by the careful interpretation of existing data. Despite their disparity, comparison does reveal convergence, culminating in a broad picture of schooling which is largely unaffected by national boundaries.

Children under sixteen represent approximately 50% of the Gypsy and Traveller population today. The number of school-age children (those over preschool age) comprise, depending on the requirements of the state in question, about 30-35% of the entire Gypsy and Traveller population. Proceeding from these considerations, and from the table given above (see "History") indicating overall numbers of Gypsies and Travellers, it is possible to estimate the number of school-age children for each country.

In *Italy*, among Gypsy children of compulsory school age (between six and fourteen), "local polls permit an estimate that on average only 20-25% of children attend school" [Karpati/Massano]. It is also pointed out that the great majority of children in school are at the first levels of primary. Statistics collected over fourteen provinces during the 1984-85 academic year allow us to form a picture of the relationship between the estimated total number of school-age children, and the number enrolled in school:

	estimated total number	numbers of children enrolled			
		primary school	secondary school	total	%
North	1,829	652	21	673	36.8
Centre	1,115	340	11	351	31.5
South	695	477	12	489	70.5
Total	**3,639**	**1,469**	**44**	**1,513**	**41.5**

But the number of children enrolled is not the number of children who attend class. Of 1,469 children enrolled in primary school, only 70.8% attend. What is more, the rate of enrolment drops dramatically as we go upwards from the first class. The same (1,469) children were distributed as follows:

class	by number	by %
first	682	46.4
second	271	18.4
third	216	14.7
fourth	168	11.5
fifth	132	8.9

and a mere 3% enter secondary school.

The same picture is observable in *Greece*: "About 17% of girls and 24% of boys are in school (a significant change only as regards girls: in their parents' generation, 22% of the men had attended school, but only 6% of the women). But in fact very few of them continue past second class, and even less after fourth. Absenteeism is also considerable" [Korré/Marselos].

In *Ireland*, "Figures derived from a number of sources estimate that approximately 50% of eligible children attend school... Figures compiled by the National Co-ordinator for Education for the whole country over a seven year period showed a total of 8,500 to 9,000 children with 6,500 to 7,000 of school age. Up to another 1,000 children of the more mobile families have never been accounted for accurately. Records showed 3,322 children attending school regularly in 1980... Only about 10% of Traveller children (10% of the only 50% who attend school) stay at school after the age of twelve ...There is a wide range of ages at which schooling starts – some children start in pre-schools at three years while others start school as late as ten or eleven years of age" [McCarthy]. A survey carried out in 1984 in Tallaght, a suburb of Dublin, by a branch of the INTO (primary school teachers' trade union) indicates that of approximately 300 school-age Travellers in the area, only ninety-three, that is, 31%, were attending school, and therefore 207, or 69%, were not.

In *Belgium*, "Parents tend to delay (their children's entry into) primary school... In certain cases, if children are very close in age, parents will hold the elder back for a year so they can start school together; in this way the family retains its economic mobility a little longer... Almost no pupils go beyond primary level; in fact, few finish the third primary class. Persistent illiteracy results... An examination of our sample confirms the extremely high degree of illiteracy amongst Gypsy and Traveller children... 101 children out of 112 (that is, 90%) do not possess the level of literacy which corresponds to their age; fifty-two of them (46.5%) have no knowledge whatever of reading or writing" [Reyniers]. These facts, dealing with the effects of schooling, are all the more significant when we bear in mind that at least some of the children involved had attended school: further proof of "the non-adaptation of basic instruction to the needs of Gypsy and Traveller children" [Reyniers]. One specific study – the results of which cannot of course be generalised – shows that, in some cases at least, nearly all the children attend school. This study covered forty-seven families with a total of 108 school-age children, whose attendance broke down as follows [Beckers, 1969, p.51, quoted by Reyniers]:

age	primary school		vocational training		unschooled	
	boys	girls	boys	girls	boys	girls
6-9	18	26	-	-	1	1
10-14	28	26	2	2	3	1
Total	46	52	2	2	4	2

A similar picture is presented in the *FRG*, where school attendance is relatively widespread (about 75% of children of primary school age attend, and 65% of older children do so – cf. Drucksache 9/2360, 21/12/1982, quoted by Reemtsma) but again scholastic results do not correspond to these high attendance figures.

In the *United Kingdom*, the tendency over the past few years has been towards a growth in the number of children enrolled in school: "In the past twenty years at the primary school level, registration (which does not mean consistent attendance always) has increased in England and Wales from around 10% to around 50%, and even more substantially in Northern Ireland, from under 10% to around 80%. In Scotland it seems to have fallen back slightly, from around 60% to around 50%... at the secondary school level the rise in attendance is much more modest and is probably still less than 20% throughout the UK. The proportion of Traveller children who take public examinations, therefore, is vastly less than for the general population, though we saw no evidence that those Travellers who do get to take these examinations are less successful than the average" [Acton/Kenrick].

There can be no doubt that, for nomadic children, school attendance rarely exceeds 30% of five to fifteen year olds:

Total numbers of nomadic children aged five to fifteen years in the UK by country and numbers attending school [Acton/Kenrick]:

Country-by-country percentage by age-group, and variations, for school attendance:

	England and Wales %	Scotland %	Northern Ireland %
Attendance at primary school by nomads (aged 5-11/12) (a) in the 1960s (b) in the 1980s	5-20 45-55	55-65 45-55	5-10 75-85
Attendance at secondary school by nomads (aged 11/12-16) (a) in the 1960s (b) in the 1980s	5-10 10-20	30-40 10-20	- 10-20

Without being able to give precise percentages for the whole of Europe (as the situation varies from country to country, place to place, and Gypsy group to Gypsy group), we can conclude from the foregoing that *perhaps half of Gypsy and Traveller children never attend school, that only a minute percentage get as far as secondary level, and that results, even as regards the attainment of basic literacy, are not in keeping with the amount of time spent in school.*

Attendance

The following indications, both as regards rate of enrolment and of attendance, must not lead us to forget that *all attendance is relative*, that is, that children who in fact are frequently absent may be counted as "in attendance". The following figures enable us to gauge the extent of absenteeism, not forgetting that this is merely the *relative* absenteeism *of those who are enrolled*, and does not include the *total* absenteeism of those who are not. Put another way, to be counted as "absent", a child must first at some point have been present – and that usually applies to a limited number of children.

Here are the results of an *Italian* survey [Karpati/Massano] of 353 children:

	enrolled	no. present	% present
North	34	25	73.5
Central	116	102	87.9
South	203	170	83.7
Total	**353**	**297**	**84.2**

Here are comparative figures (from one year to the next) covering a greater number of children:

1983-84	1,253	1,126	89.8%
1984-85*	1,440	1,020	70.8%

(* beginning of year)

– a dramatic drop.

A survey of 162 special teachers of Gypsy children gives their rating of the regularity of their pupils' attendance:

- regular	57	35.2%
- quite regular	58	35.8%
- irregular	31	19.2%
- very irregular	16	9.8%
total	162	100%

These teachers identified the following obstacles to regular attendance:

	number	%
- lack of family interest	23	14.2
- different rhythm of life (household schedule/festivals/ visits to relatives/girls'housework, etc.)	18	11.1
- economic and social conditions	15	9.3
- low motivation	14	8.7
- distance from school	11	6.8
- nomadism	8	4.9
- refusal to conform with school's behavioural code	4	2.5
- family mistrust of school	1	0.6
- no answer	68	41.9
Total	**162**	**100.0%**

It is hard to draw conclusions from this teachers' assessment, and we shall discuss the reasons for absenteeism later. In the meanwhile, for the sake of comparison, we list the reasons given by teachers in a similar survey carried out in *France* [Ferté]:

Stated and/or possible reasons for absence:

Probably true: helping the family (21), visitors (19), family celebration (18), child ill (18), parents unwilling to put their children in school (18), no appreciation of the link between regular attendance and successful learning (18), bereavement (16), parents' professional activities (15), difficulties connected with halting place (15), difficulty in getting to school on time (13), illness of a family member (11), child unwilling to attend school (9), transport difficulties (7), scholastic failure (7), economic difficulties (5), poor relationship with teachers (3), poor relationship with non-Traveller children (3), negative attitude of parents of non-Traveller children (3).

Probably false: child ill (12), illness of family member (8), visitors (6), economic difficulties (6), child unwilling to attend school (5), scholastic failure (5), family celebration (4), parents' professional activities (4), transport difficulties (4), poor relationship with teachers (3), negative attitude of parents of non-Traveller children (3), difficulties connected with halting place (2), no appreciation of the link between regular attendance and successful learning (2), etc.

These results must be interpreted with great caution: they are, after all, a list of the way teachers explain absenteeism, rather than an in-depth study of the complex factors behind the phenomenon. For example, what criteria were used to define "family visit", "scholastic failure" or "celebration" as the "probably true" or "probably false" reason behind a given absence? We shall return to this point.

In the *FRG* a study has been carried out [by Hundsalz, 1982, quoted by Reemtsma] correlating regularity of school attendance with type of school and economic situation of parents:

	ECONOMICALLY INDEPENDENT PARENTS							
type of school	for retarded children		primary		*Hauptschule*		secondary	
attendance	No.	%	No.	%	No.	%	No.	%
very regular	11	18.3	11	7.3	4	5.3	-	-
irregular	14	23.3	16	10.6	12	16.0	-	-
regular	35	58.4	124	82.1	59	78.7	6	100.0
Total	60	100.0	151	100.0	75	100.0	6	100.0
	PARENTS IN RECEIPT OF SOCIAL WELFARE PAYMENT							
type of school	for retarded children		primary		*Hauptschule*		secondary	
attendance	No.	%	No.	%	No.	%	No.	%
very regular	53	25.5	25	11.1	4	3.3	-	-
irregular	53	25.5	35	15.5	14	11.4	-	-
regular	102	49.0	166	73.4	105	85.3	6	100.0
Total	208	100.0	226	100.0	123	100.0	6	100.0

These tables show that attendance is more regular in "ordinary" classes than in those for the retarded; that in general it is better among the economically independent families; and that it increases with the level of study.

In *Denmark* statistics on children's school attendance were compiled soon after a group of immigrant Gypsies arrived in Elsinore. Here is the relationship for some children between the number of compulsory school days, and the number of days attended – with variations stemming "from the fact that many children arrived late from summer holidays somewhere in the Balkans, or left early for next summer (nomadism)" [Gudmander/Rude]. The period covered is the school year August 1973–June 1974:

form	compulsory days	days away number	days away %
2	200	156	78
5	182	157	86
6	200	63	31
5	155	122	78
2	155	140	90
3	200	156	78
5	155	97	62
7	200	83	41
5	200	109	54
4	200	164	82
5	200	108	54
3	200	160	80
3	200	103	51
5	182	77	42
4	200	166	83
5	200	92	46
4	200	166	83
3	160	97	60

Average percentage of days away: 62%.

"Furthermore, attention should be drawn to the fact that almost all teachers complained that the Gypsy pupils often came sauntering in late in the morning, and did not meet at the meeting time agreed upon. Just as frequently they left school before the time they had agreed to finish at. Such days also count as school days, when the pupils have been present" [Gudmander/Rude].

In the *United Kingdom*, detailed notes were kept in one secondary school: "A close look at individual attendance records showed that whilst 226 pupils had less than twenty half-days' absence, fewer than fifteen had more than 100 half-days. The most significant features are that no Gypsy child had fewer than 120 half-days absences and that the average for the Gypsy group was as high as 196 half-days compared with fifty-one half-days average for the whole school" [Ivatts, 1975, p.9]. The same study shows very clearly that, from Monday to Friday, the rate of absenteeism increases considerably, from 50% to 80% approximately; the latenesses of early in the week are transformed into absences. Attention is also drawn to the fact that absenteeism increases relative to the number of years spent in school. (Let it be emphasised that these figures concern a secondary school, where great stress is laid upon regularity of attendance; these facts partially explain the high rate of absenteeism.)

Equally, and doubtless in all countries, there are seasonal variations in attendance, linked primarily with travel and with economic activities; sometimes a clear pattern of cyclical attendance emerges, with a high rate during the same months each year, followed by increased absenteeism; there are also periods of difficulty (evictions, economic problems, etc.) during which schooling becomes a secondary consideration, and periods of intense attendance... *Each child, within various parameters, accumulates over time a certain number of days, weeks, months or years of school experience.* Here, for example, are the estimates given in *Ireland* by thirty-eight teachers with Traveller children in their classes [McCarthy]:

What do you estimate to be the average amount of time spent at school by your pupils?

Less than 6 months	5
Less than 2 years	5
2-4 years	15
4 years +	9
6 months each year	1
No answer	3
Total	**38**

Various factors influencing each child's school attendance (when this occurs at all, as it often does not) and the difficult conditions under which it takes place, combine with the result that *as a rule there is a gap of several years between the scholastic levels of Gypsy and Traveller children, and non-Gypsy children of the same ages.* "Their average reading age at eleven is seven" [Ivatts, 1975, p.20]. This is a widespread phenomenon, though usually less marked; the observed difference is most often of two to three years.

A statistical study carried out in *France*, in the Paris region, in forty classes with 1,088 pupils (including 114 Travellers in twenty-seven of the classes) reveals that 80% of the Traveller children showed scholastic backwardness, with the following distribution:

23%	1	year behind
30%	2	years behind
19%	3	years behind
5%	4	years behind
3%	5	years behind

Some pupils spend their entire school career on the "Preparatory Course" (the class where pupils learn to read, the first level of compulsory schooling in France) [*Jeannette et l'École Obligatoire*, collective work, MS., 1983].

There has doubtless, with the passing of the years, been an increase both in the number of children attending school, and those who come out of it literate. But this progress is slow, and, having described the effects of this situation, we must pursue further analyses to attempt to better understand the reasons behind it. As the United Kingdom report emphasises: "It also remains true that in this modern industrial state around half of the Traveller children never get the chance of schooling at all" [Acton/Kenrick].

Different groups

Gypsy/Traveller populations form a mosaic of diverse groups. As a result, several different groups may be present in a given school, and the teacher may find himself dealing with several cultures even if the class comprises Gypsy/Traveller children exclusively. This is particularly likely in all-Gypsy "special" classes; Gypsy children attending "ordinary" classes tend to form a rather homogeneous group, being drawn from families who travel or settle together in accordance with cultural similarities. Of course even "special" classes may find themselves with a homogeneous group of pupils, but diversity – be it in a mixed group, or in "waves" of different groups – is common, particularly in those countries where nomadism is widespread.

Intra-Gypsy diversity as it affects school life may be socio-cultural (different practices in connection with different areas of life), linguistic (different dialects, mutually intelligible to a greater or lesser degree), and/or economic in nature. It is this last factor which is most critical in influencing schooling, and attendance in particular: showmen, or travelling tradesmen, or scrap merchants, or seasonal agricultural workers, will have neither the same access to school, nor the same attitudes and expectations regarding it.

Nomadism is an important element of lifestyle – but is it an important factor as regards school? As we have shown, the proportion of nomads and semi-nomads varies greatly from country to country and from area to area. For example, in *Belgium*, of the forty-seven families covered by a school questionnaire [see above], twelve (or 25%) were regularly on the move, while the remainder practised seasonal nomadism. In *France*, teachers questioned about their pupils' types of dwellings gave the following picture: caravan (32), lorry (7), temporary housing awaiting transfer (6), horse-drawn caravan (3), shanty-town (1), mobile home (1), urban flat (1), hut (1) [Ferté]. The proportion of nomadic families may vary from region to region. For example in *Italy* a survey of 13,435 Gypsy pupils in fifteen provinces showed the following distribution [Karpati/Massano]:

Region	nomads		semi-nomads		sedentary	
	number	%	number	%	number	%
North	2,025	44.6	1,650	36.5	860	18.9
Central	2,400	40.0	400	6.6	3,200	53.4
South	-	-	60	2.0	2,840	98.0
Italy (total)	4,425	32.9	2,110	15.7	6,900	51.4

It is obvious that the school experience of nomadic children is quite different from that of sedentary ones. Research in most countries shows a clear increase in school attendance between November-April, the months when the least travelling takes place. School attendance can also be interrupted for professional reasons: the family may travel to participate in an important fair or market. Social factors – a family visit or celebration, etc. – may have the same effect. In the case of nomads whose halting places are often insecure, interruption is frequently a direct result of eviction. The teachers – generally "specialist" – who answer these questionnaires do not always seem to be aware of the fact that although the nomadic child has left the school when his parents resume their travels, this does not necessarily mean that he has ceased to attend school altogether: he may attend less frequently, but he will be back from time to time.

There are two important points to be borne in mind when considering the relationship between schooling and nomadism. On the one hand, nomadism does not of itself necessarily mean that children will have less complete schooling than their sedentary peers. On the other, little or no account is taken of nomadism in school policy and practice.

Nomadism and school are not incompatible. It is essential to debunk the myth – propounded in justification of assimilationist policies – that schooling is impossible without sedentarism. The available evidence, from various sources, is strongly to the contrary.

For example in *France* "The trend towards sedentarism entails an increase in absenteeism. The parents, knowing that they will be in the area for a long period, become less stringent in seeing that their children attend, all the more so as they feel ill at ease in the sedentary situation... In no case can it be claimed that nomadism is a cause of illiteracy." Moreover: "Regular attendance is no guarantee of successful learning" [Kervadec, 1982, pp. 33-35].

In *Italy*: "Nomadism has a relative influence on school attendance; in fact only 4.9% of the teachers questioned cited it as a cause of irregularity, and what is more, half of them were in the south, where the Gypsies are sedentarised... Nomadism appears to be an ambivalent factor: if on the one hand it keeps children out of school for considerable periods, on the other it affords them greater self-confidence and a positive sense of identity. There is evidence that school attendance among nomadic children is more regular than among their sedentary peers... The nomadic children had markedly superior test results to the sedentarised" [Karpati/Massano].

In the *United Kingdom* "It is widely stated that either sedentarisation, or least stable living on an official or legal caravan site is a prerequisite for successful education... but historical experience... would seem to indicate that it is not nomadism in itself, but only frequent forced evictions, or discrimination against nomads, that is an obstacle to education" [Acton/Kenrick].

It would be easy to give many more examples repeating the above conclusions, both about the important dynamism of nomadic children, and the fact that it is not nomadism, but eviction and related practices, which impede schooling.

Nomadism is not, either in general [see "Policies and Politics", above] nor as regards schooling in particular, taken into account in practice – which is, after all, formulated by Settled policymakers. Here too examples from all states abound, practised with varying degrees of intensity but converging in both detail and overall tone. Let us give a general example. In *Belgium* Article 4 of the Law of June 29 1983 "imposes very strong constraints on pupil mobility in the course of the school year, and thereby on parental mobility likewise, since the Act forbids all nursery and primary schools to accept after the thirtieth day of the school year, without valid reason, any pupil who has been enrolled in a different nursery or primary school... the nomadic lifestyle is not taken into account" [Reyniers]. And now for a concrete – and very indicative – example: in *France*, a teacher, having compiled and submitted scholastic records for some of his pupils with a view to enrolling them in sixth form (the first class of secondary school), had the papers returned with the question, *"Where does the family live?"* – which, in the case of nomads, is impossible to answer [anecdote related by A. Cotonnec, speaking at a public meeting, 1985].

What provision does exist in the various states is generally aimed only at "recognised" professions, often as a result of organised pressure from the groups themselves to assure their children's schooling despite frequent moving about. This is the case, in Belgium, France, Italy, the United Kingdom, etc., for bargees, circus people and certain categories of showmen. Often provision takes the form of special boarding schools for these children. But such measures cover only a handful of itinerant professions, and even within these categories often apply only to families who can prove they have a regular income from same. What is more, the forms they take – boarding school in particular – are generally incompatible with the wishes and lifestyle of Gypsy parents. Later on we shall analyse existing measures to see how they could be applied more favourably towards nomadic Gypsies and Travellers.

It is usually the absence of mechanisms for accepting nomadic children into schools that is the cause of poor attendance and lower literacy rates. Their illiteracy is thus the effect of the overall situation, not, as many analyses assume, solely of nomadism itself. When we observe in some countries (mainly Greece and the FRG) that the scholastic level of nomadic children is particularly low, the tendency is to generalise it, whereas in fact the result (low scholastic level) cannot be attributed to a single parameter (nomadism). *Where a correlation between the two facts (illiteracy and nomadism) is to be found, it does not signify that there is a causal relationship between them.*

From all the above considerations, it is clear that *to promote settlement as a means of promoting schooling is not only ineffective, but erroneous*, for three main reasons:

- *To postulate a relation between sedentarisation and school attendance is false:* on the whole, nomads attempt to attend school just as much as sedentary children do (while on the other hand there are groups which have been sedentary for considerable periods, and of their own choice, who do not send their children to school). "Sedentarism = better schooling" is false, because forcing nomads to settle has never improved their scholastic performance – quite the contrary.

- *To postulate a relation between sedentarisation and scholastic achievement is false:* nomads do at least as well and, according to many observers, better.

- To postulate a relation between sedentarisation and improved living conditions is false, when the sedentarism is involuntary. Nomadism permits an adaptive dynamism in both the economic and social fields; this dynamism also manifests itself in the school experience of the nomadic child.

As regards schooling, nomadism is one variable among many, to be taken into account without exaggerating the consequences it may have. Taking it into account is firstly the technical problem of modifying enrolment and acceptance procedures to accommodate nomadic children, then of a suitably adapted pedagogy, and then of pedagogical follow-up for the child. It is all the more important to respect this way of life which is on the decrease as a percentage in all countries (despite the overall rise in the numbers of nomads) as a result of combined factors: socio-economic and legal changes, assimilationist policies postulating sedentarisation, lack of halting places, public antipathy. New forms of nomadism are emerging, notably in the increased distance between one halt and the next, and increased length of stay if this is possible. As a result, schools are coming into contact with new patterns of attendance – not as yet general, but on the increase overall – as this example (from Belgium, but observable elsewhere) shows: "In the country as a whole, the problem is thus no longer how to accommodate pupils for a brief stay, but how to integrate different pupils into the school structure, sometimes for a considerable period" [Reyniers]. Nomadism is thus a relative phenomenon and, in general, "Gypsy children pose a problem for schools... not because they are nomadic but because they are Gypsies and significantly different in culture and outlook from other groups of children within our schools" [Ivatts, 1975, p.41]. In spite of everything, Gypsies and Travellers do hope to reconcile schooling with nomadism:

"Well, they can't stop us travelling. If they do that, there'll be ructions. That would be the end of the world. They can't do that to us" [a young Gypsy, father of two children, quoted by Reyniers].

"Being Travellers it is hard for us to get our children into schools during the summer months as we are working. Although we love our children very much we can't give up our way of life for the children because we know no other way of making a living. I don't feel they need to know everything that is taught in secondary schools... (but) knowing about computers and electronics is getting more and more important in today's world, especially for us Travellers, as we have to work with and repair all the new electronic equipment coming into the fairgrounds" [from *Why Traveller Children Need Education,* by Alfreda Holmes, an English fairground Traveller parent, in *Traveller Education,* no. 20, 1985, quoted by Acton/Kenrick].

Reception in school

Certain practical aspects of schooling which may well be taken for granted by Settled pupils, pose fundamental problems to Gypsy and Traveller children. In order for Gypsy children to go to school, they must first have access to it – that is, the right to attend – and then be allowed to stay. Such questions do not even touch on pedagogical considerations. How Traveller children are accepted (or otherwise) into the school system could of itself be the subject of a long and depressing report. In effect, the most widespread practice in Europe as regards school provision for Gypsy children, is rejection. And this phenomenon cannot be separated from the overall picture of the Gypsies' situation: it is merely the school's expression of general attitudes, which indeed often take more violent forms outside the school.

Some years ago, when analysing the attitudes of local bodies towards nomads, we gave a detailed picture of the various forms that rejection takes in practice [Liégeois, 1981b; Liégeois, 1983a]. These same forms recur within the context of school. There is straightforward rejection under a simple pretext such as "lack of space" – even when this is not legal. It is rejection which may take any form, from a simple negative attitude to violent expulsion on any one of a number of easily evoked pretexts: disciplinary, for example ("He's disturbing the class") or failure to comply with the dress code. But it is also, more and more, an indirect rejection which replaces blank refusal or expulsion with effective barriers to entering/remaining in a class. It can take an administrative or pedagogic form: of the first type when, for example, the parents are required to produce a plethora of documents and certificates (references or assessments from the previous school, vaccination records, etc.); of the second when, for example, the children are put at the back of the class, or the teacher refuses to deal with them on the grounds that they require special provision for the educationally subnormal. It may also happen that routine rejection may be transformed into a cause célèbre when outside bodies (a Gypsy association, a human rights or anti-discrimination organisation, etc.) brings the case to public attention. And it then becomes apparent that it is not harshness, violence or arbitrariness which renders rejection excessive and recognised as such, but simple visibility. At the same time, in the realm of schooling, such visibility is rare indeed, and in the majority of countries even now "a diffused climate of discrimination relics in informal attitudes" dominates [Korré/Marselos].

Difficulty of access to school for Gypsy/Traveller children is by no means a recent phenomenon. As an illustration we will give but one case, dating – exceptionally – from as far back as 1811 (published 1816) and collected in the *United Kingdom* by a Quaker advocate of schooling for Gypsy children:

"Trinity Cooper, a daughter of this Gypsey family, who was about thirteen years of age, applied to be instructed at the school; but in consequence of the obloquy affixed to that description of persons, she was repeatedly refused. She nevertheless persevered in her importunity till she obtained admission for herself and two of her brothers. Thomas Howard [the teacher] says that... of all his scholars there were not any more attentive and affectionate than these; and when the children broke up house in the spring to make their usual excursions, the children expressed much regret at leaving the school" [John Hoyland, quoted by Acton/Kenrick].

"How many latterday Trinity Coopers have we not encountered, saying to us wistfully 'When can I go to school, mister?' And how dreadful, that 174 years after Thomas Howard established his part-time voluntary school for the poor, volunteers still offer some Gypsies the only education available to them! (…) The demand for elementary human rights made by thirteen-year-old Trinity Cooper for herself and her two younger brothers 174 years ago has yet to be met by British society" [Acton/Kenrick].

The same holds true in most of Europe today.

Each of the participants within the school system contributes to the climate in which the Gypsy child finds himself. Firstly there are the *other children*, who gang up on him, to beat or tease him; since the Gypsy child is rarely on his own, these conflicts frequently take the form of pitched battles, on or off the school grounds. It is perhaps to avoid such situations that in a number of schools it is forbidden for Gypsy and Traveller children to play with the others.

In *Ireland*, "The results of the questionnaires sent to the teachers indicate that the Traveller children are rejected and stigmatised by the Settled children. They are subjected to name-calling – 'dirty knackers' – and abuse from other children. Chrissie Ward, a member of *Mincéir Misli* [a Traveller organisation] and a mother of ten, interviewed for this study, spoke about one of her daughters being humiliated at school when a joke competition was held and one of the pupils told a joke denigrating 'knackers'. Both Chrissie and Nan Joyce, also member of *Mincéir Misli* and mother of eleven children, spoke of Traveller children being ashamed to admit they were Travellers. Nan told of her sister's child hiding in the trailer when he saw boys from his class playing in the area" [McCarthy].

In the *FRG* "Sinti children, coming from an environment based on other cultural structures, run the risk, in a school system based on middle-class norms, of becoming the victims of a stigmatisation process on both the individual and collective level... In his research, Hundsalz [1982] remarks that discrimination – both from teachers and from other pupils – is one of the reasons for lack of motivation for school... But according to the evidence of the parents (in the thirty to forty age group) it does seem that discrimination was much more evident in their youth, than now" [Reemtsma].

"We've always gone to school [i.e. we always used to]. That's different to Travellers' children now. Oh God! It was murder going to school. They wouldn't sit beside you in the seats. They wouldn't play with you in the playground, you was always getting knocked about. Many and many a time I went home crying to my mother" [Belle Stewart (the famous Scottish Traveller folksinger) quoted in J. Sandford (ed.), *Gypsies*, Abacus, 1975, quoted by Acton/Kenrick].

> "My little brother goes to school
> And the boys do bully him
> They call him Gypsy Tramp
> and Thieves and he's only eight
> And cries at the night."

[poem by Julie Mitchell, a Gypsy pupil, submitted for a secondary school assignment, quoted by Acton/Kenrick]

"When we visit schools at playtime we often hear racist taunting from other children... When in 1971 non-Gypsy children at one school found that Christopher Reiss was visiting their school during the Schools Council Research Project on Traveller Education, they even stoned his car as he drove off" [Acton/Kenrick].

The indiscipline and aggressiveness of Traveller children within the school framework, remarked upon in different countries, must be considered as a protective mechanism against the real and imagined attitudes of the environment. All interaction between two antagonistic communities is tainted by this ongoing polarisation, and such conflict situations are often internalised by those who are constantly subjected to them.

"They accuse the other children of being prejudiced against them. 'They're always laughing at us.' 'They call us 'dirty Gypsy' – if they do, we 'it 'em, no messin', we bash 'em.' 'They call us 'dirty Gypsies', we get 'em, that's why we come to discos – 'cos we can get 'em there.' They talk freely about getting out of school as soon as the last bell has sounded so as to lie in wait for the pupils with whom they have vendettas. 'I'll smash 'er when I see 'er,' a Gypsy girl said. They say that they only retaliate when provoked – they are never responsible for provoking other children. They have successfully made a local youth club their own province by 'frightening' most of the non-Gypsy children away. The Gypsies' social mixing in the school is limited. They tend to socialise as a homogeneous group but they do have some external relationships" [Ivatts, 1975, p.18].

Frequently, the relations are ambivalent, mingling attraction and rejection: "I know that when I was in primary school, I was treated like a leper, and that by contrast, at fourteen, in secondary school, it was all 'Oh! You're a Gypsy! How wonderful, I would have liked to be one too', etc. – There's two sides to it, you see" [Cani, aged twenty, collected in *France* by Belloni, 1981, p.71]. And the fact of long-term association does occasionally lead to better mutual comprehension:

In the *Netherlands*, in certain cases, it has been observed that "In the beginning, there was a tendency in the schools for Gypsy children to stick together, and there were also instances of Dutch children closing ranks too. Such behaviour was brought about by lack of mutual familiarity, stereotyped views and prejudice. The longer the two groups went to school together or shared the same classroom and worked together on class projects, the more contacts were built up, in many cases extending beyond school. The Dutch children abandoned their initial mistrust fairly quickly, although in some cases the development of normal relationships between the children was held back by the views held by Dutch parents. This could be partly remedied by the provision of information to these parents by teachers, especially when the parents could be convinced that the quality of their children's education would not suffer from having Gypsies at the school. Gypsy history and culture are taught in the schools in an effort to reduce stereotyped thinking and prejudice among Dutch children" [Hovens et al].

It is apparent everywhere that parents' attitudes determine children's behaviour. *Non-Gypsy parents* use pejorative terms – even to teachers – in describing Gypsies, and reject (in word, and sometimes in deed) the very notion of Gypsy pupils in the school. However, it is equally often the case (as the example from the Netherlands, cited above, demonstrates) that prolonged co-attendance in conjunction with exposure to information leads to peaceful inter-group relations and, perhaps, increased mutual understanding. But that, of course, depends on circumstances and goodwill permitting this long-term contact and information exchange to take place.

Teachers' attitudes are not – and cannot be considered – detached from the wider environment's general attitudes and policies concerning Gypsies and Travellers. *Teachers* are part of the school institution and it is they who in the most direct sense represent and promulgate ideology. Their training, knowledge and practice are linked to and in harmony with the political tendencies of the moment. This is doubtless one of the reasons why school provision for Gypsy and Traveller children was first initiated sporadically from outside the existing school system, and why in most states innovation and adaptation continue to originate outside the school system – all the more so because of its rigid and monolithic character.

"There are, happily as we think, caste distinctions and class distinctions, which deserve great consideration and respect, and personally we sympathise with the teachers who protested that it would be a great moral wrong to flood their schools and bring their scholars under the contaminating influence of Gypsy children, who, according to George Smith's own persistent showing, were the very scum of the earth, brought up in the midst of the grossest indecencies and profanities" [Edwin Godder, *George Smith of Coalville – the Story of an Enthusiast*, 1896, quoted by Acton/Kenrick].

Still in the *United Kingdom*, but a century later: 1985, in response to the survey carried out in connection with this study: "One family in Scotland said that whereas at a school in England their two sons had been hit, forbidden school meals, and made to stand in the corner of a classroom after minor offences, in Scotland things were better. Some young Irish Travellers in Scotland commented, however, on the school they had recently left: 'They put all the Gypsies on one side of the class… they just throw the books at them: no teaching. They make Gypsy children stand up and read when (they know) they can't read.' Corporal punishment is generally more frequent in Scottish schools ('When the children went to school in X, they came out black and blue', said one mother) and this can clash with Traveller values against hitting children.

We only came across one specific case of discrimination in Northern Ireland, a boys' secondary school where Traveller children were made to sit at a separate table at lunch time.

Twice during our researchers' school visits children ran off from school. In the first instance a child ran after a dispute with a teacher in class… in the second instance a Gypsy boy, aged about ten, was about to attack another boy who had insulted him, and was restrained by a playground/dinner supervisor who hit the child, allegedly accidentally, with a heavy brass handbell…

It is probable that incidents such as those recorded above are not infrequent. In both cases the reaction of the ordinary schoolteachers seemed to indicate that nothing very unusual was happening; their attitude seemed to be 'You see what we have to put up with from these people.' Clearly where parents come to believe that schools cannot exercise adequate care and oversight of their children in school hours, or that they may be subjected to physical assault by staff or other pupils, this has an adverse effect on school attendance" [Acton/Kenrick].

"'We may be Gypsies but we aren't "dirty Gypsies".' This phrase was mechanically repeated. When questioned about the staff, the response was immediate: 'Oh yes, of course they call us "dirty Gypsy"'… 'He called us dirty pigs – get back to your pig-sties, he said.' 'The deputy 'ead mistress up there called 'er a Gypsy cow – she said once a Gypsy always a Gypsy – I wouldn't stand for that I can tell you – I'd just walk out'" [Ivatts, 1975, p.19].

In *Belgium*, "Among the difficulties linked with the school system, rejection is the most often expressed. It takes various forms: confining Gypsy pupils to the back of the class, mockery from teachers and Settled pupils, being forced to perform menial tasks such as sweeping the class or even scrubbing floors while the Settled pupils are learning to read and write… How do we react when a family, stopping – for want of a better place – in a car park near a school, is evicted as a direct result of a petition circulated by one of the teachers, annoyed at the loss of his usual parking-space? Any expression of rejection coming from any representative of the school system can create in the child a lasting mental block towards anything connected with school" [Reyniers].

An example from *Greece*: "A Gypsy of Rumanian bearkeepers origin, graduate of Polytechnic, told me that his teacher, in the secondary school, called him 'gypsy' with an expression of disgust, and was suspicious of the 'gypsy' in any case of disorder and 'crime'" [Marselos, MS., 1984].

In *Italy*, "A very clear symptom of school's resistance to accepting Gypsy pupils is the attitude observed during the period of the 'special classes' policy, when frequently (and in direct contravention of ministerial directives) these classes were held in completely separate, often inadequate, premises, or held at different times so as to avoid contact with other children." Even after the "special classes" were officially disbanded, some do in fact continue to function, "so as to avoid the problem of having Gypsy children in ordinary classes" [Karpati/Massano].

More of the same, from *Ireland*: "The majority of special classes in primary schools, of which there are now 100, are separated from the rest of the school. This segregation takes various forms, the commonest being separate break times and play times for the children of the special class to those of the rest of the school, and often separate washing and toilet facilities. There does not seem to be very much mixing with the rest of the school population at all, even in such subjects as sports, art, music, or physical education... In an interview for this project, Nan Joyce spoke of the degrading practice of washing and bathing children in some schools even when their parents had sent them in clean, of Traveller children being singled out to have their hair checked publicly for infestation and of the practice in schools with uniforms of keeping the Traveller children's uniforms in the school so that they have to change out of their own clothes and then back into them before going home" [McCarthy].

Before being in a class, one must first gain admission, and here teachers play a vital role. It is common indeed that under various pretexts, usually taking the form of the indirect rejection outlined above, Gypsy/Traveller children cannot get into school: demands for vaccination certificates, various official forms (which a child who has changed school frequently simply cannot obtain) etc. In certain states, where legislation governing such requirements is very detailed, the teacher faces a dilemma: stick to the rules and refuse the child, or accept the child in spite of the possible consequences of this breach of regulations? This situation constitutes a serious barrier to school attendance, even – and perhaps above all – where the initiative to get the children into school is voluntary, from their parents:

Let us give two examples from *France*: at a meeting, social workers claimed that thirty-five different procedures were required to get eight Gypsy children into school [*Journées d'Étude des Techniciens Sociaux*, CNIN 31 January, 1-2 February 1973, p.16]. And with older children: "Two teenagers wished to join the class; admission formalities, begun on 5th November 1982, were finally completed at the end of June 1983. The complexity of procedures and the length of time they take show how unsuited the workings of the system are in such cases" [from: *Tsiganes, Qui Êtes-Vous?*, brochure for teachers' training college in Cergy-Pontoise, 1985].

An example from the *United Kingdom*: "School, if only for a week or two, and most of our happiness seemed to come to an end. We were not put on the register book. If the schoolmaster said: 'What standard were you in last school?' and we answered: 'Standard Three!' it was 'Put him in Standard

Two, teacher – they're not here for long.' This is what always seemed to happen, and I was always the big boy in a class of little ones, and my sisters too. We were called 'dunces', and we all had a fight first day, and every day alike. Next school we would say: 'Standard Four', one class higher than we had been ever, and it would be Standard Three then, and we told lies to do it and we were told never to tell lies. I'm sure it was at school we started telling our first serious lies – in trying to get into the class we were entitled to be in. But we knew it would end when we moved on, and were happy to be free again" [S.G. Boswell, *The Book of Boswell*, Gollancz, 1970, quoted by Acton/Kenrick]. Although the situation described here occurred nearly two decades ago, it shows that (in substance if not in form) little has changed in the interim.

The *administration* contributes in various ways to the quality of the Gypsy/Traveller child's reception in school. Not infrequently it is, in practice, yet another block to school attendance – either in its own policies or in the way it interprets regulations. In certain states teachers express annoyance when prohibitively complicated rules prevent them from adapting the teaching programme to meet Traveller children's needs, or hinder them from admitting the nomadic child who turns up unexpectedly. And, in the Gypsy's eyes, administrative blocks constitute an important dissuading force. Moreover, where a compulsory schooling policy is actively promoted, and where schools are obliged to accept Gypsy children, administration is often still reluctant to validate the children's rights. Here are a few examples:

In *France*: "You know all the red tape involved in grant applications? And then it's refused because the only declared source of income is social welfare. The administration sent me back (the Gypsy applicant's) file, saying, 'They can't be living on this. How are they earning their living?' I make enquiries, I tell them, 'They're not earning, they just get welfare. They can't do anything, there's only the mother.' I return the file, and they send it right back to me saying 'Impossible. Grant is refused because it is impossible to live like this.' – Insufficient income, so no grant" [M. Ranucci, in Liégeois, 1980d, p.141].

In *Italy* "The authorities, who should enforce compulsory school attendance, don't bother checking whether Gypsy children are attending or not, and there is no lack of instances where under one pretext or another they oppose the admission of Gypsy children – whom they continue to regard as a problem" [Karpati, MS., 1984].

In *Ireland* an investigation was carried out in Tallaght (a suburb of Dublin) in 1984, by a branch of the INTO (primary teachers' trade union): "Sixty-one families out of a total of 100 responded to the survey. It revealed that 102 out of a possible 165 children were on the school rolls (this turned out to be an overestimate by ten when checked against the school rolls). Several families said they had tried to enrol their children in local schools but were told the schools were full. The conclusions were that (a) many Travellers view the local schools as inaccessible and the schools do not seek their enrolment and attendance, and (b) few Travellers regard education as a right...

The School Attendance Act of 1926 obliges parents to send their children to school between the ages of six to fifteen or to educate them at home to the satisfaction of the Department of Education... Travellers have always been exempted from these regulations, not out of any desire to accommodate their lifestyle but because most schools did not want to take them. However, they were never officially exempted, the law was simply not applied to them most of the time. There have been a number of instances in the past of Traveller children being removed from their parents for non-attendance at school. The Act could therefore be applied in a discriminatory way" [McCarthy].

In *Belgium* "There are also other, more disturbing practices: in September, primary schools make every effort to enrol Traveller pupils, because each child on the rolls means additional government funding; indeed the recruitment of Travellers may be crucial to maintain pupil levels and thus teachers' jobs. Young nomad children are at one moment eagerly sought out by different organising bodies, but at the next their parents are run out of town. If they do leave during the school year, the places left vacant are not allocated to other nomad children (ostensibly because they are different ages, at different scholastic levels, etc.). There are also cases of non-admission during the school year, justified by quoting the law, etc." [Reyniers].

In some countries it is only very recently that the *central administrative authorities* have declared explicitly that all children, even Gypsies(!), have a right to attend school. Such is the case, for example, in England, where in 1981 a circular was issued by the Department of Education and Science in the wake of a refusal by a local authority to accept Gypsy children whose parents were on an unauthorised halting site, into class. But everywhere, the practical application of directives issued by central authorities is a long and chancy process. What is more, living conditions for Gypsy families are difficult everywhere, and rejection by school is just one of many problems. Reports from many countries stress that Traveller children who do attend school, used as they are to frequent eviction, are haunted by the fear that they will not be able to find their parents when they leave at the end of class-time; it is easy to imagine that such an atmosphere of stress and violence must have a negative effect on the child's ability to benefit from his hours in school. In France, at a meeting of a Gypsy organisation, the parents – caught between the obligation of sending their children to school, and the impossibility of doing so because of endless evictions – suggested that local authorities might be required to issue a "certificate of eviction" which could then be shown to social welfare officials in place of the currently required school certificate. The idea could be applied in all countries and is full of potential: it would force local authorities to think twice before carrying out evictions, since such a certificate would have to give the reasons, and these would have to comply both with local anti-discrimination legislation and with overall European directives prohibiting measures aimed at any population group as a whole. Such a pause for reflection would certainly help to break the present reflex action: as soon as a caravan appears, prohibitions rain down.

This awareness of the rejection suffered by Gypsies and Travellers is rather new, and little developed as yet. This shared habitual experience of rejection is rarely apparent to those who inflict it. Thus, in the realm of school, questionnaires filled out by teachers are, accordingly, biased. The teachers who respond most willingly tend to be those with the most contact with Gypsy and Traveller children, who are most sensitive to the children's needs and who try to adapt to meet them. But such teachers comprise only a tiny handful among those involved in school provision. It is therefore difficult to interpret teachers' answers concerning the quality of their relations with Gypsy pupils: whether they do in fact reflect reality or smug self-satisfaction, available data indicating overall good relations are at any rate exaggerated due to the characteristics of those who provide them. It must be added that it is once again the specialist teachers who tend to be most critical regarding official school policies – it is they who, along with the children themselves, feel the negative consequences on a daily basis.

It is also worth adding that, while the overall situation is one of rejection, there are exceptions: schools, headmasters and individual teachers who demonstrate acceptance and understanding, and who are all the more noteworthy in that they do so in an environment which continues to reject both Gypsies and those who side with them. Parents and children cite such exceptions with pleasure and gratitude. We will give only one example:

"I really did improve at school, too – much to the delight of the headmaster who really took an interest in me and gave me confidence and encouragement. He implored my parents to stay in the town until after the Qualifying Examination for secondary school. I didn't let him down, either, being one of the three in my classes who won bursaries. He told my parents he would pay what else was needed for me to go to High School... Poor headmaster! He was pestered and bullyragged by irate parents who were convinced that my getting a bursary had been his doing... How was it possible for a Tinker child to pass and not their child? They wouldn't believe the poor man that the examination papers went to Forfar and that he wasn't responsible" [Betsy Whyte, *The Yellow on the Broom*, W&R Chambers, 1979 (Mrs. Whyte is a Scottish Traveller, who went to school in Scotland in the 1930s. Shortly after the events related above she was falsely accused of stealing at school, and her family fled from the town) quoted by Acton/Kenrick].

At the same time, generally speaking, "The parents are inexhaustible when it comes to giving examples of humiliation suffered by their children, of false accusations with drastic consequences both for the child and for the group, even if it is afterwards (too late) admitted that the charges were unfounded. The child's school dynamics have been broken; he will not return to class" [Liégeois, 1980b]. The child may go on to develop characteristically introverted or aggressive behaviour: such conduct is reactive, it is an *effect* of the situation, but all too often taken as the *cause* of failure at school. It is important to stress this yet again.

"The Gypsies suffer considerable embarrassment in the classroom where they are frequently identified in terms of inability, with subsequent segregation and differential treatment. Some of the Gypsies misbehave in order to precipitate the punitive response which can then be used as evidence of the staff's prejudice. This, therefore, justifies further misbehaviour and absenteeism. The blame for lack of personal progress and wider social acceptance is transferred to staff and non-Gypsy pupils. From the Gypsies' point of view, it is the school's prejudice which besets their progress and acceptance. Thus a behavioural pattern is established which supports a continual and mutual transfer of blame" [Ivatts, 1975, p.28].

"The 'Vagabond', 'not disciplined', 'aggressive' sometimes, and 'cunning' behaviour of children, which disturbs the Settled society, rather adults than other children, must be considered as an interaction of 'self-defence' against a real or 'supposed' and 'expected' verbal or gestural aggression on the part of non-Gypsies, as a complex of existing or consciously and subconsciously inherited experiences of rejection. Their permanent marginalisation has formed in their minds a spectre of 'blind alleys' and has led them to marginal mentality, parasitical occupations and indifference for their future" [Marselos, MS., 1984].

To escape this circle of marginalisation and the reactions which it in turn evokes, the pupil who has the determination to stay on at school must disguise his identity to avoid being ostracised; evidence from a wide range of sources confirms this.

For example in the *FRG*: "Only those Sinti who disguise their origins and who avoid contact with the group have succeeded in learning a trade requiring prolonged apprenticeship or studies" [Marion Papenbrok, MS., 1984]. Or in *Greece*: "The F. of Athens did not permit me any research in their village, although they had previously accepted spontaneously, when they watched a reportage, where I mentioned them as an example of progressive Gypsies, just because I included them with the Gypsies, and they were afraid that their children would be looked down on at school. Fortunately this did not take place, but the F. kept being suspicious of me" [Marselos, MS., 1984].

One may well ask if discrimination does not lessen as the "differentness" of the victim diminishes – in which case one need simply conform to be accepted. But let us glance at some related issues. We cannot ignore the possibility that, given the experience of his parents and his whole group, the Traveller child who is successful at school may well find himself, both during and after his school career, in a psychologically and socially ambiguous position:

"You know, at school I got treated like a Gypsy – but at home my own people treated me like a Gadji (non-Gypsy) and I didn't like that at all, it really insulted me! A child, the way he's brought up, that means a lot to him; afterwards, he may want... but it's much too late" [Mona, aged seventeen, in Belloni, 1981, p.75].

Having presented these general data (the state of adult literacy, socio-historical and socio-political analysis of schooling, the current situation with regard to school provision, compulsory schooling, nomadism, how Gypsy children are accommodated within the school system, etc.) which give us an idea of the situation as a whole, it is time to turn to more detailed considerations – case studies and other broad observations such as the situation of teachers and reflection on pedagogic projects and methods – towards our goal of an in-depth and comprehensive overview.

Structures

In the first few pages of this report we pointed out that, as regards school provision for Gypsy and Traveller children, everything (or nearly everything) has already been tried. It is appropriate then to take account of this plethora of attempts – which add up to so many "experiments" – and to draw conclusions from them. *There has been a variety of initiatives in two spheres: proposed structures for schooling* (e.g. caravan-school) *and proposed methods or, more broadly speaking, philosophy, to be pursued in teaching* (e.g. intercultural pedagogy). For the sake of clarity we shall treat these two questions in separate sections. They are, however, closely linked, and a degree of overlap is unavoidable.

We shall begin with structures. Case studies were chosen as the best means of covering the whole of Europe as well as all the relevant structures, and at the same time presenting data within their own context. They were carried out in each state, with the aid of a workplan jointly formulated by the participating experts in summer 1984. After giving a broad overview of the variety of structures, we shall illustrate with summaries of some of the case studies.

According to the typologies formulated in the light of observations from the different countries, it appears that there is almost always a dichotomy between "special classes" and "ordinary classes" [cf. Liégeois, 1983b]. But a number of nuances must be borne in mind. We must also be wary in our use of the term "special class", since everywhere there are classes which are de facto "special" because of the children who are in them, and others which are de jure "special" by administrative status; this likewise determines how "special" the teachers in them are. In some cases there is a strong, even antagonistic difference between the two types, while in others the criteria for "ordinary" and "special" status are practically indistinguishable. We shall return to the importance of these facts after presenting an overview of the various possibilities, and a few specific cases.

In *France*, the answers of thirty-three teachers on the subject of "educational structures which accept Gypsy children" were as follows:

special classes for Gypsy children, linked with normal classes	13
ordinary classes in ordinary schools	12
classes with official "special " status	5
special classes for Gypsy children, not linked with normal classes	5
permanent premises on official halting site	4
mobile premises visiting unofficial halting sites	3
mobile premises visiting official halting sites	1
total	**43**

In this sample, the number of specialised structures (thirty-one) is greater than that of ordinary classes (twelve) [Ferté]. There seem to be no overall French statistics concerning schools (or teachers) who deal exclusively (or nearly so) with Gypsy and Traveller children.

In the *Netherlands* there were twenty-eight "regional caravan centres" with "specialised educational facilities for the children of caravan dwellers" in 1985 [Hovens et al]. The total number of pitches in these sites is 2,235, an average of eighty per site (in fact the number of pitches varies from 153 to 9). These "centres" are, as indicated above, generally considered to be far too big. Children to whom no "specialised educational facilities" are offered, must attend ordinary classes.

In *Ireland:* "At present there are thirty-two pre-school classes catering for about 320 children in the three to five age group. In 1981 about 2,000 of those attending primary school were enrolled in ordinary classes. There are now about 100 special classes with up to fifteen pupils each throughout the country" [McCarthy; the Irish report includes a map showing the locations of these different classes]. We must also add the sixteen "training centres" for adolescents and young adults. Thirty-nine teachers responding to the questionnaire described the type of class in which they work, thus providing us with an overview:

special classes in primary schools	25
special school	3
ordinary classes	3
preschools	6
special school/day care centre	1
special school/junior training centre	1

In *Italy*, since the discontinuation of "special classes", Gypsy children are placed in "common classes"; there seem to be only two classes (Bologna and Turin) which accept only Gypsy pupils, and three "bridging classes" (Turin and Udine) to help children who are considerably behind scholastically, to catch up, and as "a first approach to school for immigrant (Yugoslav) Gypsy children who do not speak Italian" [Karpati/Massano]. There are also four mobile classrooms attached to circuses.

In *Denmark:* "There are no schools where classes have been established with the specific aim of teaching Gypsy pupils, because they are Gypsies. This would be contrary to the intention of the objective Denmark has concerning integration of immigrant pupils... Nevertheless classes have been established exclusively for Gypsy children, both in Copenhagen and in Elsinore, during the first years after the immigration" [Gudmander/Rude].

United Kingdom statistics combining documented minimums with some estimates taking many variables into account, are available, and can be synthesised as a table [Acton/Kenrick]:

Types of Educational Provision for Traveller in the UK					
Countries	England and Wales				Scotland and Northern Ireland
	1967	1973	1977	1985	1985
Number of LEAs* making special provision	2	13	53	65	5
LEA specialist teachers in schools/units	2	24	54	110	10
LEA peripatetic teachers	–	–	8	56	3
LEA other specialist staff	–	–	1	15	2
Total extra LEA staff	2	24	63	181	15
LEA non-mobile special units, school or site	–	5	35	11	–
LEA mobile units	–	1	7	16**	3
LEA special expenditure***	0.005	0.1	0.4-0.5	2.0-2.5	0.15-0.20
Voluntary/independent expenditure***	0.001	0.02	0.08	0.1	0.005
Voluntary/independent project numbers	2	30	7	12****	2****
Approx. no. & % of Traveller children reg. at LEA schools	750 (4%)	1,000 (6%)	1,200 (8%)	5,000 (30%)	800 (40%)
% of nomadic children on legal sites	5	15	25	65	45

* LEA: Local Education Authority
** This figure includes three mobile schools with circuses
*** Approximate figures, in millions of £ sterling.
**** This figure counts "Save the Children Fund" projects in different locations as different projects.

Many detailed maps, conveying much data, are included in the United Kingdom report.

In *Belgium* it seems that, apart from the now-discontinued experimental class at Esneux, there are no official special classes, but no shortage of them in practice: "Inserted into the ordinary school complex, they accept only Gypsy and Traveller children"; as for "preparatory classes geared towards insertion in the mainstream school system, organised on halting sites, they provide experimental teaching geared towards giving Gypsy children the basics... so they can benefit from ordinary class when they enter it. The experiments in Mortsel and Neder-over-Heembeek (Brussels) have been discontinued." Schooling in "ordinary classes" takes place to some extent everywhere, with some areas having greater concentrations of nomads than others, and in a few rare cases Traveller children are in boarding schools intended for bargees and showmen [Reyniers].

Mobile classes

For families on the move, it is easy to see how adapting school to meet their wishes (mainly that they not be separated from their children) and their lifestyle (mobility) can lead to the setting up of mobile classes. These can either travel with a group of families or go out to meet people on different sites – or indeed combine the two.

However, despite the significant numbers of nomads in various countries throughout Europe, mobile classes are very rare. The main reason behind this is that it is only recently that serious thought has been given to adapting school structures to meet Travellers' needs. Up to now it has been up to the child to adapt to the school – and this precept, with all its implications, is still very much with us: school is a Settled people's institution, itself Settled. The first group on the move to obtain mobile school facilities were circus families and some of the bigger fairground operators. There are, it seems, two reasons for this: such families practise a recognised profession, well organised into associations representing their interests; secondly, a circus is such a large-scale enterprise that it can undertake to move, and if necessary even purchase, a mobile school unit – and also provide the teacher's board and lodging. Moreover, circus children form a cohesive group, travelling together for very long periods. This may also be the case for fairground children whose families tend to travel in a group, but the system does not seem to have been adopted for them. The case of nomadic children who are attached neither to a circus nor to a fair, and who are thus more dispersed, is different again.

In *Ireland* there are no mobile schools, only a "playbus – a mobile playgroup which operates on two sites", financed by Dr. Barnardo's, a private organisation. The Van Leer Foundation also plan to set up mobile playgroups [McCarthy]. In *Greece* the Save the Children Fund set up a caravan-school at Ano Liossia, near Athens, in 1981.

In *France* there are a number of mobile classes. The first was set up in 1972; like all the rest set up or planned since that time, it is attached to a private organisation and arose from private initiative. Apparently only one description – brief, but very detailed – of these schools has been published to date [Gille, 1984, pp. 43-45]; the following quotations are taken from it.

"The status of these schools varies… yet they have points in common:

- subordination to the Ministry of National Education
- the intervention of a private organisation, be it by formal contract or simple agreement
- responsibility for providing materials and the mobile premises remaining with the association
- mobility [be it following one group, or going out to meet several] (...)
- all operate by the 'single classroom' [for all primary school ages] method, with small groups being given individualised attention. The pedagogical techniques used are similar to those of other specialised all-Traveller classes."

For the author, "Attendance at school-caravans is transitory – and foreseen as such. It is incontestably effective in rapidly imparting literacy and basic techniques. ...Far from constituting a ghetto, the mobile schools are the result of a sincere desire to fit into the reality of the people in question, and see their role as opening doors, breaking down barriers, improving efficiency." However, due to their very mobility, "The setting up of mobile schools is fraught with difficulties of an administrative nature as regards personnel, premises and teaching materials" [Gille, 1984].

Two detailed case studies are cited in the *United Kingdom* report. First, the "Central Region Mobile School" in Scotland. Following a report by the Scottish Secretary of State's Advisory Committee on Travelling People, a working party set up by the Central Region Council noticed, in the course of a general study of Scottish Travelling People, that more than half the children did not attend school – not because of their parents' work-related mobility but because the parents "were afraid of the children being ostracised at school, or that they would be moved on from their unofficial roadside sites, while the children were in school". As a result of the study the Region employed a mobile teacher who, working "in all sorts of locations such as the children's own caravans, under trees, and child guidance centres" as a link between families and school, quickly demonstrated the necessity of creating "some sort of mobile resource unit". In 1980 the Save the Children Fund, a private organisation, demanded financial aid towards developing the project, and the Scottish Development Department agreed to provide 75% of the financing for three years – and renewed the agreement in 1983.

It is worth pointing out the use, in this report, of the term "mobile resource unit", a concept which transcends "class", or even "school", and envisages a coming together of various elements to form an educative whole, in itself largely open. To give a clearer picture, we include extensive extracts from the complete report:

"A monitoring committee had government, local authority, Save the Children, police and health board representatives. By 1983 the project was using three vehicles – a mobile classroom in a Bedford van belonging to the Region, a Ford Transit minibus loaned by the Save the Children Fund and a car for the Save the Children Fund-appointed Project Leader. It had also acquired for play and exhibition purposes two old caravans, both needing repair, and used a classroom in one primary school, and a temporary classroom which has been placed in the grounds of another primary school. An office base was found in a Teachers' Centre.

The staff included the Project Co-ordinator, assisted by a voluntary secretary and a voluntary community worker, two advisory teachers, two teachers assigned by the mobile school, two full-time and a part-time teacher working in school (including a teacher for secondary-age children who had shifted her work from the mobile unit to a spare classroom in a primary school), three part-time adult 'basic education' (i.e. literacy plus) tutors, and a part-time physical education teacher... The teachers in the mobile van made around three visits to camps each day, seeing up to fifty children weekly. In the van they encouraged aspects of Traveller culture..."

The teachers had the aim of fostering "a love of learning beyond the expectation 'Education is learning to read and write'. A mobile school can foster such a love, but not satisfy it... Parents would often begin to complain that the van did not visit each site often enough, and did not stay long enough at each visit. Such complaints provided an opportunity to arrange a visit to school, where the much greater possibilities of full-time education could be explained. Teachers also made it clear to parents that the long-term policy goal was 'integration, not segregation'.

The mobile school thus became a stepping stone to other kinds of provision... Respect for Traveller culture was carried into the ordinary schools... Between 1979 and 1983 the number of children enrolled in schools rose from forty-three to two hundred and twenty-five per year, with the number of children attending ordinary school at any one time rising from seven to sixty. The children attending the mobile school are in addition to this last figure... Pupils came from families nomadic across the regional boundaries. Lack of adequate provision in neighbouring regions obviously contributes to the problem of preparing children for school in Central Region... The success of mobile school provision in the Central Region of Scotland is clearly due to and part of the success of the wider range of provision of which it is part" [Acton/Kenrick].

Generally speaking, mobile schools elsewhere in the United Kingdom – notably the West Midlands, Inner London, Oxfordshire and Berkshire – seem to follow the same general principles.

The second case study is from England, in an area where local authorities have a reputation for rejecting Travellers; however, in addition to a few small private sites, there is a large official one set up by the same authorities. But, "Although there are well over 100 children of school age in the area, we heard of only one local authority school taking Traveller children. The LEA chose, rather, after making its temporary site, to provide a mobile school unit in a large and well-converted van, staffed by two full-time teachers, as an alternative to encouraging children into local schools.

The teachers are forbidden by a policy directive from the LEA (in clear contravention of DES Circular 1/81) to go to any unofficial sites, and may visit only the local authority site, private sites, and housed Gypsies. During our visit to the school while on the official temporary site, an Irish Traveller boy aged about twelve came across from a nearby unofficial site and begged the teachers to come across to them. The teachers were clearly agonised by having to refuse... Children visiting the school in the session when we were there were clearly making good individual progress to literacy, each with their own folder, and there was considerable utilisation of Traveller culture in the materials available and on display...

The teachers... felt sure that they were being used as an alternative to admission to school, or to provision of a multicultural policy in school, and felt that the injunctions the authority had put them under, not to engage in any politics, not to be funded to go to any courses or training, not to join any associations, was indicative of the lack of support from the authority to these teachers. They felt unable to meet the clear demand from Travellers and felt isolated... The purpose of this provision was segregation, not integration. The teachers were obviously dedicated and immensely hardworking; but their labours were being misused by the LEA to keep Travellers at arm's length from real educational opportunities. We estimate Traveller attendance in ordinary school in the area at around 5%, with perhaps another 25% of Travelling children in the area getting the chance of four to six hours a week in the mobile school" [Acton/Kenrick].

We shall not attempt to draw conclusions from this examination of mobile classes before having considered other structures. We shall limit ourselves for the present to a few immediate observations.

Firstly, as the authors of the United Kingdom report themselves point out, such case studies offer valuable insight into aggregate statistics. As it happens, the overall picture given earlier is of appreciable progress in England and a falling rate of school attendance in Scotland, while these two cases present the opposite picture, "an example of good practice in Scotland and of bad practice in England regarding the use of mobile schools"; case studies also serve to illustrate the independence of local authorities in scholastic matters, in comparison with institutions and policies at national level.

Furthermore, the two contrasting examples given – corroborated by evidence from other countries with mobile schools – demonstrate the ambivalent position that everyone, and particularly the authorities, can have towards them. As in the Scottish example, they can be an instrument of acceptance, and of individual and collective progress, "support to mainstream provision", a *"pont"*, "bridge", *"puente"* towards "ordinary classes" and "integration". Or, as in the English example, a means of segregation, a "substitute for mainstream provision". However, the dichotomy need not be absolute: in either case, the teachers involved may be doing their best to provide high-quality instruction; in either case they may draw largely on elements of the children's own culture both as a pedagogic device and as a means of recognising and validating that culture; in either case the teachers involved may approach their task with an attitude of respect; in either case they may take account of the wishes of the parents.

No example can be fully understood outside the political context which determines it. The same pedagogical act or the same structure can in this way acquire radically different functions. *If pedagogy or structure provides the form, it is policy which forms the base, and a few connecting elements which determine the tone.* It is a question both of structures and of the methods employed within them – which explains in part, as we stressed earlier on, how the same structure can serve different, even opposite, policy goals; in essence, any method can be used in any structure. To put it briefly: don't take things at face value. School in a caravan can be a good thing or a bad one. The important thing is that it can exist – then and only then can one ensure it is operating for the good, in accordance with criteria we shall be examining later on.

Finally, for our last provisional consideration: examples such as the Scottish project, conceived as a "mobile resource unit", clearly demonstrate the usefulness (from all points of view) of an inter-institutional approach, a classroom in a caravan being only one element of what one might visualise as a very open system. It could, for example, go on towards vocational training, a resource centre housing teaching materials for Gypsies and Travellers, etc. We also emphasise yet again the necessity of bearing in mind the fact that a mobile school can both follow families, and go out to meet them – that is, it would doubtless be extremely useful in some circumstances even in areas where Gypsies and Travellers are supposedly nearly all sedentary. Such a school, equipped with adapted teaching aids, could go to a district or site to meet children as a means of familiarising them with the school situation, to help in assessing and placing children and/or as supplementary provision. We return to this last question in the next section.

On-the-spot provision

Many different practices come under this heading:

- "unattached" teachers who visit Gypsy homes. Often these are voluntary and deal specifically with literacy. But in several countries this type of provision is made by the authorities (notably the "home teachers" of the United Kingdom) – we shall return to this form of support;

- mobile classrooms, already described, can also be considered in this category, since it is they who come to the pupils and not vice-versa. Some mobile classrooms visit only one site day after day, usually because those in charge choose not to leave it there, so their mobility is really only between site and garage;

- classes and schools especially created for the needs of Gypsy and Traveller children, whether on or near a halting site or within a housing district with a high Traveller population. We shall be concentrating on this type of provision in the present section.

Self-evidently, provision exclusively for Gypsies and Travellers has arisen where such families exist: the school has geographically come to them. The entire research for the present study did not uncover a single case of a centralised "Gypsy" school attended by children from widely scattered sites. For many parents, proximity is an important consideration. Only in very rare cases do Gypsy and Traveller children attend boarding schools established for the children of nomadic parents – for example the *"homes"* of Belgium. This despite the fact that such establishments are open to all who fulfil certain criteria (of work-related nomadism); Gypsy and Traveller parents simply refuse long-term separation from their children. Numbers of "special" classes set up in proximity to Gypsy dwellings vary from country to country – from nonexistent to quite widespread. We have been unable to obtain overall statistics regarding such classes. The brief synthesis we give here is thus basically an indication of trends in Traveller schooling as part of overall scholastic policy. Having examined these individually, we shall then see if any general tendency can be identified.

In the *Netherlands* for example, "Provision for specialised schools was made as far back as the 1950s, the reasons given for setting them up being that:

- unlike the rest of the community, caravan dwellers did not have any tradition of education of their own. This meant that the initial educational situation of caravan children differed sharply from that of other children;

- in both a geographical and a social sense, caravan dwellers were very isolated from the rest of society. These factors made joint education extremely difficult" [Hovens et al].

Two acts (1951 and 1955) permitted the opening of "caravan-centre schools": "It was from this point onwards that participation by caravan children in primary education got under way, with subsidised caravan-centre schools being set up at dozens of places in the Netherlands." Other steps were also taken: "In order to promote the continuity of education for Travellers' children, the Central Curriculum Committee drew up a system of tests and assignments for use in centre schools. If the parents moved, the centre school would give them the assignments book, so that the new school could quickly see what stage the child had reached" [ibid]. Twenty years later there were over fifty such schools. Later, towards the end of the 1970s, the policy of large halting sites was reversed (as their total unsuitability became apparent in more and more ways) to be replaced by a small sites (twelve to fifteen places) policy. This is still in force, but hard to put into practice because of the difficulty in finding the necessary replacement sites.

As a result, specialised schools attached to the large sites were to be disbanded; by 1985 fewer than thirty were still operative. On the whole, such schools are judged favourably, both because they permit close contact with the parents and because they allow the flexibility without which the children's special needs cannot be met: "The norms and values of many caravan parents and hence of their children are by no means always suitable for or adaptable to school. Conversely educational norms and values are by no means always applicable to the daily life of caravan children and their parents... In the caravan-centre school the classes and groups are small and the teacher has a clear idea of each child's abilities and problems. Intensive contact is maintained with the parents by talking with them, either in the caravan or at school, and immediate remedial action can be taken where necessary. A teacher in the normal system has much less flexibility: each pupil merits equal attention; the classes are large; teaching often has to proceed along set lines; contact with parents is necessarily limited; and there is little familiarity with the caravan child's home environment" [case study by A. Kuijpers-Haans, cited in Hovens et al]. And despite the present integration policy, "Caravan-centre schools still provide a good deal of scope for bridging the gap between the home and school environment. In regular education, a dangerous gap arises between the two worlds which is underestimated by nearly all concerned" [ibid]. Integration of Traveller pupils into ordinary classes is not easy, and backup teachers are essential.

In *Belgium* a preschool and literacy class initiated by a private organisation operated for two and a half years starting at the beginning of 1978; it was set up in an old railway carriage on a halting site. Resources were minimal and working conditions atrocious – a situation reported from many countries as regards special classes. "There was only a blackboard, a couple of sticks of chalk, some paper, a little paint and a few pencils. The pupils were divided up in four groups. The youngest (aged five to seven) came to class at ten o'clock. The seven to thirteen year olds came in at half past eleven. In the afternoon the teacher dealt with older adolescents and finally with adults; in the evening, he did follow-up work with Manouche children who attended the village school" [Reyniers].

The conclusion reached was that such a specialised school is indispensable: "The children don't understand why they should sit together in silence and listen to the teacher. They don't understand why they have to stay cooped up in the classroom... Certain children were physically incapable of picking up or holding a pencil (a culturally foreign object), others – even as old as nine – could not stay within the lines when colouring in traced pictures. Parents were wary of the teacher's intentions towards their children, and kept a close eye on him. He had to simultaneously establish a climate of trust with the parents, and evolve the necessary flexibility for adapting to the children's changing moods... In fact the rhythm was imposed by the pupils: when they decided it was time to leave the class, they made such a din that the teacher had no choice but to give up" [Reyniers]. The class ceased to exist in May 1980: "In the absence of the teacher, the railway carriage classroom was vandalised by the children; another factor was that most of the Rom families had left the site."

Nearly all countries have some special classes for Gypsy and Traveller children, and we could give many more examples, particularly from France, Ireland and the United Kingdom. But in all cases such classes are in a somewhat precarious position, caught between the general push towards integration and the desire to meet the needs of children who are not ready for "ordinary" schools. Another two illustrations:

Here is the account of a woman teacher working in a caravan on a site in London. After giving a minute account of a working day, she concludes: "Evaluation: it is more by the contrast with a session of two months ago that the success of this session can be appreciated. Formerly there was total chaos. Although the children were motivated, there was little co-operation: they would dance on the tables, swing from the windows, fight, tear their work and others'; fight me, spit at me, pull my hair, throw things at me… in summary there was total defiance to my wishes and it was a time when they were testing me to the full. In addition, the parents believed the project was doomed to fail, and there was only superficial support.

Today there was good co-operation and parental support. The children awaited their turn, and when they couldn't get the attention they needed, they used another outlet rather than vandalism and aggression. The noise was less and we could hear ourselves speak; the level of concentration was higher and frustration was lower; they showed pride in their work and what they had accomplished; they showed greater trust in that they openly admitted they could not do something when previously they would have pretended they were able; I left my belongings about without fear and materials were on the whole returned; they helped clear up" [quoted by Acton/Kenrick].

The context of the overall *United Kingdom* study reveals that this teacher is not being alarmist in her first description, nor smugly self-satisfied in the second; the *Belgian* example above offers further corroboration. One could add others, for example this one from the *Netherlands*: "To start with the Gypsy children's behaviour such as sitting still, talking quietly instead of shouting, cooperating instead of squabbling, listening to the teachers, playing with toys without breaking them and so on, had to be learned... The initial contacts between teachers and Gypsy children were characterised by caution on the part of the children... as time went by, however, the teachers gradually won the children's confidence and a strong affective bond was often established with the teachers, sometimes to the point that the children would not go to school if the teacher was ill... for most children a new environment, individual attention from teachers and the acquisition of new knowledge and experience acted as an incentive to go to school" [Hovens et al].

Generally accounts of the workings of specialised classes are favourable, and can be summed up in the fact that such a class permits a flexibility which is indispensable, at least in the early stages. *The "specialised" class would – with exceptions – seem, considering the present state of schooling of many Gypsy and Traveller groups, and the overall context described above, to be suitably adapted to the children, and thus in turn to favour the child's adaptation to school.* To put it another way, it allows for adaptability in teaching which in turn encourages the child's own adaptability. Thus both sides share in the effort to gain common ground. This becomes clear when the flexibility is withdrawn; for example if the special class is suddenly discontinued, the number of children attending school drops dramatically; from Greece to Ireland, whatever the reasons parents give for it (transport difficulties, needing the children's help, discrimination in the ordinary school), the fact is that children will be attending less. If there is a wish to pursue school provision, it then becomes necessary to implement a whole new adaptive formula, for example support mechanisms and ongoing consultation with both parents and the schools in which their children may be enrolled.

To say that specialised classes are generally adapted classes is not to say that they are the only ones to be so. And parents themselves may sometimes feel differently.

Let us give a few observations from *Ireland*, where forty-four families asked to name their preferences responded as follows:

a) school for Travellers only	7
b) special class in an ordinary school	13
c) ordinary class in an ordinary school	17
d) no preference	7

giving the following reasons:

    a) in the all-Traveller school nobody calls the children "knackers"
    b) the ordinary school is nearest and should be available to the Travellers
    c) Travellers' children go wild in an all-Traveller class or school [Tallaght Report, 1984].

These results corroborate those of a small sample study (twenty children and twenty parents) carried out for this study, also in Ireland: "A majority of the parents interviewed expressed a strong preference for their children to attend 'ordinary' schools rather than special classes. The reasons given came under a number of headings:

- there was not enough discipline in the Traveller classes – Buffer teachers did not know how to handle a large number of Traveller children

- the educational standards in the special classes were low

- children learn more if they are mixed in with 'country' [non-Traveller] children.

However, three quarters of the parents interviewed had children in special classes and said that generally speaking they were happy with the way they were getting on...

A minority of parents said that they preferred their children to attend Traveller-only schools because there was no discrimination against them, no name calling or abuse or humiliating segregation practices. They also felt that the teachers in these schools understood Travellers better and were more sensitive to their needs" [McCarthy].

It is interesting to note some further findings of these same interviews, in that they reflect analysis emerging from other countries as well, and illustrate the diversity of opinion over different types of structures: "Parents' aspirations from these interviews are for their children to become literate and familiar with the operations of the Settled world. A great deal of frustration with their children's slow progress was expressed. Some felt that it was a waste of time sending them to school as they did not learn anything. Several complained about lack of discipline and messing in the special classes. There were also complaints about insensitive teachers embarrassing children or of bullying them. Discrimination, name-calling and physical attack by country children was a common problem. Many of the parents said that teachers, social workers, and other buffers had no idea how hard it was to send children to school in the winter when they are camping in muddy fields without water or toilets. When one child gets sick, they all get sick and several of the mothers said that they spend the winters going from doctors' surgeries to hospitals and that it was not surprising that their children missed school more often than country children. They would like their children to be able to read books and magazines. However, they did not want them to be so educated that they could not relate to them or that the children would feel ashamed of them. None of them saw their children's future in jobs in the Settled community... Parents and children should have a choice of attending ordinary school or special school. All the parents interviewed said that education was extremely important and that they had put a lot of effort into getting their children to school. They felt their own illiteracy (only three of the parents were literate) was a great handicap and wanted something better for their children" [McCarthy].

By way of contrast, we present findings from two other countries. In the *FRG*, "The mistrust of parents is rarely dispelled even by successful schooling programmes, as appears to have been achieved at Landau (Palatinate). Within a purpose-built all-Traveller housing estate, a kindergarten and preschool were constructed as an integral part of the scheme. The school was accepted as readily as the houses, since its proximity meant that parents could keep an eye on it. From the outset the teachers endeavoured to involve the parents as much as possible in school life, consulting them when problems arose, etc. The parents in turn did not feel excluded, particularly because of the close cooperation of the regional Gypsy organisation in setting up the school. The results: all the children attend very regularly (four years ago not one of them attended school!) and with remarkable progress" [Reemtsma].

In *France* among certain families who are sedentary in poor living conditions, there is a quest for a validating social identity: to be a Traveller "within the school, for a child who does not in fact travel, means a search for some other identifying criterion to differentiate him from the Settled norm: illiteracy. In such a case illiteracy can in fact be interpreted as a cultural trait and serves as a symbol of refusal to integrate into Settled society. In this regard, the failure of sedentary Gypsy children on the preparatory course is most remarkable. Some of these children have spent two full years in a traditional class without any result at all. Yet when they transfer to an all-Traveller class, this 'mental block' dissolves. The specifically Traveller nature of the class ensures their retention of non-Settled social status, so that literacy is no longer seen as synonymous with assimilation" [Kervadec, 1982, p.73].

Yet in another report from France, mention is made of "reconciling Traveller parents with specialised (all-Traveller) classes:

- Despite having been rejected and humiliated by it, they continue to see the school in very traditional terms, and to consider specialised classes as second-rate, i.e. as ghettos. This opinion colours parental attitudes which in turn have an enormous influence on their children's behaviour (who in effect boycott a way of teaching which attempts to adapt itself to their reality).
- Attention must also be drawn to the mistrust of parents (Settled and Traveller) of the latest teaching methods.
- Plus the fear, which persists with justification among Traveller parents, that school will inculcate 'foreign' values in their children.

It is for these reasons that the achievement of 'reconciliation' seems important to us" [*Le Voyage*, a newsletter printed in Rennes, no. 3, 1985].

It is important, when reading and analysing these reports, to maintain a *distinction* between *desires/ideals* on the one hand, and what we shall term a *principle of realism* on the other. If for example it appears that teachers, parents and policymakers all share a desire for the school to be an open, integrated one, the principle of realism suggests that we be both cautious and a little sceptical, considering the actual state of school provision for Traveller children. *Caution* as regards the suppression (in the name of an equality which is often a euphemism for "normalisation") of structures contributing to adaptation, and *scepticism* as regards projects which are too ambitious or large-scale, where idealism runs the risk of masking the difficulties entailed.

In the *Netherlands*, about fifteen families shared a halting site. In 1977, a literacy project for adults was started, then the children joined in and the idea of a school took shape. The parents, who had had bad experiences in the past, did not want an ordinary school, and in 1978 a school was set up with a principal and several volunteer teachers. The families took pride in "their school" and participated in every level of its functioning, including choice of teachers and classroom layout. The parents themselves came daily to learn reading and writing. But the families were not satisfied with their living conditions, and demanded a change of site. This was accomplished in 1981, and, during the transition period, the old school continued to be used. However, the move brought the group under the jurisdiction of a different set of local authorities, who proposed two special classes near a school complex with the goal of "progressive integration", outlined as follows:

"- that the children should, over a five-year period, be integrated into the ordinary school system;
- that the effort should be made to permit Gypsy children to get on in society while conserving their Gypsy identity."

A familiar enough scenario.

The parents seemed to be in agreement. But the authors of this case study [cf. Hovens et al] indicate that "Three years later, we are obliged to concede that the integration process has not succeeded" and go on to analyse the situation. Parents gave the distance of school from site as the reason for not sending their children. Various solutions were tried: at first teachers picked up the children, then group transport was arranged, then the children attended police-run cycling courses so they could safely make their own way to school. The parents remained uncooperative and by 1983 the municipality issued an official report stating that they were not fulfilling their obligation to send their children to school. In 1985 the Court of Appeal found against the Gypsy families, which led to a further hardening of attitudes against the school, and to their feeling threatened. During a consultation in 1984 they declared clearly, "We want to remain Gypsies, we want to be able to travel during the summer", etc. The result was thus mutual alienation between parents and teachers, a growing mistrust with the teachers being perceived as acting in connivance with the police, local authorities and government, and no longer on the side of the Gypsies.

Even if we confine ourselves to a consideration of the purely physical aspects of the specialised school structure, particularly if it is located within a Traveller community, we should note the following observation from the *United Kingdom*: "If Travellers are excluded from the decisions about the school, and not allowed to use it for community purposes out of school hours, as happened on one Surrey site, then it is hardly surprising the premises were destroyed" [Acton/Kenrick].

Consultation with parents is essential. This is a strong point of specialised classes: in principle, this type of structure allows for close contact with families, but it is a weakness and a source of discord if consultation does not take place. This brings us to an important point, to which we shall return in greater detail later on: administrations which allow for the existence of a specialised school structure, must also allow it leeway in which to function in a specialised way. For example, many teachers complain that despite their classes being "special", they are expected to run them exactly like ordinary classes. In connection with the present topic of consultation and contact, if no backup personnel are provided within the specialised structure, then this role falls to the teacher himself. This is only one of many delicate tasks which a "special" teacher must have the structural flexibility to accomplish, if the "special" class is to function in accordance with this label. Yet at an official level little cognizance is taken of this fact; this is why special classes, when they are successful, usually achieve their results through teachers' ignoring regulations and/or doing things at their own initiative, rather than thanks to the special structures themselves.

By encountering and overcoming numerous pitfalls, the teachers of all-Traveller classes have, over the past twenty years, amassed an invaluable bank of experience, from which others should benefit. Such classes have also enabled many children to enter the mainstream school system, as they offer Gypsy parents a chance – often the only one – to familiarise themselves with the scholastic world which their children may be entering. But, being special, they are often the subject of special criticism: accused of being ghettos, or never-never lands promoting a cultural myth, or places where nothing gets done. Where such classes exist, they are denigrated; where they do not exist, or have been discontinued, they are missed.

In summary we conclude that, in most situations, given both the context of conflictual relations in which Gypsies and Travellers live, and the development of new educational philosophies, *special classes which are made accessible in every sense (geographical and pedagogical) to Gypsy and Traveller children appear to be necessary – but not sufficient.* They are entering a new era, since (like the mobile schools) they are operating less and less in isolation, but are – or should be – becoming a part of the school system as a whole. *Neither ghetto nor panacea, sometimes a solution, sometimes a means of transition, sometimes a mediating force, they appear to be the indispensable complement of other measures – neither more nor less.*

Other specialised provision

There is yet another form of specialised class: that which, despite accepting only Gypsy and Traveller children, is integrated within a school setting comprising other, "ordinary" classes. The existence and functioning of such classes produces varied, even opposite effects, which our analysis must take into account.

In many cases such classes offer some of the same benefits as the special classes described above. These benefits might be described as being of a "technical" order – for example when the children do not arrive punctually, or when their ages and scholastic levels are at variance. Such advantages have led to the setting up of such classes even in some countries where official policy is opposed to "special" provision.

For example in *Denmark*: "In Elsinore it had to be admitted in 1972 that integration of the newly immigrated Gypsy pupils into the school had been a failure in spite of all good attempts. Therefore it was decided to establish a special class" [Gudmander/Rude]. As an indication of the range of ages, we note that in 1982-83 the children in this experimental class had been born between 1966-73, that is, with an age difference of up to seven or eight years [Gudmander, 1983].

Advantages of a "cultural" and pedagogical nature are equally important: using culturally familiar material, validating the children's way of life through manual and intellectual projects "allowing and facilitating their positive identification" [Ivatts, 1975, p.31]. Almost everywhere, relations with the school tend to develop along positive lines, as do relationships between Traveller parents and children, and the teachers. Conflict situations and mutual rejection are thus avoided. The school adapts to the child.

Staying with the Danish example: "We should emphasise that, for a very long time, the experimental class has not been a permanent entity but rather a small group with a number of arrivals and departures. On the other hand it has become clear that brothers and sisters – indeed whole groups of siblings – should never be split up" [Gudmander, 1983].

At present there are three ways in which such classes (specialised, but integrated within a school group) function. Some are conceived as a stage – essential, but to be kept as brief as possible – between no schooling at all, or unadapted and thus ineffective provision, and going straight into ordinary classes. The child thus spends a certain amount of time in one of these classes (or several, if he is on the move), before being "integrated" into an ordinary class.

Other such classes offer part-time teaching, the proportion of which varies. It may depend on the capacity and desire of the child himself to "integrate" into an ordinary class; or the degree of conflict characterising relations between Traveller and non-Traveller pupils in a given period; or the subject-matter taught at different periods during the day, with the child attending some "special" and some "mixed" classes.

Let us give an example from *France*: "If the child is behind, he needs a structure flexible enough to take this into account, gearing teaching to his individual needs. The 'special' (all-Traveller) class, with its lower pupil-teacher ratio, is better geared towards this need. As for ourselves, we have sometimes opted for a 'mixed' curriculum for children who are further behind in French than in mathematics – a very common situation among Travelling children. Thus, these children attended our remedial language classes in the morning, returning to normal class structures in the afternoon" [Michel Hermine, in *Le Voyage* no. 3, 1985, Rennes].

Under these conditions, inter-system flow can work both ways, allowing non-Gypsy children to be invited to participate in "the Gypsy class", with a twofold, and doubly positive, result. Namely, the Gypsy class is validated on its own terms, and/or it comes to be seen as simply one class among many (rather than an alien/exotic ghetto).

But – the third possibility – the class may also close in on itself and become a ghetto, with "the Gypsy class" remaining separate, and even the teachers working in it being marginalised by their colleagues. It may even come to the administration setting up separate recreation periods and mealtimes. This apartheid system prevents all contact and thus all exchange between the two groups of children. It is most often in connection with this sort of set-up that inter-group contact outside of school will take the most violent forms.

In summary, then, all-Gypsy classes integrated into the school system may, like other types of structures, exist for the better or for the worse. They can be a bridge, but they can also be a prison. The physical proximity which they permit is not in itself necessarily a synonym for socio-cultural contact. On the contrary, it would seem that in some cases it is the physical proximity itself which creates isolation, or at any rate which brings about a stigmatisation of the children, their class, and their teachers. In many cases it would appear that the more "specific" and clearly specialised the class (for example in a caravan-school), the less it appears to be "special". Within the school itself, the very proximity of the Traveller class – if there is no inter-group movement or exchange – makes it appear to be "special", i.e. for "maladjusted" children. *Differentiated classes are thus sometimes differentiating.* However the dominant tendency, at present, is along the lines of the first two models: as a stage, as a part-time measure, or as a mixture of the two.

"Ordinary" classes

Ordinary classes attended by Gypsy and Traveller children are numerous; the proportion of Gypsy children attending them varies from country to country, but there is nonetheless a wide overall discrepancy between the number of Gypsy children in school and the number of places in "special" classes. Unfortunately we have no statistics which would permit us to ascertain the proportion of Gypsy children in ordinary classes. At the same time in some countries there are no special classes at all (Luxembourg) or very few (Belgium, Denmark, Greece, Italy). Elsewhere we depend on estimates: "At the present time roughly half the children go to specialised caravan-dwellers' schools and the remainder to normal schools along with non-caravan children" [in the Netherlands – Hovens at al.]; or in the United Kingdom where schooling in "ordinary" classes "is by far the commonest situation in which Gypsy children receive education" [Acton/Kenrick]. In the FRG Gypsy classes are rare but in Ireland they are common, while in France there seem to be numerically quite a lot of them – although few enough, considering the number of children concerned. At the same time, for reasons gone into above, little information about "ordinary" classes is available: their teachers are rarely approached for information on the schooling of Gypsy children.

At present, on the whole, schooling in ordinary classes in ordinary schools is the common wish both of Gypsy/Traveller parents and of policymakers (though the reasons behind it are not always the same). But let us recall the earlier warning to bear in mind the difference between a shared desire and a principle of realism which impels us to exercise caution. Let us also remember the tendency of the schools to "integrate" Gypsies by classifying them as handicapped – and classes geared towards the handicapped or feebleminded are not adapted to the needs of Gypsy children.

It is essential to bear in mind that ordinary classes may, now as in the past, be linked with assimilationist policies: *"normal" schools are still, in a broad sense, "normalising"*. We shall return to this question when examining pedagogical issues; for the moment we limit ourselves to pointing out that the breaking up of Gypsy groups is always a part of the process – sometimes deliberately and explicitly, sometimes not.

This can be for "good reasons" – for example in one case in the *Netherlands*: "Opposition based on prejudice resulted in protests against the arrival of the Gypsy school. The school responded to the problem by organising an information evening on Gypsies and their education, which had a beneficial effect. Nevertheless, it remained impossible during this initial phase to make use of the local school for integration purposes. The distribution of the Gypsy children over the five different schools left them too split up to form 'fronts'" [Hovens et al].

Similar situations have occurred elsewhere: "Liaison teachers and Educational Social Workers try to avoid exclusion, placing children in schools where the head teachers object, thinking, probably rightly, that this may lead to a bad experience of education for the children. In London and elsewhere liaison teachers also sometimes adopt an informal quota system, not placing 'too many' children with any one school, even if no other school is available. Although no formal policy of dispersal can be deduced from Local Authority documents, this informal policy where it operates clearly stigmatises Gypsy children, and reduces the possibility of their using their own group solidarity as a defence against persecution by other children, and lessens the chance of their successfully bringing their own culture into the school" [Acton/Kenrick].

The presence of Gypsy children in ordinary classes is always strongly influenced by the overall situation at the time. It would be grave nonsense to ignore this fact, and illusory to pretend that such considerations do not intrude into the classroom. In this regard, with few and notable exceptions, ordinary classes really are "ordinary" – that is, they form part of a whole which remains antagonistic and ill-adapted to cultural plurality, particularly as regards Gypsies and Travellers (we have already looked into the historical reasons for this, and will soon be analysing the pedagogical consequences). On the contrary, classes or schools where Gypsy children are made to feel welcome are seldom "ordinary", but shining exceptions to a rather dismal norm.

The usual situation in ordinary classes is that cultures co-exist but do not enter into meaningful exchange.

Two examples from *Belgium*: some families placed their children in a *"home"* (boarding school) not set up specifically for Traveller children. "All of the children in the establishment show a profound need of affection, but (Travelling children) do not display the type of psychological problems one encounters in some children of Settled origin, and they stand out from the crowd for their goodnaturedness. On the other hand they are remarkable for their strong integration into the preoccupations of their group: the children are always on the lookout for scrap metal, for chairs needing re-bottoming, old clothes and the like, to give to their parents when they come to visit... The sojourn of these children within the *home* has no long-term impact on their scholastic achievement: they do adapt to the conditions of the *home*, but as soon as they return to their families they cease school attendance altogether and fit right back into their traditional lifestyle, participating in their parents' economic and domestic activities... The time spent in boarding school is merely an interlude without visible or measurable consequences." Elsewhere, at a state primary school situated near a halting site: "Even within the framework of an exceptionally welcoming school such as this one, the overwhelming majority of Gypsy and Traveller children develop within a different system... Their own educational system is not on the wane. Quite the contrary... we are witnessing a sort of 'colonisation' of the school system by young Gypsies and Travellers" [Reyniers].

This "colonisation" by Gypsy children when they do find a school that makes them feel really welcome, can in turn lead to an exodus of non-Gypsy pupils. For example in *France*, in the Paris region, one school had a 20% Traveller student body in 1978; by 1984 it was 85% Traveller:

"By welcoming Traveller children on equal terms, we have become victims of our own success and generosity. Since other schools in the locality do not receive them so readily, Traveller children enrolled here en masse, and local children, finding themselves in a minority, began to leave. Neighbouring schools continue to discourage Traveller children and also tend to steer their 'problem' pupils towards our 'tolerant' school. On the other hand they will accept our 'good' pupils who wish to transfer. All these factors combine to make our school a ghetto" [Lafaurie, 1984, pp. 33-34].

Similarly, in *Northern Ireland* the ratio of Traveller pupils reached 100% in an ordinary school where, little by little, up to 135 (Travelling) children enrolled. The attitude of neighbouring schools was the same as in France:

"Some parents have tried to transfer their children to other primary schools, but have returned them to St. Z. The teachers at St. Z. believe this is partly because they encounter discrimination in other schools, and partly because the other schools make demands for punctuality and cleanliness of school uniforms which Travellers find it hard to meet" [Acton/Kenrick].

In this manner it can happen that "ordinary" classes or schools become "special". Perhaps this is a sign that the moment is not yet ripe for Gypsies to fit into a uniform system, accepted by and acceptable to all. At any rate it does prove that the situation is still in flux and that adjustment to often contradictory factors requires great flexibility, particularly as regards structures. Ordinary schools must be seen as one option in a complementary range. The alternatives may seem less ordinary simply because we are less used to them, or they are less numerous – but they are equally valid and legitimate all the same. For example, evidence from a variety of sources confirms that successful integration of Gypsy children into ordinary class is often founded on a period in a special school.

Supplementary provision

Supplementary provision is by definition complementary to the various structures discussed above: it can operate independently or as an integral part, and can be exercised in a variety of ways. But a very strong consensus exists from all the countries (regardless of structures and policies) and from both parents and teachers, emphasising its necessity. Analysis of supplementary activities confirms their usefulness, and school authorities who do not support them in one form or another are, by now, rare indeed. However, these authorities can be divided into two groups: those who recognise the importance of supplementary teaching and provide it, and those whose support remains purely theoretical.

Here are examples from several different countries:

In the *FRG*, "The experience of the Sinti Union in Bremen shows clearly that provision as made by public authorities does not as a rule fulfil the conditions which could lead to effective schooling for Sinti children. In this context, supplementary help is needed. Towards this end, the Sinti Union hired two supplementary teachers, financed by the Federal Department of Labour. The idea is that these teachers, in close cooperation with the schools and nurseries, should operate as mobile instructors, giving the support to allow Sinti children to keep up in normal school and, in individual cases, to transfer from specialised teaching to the normal system" [Bremer Volkshochschule, 1983, p.44].

"Most parents want integrated schooling with separate backup outside the school... supplementary teaching, where required, should take the form of individual help or small workgroups" [Reemtsma].

In *Italy* "The creation of supplementary teaching for Gypsy children in difficulty is a new departure, and also serves as a link between the school and Gypsy families." In response to a questionnaire item concerning "methods and techniques adopted to surmount obstacles", sixty of the ninety-six teachers responding named "individualised methods", these being:

individual remedial instruction	50
work with Gypsy families	6
collaboration with class teacher	1
work with local authorities	2

Six teachers felt that collaboration was ineffective because it was irregular and limited to a few hours per week; two felt that the children had no need of it, and two rejected it because they felt that the employment of supplementary teachers was a form of segregation [Karpati/Massano].

In *France* as well, supplementary teaching for Gypsy children, although not yet widespread in practice, is considered important, particularly in helping children to adjust to school, and in their correct placement [cf. Ferté, 1984]. Also, "The presence of supplementary teachers is extremely important as a link with the families" [Gille, 1984, p.14]. In *Ireland*, "The visiting teachers appointed by the Department of Education within the last few years are effectively educational social workers. There are six such posts at present. They liaise with the schools, the parents, social workers and all other relevant services. Their input is generally very well received and the service is seen as very well worthwhile (but) given the present emphasis on decreasing costs it is not likely that more of these posts will be created in the near future" [McCarthy].

In *Denmark* supplementary teaching forms an integral part of the overall school system. Immigrant children are initially admitted to reception classes: "The work in the reception classes is supported in various ways by specially trained speech therapists and the school psychologists. From the social welfare system assistance is often given through social workers who can provide advisory guidance to the homes... When the pupils have a reasonable command of the Danish language, they are ready for integration into an ordinary Danish class... The integration is planned in the case of each individual pupil. Supplementary education can be given to the pupils during the first period after the transfer to the new class... in the form of allocation of a number of teacher lessons during a shorter or longer period. These remedial lessons may be used in various ways. Many lessons are e.g. used as individual supplementary education of the pupils in new subjects. Others are used in such a way that the new teachers work alone or in small groups with the new pupils for some weeks, while the remedial teacher works with the rest of the class" [Gudmander/Rude].

In the *United Kingdom* the tendency is also towards supplementary teaching in various forms: "extra staff", "liaison teacher", "home tuition". At a primary school in London, "the practice is to meet special needs by extra staff time as need arises rather than on a special time-tabled basis"; elsewhere, "the LEA have appointed a part-time liaison teacher who assists integration into ordinary schools, which has become the most prevalent pattern for children on official sites". There is also the use – poorly developed as yet – of "home tuition", although in practice it is often carried out by "liaison teachers". It appears difficult, even in cases of obvious need, to guarantee measures "providing individual tuition for specific individual children with a need that cannot be currently met in school". Work is not easy, either, for the "peripatetic teacher who is the sole liaison worker for a number of schools and sites, and who does not have a mobile unit. One of our researchers spent a day with one such teacher who normally commutes between three schools and four or five sites on a bicycle. Great resourcefulness and considerable sensitivity in dealing with teachers in the various schools, even more than in other situations we have discussed, is needed in such a post" [Acton/Kenrick].

In the *Netherlands*, supplementary teaching is used intensively, and is well-coordinated with the rest of the system. It is organised with the goal of "integration" into ordinary classes in ordinary schools – both of local Traveller children (in the wake of the breaking up of large halting sites and the consequent dispersal of the children) and of immigrant Gypsy children. Here are a few details of the types of supplementary teaching used:

Firstly, in connection with the policy of breaking up the larger sites: "The teachers are full of good intentions to make the best of it and above all not to discriminate. Caravan parents also want to do their best, especially if the children are still little. Everything seems a bed of roses; the integration teacher shouldn't be so awkward!

But the integration teacher is not so quickly taken in. She's not a born pessimist but has learned the hard way – for the integration teacher is me. I was appointed on 1 August 1980... Since the beginning of the decentralisation process in 1980 up to the present time (May 1985), some 120 children have made the switch from caravan-centre school to various kinds of normal education... They were fitted into four pre-school playgroups, ten nursery schools, sixteen primary schools, three schools for the educationally retarded, two technical schools, six domestic science schools, two junior secondary schools, one junior commercial school, two secondary special schools, an employment project, an apprenticeship training institute and two non-vocational training institutes. My duties have been and are to guide the changeover process. The intensity and nature of guidance required vary greatly. Some children and their parents and the recipient schools rapidly no longer need my help. In most cases interest is greatly appreciated, especially by the children and the parents... Such guidance consists of:

a. Preparing children and their parents and the receiving schools for the changeover. This is a matter of mentality and the particular teaching situation the child will face.
b. Watching over the interests of the caravan child in normal education. Here again a clear distinction needs to be drawn between social and educational factors.
c. In many cases I act in my counselling role as a link between the two environments and am able to exert a beneficial influence in both directions.
d. To carry out the counselling and guidance properly, help and information are required from such bodies as the local Educational Advisory Centres, welfare organisations, the caravan community and the municipality. There is particularly close cooperation with the Education Welfare Officer" [case study in Hovens et al].

Following an influx of Gypsies into the Netherlands in 1977, "In the ten reception municipalities, so-called 'education familiarisation projects' were set up. Remedial teachers were recruited who, in collaboration with existing schools, organised the tuition for Gypsy children, worked out the curriculum and provided the instruction. One teacher was appointed for every eight to ten children.

In view of their educational backlog, lack of Dutch and different social behaviour, the Gypsy children were initially given separate tuition. The aim was, however, to integrate them as quickly as possible into ordinary education, for which reason most education projects were tacked on to existing schools and gym lessons and arts and crafts lessons provided on an integrated basis from the beginning. Gypsy children also took part with Dutch children in any extramural activities. After between two to five years most Gypsy children proved able to keep up with Dutch classes, although with remedial teaching by the extra teachers...

The support provided by the remedial teachers was a particular source of help, especially when it became apparent after a few years that practical problems persisted and that the Gypsy children would need more time to overcome their educational backlog than had originally been anticipated, and a number of teachers in the ordinary system began to grow more sceptical about their prospects. This applies particularly to school in which the system of education does not permit much distinction to be drawn in terms of individual knowledge and skills. The remedial teachers assisted normal teachers in establishing contacts with Gypsy parents, although in most cases these contacts remain strictly limited" [Hovens et al].

Many other analyses within the report confirm the usefulness of supplementary teaching; moreover, "Surveys reveal, for example, that significantly more caravan/Gypsy children proceed to secondary education in regions with integration teachers."

There are few parents or teachers – or even, for that matter, school authorities – who still contest the usefulness and indeed necessity of backup services, but, the principle having been conceded, practice varies greatly from country to country. It can be used as an instrument of assimilation, all the more so as it is frequently one-to-one. It can also overburden the child with extra schoolwork, or conversely deprive him

of "normal" schooling by filling his time with support classes. A difficult dilemma to resolve; for the moment we confine ourselves to two general remarks.

First: supplementary teaching must, like every other element, be seen within the context of school practice *as a whole*. This means for example, that supplementary teachers must work in cooperation with, rather than opposition to, ordinary teachers – yet case studies from country to country draw attention to the frequency with which such opposition does in fact occur. Yet if opposition or distinction is justified in the case of physically or mentally handicapped pupils, it cannot be in the case of cultural minorities; such a situation requires continuity of structure and even of personnel. In fact, in certain very successful cases, supplementary teaching takes the form of three teachers between two classes, thus permitting liaison with parents, personal follow-up of pupils who require it, meetings with administrative bodies, social workers and the like, attending conferences and training sessions and so on and so forth. Who, in this situation, is an "ordinary" teacher, and who "supplementary"? All share both roles.

Backup must, moreover, be understood in the broadest possible sense: teachers themselves need it just as much as their pupils do, and can support each other as well as receiving support from other sources: administration has a role to play in providing training, information, and pedagogical counsellors. "Visiting teachers", "liaison teachers", "integration teachers" – call them what you may – have an important role to play both in mutual support and in aiding overall coordination.

Our second remark concerns what backup ought not to be. In connection with this, we reproduce a recent reflection on school provision for immigrant children in Europe:

Backup may consist of "allocation of supplementary teachers, on a day-to-day basis to help them in their work, providing and correcting supplementary exercises, home visits, follow-up schoolwork, etc." But in fact it is usually a reaction when things have already gone wrong, a sort of after-sales service or emergency break-down service, putting patches on holes as they appear. "There is no broad vision of transforming the educational system as a whole, rendering it adequate to the needs of all children and flexible enough to go on adapting as required. Things are left as they are, but with a few bits and bobs tacked on. Under such conditions it is inevitable that results are mediocre, and that immigrant children comprise the majority of pupils with scholastic difficulties. The situation can be summed up by saying that they are treated as *charity cases*, and as everybody already knows this cannot be conducive to the development of learning autonomy. Instead of a pedagogy centred on the learner, we have instead a pedagogical patchwork" [Porcher, 1979, pp. 62-63].

The same conclusion has been drawn in connection with Gypsies: "Supplementary teaching is nothing but a pair of crutches, made to fit not the one who needs them in order to walk – the learner – but the one who provides them – the school" [Balas, 1984, p.126]. The same analysis was made in Spain by an Inspector General and National Counsellor on Gypsy Education who firmly rejected supplementary teaching, at least as it is capable of being practised within the ordinary system as it now is; he calls it *"curanderismo pedagógico"* (pedagogical patching-up) and rejects it as a bastard system which appears to bring pupils into contact but in fact perpetuates discrimination and continues to expose minorities to rejection and stigmatisation [Iniesta, 1982, pp. 42-43]. Instead, he gives his firm support for *las escuelas puente*, that is, "bridging classes" especially for Gypsies [and there were about 200 such at the beginning of the 1980s. For further details on these classes see the Report of the Institute of Applied Sociology of Madrid, 1982.]

We dealt with these themes in detail as far back as 1977, concentrating on the question of social work. When analysing "preventative" social work (as it is known in France), we emphasised that "the art of the social technician, promulgator of new needs, is modelled more on marketing than on after-sales service – which would at least put it at the disposition of those who, subjected to the vicissitudes of acculturation, really do need some such backup" [Liégeois, 1977, p.92]. To summarise: the overall situation, in a context of assimilation, creates new needs, and "after-sales service" must be guaranteed, both from social workers and from a pedagogy of "ongoing patching up". On the subject of this "patching-up", and the fact that it is a permanent state of affairs, we have pointed out that the activities of social welfare, as conceived, "confine the Gypsies not only to a role of dependence, but to perpetual maladjustment – since changes in the surrounding society will always continue to occur at least as fast as within the Gypsy community, which will therefore always be out of sync. Social workers set the Gypsy running towards an unattainable goal. Why not shake off this evolutionist bias, which assumes that all societies must go through the same stages in order to 'progress'? Why not just accept the concept of parallel evolution, different rhythms?" [ibid, p.128]. One can see how such principles apply to intercultural pedagogy. And, on the subject of "autonomy", we noted that "Imposed autonomy is a parody of spontaneous autonomy" [ibid, p.135].

We could pursue these parallels. It is interesting to note the convergence of analyses – even down to the detail of using the same figures of speech. In other words, backup to school services in many ways resembles social work. Institutionally, in fact, the two may overlap: in a significant number of cases (and largely because social work systems are by nature more flexible than school systems), the personnel responsible for support work are trained and employed by the social services sector, as *"éducateurs scolaires"*, "educational social workers", etc. Certainly it is desirable that the two systems complement one another, but we must be wary that this does not lead to a compounding of their defects.

Preschooling

Preschooling, being non-obligatory, offers the parents involved a real choice. Two complementary effects result, which seem contradictory only if glanced at too superficially. On the one hand, parents are unenthusiastic about consigning their toddlers to a school institution which appears alien and often threatening (both physically and culturally), particularly as education at that age is primarily a function of the family. On the other hand – and this is a recent phenomenon – preschooling is noticeably on the increase, due primarily to the fact that the children are given a warm and indulgent welcome within a structure geared towards flexibility, improvisation and innovation; this warmth, combined with the voluntary nature of preschool, leads to higher attendance rates. This tendency is not universal, but it is a definite trend.

It appears that the differences between all-Gypsy and mixed classes are less at preschool level than at primary: the functional flexibility of the preschool makes for relatively easy adaptation, as does the principle of "stimulating" activities – which are culturally more polyvalent than the more structured and more culturally "charged" activities of primary class. Toddlers often take less notice than older children of the fact that their schoolmates have a different lifestyle, and sometimes a different colour of skin and hair. Two essential criteria for Gypsy parents, even more as regards preschool than primary, are proximity and accessibility. This implies that the class must be located near the children's homes (both for ease of transport and above all so parents can keep an eye on it) and that it be open to parents who wish to see the conditions and company in which their child will be spending time outside the family. Because they meet these criteria, it is specialised classes on or near halting sites which most often gain parental approval.

Specialised preschool classes, from a few to several dozen units, are to be found in several countries, notably Ireland, the United Kingdom, the Netherlands and France. They are established in proximity to both long- and short-term accommodation, and cater for nomadic and sedentary families. If they are linked with some provision for specialised primary schooling, the children go on to attend this (assuming they have not moved on in the meanwhile). But more and more the trend seems to be to retain, and even to intensify, on-site specialised preschooling as a preparation for integration into "ordinary" classes. At the same time it must be mentioned that financial restrictions have curtailed preschooling somewhat, notably in the United Kingdom and Denmark. The Danish report mentions that this has repercussions at other levels: when the toddlers stay at home, so do the twelve to sixteen year old girls, to mind them.

The trend towards preschooling must be seen within the overall context sketched in the preceding chapters. Certainly, attendance is on the increase, but not so long ago, it was nil. The majority of parents do not wish to send their very young children to school, and they do not do so. We include a few brief extracts from the national reports:

In *Greece*: "There are special difficulties in Gypsies entering pre-school education:

a. Since Gypsy mothers move also very often because of seasonal work, they are obliged to carry their children with them;
b. Bureaucratical functions (registration, etc.) are hardly accessible to Gypsies;
c. Gypsy parents can rarely see any important need or purpose in sending their children to crèches and nurseries cutting them off from their family home;
d. Traditionally family-focused education remains extremely important to Gypsies;
e. It is not so simple for Gypsy children to adapt to a non-Gypsy organised community, even a nursery (since it is governed by unfamiliar adults)" [Korré/ Marselos].

In the *Netherlands*, "The Gypsy parents display great concern over their little ones. They come in specially to say that the children should not go outside or to the playroom and ask whether the outside door could be locked. Some of the older girls are given strict instructions to keep a constant eye on one of the little ones and to 'protect' them against other children. The parents do not send their infants to a pre-school playgroup on the grounds that it is too unfamiliar. For this reason some of the three-year-olds are sent along to school. Because they speak Romanès there are often initial communication problems" [Hovens et al].

In the *FRG* "Sinti parents do not generally send their children to preschool" [Reemtsma]. In *Italy*, "Gypsy families do not favour sending their children to preschool, be it because of nomadism, or to protect them, or to avoid a clash of wills with them. Moreover in many families ethnic consciousness leads to a preference for in-family education in earliest childhood" [Karpati/Massano]. In the *United Kingdom*, "It is unlikely that many Travellers would wish to surrender their infants to teachers for more than short periods" [Acton/Kenrick].

To the reserved attitude of Gypsy parents we must also add the rejection of non-Gypsy parents, as detailed earlier. In the case of preschool this antagonism may be even more marked, as places are limited and Gypsy children may get priority.

The characteristics commonly associated with preschool classes (acceptance, warmth and flexibility – which make it easy to accommodate the differences between children) generally make them attractive to those who have attended them, and to their parents. Parents have been known to try to keep their school-age children in preschool; children with preschool experience do better in primary; those who have got to know them convince others to send their children [cf. for example Deligné and Miscoria, 1984, for the experience of one school in France]. In many different respects, then, preschool operates in ways which could be applied within the school system proper – yet too often, there is little continuity between the two.

Preschool, as its name indicates, precedes schooling proper, and is geared towards preparing for it. This may lead to certain ambiguities. Intensive preschooling may be followed by inadequate, non-adapted schooling, or may itself be a tool in the coercive assimilation of children from whatever cultural background. Indeed, certain of the national monographs are quite explicit about the official function of the preschool being to "initiate children into the discipline they will encounter later, in ordinary classes". Should the child become skilled at more quickly and easily dissociating himself from his background? Before stepping up the practice of preschooling as a means of enabling the child to enter primary school on an equal footing, we must first ask what goal the preschool sets for itself, as well as what sort of schooling will follow it.

Secondary schooling

"I was five years going to the special classes in the Convent with a lot of other Travelling children. When I made my First Communion I was sent over to the boys' secondary school. I liked it for the first few days. Then I got sick of it. I was left sitting in the back of the class all day doing whatever I wanted to do. I was like this for six months. I had no books, and I got no homework and I was learning nothing. Then I started going in late. That was still alright with them. The only thing I could do was draw pictures, and I knew that before I went there. The year passed by and I had forgotten everything I had learned in the special classes. All the rest of the town lads were moved into sixth class, but I was held back for another year with the same teacher. I wasn't putting up with it for another year.

One day I was on my lunch break and all the lads were playing with a tennis ball and I joined in the game. One of the lads said: 'That Tinker is not playing.' I went over and hit him. I was brought up before the teacher and he asked me what happened, and I told him. Then he said I was suspended off the [ball] alleys for three months. I started missing school. I was six months out missing and they knew it. When my mother found out she went over to the school and asked them if I was coming to school. They said I wasn't. They let me go for my Confirmation because I told them I was leaving after the summer holidays were up. I didn't go back after the holidays. That was the end of the school. I didn't know A from B. It was two years wasted. Looking back on it now it could have been time well spent. If I had gotten the attention from the teacher, I would have tried all the things the rest of the boys were doing. Maybe I could have learned them, maybe not. I only went to school to learn how to read and write. I didn't want to become a doctor or a school teacher. It would be a good idea if there was a Traveller teacher, because young Travellers would learn more" [Ned McDonagh, in McCarthy].

This testimony is fairly representative of the experience of Gypsy children who go on to secondary school. What is more, there are few such children, as the overall data have shown.

In *Greece*: "In secondary education there are very few cases" [Korré/Marselos]. In the *FRG* "Few (1-2%) Sinti children go to secondary school... The percentage of pupils leaving school with no certificate is extremely high" [Reemtsma]. "In all of the FRG today, there is not a single Sinti or Rom with a college diploma or university degree. However, thanks to the civil rights work done since 1979, many Sinti children are now attending college and perhaps will soon go on to university" [report from the *Zentralrat Deutscher Sinti und Roma*, June 1985, quoted by Reemtsma].

In *Ireland* "Very few children get as far as secondary education. Most finish school at around twelve... to date no Traveller has ever attended a third level course... most children in secondary education are in training centres or special schools... at present there is a strong vocational training element in the special secondary education that is available" [McCarthy]. In *Italy*, "Secondary school remains, for the majority of Gypsy families, inaccessible and almost unimaginable" [Karpati/ Massano]. In the *Netherlands* "Only 35% of the children proceed to some form of secondary education (and) fully half drop out after just one year. Almost without exception, this spells the end of their educational careers... over the years the problem has remained unaltered: school attendance steadily tapers off" despite the efforts of specialised classes, supplementary teaching, and contact with parents. One case study shows that "The education provided for caravan children had been satisfactorily arranged for many years. There was one major drawback: the day they turned fourteen, children would arrive at school with a big cake or bag of sweets to say good-bye. That was the end of their schooldays: no-one kept going!" [Hovens et al].

To the above considerations (that few Traveller children go on to secondary, and do not stay long once there) must be added the fact – which partially explains the above – that secondary schooling is ill-suited to their needs, and fraught with difficulties from several points of view. Schematically one could demonstrate that all of the positive characteristics of preschool appear in a negative form in the secondary system. One enters through a cold, impersonal administrative system; structures and programmes are rigid; inter-personal and particularly inter-ethnic tension are rife… As a result, there is a massive tendency towards "remedial units"

– which are not geared towards taking cultural differences into account, and which only widen the scholastic gap between Gypsies and the student body in general. Nonetheless such classes are often accepted as the lesser of two evils, even by parents [see "Integration by Handicap"] when confronting the practical inability of secondary instruction to accommodate pupils of different cultural backgrounds, as well as the discrimination to which Gypsy children are subject. The remedial section may appear as a sort of sanctuary, as well as, at first glance, slightly less unsuited to the children's needs than the wider structure. Before long, it becomes apparent that in practical terms it is a dead end and a waste of time for Gypsy and Traveller children, who by this age are ready for vocational training – by their parents.

Parents are perfectly conscious that it is they and not school who will provide the child with the skills by which he will earn his living. There are many reasons behind this, including the poor quality of the schooling the Gypsy child receives, the prejudice which ensures that the Gypsy really is incapable of "getting a job", Gypsy preference for self-employment. Other factors to be taken into account concern lifestyle and education within the Gypsy family (see below).

"Some of the things that make us keep our children out of secondary schools are the bullying that goes on, sex education, glue sniffing, smoking and swearing, and often the schools are far too advanced for them… Many schools think that fairground parents are not very interested in education for their children but this isn't true. However, I think primary schools are very very good. The trouble starts when they have to leave to go to secondary school. These schools are too military in their organisation. Smaller, more friendly schools are needed that are more concerned with the children and use the primary schools' methods" [Alfreda Holmes, "Why Traveller Children need Education", in *Traveller Education* no. 20, 1985, quoted by Acton/Kenrick].

Taking into account the present situation as regards Gypsies and Travellers in secondary education, the range of existing structures within the system, and the wishes of Gypsy/Traveller parents, we are led to consider two types of training. Firstly, *vocational training*. Initiatives undertaken to date have not always been successful, but they do offer a valuable pool of experience for further ventures. Such vocational training can be organised along flexible lines, to incorporate traditional in-family training and to continue basic scholastic (e.g. literacy) instruction, thus providing young people not with "alternative" but with additional means towards economic development, and for successful adaptation to their environment as a whole.

Secondly, *adaptation of secondary schooling*. As practised in various countries, this seems to take the form of a specialised class which may be only short-term, or part-time; children stay in as long as it takes for them to be ready to go on to normal classes or else attend it as a supplement to their activities within the wider system.

We include here only a few observations from the *United Kingdom;* they draw attention to many important considerations and are similar to what can be observed in other countries. In January 1984 a post for a part-time teacher was created by the Inner London Education Authority in one of its secondary schools, for the purpose of developing provision for Traveller children stopping on a site about a mile from the school. "The school in question had an international reputation for its progressive approach and had been attended by the children of Labour Cabinet ministers in the 1970s." Of the nine eleven- to thirteen-year-olds who at the beginning attended frequently, the number quickly dropped to five, who divided their time between ordinary classes and the group created especially for them. Support, in every sense of the word, played an important role, and included several "peripatetic teachers for Travellers" providing information and insights to other teachers, with a view to helping them to understand Travellers better. Transport of children to school posed considerable difficulties, overcome now thanks to outside help and the parents' determination, and although it is still "too early to say how far the children will be able to progress up the school", the experience has on the whole been positive. This example [quoted by Acton/Kenrick] is important since it demonstrates that even within an exceptionally favourable scholastic environment, a number of special measures must be taken in order to overcome obstacles – which, if ignored, can bring the entire project to naught.

Here is another illustration, this time from another comprehensive school in the London area, which has been accepting Gypsy pupils since 1980. In 1983 the coordinator of the project (which involved both primary and secondary levels) evaluated the experience [in *ILEA Multi-Ethnic Education Review*, vol. 2, no.1, 1983, quoted in Acton/Kenrick]. In connection with secondary level, she wrote: "A few Travellers settle into the school and do well; others need remedial help with reading to facilitate the settling-in process. Some Traveller children, however, feel that they suffer prejudice and victimisation from other children because they are Gypsies and they tend to react aggressively or to run out of school thoroughly upset. The school has a policy against racism and attempts to deal with pupils who perpetrate racist abuse. I have become something of a focal point for the Travellers in the school; hopefully they will come to me for help with problems rather than becoming aggressive or staying away from school. Staff who are having problems with Traveller children can also seek help from me.

Part of the Travellers' difficulties in settling into secondary school centre on the curriculum. While most Travellers appreciate the value of literacy they tend to see exams and qualifications as unnecessary and irrelevant to their lifestyle. Of the few Travellers who have stayed at school until the fifth year in recent years, all have dropped out before taking any exams. As with some other pupils, if lessons lack interest or seem to be irrelevant, disruptive behaviour can follow. Some Traveller pupils opt out of lessons that they dislike and we have sometimes allowed them to spend these lesson times in the basic studies department rather than risk total non-attendance because of one disliked lesson. Such problems are not, of course, unique to Travellers, and I have had to walk a diplomatic tightrope, as the school is anxious that Traveller pupils should not be treated substantially differently from other pupils. However, my very existence as the Traveller teacher indicates a measure of positive discrimination. I hope that as the school develops its multicultural curriculum the needs of the Travellers will be taken into consideration."

As our final example, we turn to the Manchester Travellers' School, "which is a special class for secondary-aged children located in a temporary building in a primary school. This apparent example of segregation is in fact the result of integration at the primary level. In the early 1970s primary schools successfully took many children from the now closed Dantzic Street site, and became concerned about their failure to pass on to secondary education. In 1975, one, Abbott County Primary, decided, against regulations, to retain children over the age of eleven, rather than see them leave school. In 1976 the LEA responded by agreeing to set up a special unit in the grounds of Abbott CP school, as a bridge to two local secondary schools, one for boys and one for girls.

At first the syllabus of the school was mainly secondary, but a change in families on the site led to an influx of children with no previous schooling, and a great deal of basic literacy work had to be offered. After the site was closed, this became even more the case, but Traveller parents continued to send their children to the school, and to friendly primary schools, from illegal sites some distance away. At the same time, secondary-level work is still on offer to children who fail to make the transition to secondary school from primary schools. Some of these have been placed successfully in secondary schools, but apart from a few children whose families moved into houses, none have successfully completed secondary school. Visits to secondary schools are carried out, but these are not entirely satisfactory. Children often have to be placed in the secondary school's remedial unit, and the problems of bright Traveller children who happen to have had very little schooling are not the same as non-Gypsy children who have failed to learn to read despite having had a full primary education. In addition most secondary schools in Manchester have school uniforms, and buying these could prove expensive for Travellers if their children were to attend a new secondary school every time they are evicted.

The number of pupils attending varies according to the current state of evictions between ten to fifty, and attendance is around 80% of those enrolled. In 1983 the HMI discussion paper, 'The Education of Travellers' Children', commented 'There are few examples of successful provision of secondary education for Travelling children, but this small project provides some indication of how the early stages might be attempted.' It must be emphasised that this segregated provision is thus part of a strategy of integration... The school clearly encourages respect for Traveller culture not only in its own class and in Abbott school which has up to twenty Traveller children in ordinary classes, but throughout the North-West of England" [Acton/Kenrick].

What structures ?

The preceding survey amply illustrates the variety of structures involved in school provision for Gypsy children. This variety is the result both of choice and of necessity, a blend of ad hoc, rarely well-considered (and even more rarely coordinated) responses to the "question" posed by the presence of Gypsy children in an institution continually bemused by its inability to attract them, accommodate them, hold on to them, or do them any good. *This mosaic of attempts, whether successes or failures, comprises a considerable sum of experience. It is vital, and urgent, to draw upon this experience, to replace guesswork with informed planning and compulsion with a will to provide – and receive – schooling, rather than a hasty reaction to a pressing situation.*

It is interesting to note that, in the different countries, with no consultation or exchange of ideas at any level (neither school authorities nor policymakers base their projects on studies of what has been tried elsewhere), despite different school systems, different views on schooling children of different cultures, and after nearly two decades of trial and error, similar conclusions have been drawn everywhere by those who have sat down and pondered these questions. This consensus must be made known, discussed and shared, to avoid the repetition of errors which are costly in every sense (psychological, social and financial) and which moreover contribute to the perpetuation of the conflictual relationship between the two communities.

The structures involved – even if we consider them purely from a material viewpoint – must, if they are to avoid dead ends and open up, adapt themselves to certain practices of those who attend them. Eleven-year-olds arrive in school not knowing how to read and write. Children arrive in bunches (typically, brothers and sisters of different ages) and refuse – with their parents' support – to be split up, so as not to feel lost and helpless in the alien environment of the classroom. Small children arrive, unable to speak the teacher's language, and he must turn to an older child to act as interpreter before any instruction can take place. A group of children arrives, stays for a day or a week, and is never seen again. Commonplace events in some places. Let us add a few considerations to complete what has already been said, and anticipate what is to come:

"There is still a great deal of discrimination against Travellers in the educational system. Children are tormented at school by other children calling them abusive names, attacking them. Frequently they are totally segregated in schools, not allowed to play at the same times as the other children, not allowed to use the same facilities as the other children, etc. Many teachers say that Traveller children have educational blocks and that they cannot learn to read and write, even after years of regular school attendance. It seems much more likely that these are cultural blocks. For example, Travellers' own language is not recognised at all and in most schools their separate culture is treated as totally inferior or non-existent" [McCarthy].

> "Our lot don't know how to read and write.
> They say we're thick, 'cos we can't read.
> We've never been to school except stuck at the back (of the class).
> The teachers aren't interested in us.
> They don't pay any attention to us." [*Jeannette et l'École Obligatoire,* 1983, p.30]

Gypsy children, "influenced by the attitudes inherited from outside school (attitude of their society towards latent discrimination) and derived from a different cultural environment and psychology, are more sensitive not only to obvious racial attacks but also to ordinary children's aggression which is not addressed to 'Gypsies' nominally" [Korré/Marselos].

"Teachers who expect to have children in their classes are perturbed by the presence of Gypsy pupils whose behaviour is adult" [Michel Pragnère, MS., 1985].

"In some situations, most of the teachers will be against admitting caravan and Gypsy children to their school. More commonly, a number of teachers will be cooperative, others more or less neutral and a small minority outright against admitting the children. The latter tend to be easily the most vocal. Arguments against admitting caravan/Gypsy children to a school are often based on presumption, such as 'The parents of our children will say they don't want the caravan/Gypsy children at their school, because…' It is rare for all the teachers of a particular school to support the admission of caravan/Gypsy children to their school. Reluctance is often especially marked towards Gypsy children" [Hovens et al].

These observations – we could add many others! – would seem to point in the direction of specialised classes. Yet there are plenty of observations to the contrary, which emphasise the inherent risk of such provision being used as, or becoming, a ghetto. Parents themselves try to avoid such classes, and try to get their children in where "there aren't too many Gypsies". They may also argue that, although a class is "special", it is not necessarily adapted to their children's needs – so why send them? Both teachers and parents point out that intergroup and interfamily antagonisms are brought into the classroom, and may have disturbing effects. Many parents feel that "special" schooling is "cut-price" schooling, at a much lower level than ordinary classes. Moreover, the general dispersion of Gypsy children (be they nomadic or sedentary) and their number compared to the availability of "special" facilities, imply clearly that their schooling (if it is to occur at all, and particularly if it is to extend to children with little or no schooling to date) will have to take place in whole or in part within non-specialised structures.

If we are to take account of the "principle of realism" outlined above, we must consider two apparently contradictory imperatives: the necessity of schooling (at least partially) within ordinary structures, and the impossibility of doing so. Is there a way out?

Where we have found examples of successful "integration" of Gypsy children into ordinary classes, we have seen that such integration is the end-product of a (sometimes lengthy) process which occurs on several different levels and consists of several stages which simultaneously and consecutively make use of various structures and formulas. On this subject, we add a few examples – two of them from outside the European Community – to complement those given above.

In *Norway:* "The school administration of Oslo began teaching Gypsy children through two existing primary schools in 1971-72. The first essential step was the creation of a climate of confidence between the two instructors and the children's parents; in effect the teachers became social workers. The Gypsy children did not 'mix' in class. The teachers had to get them out of bed, bring them to class, and take them home again. The children often seemed to enjoy school first and foremost as a welcome change from the harsh conditions of the campsite.

When the Gypsies left Oslo in spring 1972, a mobile school was set up to provide continuity for what had proved a promising scholastic beginning. This project was funded by the Norwegian Research Council. The teachers had a letter of introduction from the Oslo Chief School Administrator, granting them the right to use local classrooms wherever their travels took them. In fact, this only occurred in connection with long-term halts; otherwise, classes were held in the caravan.

When the Gypsies set up camp in the Gaustadbeck Valley, the local school was able to provide them with a premises all their own. Instruction continued here until 1977, for the children who remained in the area. Afterwards, children – at their own request – went into state schools near their new homes in Oslo. Integration took the form of children attending ordinary classes with the continued backup of their 'own' teachers, while they undertook some courses (for example crafts and sport) with no backup. This 'unsupported' situation became generalised by autumn 1978, with the goal of integrating all the children at secondary level" [Schlüter, 1983, p. 3].

In the *Netherlands*, a case study gives details of the different stages leading to the scholastic integration of children from a group of recent immigrants:

"a - The initial reception of the children at the temporary school at the camp-site was extremely difficult. There were too few teachers and no similar experience to go on anywhere else in the country. The school was required to deal with some forty children aged three to fourteen with a totally different cultural background and unable to speak Dutch, and who lacked many of the usual prerequisites for schooling. Educationally they were right at the beginning and their attitude towards learning was very poor. There was no specific teaching material, which made it impossible to achieve continuity in teaching. Nevertheless teaching was achieved and, in their own way, the Gypsy children were motivated to learn and regarded the school as their school. The teaching staff were also motivated. Leaving aside the complicated situation, the children formed a cheerful and inspiring little club. The education was geared to the children's capabilities. The demands were not pitched too high, children were dealt with at their own individual level, and teaching periods kept short...

b - In October 1978 the Gypsy school was transferred to the neighbourhood to which the Gypsies had moved. A number of children were deemed able at this point to cope with ordinary schools. The arrival of the Gypsies and their school aroused a good deal of commotion in the neighbourhood, for which reason it was thought inadvisable to send the children to the local school. Approaches were made to five other schools within a two-kilometre radius. The response in this case was more positive, although each school laid down conditions. In particular, the schools could be persuaded to accept them. The real break-through, however, did not occur until the children actually went to the schools, when there proved to be no cause whatever for panic.

c - The separate Gypsy school was disbanded in August 1980 and the pupils all transferred to ordinary schools. The Gypsy-school teacher no longer has any teaching duties but provides counselling and guidance. The main focus of attention now is on improving relations between Gypsy parents and the schools, reducing school absenteeism and helping the Gypsy children in class situations with modified remedial programmes" [Peerke Bos and Jules Wolthuis, in Hovens et al].

In *Sweden*: "Gypsy pupils, like all other children, are generally placed according to age. They are enrolled in ordinary classes. If they do not speak Swedish, many districts can provide them with 'preparatory' classes to help them over the transition. In these classes they learn Swedish and are also taught about their new environment – 'the world outside' as well as the school. For certain lessons, for example crafts and sport, they usually rejoin their ordinary class, to help them get to know their future classmates. As the child's grasp of Swedish improves, he spends less time in the preparatory class and correspondingly more in the ordinary one; the goal is to allow him to participate fully in his own class as quickly as possible. Supplementary teaching is an ongoing process however; it provides the child with backup in the following forms:

- advanced, in-depth study of the Swedish language;
- supplementary teaching in other subjects (through the child's own mother tongue if a teacher is available);
- study of the child's mother tongue.

For the past few years Gypsy children, like all children with a mother tongue other than Swedish, have been entitled to instruction through the language spoken by at least one of their parents. This can begin in primary school and continue throughout the school career" [Lambert Scherp, report to the Council of Europe, Donaueschingen, 1983]. The author adds, however, that there is still a lack of materials and teachers in Romani.

In Ireland the *Irish Times* (10/3/83) describes Galway as being very advanced as regards school provision for Travellers. About 250 children attend, within the following structures: two all-Traveller preschool classes, six specialised classes, and the rest in ordinary classes with some backup; moreover, Galway has a "visiting teacher" – the first in the country.

The above observations fully bear out the conclusions of a Council of Europe seminar (with participants from eight countries). Here are some of its recommendations concerning structures [Liégeois, 1983b]:

"At present there seems to be general agreement, both from parents and from teachers, that Gypsy children should attend the same schools, and even the same classes, as other children. This is out of concern to avoid marginalisation, and to accomplish a mutual enrichment.

However:
- 'supplementary' instruction, both complementary and specialised, is always required,
- preschooling must take place within a specialised (all-Traveller) structure,
- certain preconditions are essential in order that the school may provide properly inter-cultural conditions. Primary among these is that teachers be thoroughly trained and informed – otherwise how can they understand and deal with various elements of the children's culture? – as well as information exchange between Gypsy and non-Gypsy (parents and children) to avoid conflict and rejection,
- realism demands that we do not recommend the immediate abolition of 'specialised' classes, until the above-mentioned criteria are fulfilled. 'Ordinary' schools do not, as yet, offer either the teaching quality nor the cultural respect characteristic of specialised schools, nor have they the essential flexibility of rules and timetable,
- school provision for *nomadic* children must be suitably adapted: caravan-schools, school on or near the halting site, and scholastic continuity (mainly in the form of an assessment booklet) for children who move frequently,
- intercultural education, if misinterpreted and misused, can be full of ambiguities: 'the same school for all' can rapidly become a means of standardisation and elimination of differences, all in the name of equality."

The present situation in most countries is that there exist several different structures – each of which may, as applied to Gypsy and Traveller children, function for better or for worse. The very fact that there are different structures, is a positive one: situations vary, as do the wishes of parents. Yet none of them appears to be sufficient on its own, nor wide-ranging enough to cover all the possible variations. None is fully useful until taken in tandem with others, either diachronically (passage from one structure to another) or synchronically (simultaneous use of several structures, for example lessons in "ordinary" class plus lessons in "Gypsy" class, with ongoing backup). *The adaptation of structures should take the form of variety and flexibility, not the sort of either/or monolithic models which the authorities may tend to favour.*

As a first step, in order to improve unsatisfactory conditions and inadequate structures operative at present in school provision for Traveller children, *it is indispensable that the special provision described here be recognised and developed.* Preschool classes, primary classes (including mobile classes), provision at secondary level, supplementary and liaison personnel, etc. are all essential yet such formulas are still too often treated as a necessary but temporary evil. Since they are seen as small-scale annoyances, they tend to be allocated resources on a correspondingly small scale. It is also frequently the case that they are subject to periodic review as a precondition for renewed funding – a situation which prevents them from working with stability and continuity. The derogatory perception of specialised facilities often leads to a lack of will to create them, and initiative in this field continues to come, to a large degree, from private bodies, which also provide a significant amount of the necessary funding.

By its very nature, the functioning of specialised structures necessitates *trained personnel*. In fact this is far from always being the case. Yet a "specialised" class without a "specialised" teacher loses a great deal of its rationale. The same applies if the class must function according to a rigid schedule: since it is incapable of adapting to the children, in what way is such a class "specialised"? As we pointed out above, such a class has every chance of accomplishing nothing but the failure and frustration of all concerned. Sometimes it is infinitely preferable for Gypsy children to attend ordinary, "integrated" classes than "specialised" classes without funding or trained personnel. Such "specialised" provision serves in practice to hide the fact that no appropriate provision is being made, or as an alibi for assimilationist policies, or as a dumping ground for children labelled "problems" or "maladjusted" without anyone trying to understand them on their own terms.

But it must be stressed emphatically that *specialised classes need not be considered "special" classes nor specialised teachers as "special" teachers.* Complementarity of "ordinary" and "specialised" structures allows for continuity and interchange between them, in content as well as personnel – which should include both pupils and teachers. Such an approach helps to avoid two pitfalls: firstly that of hyperspecialisation, stigmatising and isolating those involved in it (a frequently voiced fear of those who object to such classes), and secondly that of segregation (rejection, teasing, etc.) coupled with imposed "normalisation" (non-acceptance of difference, lack of flexibility) which at present characterise the majority of "ordinary" classes. To recall a distinction made at the beginning of this chapter, we should be thinking more in terms of structures specialised in practical terms by the children who attend them, than in the perpetuation of structures specialised because of the rules under which they are set up. Observation bears out that the first type tends to be flexible enough to deal with influxes of different groups of children, and the teachers themselves are more flexible too. Such classes/structures can be more or less differentiated, as circumstances require. Prescribed specialisation, on the other hand, is generally synonymous with "special classes" with all the rigidity and various negative effects that this implies; this makes them ill-suited and difficult to adapt. They may seem viable from an administrative point of view, but not from that of Gypsy reality.

In time we ought to be able to speak simply of *adapted classes* to get away from the false dichotomy of "special(ised)" versus "ordinary" – which owes more to preconceptions than to an examination of reality [cf. the chapter "L'institution scolaire" in Liégeois, 1985a]. A structure is "adapted" from the moment that parents no longer have reason to withdraw their children from it, nor hesitate to send them for fear of rejection, ineffective or objectionable teaching, lack of results… In this concept (or is it a hypothesis? or utopianism? at any rate it can serve as a general guideline and springboard for discussion), which emphasises the adaptation of the class to suit its pupils, all classes might be called specialised insofar as this adaptive effort is made. And this way no one is branded "special". Should a Gypsy child spend years, perhaps his entire school career, in classes on halting sites? Well, why not, if conditions are favourable and parents approve?

"Segregation has a negative ring, but here we are concerned with voluntary segregation, which may be said to have the same implications as when other ethnic groups create educational systems of their own" [Gustafsson, 1973, p.104].

No structure should be rejected or classed as "temporary" if it proves to be suitable for some. Why should all existing "specialised" classes necessarily be gearing all their pupils towards "ordinary" ones? We mentioned earlier that some Gypsy children attend "ordinary" classes from the start, while others go into them after a long process of "special" schooling. This does not however imply that "ordinary" classes must necessarily be the ultimate goal for all, nor that passing from "specialised" to "ordinary" need necessarily be "progress" either from the scholastic point of view or in the eyes of the pupil himself. Two points may be mentioned briefly, in connection with this subject. On the one hand, "What does 'normal' schooling mean to a child whose world lies outside the fundamental precepts of 'normal' classes?" [Cotonnec, 1983, p.118 – this question will be further developed in a later chapter]. On the other hand, to require that "specialised" classes be conceived as "bridges" assumes that there is a passable road on the other side of the bridge. When – as so often – this is not the case, it is better not to cross that bridge.

A desire to organise all classes along similar lines may well spring from a desire to simplify at the administrative and teacher-training level; it is an economical and soothing solution, often defended in the name of equality. But can different cultures in fact find a place in such classes? Flexibility is the enemy of monolithism. We must also consider the teachers: can they possibly know so much, be so adaptable, so welcoming and so attentive to each child, while at the same time remaining attentive and understanding towards parents and school authorities?

"Normalisation is the byword today in immigration policy, and here, 'normalisation' has some connotation of equality, of avoiding marginalisation and the ghetto (even in a deluxe version!). But how can we be sure that a policy of normalisation actually has the normalising effect expected of it, and which is supposed to justify it? In fact it is a spurious option. All it does is switch the two terms about: as soon as normalisation is declared, there is a longing for specialisation, yet as soon as specialisation comes into force, it is suspect" [Sayad, 1983, p.45].

For the past few years there has been a tendency to "normalise" scholastic integration, in theory if not in practice, so much so that one ends up with the impression that it is a simple process: that one need only open the classroom door for former outsiders to enter and sit down quietly, with all their cultural baggage, and get on with it. But will they get a chance to open up this baggage and share it with others? Won't some of them be required to leave it shut, and only pick it up again on the way out, so that one day perhaps they'll forget about it altogether? To pretend that scholastic integration is easy is for all concerned is to run the risk of failure and delusion; let us bear in mind what has already been said in connection with the attitudes Gypsy children encounter in school, and the heavy socio-historical burden complicating all relations between the two communities.

There is also too frequently a tendency to consider "integration" as if it were a goal to achieve, whereas it should also and perhaps above all be seen simply as a means of schooling. The same goes for structures. Are they geared towards the child's scholastic needs, in which case he can hope for better-adapted ones? Or is the child expected to conform to imposed structures before he can even begin his schooling? *Recognition of children's culture and cultural practices must first be present in the respect shown for them in the way the child is received, before we can speak of what pedagogical use can be made of them. The intercultural attitude recommended for the classroom must also be manifest throughout the school system: a diversity of structures adapted to diverse cultural practices is a precondition for this. Complementarity of structures, making it possible to pass from one to another, or to use them simultaneously, guarantees it.*

As concerns structures, we have demonstrated that the key words should be: *complementarity, openness, flexibility, progressiveness*. Any structure can lead to success – or to failure. This is only another way of saying that there is no overall "solution" to this problem, and that preconceived and exclusive advocacy of any single type of structure is more likely to stem from political/ideological motivation, than from pedagogical considerations.

Teachers

The choice

The presence of a teacher in an all or mostly Gypsy class should be the result of a double choice: the teacher's personal choice that this is the class he wants to teach, and the appointment of the teacher in accordance with certain criteria, to ensure maximum adaptation of the class to the children and their needs. Such criteria vary; the important thing is more the profile that emerges from the teacher's characteristics, which may then be compared to a theoretical "ideal" teacher for that particular situation. This is why teachers ought to be appointed from among voluntary candidates, by a committee – the composition of which may vary from country to country and from system to system, but which must have some knowledge of the specific aspects of schooling for Gypsy children. Among the determining criteria, there are the teacher's motivation in seeking the post, his experience, training, and knowledge.

The above criteria are hardly ever met in practice. Either one of the two "choices" mentioned may be lacking, or appointment may be made by arbitrary administrative criteria. It is not at all uncommon for teaching posts to be allocated according to seniority, family considerations (for example spouses wishing to work together), etc. – resulting in "Gypsy" classes with teachers who are neither voluntary nor trained nor even informed, and whose foremost desire may well be to get out of that class as quickly as possible. The fact that, to date, school provision for Gypsy children is considered a "marginal" or "minor" issue, or a "provisional" measure (on the path towards "normalisation") means than it tends to be treated as "low status" administratively. As a result, appointees often come from the bottom of the scale, be it because they are just out of training college and lack experience, or worse, because they have had problems in other posts. This practice contributes towards the general low regard in which those working in this field are held: they become marginalised along with the class they teach, and in their turn do much to make Gypsy classes into "special" classes, "ghettos" with negative connotations. As a result, applicants for work in this field are even less forthcoming: a vicious circle which must be broken.

This general belittling of such teaching means that, in *Ireland* for example, "It is common for untrained or retired teachers to work with Travelling children (though this practice has decreased now due to the difficulties young newly-qualified teachers experience in finding employment)" [McCarthy]. On a major site in *Belgium*, "The teaching staff consisted mainly of persons of rather shaky standing: social work trainees, conscientious objectors, unemployed people on an 'experimental workfare' scheme – plunged into a cumbrous bureaucratic system... School personnel (in 1980-81) consisted of one conscientious objector and two final year trainees from the Institute of Social Work" [Reyniers]. Recruitment can take the form of advertisements in the educational press: their wording is explicit but the marginalisation inherent in the work means that there are never many applicants – and aren't they applying because they can't get anything better? A case is mentioned in the *United Kingdom* report of a teacher hired after he had already been dismissed – for incompetence – from another "Gypsy" post. Then again the selection committee may have a very unclear idea of the profile required; they are more likely to be thinking in stereotyped terms about "those children", than in an informed and realistic manner.

At the same time we hasten to point out that this is a relative rather than an absolute picture. These are the dominant tendencies, yet there are proportionately more and more cases of teachers who really choose to work with Traveller children, being appointed to do so, and of teachers appointed involuntarily staying on in the work and developing enormous experience and competence despite encountering numerous difficulties for which they are not responsible. There are also signs, here and there, of an evolution in recruitment practices, in the general direction of the recommendations given above. Such localised and exploratory procedure must become the general practice. The main opponents of the still too prevalent absence of choice are experienced teachers who have had years of difficulties in developing appropriate teaching methods, and whose task was rendered the harder by the fact that (with few exceptions) they were neither prepared, trained, nor informed, and remained unsupported by the administration and misunderstood by their colleagues.

Administration

The teacher's task is a particularly difficult one; if he is to succeed in it he needs the interest, comprehension and encouragement of the administration, local and national, in various forms. All the more so because such teachers work in conditions considered "atypical" by their colleagues, and which are indeed – objectively – complex, with their own demands pedagogical and otherwise. But we have repeatedly emphasised that due to the treatment to which Travellers have been subject for centuries, the general misunderstanding surrounding them, and because schooling cannot be considered as "detached" from the larger context which determines it, Gypsy children are generally perceived en masse either as requiring no special treatment (all the children to be enrolled in ordinary classes) or as requiring short-term special treatment (in specialised classes). Having "resolved" the issue, the administration often fails to consider it again. The teachers involved are forgotten when all is going well, but, when some difficulty arises, although the teachers themselves may be the first victims, it is they who are first to be held responsible.

Illustrations of the administrative marginalisation of Gypsy provision exist right up to the highest level. We give two examples:

After publication by English (school) inspectors of the document, *The Education of Travellers' Children* (1983), "Contrary to usual practice with HMI discussion papers, the DES did not hold any press conference about this report and has done very little to publicise it" [Acton, 1985a, p.6]. In the same country, a few years ago, for a number of teachers, "a post in Traveller education was their first professional appointment. They often found that the DES would not recognise such a specialised post as qualification for the completion of their probationary year, and that their career prospects were thus blocked" [Acton/Kenrick].

It is not necessary to give details here of the trying conditions in which most teachers of Gypsy children must operate. They may for example be *of a material nature* – tables and chairs have to be "borrowed", and teaching materials may be grossly inadequate. A frequently recurring problem in most of the states is sudden withdrawal of promised funding, often by the very bodies that initiated a project in the first place – which means that promises cannot be kept, teachers lose credibility, and the Gypsies once again – and not without justification – feel that they have been foolish to believe that things would be different this time. Difficulties can be, in the broad sense, *of a statutory nature*: teachers of Gypsy children may be put on the lower end of the payscale; staff numbers are insufficient to perform all the necessary roles (liaison with parents, developing new teaching methods, further training, consultation with others in the field…). The national reports mention cases of teachers who, determined to do their job properly, become ill through overwork. Difficulties may also be *of a moral nature:* incomprehension from colleagues, an administration that refuses to listen and instead pressurises the teacher to apply directives and programmes which they know are unsuitable.

Difficulties *of a structural nature* are apparent too. Schooling often occurs, not because of administrative structures and their programmes, but in spite of them. In fact, and particularly as concerns teaching which endeavours to adapt to cultural diversity, it is important that the innovative spirit this requires be free to express itself. This means, particularly in states with highly centralised and rigid bureaucracies, that a margin of autonomy must be foreseen for schools open to different cultures – which is to say, all schools, if one truly wishes to develop intercultural education. Sometimes school regulations are so rigidly detailed that it becomes impossible to adapt to meet different children's needs without running up against them. This situation is especially inherent in highly centralised systems, but even local authorities can take too much decision-making upon themselves.

On the other hand, when administration and inspection see themselves as partners in the service of teachers, they give the school what it requires for successful adaptation, namely flexibility – even if only to a degree – and support. When administration keeps a concerned eye on the actual effectiveness of policy and practice, it becomes apparent that if certain steps are not taken, failure is inevitable and repetitive. Greatly improved results have been noted when the recruitment campaign for "Gypsy" teachers has consciously sought out experienced and willing candidates – and paid them better. Support systems may lessen the teacher's workload while providing pupils with an improved service. In such conditions the children make better progress, teachers stay in the job longer, and there is more opportunity for information exchange and making contacts. More and more, in different countries, inspectors come to the aid of teachers in various ways – counselling, obtaining funds, providing training, liaison, etc. but also by undertaking a thorough analysis of the situation and passing it on to the authorities. But central authorities rarely take heed of the arguments presented by inspectors. This description from Britain reflects the situation in most countries:

"When the fires of enthusiasm lit by the HMIs reach the wet blankets in the DES at Elizabeth House, all that results is a smokescreen behind which very little gets done" [Acton, 1985a, p.8].

Administration plays a key role in financing, teaching materials, training, coordination, recruitment, etc. Administration is thus present directly or indirectly in every chapter of this report, and the majority of final conclusions and recommendations will be of concern to it. As noted in the introduction, the 1980s seem to be a period of important changes – perhaps by choice, undoubtedly by necessity – in official attitudes towards the "problems" posed by the reality of multiculturality, which has become a fact of life in many European countries. Those countries with the greatest degree of multiculturality are evolving responses which can provide ideas and examples to countries where the phenomenon exists on a smaller scale. Gypsies and Travellers in all countries stand to benefit.

Marked change is occurring – albeit slowly – and most importantly as a change of mentality. An indicator of the slow pace of change is the terminology employed in connection with school provision for Traveller children. In almost every case, Gypsy classes (be they on a halting site or within a larger school complex) are described as "experiments" even as their numbers increase, or as "projects" – even when they've been operating for a decade or more. It is as if there were an unwillingness to confirm – to accept – the existence of school provision for Gypsies. It is to keep such provision, in spirit and in fact, outside the norm; it is to see specialised classes as "special". It is time for this schooling to be "normalised" in the sense covered earlier, in our discussion of structures: all classes should be adapted to the needs of the children who attend them.

Stability

It is impossible to give exact figures on job stability among teachers of Gypsy children; ministries seem to have paid little attention to this question, despite its obvious relevance. We can, however, present some indications, which give us grounds for further reflection – all the more so as they corroborate each other.

In *Ireland*, "Analysis of the questionnaires shows a high degree of stability. However the number of special classes is growing every year, there is a problem of unemployment among primary school teachers and it seems very likely that some teachers are in Traveller classes primarily out of a need to be employed... Stability in a post in a time of recession and unemployment does not say very much about job satisfaction or about a preference for working with a particular group of people. In fact there is some evidence in the Dublin area of increased efforts to get Traveller children into schools to maintain teaching posts. The teacher/pupil ratio is much lower in Traveller classes, averaging 1:12 whereas it can be as high as 1:40 in ordinary classes. However there is usually a much wider age range in the special class. Over the past three years there have been extensive cuts in education spending, especially in the remedial services available to ordinary schools. Traveller education is still relatively free from these financial cutbacks because of the stated government policy to encourage education for Travellers. However all the teachers who responded to the questionnaires complained that the grants available to special classes were far too low. This money is used to buy material for the class and can be as little as £20 a year!

It would be reasonable in these circumstances to find a high degree of stability in these posts. An additional factor is that there are a substantial number of nuns involved in these posts. They are, of necessity, trained teachers but their religious vocation would ensure a high degree of stability. Some Travellers have voiced the opinion that some of these nuns are too old for the job and there is a disproportionate amount of religious education in special classes" [McCarthy].

In the *Netherlands*, "Teacher turnover has not been very great, not least because of the difficulty of getting jobs throughout the teaching profession, which has reduced turnover at all levels." But there are plenty of grounds for dissatisfaction: "Where a special reception class is set up for the children the teachers willing to take it often turn out to be the young (and hence enthusiastic) ones. One problem in the current situation with the decline in school numbers and education cuts is that it is precisely these sorts of teachers who (on account of their short length of service) are the most liable to be made redundant. This is often a source of dissatisfaction, both among the remaining staff ('Who do they expect to teach these children now?') and among the caravan/Gypsy children and their parents ('The one teacher we've built up a relationship of trust with has been dismissed'). In order to make a success of the teaching, those teachers responsible for children in separate (reception) classes tend to be particularly dedicated. Their colleagues often display a lack of understanding, which they generally find most frustrating. The same applies to some teachers with just one or a few caravan/Gypsy children in their class. Others are either over-tolerant because they fear difficulties with the parents of the caravan/Gypsy children or else seize every opportunity they can to 'bring the children into line'" [Hovens et al].

In *Denmark*, in the reception class for Gypsy children in Elsinore, "Throughout some years incredibly big and very little appreciated (by the pupils and their parents) efforts were made to achieve at least some results. Through a very important effort on the part of the Yugoslav teacher, which included home visits in the routine, he succeeded to some degree in reducing the absenteeism. Time and again the Danish teachers had to compromise with their own expectations to the pupils' interest and own efforts. This is frustrating, and the result was unavoidable: the teachers in the teaching team had to be replaced to avoid that everything went haywire. This is quite pardonable, for in the long run nobody can stand seeing all promises and deals broken, or directly opposed" [Gudmander/Rude].

In the *United Kingdom*, in the 1970s, teachers "were often thrown into situations where they were thoroughly overworked. Many made surprising progress, but the rate of burnout was high; an opinion became current that no one should work in such a post for more than two or three years" [Acton/Kenrick]. The situation has changed somewhat since.

In *France*, the closure of a site brought about the dispersal of the several classes which had been attending school there. "This situation forced us to reflect on the school's ten years' existence… On the whole, the Travellers' attitudes towards the on-site school had deteriorated, with increased mistrust of teachers leading to a rise in absenteeism, indifference and criticism. When a post fell vacant, no one dared 'venture' into work on the 'chain-gang'. On the other hand, the ghetto/cocoon situation, coupled with purely lip-service admiration from the outside world, did not combine to favour an attitude of self-criticism. In connection with this, let it be added that general indifference towards the work the teachers were doing, comforted them in their pedagogical smugness, and that the ABC book was the only thing that tied them (to the school), with the possible addition of a feeling of a moral contract with the families on the site. If teachers themselves are largely responsible for the tone of a school (i.e. in forging a true teaching team, and as regards individual attitudes), then it is the duty of the national authorities to ensure that personnel appointed to such posts are carefully selected, experienced and highly motivated" [Michaud, 1984, p.41].

Many other factors, over which the teacher may have no control, may cause him to leave: teachers may be arbitrarily reassigned as part of personnel shuffles with no account being taken of the specific nature of their work. Administration does seem to be increasingly aware of such questions, yet often for "technical" reasons (at least, that is where the blame is usually laid) its hands appear to be tied. A dramatic example is when a teacher, having improved his qualifications (for example by completing an additional training course) is automatically promoted; so say the rules, and nothing can stand in the way of their implacable logic. As one teacher (in France) who passed a competitive examination and was subsequently "promoted" (transferred) despite his wish to stay on in the same job, put it, "Good old progress!" [quoted by Ferté].

Since we have no statistics, it is impossible to compare job mobility among teachers of Travelling children with that of teachers in general. However, many sources indicate a high rate of transfer after only a brief period in the job:

For example, "From 1976-79, the Marseilles CEFISEM (Training and Information Centre on Schooling for Immigrant Children) trained a total of 220 teachers in introductory classes and refresher courses... By 1979-80, only 3% of the teachers who began to practise in 1976 were still working with such classes" [Couillaud, 1981, p.28].

This would indicate that funding such training is a waste of resources, since teachers left jobs for which they had received supplementary training having given them little or no benefit of their expertise. Moreover, the fact that employment difficulties are repeatedly mentioned, in country after country, as the explanation for a new (relative) stability, offers no grounds for optimism; this simply means that the teacher stays on because even an unsatisfactory job is better than nothing. This is related to other overall trends in the teaching profession: recent research reveals that the concept of vocation has practically disappeared as a motive for entering this career, to be largely replaced by more practical considerations. For example, many women mention choosing it because it is relatively compatible with the demands of family life [cf. for example the Carraz report, 1983, p.244]. However, when considering the teaching of Gypsy children, these observations must be modified somewhat. On the one hand, a general trend emerges: there is massive turnover (voluntary and otherwise) of newly-appointed teachers; the remainder leave little by little (voluntarily or otherwise) except for a few who stay on for very long periods. It seems that those teachers who can overcome their initial demoralisation become very attached to the children, their parents, their lifestyle, and the task in hand, all in spite of difficult working conditions: the incomprehension of colleagues and/or parents and/or administration and/or material difficulties of every description. Yet there are cases of highly qualified and experienced teachers, deeply committed to the work, who resign out of physical and moral exhaustion, unable to continue when those around them remain incapable of understanding and appreciating their work. Isolated and unappreciated, they capitulate, and only then do those who should have been their partners but instead were mere observers, realise just how much they had been handling. But by then it is too late. And this *lack of personal and official recognition* towards teachers is yet another factor hampering the schooling of Gypsy children. As we have said time and again: *it is more a social problem than a pedagogical one.*

Initial training

In a recent Commission of the European Communities synthesis report, the extreme importance of training is strongly emphasised:

"The keystone of all pedagogic innovation is without question the *initial and in-service training of teachers*... Teacher training constitutes the priority of priorities. Future teachers, and those who are already practising, must be given the opportunity to acquire in-depth knowledge on the problems of immigrant children, as well as the principles of making them welcome, pedagogical support, and intercultural education" [EEC (84) 244, pp. 4 and 37].

Strategically speaking, teacher training is a choice means of adapting schools to the needs of the children who attend them. This training "controls the functioning of the educational systems and the teaching they provide" [Porcher, 1979]. Training occupies an upstream position "and thus makes of each teacher a sort of relay-station in the dissemination of new knowledge... Moreover, in relation to the preparation of teaching materials, training takes first priority: while the trained teacher is capable of utilising or creating specialised teaching aids, such materials, no matter how elaborate, can never take the place of the trained teacher" [Liégeois, 1983b, p.6]. The authorities seem to be aware of the necessity for comprehensive training and even of supplementing this with specialised training for those who will be working with multicultural classes – yet such recognition is all too often in theory only, and the familiar correlation of teaching failure with lack of appropriate training, remains.

There is a long road between awareness and putting it into practical action, and teacher training (which would, in comparison to teaching practice in the broad sense, be relatively easy to modify) is taking a long time to evolve. The following analysis of the Belgian situation applies in most countries:

"The question of initial and in-service teacher training in relation to immigrant children has had no systematic response at the level of teacher training colleges. There is a gap between immigration policy and education policy which is astonishing in a country like Belgium, which has been actively recruiting foreign workers for over forty years!" [Bastenier et al, 1985, p.74, quoted by Reyniers].

One can be all the more "astonished" when considering the situation facing Gypsy populations: they have been present in Europe not for forty, but for over five hundred, years, and yet in most states a coherent overall policy as regards their children's schooling has yet to be put into practice. What is the present situation as regards teacher training?

- "No special training of teachers at any level" [*Greece*, Korré/Marselos].

- "There is no criterion for specialisation other than the experience acquired through ongoing contact with Traveller children and their environment" [*Belgium*, Reyniers].

- "Teachers are often seconded to specialised posts without any previous experience, but it usually takes them at least two weeks in post before they start describing themselves as experts on the Gypsies. In this report and in general parlance in UK education, a 'specialist' is anyone who has been appointed to a special post in Gypsy education" [*United Kingdom*, Acton/Kenrick].

- "It is not possible to specialise in education for itinerant community children during teacher training; nor are any specialised re-training facilities provided in this field" [the *Netherlands*, Hovens et al].

- "One can speak of teacher 'specialisation' only in terms of their experience, and this occurs only when the school happens to be situated near a concentration of Gypsies... Teachers dealing with Sinti children are utterly unprepared for the task. They don't even have an opportunity for supplementary training once they are in the job" [*FRG*, Reemtsma].

- "Teachers of Travellers are 'specialised' only in the sense that their pupils are expected to be 'special' i.e. in need of remedial education. Several teachers who replied to the questionnaires stated that they had special training but this transpired to be a Diploma in Special Education, which is basically remedial teaching... Neither the basic training course nor the special education course relate specifically to Travellers. They are mentioned in a remedial context" [*Ireland*, McCarthy].

This last point is made in other countries, notably *France* and *Italy*. Insofar as "Gypsy" teachers have "complementary" or "specialised" training, it is invariably geared towards work with the physically or mentally handicapped. Even when, as in France, specialist training for the additional category of "the socially handicapped" exists, it by no means covers the specific needs of Gypsy children. Teachers themselves feel that they have not been given adequate training and in France this has given rise to an ironic but telling pun: teachers say that CAEI (Certificate of Aptitude for Teaching Maladjusted Children) really stands for Certificate of Aptitude for Maladjusted Teaching.

This lack of training is all the more glaring in that the teachers who have expressed such opinions in the course of research are the very people directly responsible for the schooling of Gypsy and Traveller children. These are the teachers who, painfully aware of their lack of training, make every effort to train and inform themselves. Yet this makes one wonder about the other teachers, untrained, uninformed, and seemingly unconcerned, underlying the rising number of "specialised" classes being run by teachers who are not. Such classes are the trendy new vessels into which a very ordinary and rigid content (the teacher bringing his own methods) is to be accommodated. Yet experience shows that it is frequently the vessel which is forced to modify under pressure of the rigidity of the content, or else the vessel shatters and the content remains, triumphant but alone and useless. The end result is failure, the causes of which are always sought and found elsewhere, notably among the children and their parents. As for ordinary classes: either the "question" of Gypsy presence does not arise at all, except in relation to the (purportedly negative) effects it has on the rest of the class, or else there is lip-service to the ideal of interculturalism while lamenting that lack of equipment or training makes it impossible to practise. A third possibility is that there are half-baked, half-hearted, uncoordinated gestures, as if one could "do a bit of interculturalism" in the same way as one might "do a bit of crafts". *Interculturalism can be spontaneous – that is how the children themselves live it – but it cannot be haphazard. The teacher who wishes to practise it,* and whom the authorities require to practise it, *must be trained in it.*

Teachers receive both basic and in-service training. In the situation as it stands, what principles should underlie initial training for future teachers of Traveller children, and permeate educational material? At present general agreement, in theory at least, has been reached on this question, and should facilitate the implementation of new types of training. The overall trend is to train all teachers to appreciate – that is, to recognise, understand and respect – the multiplicity of cultures which their future pupils may represent. Thus the idea of "categorisation" or "specialisation" in initial training is being replaced, since such specialisation at the initial stages runs the risk of limiting the teacher's options, and increases the risk of "ghettoising" his classes. It appears that the few advocates of early specialisation do not fully appreciate the consequences such an approach would have. Nearly all of them seem to do it as a reaction to the general lack of specialised training – and when we consider how unprepared the overwhelming majority of teachers of Gypsy children initially are, suggestions for radical change seem in order. But this sort of suggestion is unrealistic: when we consider the painful slowness with which most school systems are tackling the question of training teachers to deal with a multiplicity of cultures, it would be too much to hope that some would be trained specifically for dealing with Travellers.

Consensus, then, tends to favour intercultural pedagogy. This implies that, since no one can learn everything there is to know about every culture, the next best thing is to teach the trainee how to learn about the cultures he does encounter, as he encounters them. Since no training, including culture-comprehension, can be entirely abstract, it is at this point that trainees should be introduced to elements of Gypsy/Traveller culture, as well as Islamic and so on, in accordance with the cultural mix of the country in question. For Gypsies and Travellers, this would constitute an important validation of their culture, and a chance to modify stereotypes and prejudices concerning them. For their part the trainees (regardless of their future careers) will be able to pass on these new insights to those around them. In any case, to a greater or lesser degree depending on the state, Traveller culture is a constant – perhaps the only constant – in the cultural makeup of Europe. Apart from this didactic use of "the Gypsy paradigm" in training, if there is a "problem" in connection with the schooling of Gypsy and Traveller children in a given country, "the perspective of interculturalism implies that all those involved in a given school system, should be concerned with the problem" [Porcher, 1979, p.18].

During an international seminar on "The Training of Teachers for Gypsy Children", organised by the Council of Europe, participants submitted the following general proposals for all teachers:

"• Training must first incorporate into its programme, elements of general pedagogy which are highly relevant to the present question:
  - Training in teamwork, for practice in consultation under different circumstances.
  - On the other hand, preparing trainees to take account of cultural background, including such elements of this as may be in conflict with the teacher's own.
  - Moreover, on the linguistic level, training in such concepts as 'language status', and the relationship between language and culture, seems necessary.
• Since it is likely that all teachers will be called upon to teach in an intercultural situation of one sort or another, it would be interesting to touch upon the following themes/topics:
  - Other pedagogical systems and their psychological bases; other (non-verbal) communications systems.
  - Some elements of ethnology, anthropology and sociology, not to give a complete picture of the cultures one is likely to encounter, but to give the trainee familiarity with concepts and methodology he will be using later on.
  - The attitudes and tools required when teaching the official language of the class, as a second language – which it will be, for some of the pupils.
  - The necessity of establishing genuine dialogue with parents from socio-cultural minorities, the initial groundwork for which will always have to be done by the teacher himself.
  - Intercultural pedagogy as a practice of taking into account differences linked to membership of a socio-cultural minority...

Finally, it must be stressed that the central objective of the work must remain to modify dominant attitudes and the ideology from which they spring, to enable the education system to undergo the transformations outlined here" [Council of Europe, 1984, pp. 32-33].

A report from *Sweden*, by the Government Commission for Immigrants' Languages and Cultures in Schools and Adult Education (*Språk- och kulturarvsutredningen* – SKU) arrived at the same conclusions, and it is interesting to quote some of their basic points concerning the training of personnel:

"SKU has already discussed the situation of multicultural schools, and has argued that all members of the school community need to know more about other cultures and their values, to be made more aware of their own values, to acquire greater preparedness for resolving conflicts involved in cultural encounters, to cope with negative attitudes and prejudice and so forth... These changes are not confined to schools or municipalities with large immigrant contingents; they affect every school and they affect Swedish society as a whole. Consequently, all school employees today have the major responsibility of ensuring that encounters between cultures and different values in the school sector will contribute towards a pattern of social development in Sweden characterised by closer understanding between the majority and minorities. Social development of this kind will not come automatically, and school staff need and – as SKU sees it – are entitled to demand thorough preparation in order to take their share of responsibility for favourable developments... Teachers should particularly be taught:

- to become aware of different cultural manifestations in their own cultures and in those of immigrant communities;

- to learn to recognise and overcome ethnocentricity and stereotypes in school and society;

- to realise that they themselves are involved in a process of cultural interaction and to develop and utilise strategies of approaching, understanding and showing due consideration for other cultures.

These are the premises which SKU feels should be applied not only to teacher education but also in the training of all school staff, so as to achieve positive intercultural changes of attitudes in school and in society at large" [SKU, 1984, pp.69-70].

Cautiously – very cautiously – different states are beginning to implement training programmes which should contribute to developing a pedagogy better adapted to those at whom it is aimed. And, little by little, Gypsies and Travellers are appearing in these programmes. In the *FRG* at the University of Oldenburg, a seminar on the history and present situation of Sinti and Roma is being planned for winter 1985, aimed at future teachers and community workers, within a wider framework of "Intercultural Pedagogy Studies" [Reemtsma]. In the *United Kingdom*, some teacher training institutions (colleges, polytechnics, Institutes of Higher Education) have introduced some references to Gypsies in their curricula – although not always in the best context, e.g. under "Deprivation" [Acton/Kenrick]. It must be emphasised yet again – and the brevity of the remark must in no way detract from its importance – that *training must be of an extremely high standard both in presentation and in content, otherwise it reinforces stereotypes instead of reducing them.*

Attention should be drawn to the existence of complementary – specialised – initial training available within some systems. The future teacher, having completed his basic diploma, can continue his training by choosing from among options. Such options, when they exist, are almost always geared towards specialised instruction for handicapped children. Where the schooling difficulties of immigrant children have become a major issue, the general trend has been simply to extend the range covered under existing options – in France, among others, by inventing the new category of "social handicap", which remains a mere sub-option among the handicaps. Teachers themselves are the first to recognise the uselessness of such training when they find themselves trying to reason in terms of different cultures and languages; they also find an ominous undertone in the way that their training gears them to interpret everything in terms of handicap and inadequacy/deprivation. The only advantages are that the extra training permits the teacher to work in a "special" class, with a smaller number of pupils (certainly an important consideration) and better pay (no minor incentive). Working conditions are doubtless better, but the pedagogy is inappropriate. It is high time to draw a clear line between fields which have nothing in common in the first place, rather than to continue to lump together individual handicaps and the handicaps supposedly shared by all children of a given minority culture. It is preferable to keep preparation for teaching Gypsy children as far as possible from this type of option.

In-service training

In-service training is all the more indispensable since, as we have seen, as things stand at the moment nothing of relevance is provided at the initial stages. What is more, intercultural pedagogy will take some time to be put into practice, and longer still for its effects to be felt. In-service training by contrast can take quick and easy forms, contributing to an intercultural approach or building on it where it has been introduced at the initial stage. This is all the more important as the average age of teaching staff is on the rise: there is a general drop in recruitment to the profession, so much so in fact that "in the near future, the minister will have to rely on in-service training to transform teachers' teaching habits" [Carraz, 1983, p.243].

In-service training is characterised by its flexibility and adaptability: different levels (from the newly-qualified to the experienced teacher), different places (local, regional or national level), variable duration (from a conference to a long course), with the programme always adapted to fit the circumstances. These combined factors render in-service training ideally suited to the task in hand: training competent, adaptable teachers who may become specialists, but who will also be able to change direction during their career, if they so wish. Yet concerted, long-term reflection is no more apparent in connection with in-service training, than at the initial stage.

A few steps have been taken, but have been far from sufficient nor indeed always profitable to the participants. The number of teachers taking part has been very low, even in the case of teachers "specialised" by the fact of their presence in a "Gypsy" class. The situation is often ridiculous: research in one country showed that of 132 such "specialist" teachers, only three had received any kind of training – and that, by attending a single course run by an organisation approved by the ministry in charge. The same research showed that of twenty-three remedial teachers, only eight had done the course in question. Information from other countries confirms that this is the situation elsewhere, too. And in certain cases – thankfully on the decrease – those teachers who do attend even such brief training sessions must do so at their own initiative, their own expense, and sometimes without official authorisation. So what should we infer about the training of those teachers who do not deal with Travellers on a day-to-day basis?

Training, as it stands, is characterised on the whole by its *scarcity*. The teacher may take part in a conference – if he happens to know of its existence. He can take part in a seminar lasting a couple of days – maybe even up to a week. During his summer holidays he may attend supplementary training organised by an association of volunteer teachers. One of the most regular examples is that provided in England by the Department of Education and Science (and despite its merits it simply illustrates this state of scarcity, when we consider how many teachers could potentially have benefited): from 1973-75 it held an annual five-day training session open to teachers from throughout the United Kingdom; from 1976, the frequency was reduced to once every two years. Local school authorities and inspectors have also organised occasional one-day training sessions. In France, the highly-developed CEFISEM (Training and Information Centres on Schooling for Immigrant Children) network, to which the ministry has given responsibility for training teachers for Gypsy and Traveller children, has few resources to develop this; courses are rare and brief, and reach only a limited number of teachers.

This "training" also presents an image of *disorganisation*. The programme tends to be made up of bits and bobs, usually dictated by who happens to be free to come and speak at the time. It is usually organised by people whose competence, and day-to-day work, lie elsewhere than in the teaching of Traveller children and who, as much by amalgamating diverse topics (childhood maladjustment, immigrant children, Gypsy children, etc.) as by failing to recognise those who could usefully contribute to the programme, end up by providing teachers with a jumbled kaleidoscope, the pieces of which are so unrelated, or so irrelevant to the task in hand, that they cannot be applied in the teacher's daily work. What is more, many sessions are of a purely informational nature. Information is of course an essential element of training, but insufficient in itself; it needs to be supplemented by more detailed problem-solving, more links between the subjects covered, and progression into increasingly complex questions.

Moreover, recruitment of participants is haphazard indeed. Frequently, teachers with a decade or more of experience in Gypsy classes, in search of in-depth debate on, for example, alternative approaches to the teaching of literacy, who have published their reflections on the subject and know more about it than do their "instructors", find themselves side-by-side with newly-qualified teachers who have been a couple of weeks in a Gypsy class and haven't got round to reading anything on the subject as yet, posing naive questions in search of some general background information. Whatever category the participant happens to fall into, he will be disappointed because his needs are not being met. Some will attend future sessions in the hope of getting something out of them, or because it is always pleasant to meet and chat with colleagues, but others, deeply disillusioned, will no longer bother.

This situation is the result of assimilation policies pursued up to the present: postulating a goal of assimilation for a given population implies logically that its culture will not be taken into account to an extent meriting courses explaining it. Yet this situation can – if the will is there – be redressed much more easily than trying to remodel initial training. Certainly, experience and routine are not sufficient. As the Swedish report quoted above stresses: "New models of teacher training therefore need to be developed and tested where cultural competence is concerned" [SKU, 1984, p.73]. And the European synthesis report, also quoted earlier, insists on the importance of in-depth training:

"In-service training must be supplemented by *complementary training*, open both to newly-qualified and to experienced teachers. High-level complementary training should be available to the latter in particular, in order that further pedagogical counsellors and providers of in-service training may be recruited from their ranks. Such training will doubtless remain, for a considerable period, the preferred means of training specialised teachers who, back in their own schools, will promote pedagogical adaptation and cultural openness" [EEC (84) 244, p.31].

Change in this area is all the easier to accomplish since appropriate training facilities already exist in every country, and are already geared towards a full range of courses (single day courses, short residential courses, longer courses, regional and national courses, etc.). As pointed out above, the characteristics of in-service training combine to make it capable of adapting to needs as they arise. All that is required, then, is *innovation, both in deployment of existing means, and in training content*. If there is no evolution along these lines, it will be because there is no will to evolve. It is not even possible to plead lack of finance as a justification for maintaining the status quo – little additional means are required, and would be far less costly in material and psychological terms than even the short-term effects of inappropriate pedagogy, not to mention the indirect administrative expenses of following up children who are not in school, and the very considerable long-term cost of the social services they may require for want of vocational training.

Every training course should include a detailed workplan, to ensure that participants are *all at a similar level*, and that the course is *geared to their needs*: frequent mention is made of the necessity for separate introductory and advanced courses. Such proposals – already an improvement on existing practice – would seem a little too dichotomous, and perhaps it would be preferable to visualise training in the form of thematic "modules". Some of these could of course be "introductory" modules aimed at a wide public (including non-teaching staff and personnel working outside the school system) while others could be more specialised (e.g.linguistics, teaching literacy) and aimed at a broader (regional or national) catchment area, while still others could be specifically for experienced teachers to enable them to trade insights and, for example, cooperate to develop adapted reading materials.

When in-service training becomes training worthy of the name, surpassing simple information or consciousness-raising, it is important that the qualifications attained by teachers who have undergone such courses, be officially recognised, just as specialists in other fields are recognised (e.g. that they would have priority for promotion within the field). This is why the term used in the European report quoted above – *complementary training* – is worth retaining; it implies real deepening of existing knowledge and the acquisition of new competence better than the term "in-service training", which is often a synonym for simple recycling or refresher courses which every teacher must undergo.

The flexibility inherent in complementary training also enables it to make immediate use of the variety of skills available among the Gypsy and Traveller population, which can complement the roles played by others on the training team: schools inspectors, experienced teachers, university personnel, researchers and so on. As the European report notes, participation develops the competence of instructors as well as those instructed – for example the experienced teacher may become a regional pedagogical counsellor. What is required in the short term, in addition to political and pedagogical will, is *appropriate training. A small-scale provisional framework could be set up at national level, with the task of coordinating, consulting* all concerned, eventually *proposing* practical measures, *implementing training programmes and assessing their effectiveness.* In many countries such experimental units already exist, active to a greater or lesser degree. At the end of this report, having completed our overall evaluation, we will return to the question of recommending measures for implementation.

Information

Information is doubly important for the teacher: he must be informed, and he must inform others. And, in the case of Gypsies and Travellers, a great deal of available information offers only distorted images. *Prejudiced and stereotyped images permeate this information, to which the teacher has generally been exposed since childhood, and are in turn inclined to colour the images he transmits in class,* since he rarely has access to corrective material. What is more, a certain number of schoolbooks also perpetrate negative stereotypes of the Gypsy. "Popular" negative images are then overlaid by current political ideology: "the Gypsy is socially maladjusted". By manipulation of words and images, he is made to fit into existing categories. Having thus amalgamated the "causes" of various problems, the next step is to think up a blanket means of "solving" them. Difference is perceived in terms of deprivation, and a policy of re-adaptation is undertaken. Teachers, even if they do succeed in discarding general anti-Traveller stereotypes, are still not always vigilant enough when they come across them (be they of the malignant or the "folklorising" variety) amongst their non-Gypsy pupils or in school textbooks, nor are they always untainted by more modern "official line" stereotypes. Teachers' attitudes do tend to remain just as ethnocentric, in their teaching, when dealing with children of any other culture, as they are when faced with Gypsy and Traveller children. In monocultural teaching there is a tendency to dismiss cultural and linguistic factors as so many hurdles to be overcome – whereas the intercultural stance treats the same factors as a vital driving force to be harnessed constructively. This is why the monocultural teacher attempts to suppress use of the child's mother tongue, which he sees simply as a block to mastering the language of the school.

Thus the teacher's erroneous concepts of the Gypsy child and his family directly influence his teaching, which is consequently inappropriate. Such concepts can also lead to scholastic failure. There is no point in analysing here exactly what prejudices and stereotypes teachers commonly hold; it is of interest, however, to point out some of the consequences that they may have.

We shall do this by referring to the well-known but often ignored phenomenon, "the Pygmalion Effect" (quoting from the book by Rosenthal and Jacobson, 1968). The initial hypothesis is that "one person's expectations of another's behaviour may come to serve as self-fulfilling prophecies".

In a school situation, children were chosen by lot, their "difference" – invented by the researchers and confided only to the teachers who would be dealing with them – being that they would make spectacular intellectual progress over the coming year. And, for these randomly chosen children, such was indeed the case. Let us add a few remarks concerning some Mexican pupils of whom the same prediction was made: "After the first year of the experiment, and also after the second year, the Mexican children showed greater expectancy advantages than did the non-Mexican children... These magnitudes of expectancy advantages were then correlated with the 'Mexican-ness' of the children's faces. After one year, and after two years, those boys who looked more Mexican benefited more from their teachers' positive prophecies. Teachers' pre-experimental expectancies for these boys' intellectual performance were probably lowest of all. Their turning up on a list of probable bloomers must have surprised their teachers. Interest may have followed surprise and, in some way, increased watching for signs of brightness may have led to increased brightness... There may be here the makings of a benign cycle. Teachers may not only get more when they expect more; they may also come to expect more when they get more" [Rosenthal and Jacobson, pp. 177-8].

On the subject of the Mexicans who, as objects of favourable prejudice, progressed well, there was nevertheless a tendency on the part of teachers to consider them as "less curious intellectually": "It seemed almost as though, for these minority-group children, intellectual competence may have been easier for teachers to bring about than to believe... Teachers may require a certain amount of preparation to be able to accept the unexpected classroom behaviour of the intellectually upwardly mobile child" [ibid, p.178]. To put it another way – and this is the dominant reality – preconceptions are stronger than empirical evidence.

The authors list conclusions of vital importance for training and information: "The experiment described in this book shows that change in teacher expectation can lead to improved intellectual performance... As teacher-training institutions begin to teach the possibility that teachers' expectations of their pupils' performance may serve as self-fulfilling prophecies, there may be a new expectancy created. The new expectancy may be that children can learn more than had been believed possible... The man on the street may be permitted his opinions and prophecies of the unkempt children loitering in a dreary schoolyard. The teacher in the schoolroom may need to learn that those same prophecies within her may be fulfilled; she is no casual passer-by. Perhaps Pygmalion in the classroom is more her role" [ibid, pp.181-2].

Let us recall that Pygmalion was a famous Cypriot sculptor. He fell in love with one of his own statues and was heartbroken by its lifelessness. In the end, Venus brought it to life so that he could marry it. Is this not – symbolically – the story of so many teachers who are successful with Gypsy and Traveller classes? – But who is Venus?

Before the child has had any chance to demonstrate his grasp of reading and writing, he is judged – he is *prejudged* – by the teacher to whom he presents himself, all the more so if he happens to be a nomad passing through. The teacher's interpretation of the child's presumed capacities and motivations will in turn influence the child's behaviour.

"Never disbelieve a Travelling child, because if you do, he will lose faith in you and class you as a *shade* (policeman). Fear of the police is a big problem with Travelling children... that should also be tackled... But no matter who it is that approaches a Travelling child or his parents... the expression on your face must be relaxed... and before you speak you must mean what you say, because the Traveller child wants to find out if you are just an insidious person, just waiting to snare him, or if you have come to really help....

The education of Travelling children adds up to one thing. We cannot rob them of what they already know. If we change their beliefs, we destroy them. Therefore it is important that Gaujos (non-Gypsies) should believe them as much as they can. I know we cannot believe everything a child says. Knowledge on top of what they already know will teach them to read between the lines.

Galyune na monya na Pavee and Rom, Buff, Gaujo, clim skuck landoon anocha an world! (Oh God! Be good to Irish Travellers and Rom and house-dwellers and Gadjé, on water or on land anywhere in the world!)" ["Pops" Johnny Connors (an Irish Traveller), "The Education of Travelling Children", in *National Gypsy Education Council Newsletter*, no. 3, 1971, pp. 2-4, quoted by Acton/Kenrick].

The teacher's attitude will elicit a certain type of response from the child. Information is essential if these effects are to be modified, and "certainly the teacher must learn how to teach, but he must also learn how to acquire knowledge" [Liégeois, 1983b, p.6]. The notion of information, like that of specialisation, is very subjective. Some will believe themselves "informed" after reading a bit – and often regardless of the quality of the material they have read. Practice in this field remains inadequate, and for two reasons. First, the attitude of some teachers, who consider themselves to have been trained once and for all, and for any conceivable situation – and who therefore feel no need to acquire further training. It is sometimes a case of "those teachers unwilling to contemplate innovation, who sometimes seem to regard being asked to read a book (when they've already been trained once!) as an assault on their professional integrity" [Acton/Kenrick]. Others simply don't make the effort to get hold of and acquaint themselves with the relevant literature – several reports stress how little reading teachers actually do. Lack of will? Lack of time? Lack of professional dedication? Or lack of access to the documents?

Which leads us to the second cause, closely related to the first: production and distribution of information on the schooling of Gypsy and Traveller children is at an embryonic stage. The first steps have been widely varied: general or specific booklets, liaison newsletters, evaluation reports of an annual or more frequent nature, minutes of training sessions and meetings, miscellaneous reports, students' dissertations on school-related topics, video and slide shows, etc., with producers and audiences as varied as the media employed. A significant amount of information, and of material, is already available. But analysis here leads us to the same conclusions as were reached regarding in-service training: lack of coherence due to what (up to now) has been a near-total lack of will on the part of the authorities, which results in haphazard localised efforts and an absence of effective coordination. The upshot is a squandering of effort, loss of information, duplication, a relative immobility despite the potential for "pedagogical advancement", and circulation of information within a small closed circle, giving the "chosen few" a sense of isolation while those outside it may have great difficulty in obtaining information which they, as teachers of Gypsy children, urgently need.

Here too, however, *all the necessary structures are already in existence*: documentation is available to teachers through local information centres, training colleges, school libraries, regional and national scholastic publishers, etc., yet even when the urgent need so apparent in this area gives rise to a desire for action, *an approach emphasising coordination of existing means, rather than the creation of new ones, is lacking.* As with complementary training, the various educational systems already have competent personnel which, if charged with this task, could coordinate various activities and participate in liaison and innovation. The same workteam could take charge of training and information – which cannot be separated – simultaneously.

The propagation of information is always a delicate task, as regards both form and content. The information itself must be above reproach; any information intended for use within the school system, by teachers or by pupils – whether it be a film, slide-show, text, etc. – must therefore be prepared by qualified personnel. There is always the danger of replacing one stereotype with another, or even of reinforcing existing ones by the very measures taken to eradicate them. It can happen that the net effect is to "reduce" prejudice much as a sauce is "reduced" – by boiling it down and concentrating it.

Let us give a brief summary of an experiment. Some 300 schoolchildren were divided into groups of twenty to thirty and given a questionnaire about Gypsies. After these had been filled in and collected, the children were (orally) given clear and accurate information, and a few days later they filled in the same questionnaires. "The effect of the information was to homogenise opinions: children who had never heard the myths were exposed to them, and those who had originally shown little prejudice showed an increase. On the other hand, those with an actively rejecting attitude had become latent – that is, they retained their negative attitude, but had learnt to hide it. We can thus conclude that every attempt to reduce prejudice is fraught with danger, since standard anti-racist information has the opposite effect to that intended" [Dégrange, 1981, p.19; for more details see Dégrange, 1978].

In fact, the questions that information may move people to ask are as important as any convictions it may impart.

This setting right of general attitudes towards the Gypsy will have a major impact on the conditions of his schooling. The task will be long and difficult, and the school itself will have to set the example, since the methods and materials it evolves can obviously be used by a wider public. In the overall scholastic context, books portraying Gypsy/Traveller cultural reality are surely a powerful means of combating prejudice; indeed they already exist in many countries – but how widely used are they? Such information should be built upon – and insofar as possible, in cooperation with Gypsies and Travellers themselves. This in itself will entail great mutual effort, in order to transform collaboration from the rarity it is at present, to an established pattern. Moreover, "The fact that Gypsy reality is extremely diverse necessitates an overall presentation which takes the form of an introduction to the general *spirit* of Gypsy culture and social organisation, rather than attempting to give too detailed a picture. Such an approach also avoids a vulgarisation of those elements of cultural intimacy which Gypsies would rather not have all and sundry gawking at" [Liégeois, 1983b, p.37].

Mention must also be made of all sorts of books (particularly of short illustrated histories aimed at six- to twelve-year-olds) to be found in school libraries, and which can also be used in class. They must be selected and used with caution, since presentation in a classroom context greatly increases their impact on the children, and even on parents, since they feel that use by the teacher legitimises the content. It is important to consider such works very carefully, and it is worth consulting the analyses made by experts on the subject [for example Binns, 1984; Dégrange, 1980; Kenrick, 1984; see also Ferté, 1985].

We shall conclude our reflections on this subject by pointing out that it is often possible to involve a very broad public in information and/or training programmes: the pupils' parents, Gypsy organisations, all of the teaching staff (not just the "specialised" teachers), the local community, and, through the mass media, wider audiences yet may be reached.

The Teacher Training College at Levanger in Norway implemented a wide-ranging programme of this kind over a three-year period (1976-79): critical analysis of existing documents (books, films, press-cuttings); cultural evenings (aimed at students, lecturers, and the local populace) with music, dance, theatre and photographs; a press conference; liaison with local schools; exhibitions; discussing what they were doing with Gypsies; bringing in specialist teachers to talk to the trainees; using work done in connection with the programme as a basis for teaching material for future trainees; preparing teaching materials (brochures, photos, books, cassettes, press clippings) for primary schools; using "television for schools" to help children to get to know something about Gypsies. The main participants in the project were later invited to other areas, notably Oslo, to help in teacher training and other information campaigns. Teaching materials were revised with the collaboration of Oslo Gypsies. The school authorities recognised their value and recommended their use [cf. Schlüter, 1983b].

Liaison

The teacher's contacts with others in the school system contribute to his store of information and help him, even if only by acquainting him with new ideas and teaching techniques, to adapt his own teaching more appropriately. Liaison is an important form of support for teachers.

"What upsets me the most is that one gets caught up in a sort of diabolical treadmill, with no chance ever to stop and take stock, look back at what one's been doing, at what's working and what isn't. So – call it synthesis, teachers' conference, whatever – but we absolutely must get the time to evaluate our work, ask ourselves questions. When you asked us for commentary on what we're doing, I just couldn't answer, I had to say, 'I've never had the time to sit down and take note of what I've been doing over the past ten or twelve years – never!' The whole thing is incredible; we try to keep up, but we do no assessment whatsoever" [M. Ranucci, in Liégeois 1980d, p. 331].

Liaison can be brought about by various measures, preferably complementary. Among the most obvious possibilities are those teachers – hopefully with personal experience – whose role is to act as a link between teachers and other relevant bodies, while also bringing support to children in need of it: "liaison teachers", "visiting teachers", "integration teachers" as they are known in the various states where this provision is most widespread – notably the United Kingdom, Ireland, and the Netherlands. The principle remains the same from country to country:

"Government funds are provided to release a teacher from the caravan centre school, either full-time or part-time... This teacher – known as an integration teacher – provides information to the receiving school and practical support to teachers responsible for educating these children" [the *Netherlands*, Hovens et al].

"One of the most encouraging and effective steps which has been taken in the last three years... has been the appointment by the Department of Education of a visiting teacher service. These teachers work with the families, the teachers and the social workers in the whole area of Traveller education. They co-operate with teachers who have Traveller children in their classes, sorting out individual problems, visiting families who are not sending their children to school, notifying the relevant authority of specific needs, helping to provide a homework service where necessary, identifying further needs for educational provision in the area, and in general ensuring the successful attendance at school of as many Traveller children in their areas as possible. As Regional Representatives of the Association of Teachers of the Travelling People, they also enable groups of teachers from schools in their areas to meet together and discuss their problems and aspirations" [*Ireland*, Dwyer, 1984, p.8].

The following description from *England* (Inner London Education Authority) allows us to grasp the essential role of the "liaison teacher": "When the Travellers move onto an empty piece of land, teachers visit them to find out which families are there and how many children will require school places. The nearest schools are then located and a meeting arranged with them to find out how many places are available. Once places have been allocated, the teachers meet the school staff to discuss the children's work and educational experience, and to talk about their way of life and the day to day pressures on them.

The ILEA recognise Travellers as an ethnic minority and, as such, it is essential that schools acknowledge this. Like most other minority groups they are subject to harassment, stereotyping and myths. It is, therefore, important that in schools Travellers should be seen as part of the multicultural curriculum which reflects and values their lives. A good, practical anti-racist policy will greatly assist Traveller children into settling down in a school. To help provide continuity the children have folders of work which go with them from school to school. This is to help the class teacher provide appropriate work as a continuous process, even if it goes on in a number of schools...

When the Travellers leave a school their teachers collect their folders and the process begins again... Travellers are rarely allowed to remain in any area for more than a few weeks and are not generally regarded as part of the local community. When they do move into an area teachers and children in school may have little knowledge about their way of life and the pressures they face, and this may make it more difficult for Traveller children to be accepted and settle down in the school... A video/slide programme has been produced by the teaching team, providing background information to enable teachers to take account of the culture of the children they teach and to help other children to understand the Travellers' way of life, their history and background and the daily organisation required for living without basic facilities" [Dave Cannon, in *Traveller Education*, no. 19, 1984, pp.18-19].

In a more localised fashion, within a given school, liaison can be an intermittent process, for example with various teachers occasionally spending a half-day in an (all- or part-) Gypsy class. This will enable them to understand the children better before receiving them into their own classes, and will also increase their understanding of the teacher who usually deals with them (this type of contact was successfully developed as a pilot scheme in Blanquefort, France). At a broader level, liaison can also occur between different administrative bodies (for example between the school authorities and the Department of Health and Social Welfare in Elsinore, Denmark). At a national level, three states have taken measures in the direction suggested above for implementing training and information. In *Ireland* the post of National Coordinator for the Education of Travelling People, financed by the Department of Education, has existed since 1974. In the *United Kingdom*, there are two inspectors – HMIs – (reduced to one in 1986) working in England whose main focus is on schooling for Gypsy and Traveller children. In the *Netherlands*, activities are coordinated by the network of National Centres for Pedagogic Counselling (LPCs):

"A news-sheet entitled *Van Wagen naar School* ("From Caravan to School") edited by the LPCs is issued quarterly. The magazine, which is widely distributed among persons concerned with the education of caravan and Gypsy children, contains information on new developments, measures, studies, literature, activities, seminars, teaching materials and methods, audio-visual facilities, etc. in this field. The LPCs also coordinate regional meetings of schools, integration teachers, local school advisory services and so on and local or regional, inter-disciplinary cooperative bodies. These meetings concentrate on sharing experiences and the discussion of specific topics of common interest. Similarly there is an interchange of experience at national level. This is channelled through two national bodies, once again coordinated and chaired by the LPCs, namely the 'Committee on Secondary Education for Caravan and Gypsy Children' and the 'Central Curriculum Committee'. The committees include representatives from the Ministry of Education and Science, the Ministry of Welfare, Health and Cultural Affairs, the inspectorates for special education, nursery/primary and secondary education, the National Caravan Welfare Officers, the National Youth Educational Institute, secondary schools, caravan-centre schools, Gypsy schools and ordinary primary schools. Apart from the interchange of experience these committees coordinate activities in the fields of development, guidance and counselling, research, evaluation and so on" [Hovens et al].

Again at the national level, associations for specialised teachers exist in three countries. In *Ireland* the Association for Teachers of the Travelling People (ATTP), founded in 1972, now has about 300 members. The association plays an important role of liaison and information exchange among teachers: a biannual newsletter, biannual conferences, organising summer training courses, as well as local and regional meetings. In the *United Kingdom* the National Association of Teachers of Travellers (NATT), founded in 1979 and reserved for teachers actively engaged in teaching Traveller children, had fifty-eight members in the 1984-85 school year. Two other UK organisations also exist, with membership open to non-teachers, in which Gypsy/non-Gypsy cooperation is developing apace; these are the National Gypsy Education Council (NGEC) and the Advisory Committee for the Education of Romany and other Travellers (ACERT). In *France*, the *Comité de Liaison et d'Information Voyage-Ecole* (CLIVE – "Travel-School Liaison and Information

Committee") was founded recently, in 1985. A preliminary circular defined the association's functions as follows:

"In view on the one hand of communication difficulties between various participants in the education system, involved in the schooling of Gypsy children;
and on the other, that by nature the schooling of Gypsy children does not neatly fit the administrative and geographic pigeonholes of the Ministry of National Education;
the Yvelines group working on this issue feels it necessary to set up a regional association with the goal of facilitating a better relationship between Gypsy reality and the demands of the school.

Such an association would permit:
- better distribution of information regarding the schooling of Gypsy children;
- the creation of a forum for reflection;
- the setting up of a memory bank, maintaining a link between the people directly concerned and those who are called upon to fulfil other functions."

The initiative turned out to be a response to a nationally felt need, and CLIVE's membership now includes teachers from many regions. They have already published some "Information Sheets", and are working on "Files" on different themes, including Legislation, Gypsies Talk About School, Reading Tools, Case Studies, a Directory.

As the founders of the French association point out in referring to a "memory bank", liaison makes it possible to accumulate knowledge and avoid the endless repetition of failed educational "experiments". It gives teachers a chance to compare notes, with each other and with others in the field. It opens up possibilities for complementarity and comparing progress at every level, from the local to the international. It facilitates exchange of ideas, confrontation of methods, and discussion of end results. What is more, before undertaking any action of their own, people planning projects can only benefit from first studying what is being done in other countries, and how effective it is proving.

The need for liaison is now accepted everywhere, and in every country there are more and more meetings for discussion and evaluation between teachers and with other concerned partners, notably school inspectors, social workers and parents. They do not, however, always take place under the best possible conditions. Whether formal or informal, such meetings must be given administrative recognition – both to allow a maximum of teachers to attend, and to affirm their role of liaison with other personnel (inspectors, education advisors), other structures and organisations (training centres, resource centres, teachers' and teaching-related associations) and other measures (regular meetings, newsletters). Such recognition presupposes full administrative support and subsequent availability of facilities (which are in fact usually forthcoming, yet without overall coordination).

Liaison means liaison with parents, too. "It might seem all too obvious, but the key factor is the existence of a good relationship between the school and the parents. Without the parents' cooperation each and every initiative is doomed to failure" [Hovens et al]. This statement expresses a principle which is generally recognised as relevant to schooling of all kinds, but it becomes particularly important in the

Gypsies' situation. These few lines stand out all the more strongly when we consider them in the light of our socio-historical and socio-political analysis, and when we go on, in the next chapter, to examine the important division between the school's purposes and those of the parents.

Liaison with parents first of all means continuing contact, in which one considers the child, his or her work, play, progress and difficulties. But it also means parents' participation in school life, in formal meetings. If the first type of contact is on the rise in certain countries, establishing itself as the norm it doubtless should be, it is still all too rare in others. Partly this is due to a general lack of parental involvement for various reasons, such as "administrative oversight" about organising consultation meetings, teachers' lack of enthusiasm or time, parental difficulties or even apathy. In such circumstances it is difficult for parents to present their point of view or to explain themselves in order to be better understood, and equally difficult for teachers to overcome certain stereotyped preconceptions they have of the parents' and children's wishes.

Each community defends its own position. Contact may then be limited to administrational requirements, such as enrolments and requests for certificates. If the school is situated near the families, on a halting site for example, it may be perceived as an integral part of "Gypsy territory" [Reyniers] and taken over by parents and children who may establish – many reports attest to this – "a power relationship. The parents are in permanent control of the teacher (she is accused of doing a bad job, making money off the Gypsies, etc.) and oppose her teaching practice (for example a father who storms into the school and publicly denounces the teacher who, in his opinion, is useless)" [Reyniers]. If the school is far away, it is seen as an alien institution into which parents must (compulsory schooling) deliver up their children. No more than when the school is seen as "Gypsy territory" are they willing to be intimidated by this alien universe, and for example "When they fetch their children from school and happen to be early, they do not wait but march straight into the classroom and simply take the child away; or they drive up to the classroom window and put an elbow on the horn" [Gustafsson, 1973, p.88]. The Gypsies have their reasons, but the school does not recognise or understand them.

Informal get-togethers may be held in an effort to ease relations: "A coffee morning was organised to bring the Gypsies and voluntary workers closer together. The Gypsies, however, displayed little or no interest in the coffee morning" [Teunissen, 1982, p.45]. In another country, during a "coffee evening" with a slide-show about Gypsy life, tensions developed and the slides disappeared for good. Quite apart from the fact that no coming together of teachers and parents took place, the latter strongly objected to such public display of Gypsy life. Many similar incidents could be cited. Yet it would be wrong to conclude too quickly, in the wake of failed initiatives, that "Unfortunately the evidence indicates that the parents of caravan and Gypsy children are not greatly involved in the education of their children". Appearances can be deceiving, and in fact the children's education, of which the parents are very attentive indeed, is not limited to schooling.

The absence of preliminary consultation means that planning the school, class, halting site, etc. is not a common/shared undertaking, and as a result personnel serving as intermediaries – teachers, social workers, ombudsmen – find themselves in a strained position. Let us quote the testimony of an ombudsman involved in a pilot scheme at Oldenzaal, in the *Netherlands*:

"Ombudsmen employed by the municipality generally have (or had) a twin function as ombudsman and point of contact. The ombudsman aspect consisted of winning the confidence of the Gypsies. At the same time he was required to convey policy decisions and communications from the municipality by which he was employed. This inevitably led to role conflicts; in one instance the official in question even resigned in order to escape the dilemma he was caught in... On the one hand I am required to promote the interests of the target group and on the other the interests of my employer. These interests by no means coincide but continually come into conflict with one another. This means that I repeatedly feel – and am – isolated!" [Teunissen, 1982, pp.36-37].

It is certain that inter-community conflict crosses the school threshold, and it is thus understandable that, for the moment, parents are none too willing to help teachers. In most cases, parental attitudes to the school structure oscillate between indifference and antagonism, even when contact – and good contact at that – exists with the teachers. Teachers may be respected personally, but this does not save them from criticism as representatives of an institution which is so often threatening or even coercive in its functioning. If the child feels ill at ease in school; if he is the subject of remarks (justified or not) from the teachers; if the other children reject him – his parents, his family, his whole group will always be behind him, supportive and protecting. It can happen, too, that the child plays up the situation, deliberately exaggerating his descriptions of school life, if he simply doesn't feel like going to class. His choice will be respected by his parents. How to change all this? "Certainly not by starting with the instruction of the children, but by (gaining) the acceptance of the parents... You don't water the leaves, you water the roots; the parents are the roots and that's where you have to start. Afterwards the leaves will unfurl and grow strong" [Yung, 1980a, pp.292-5; Mr. Yung is the President of *l'Union des Tsiganes et Voyageurs de France*].

Liaison and contact, if they are to lead to cooperation, presuppose a willingness for consultation on both sides. Too often, up to the present, either no steps have been taken (leaving each side distanced from the other, both of them misunderstanding and misunderstood), or else the assumption was made that the first steps would have to be forthcoming unilaterally from the Gypsy side. Yet here and there in various countries, within the recent past, mutual efforts are developing and do allow for the surmounting of conflict, apprehension and incomprehension. A process of reciprocal adaptability has been initiated. Contacts intensify; the teacher obtains a margin of freedom in which to establish and maintain them, or a mediator is appointed to this task, at the service of both teachers and parents. Parents take more active interest in their child's schoolwork. A few administrative innovations bring about a change in class life: parents are given access, and/or the possibility of making contact by telephone… Some teachers make enormous efforts to get closer to the Gypsies, though such efforts are not always entirely apt; for example the United Kingdom report mentions a teacher who hired himself out as a labourer during the holidays, to help a Gypsy sell used cars. The overall result was that his prestige fell in the eyes of Gypsy parents – because he had been a mere employee. (He should have been a partner, of equal status) [Acton/Kenrick]. Parental non-attendance at formal meetings is not so much a sign of apathy as of the alien-ness of that particular forum of discussion; these poorly-attended formal meetings are moreover, according to many reports, of little practical interest. Parents appear to take fall into two distinct camps: either unwavering enthusiastic approval, or systematic blanket criticism. The practice of consultation does not come easy:

"Only 30% of parents followed their children's schoolwork, and despite their desire for constructive contact with teachers, the relationship was often limited to brief and superficial dialogue. A genuine communication barrier generally exists between teachers and parents, stemming from the latter's illiteracy, which makes the whole concept of school and what it means to their children, incomprehensible. Seventy per cent refuse to comply with the various regulations of school bureaucracy, with the tired old justification, 'What's the use, after all we're Gypsies, that's what we'll stay; for us, nothing will ever change.' Underlying such phrases is a sad resignation, a lack of enthusiasm and aspiration for change or progress" [Bruno Morelli, statement quoted by Karpati/Massano].

During the pilot project in Bremen, "One of the essential didactic objectives of the project was to teach the Sinti that they were equal partners. In practice this consisted of having them participate in the planning of the project, through the intermediary of a consulting committee regulated by an agreement between the Bremer Volkshochschule and the Bremer Sinti Union. Putting the ideal of equal Sinti participation into practice turned out to be extremely difficult in many regards... There needs to be permanent and motivating work in order to get continued participation that goes beyond the immediate family circle... Participation, in the sense of critical collaboration in the realisation of the project, turned out in a large degree to be asking too much of the group... When questioned on this subject, the Sinti – particularly the older ones – repeated over and over again that it was enough that they had confidence in us. The idea of offering criticism was seen as a form of impoliteness springing from aggressive feelings, and consequently considered superfluous once confidence and unity had been established" [Bremer Volkshochschule,1983, pp.41-42].

Discussion enriches all participants. It gives the teacher a better understanding of the child, his education, background, and the parents' wishes, enabling him to adapt his methods accordingly. As for the parents, it is important that they be given proof so that they can feel the school "belongs" to their children just as much as it does to other pupils. But, in the present situation, is such a feeling possible? Would it be justified? Or would it be founded on illusion?

Gypsy teachers

"The best way to whet the children's appetite for knowledge is to have them taught by their own people. They would be best at getting the children to open up" [Jean Alciati, Director of the *Centre Culturel Tzigane*, in *Ouest-France* (newspaper) 31/10/1985]. Reflection on this subject is vital, and the brevity of proposals listed in this section must in no way minimise their impact. On the whole, reports which mention the topic are favourable to the employment of Gypsies and Travellers as teachers or auxiliaries; such work is seen as collaboration, as help, as a way of adapting the school to the children who attend it. But from theory to practice is a long road, and cases of Gypsy personnel on school staff are still rare indeed.

In *Ireland*, "A Traveller man did drive the school bus for a number of years... Another Traveller man is employed as an instructor in car maintenance in a training centre. Travellers are employed as childcare workers in at least three centres around the country... the trainees on the community development course which is being run at present hope to be employed in these kinds of posts... The Van Leer Foundation intends to establish mobile playgroups with direct Traveller involvement at all stages – from the building of the mobile to assisting in the playgroups" [McCarthy]. In the *Netherlands*, Gypsies were invited into schools to give talks on their way of life. In one case, "A Gypsy was appointed on an hourly basis to give folk-dancing lessons" [Hovens et al]. In the *FRG*, "In Cologne, two Sinti women work part-time in kindergarten." On another project, "In the first phase, there were lively discussions with the schools on the subject of different work methods, estimations of the children's capabilities, lots of misunderstandings, and a clear limitation of competency. These initial difficulties could not have been surmounted but for numerous consultation sessions with, and eventual organisation of a training seminar by, the Sinti Union, for the benefit of educators and community workers; they also paid visits to the courses, once these were under way" [Reemtsma].

In *Norway*, "Two Gypsies followed the courses of the Higher Institute of Pedagogy in Sagen, as mature students. Now they are teaching children through Romani. The experimental system implemented in 1978, stipulating that all Gypsy children should have Gypsy teachers, is progressing well" [Schlüter, 1983]. In an Oslo preschool, "Gypsy women were employed as assistants, which ensures the children both instruction in their own language, and their socialisation within their own culture" [ibid]. "If there is a Rom assistant, the children will come to school more often, they understand the teacher's instruction better and the cultural clash is softened. However, we lack Rom assistants, which in turn reflects cultural differences between the Norwegian society and the Rom-society" [Schlüter, MS.]. In *Greece* a pilot project was launched to train Gypsies as teachers; this is still going on, but the beginnings have been fraught with difficulty: "The results have inevitably been very limited because of the following reasons: a) there are few qualified Gypsies, at any level; b) their itinerary jobs don't allow them to be regular during the courses; c) their presence in the first seminar was very limited, though it took place in their own centre and they had been long aware about the subjects. The level of the procedure during the seminar was simple and accessible; d) there is enough hesitation on the part of Gypsies to be instructed by persons of their own community; 'Let's begin, even with "Gadjé"' they say. 'We'd prefer so' " [Korré/Marselos].

In *France* cultural, artistic, and crafts exhibitions are presented in school by Gypsy parents invited in to do so. Field trips also give Gypsy parents an opportunity to participate. Some auxiliary teachers are also employed [Ferté]. In the *United Kingdom* Travellers – often mothers – are sometimes employed as assistant teachers. "The most successful involvement of Travellers in education took place in the independent Van Leer-funded West Midlands Travellers' School. This first appointed paid Traveller helped with pre-school work in 1974, at a time when some teachers had resigned and the appointment of others was still pending. This proved very successful, and some Traveller mothers took Playgroup Supervision courses at Bilston College of Further Education, which were open to those without formal educational qualifications. Travellers were then employed as assistant teachers... One Traveller had been illiterate before starting to learn within the adult literacy project; after eighteen months, she was a paid teacher... By 1975 the Travellers were running the pre-school class entirely by themselves. In 1976 ... a Traveller became chairperson of the project. Obtaining the playgroup supervisor qualifications also enabled these Traveller teachers to obtain local authority subsidies and carry on the project for a while after the end of the Van Leer grant. It soon became entirely Traveller controlled, and under the name of the 'West Midlands Traveller Education Council' continued the pre-school work in Walsall until 1978." But, for financial reasons – notably the cost of school transport – the class was discontinued. "A valuable contribution here has also been made by the Scottish Arts Council Writers in Schools Scheme who funded two Traveller authors, Duncan Williamson and Betsy Whyte, to visit schools and tell folktales to both Travellers and non-Traveller children. Occasional visits by Travellers to speak to non-Traveller children have also been arranged in England" [Acton/Kenrick].

It is also necessary to take into account that certain families do not wish, or even refuse outright, to have Gypsies on the school staff. And young Travellers who have followed a long school career may not wish to teach Traveller children [cf.among others Karpati/Massano; Louis 1971; Korré/Marselos]. The following analysis is broadly applicable in all countries.

In the *United Kingdom*, a young Traveller "is still active in voluntary work. This person has applied for paid community work posts but has failed even to be shortlisted. Perhaps the idea of a graduate Gypsy is just too unsettling to local authorities. Given the experience of this person, the majority of teachers of Gypsy origin are perhaps wise in keeping those origins secret. We know of only one who has publicly declared his own ethnicity to take part in Traveller Education, and he left the field after frustrating experiences with his LEA. Others have become involved, even attending the DES short course, but without revealing their origins. We also know of others who are teachers of student teachers, who keep the fact that they are Gypsies secret, as we know of Gypsies with professional positions who even though they are prepared to come forward themselves to assist voluntary work, tell their children not to reveal their identity in school. All these phenomena are as much a part of the oppression of Gypsies in our society as the more overt harassment of nomads" [Acton/Kenrick].

It is obvious that, from the perspective of the development of intercultural education, the participation of older members of the pupils' community is a precious asset – in addition to the fact that it makes for better reciprocal understanding.

The conclusions of the 1983 Council of Europe seminar on "The Training of Teachers for Gypsy Children" emphasises that "The training of Gypsy teachers is considered by many delegates to be greatly desirable. In order to achieve it, there is on the one hand the need for Gypsy organisations to help those who wish to teach, and on the other a necessity for administrative flexibility to allow – at least during an initial transition period – young Gypsies to teach without necessarily having first gone through all the standard channels of training" [Liégeois, 1983b].

Sometimes measures have been taken along these lines. For example in *Italy* the National Council of Public Instruction, in a recommendation dated 14/4/81 on school provision for Gypsy children, stated that it is necessary to "evolve adapted measures to promote teacher-training from within the Rom community, as being the best equipped to safeguard the cultural heritage and ethnic identity of the Rom, especially in courses for adults" (Article 3); "Instruction in and through Romani is foreseen when qualified personnel are available for the task" (Article 4) [Karpati/Massano]. Yet everywhere, at this very moment, there are possibilities which are not being sufficiently exploited and would require no special exemptions: for example in the field of preschooling, the employment of auxiliary teachers, in training centres, as monitors, support in various forms, or in mediating roles – there are no school systems today which could not employ Travellers. And as for appointment to teaching positions, there are ways and means of achieving this as well. For example, in *Denmark*, bilingual instructors may be employed without necessarily having a Danish teaching diploma; in *France* ELCOs ("teachers of mother tongue and culture") can be appointed once they undergo special training. Which is not to lose sight of the importance of initial training:

Measures geared towards young people from immigrant cultures are all equally applicable on this question of training: "Integration into the teaching body of the host country of second-generation immigrants, by means of initial training, is to be encouraged. 'Access Courses', as in England, with the goal of preparing young immigrants to obtain the necessary qualifications to embark on teacher training, are a first step. Mention must also be made of the practice, in several *Länder* of the FRG, of allowing second-generation immigrants access to practical training once they have passed their first secondary school state examination" [CEC (84), 244, p.33].

Pedagogy

An alien institution

Sending children to school is a cultural option. It is a practice associated with a certain cultural context and a certain historical experience. The school institution both as a system and as a means towards certain ends cannot therefore be perceived in the same way by all. A school system that suits some will not suit others, but it is very common (and very ethnocentric) to believe otherwise. This may be the root cause of many failures.

Acceptance of school, its methods and its goals, is not universal. It is all the more vital to emphasise this, as it is so rarely taken into account, for various reasons. One of these is that the aims of school are always presented in their noblest light: one has only to read declarations in which it is presented as an instrument of social progress, broadening horizons and developing personal autonomy. This assumes too readily, on the one hand that everybody sees these as desirable goals, and secondly that every child who attends school is necessarily going to attain them. To promote these ideas without submitting them to critical analysis – even if it is only a critique of how they are applied in the real world – is to risk (the end justifying the means) obscuring the ill-effects of practice behind the nobility of goals.

The institution of school occupies a central role within the host societies of Gypsies and Travellers. A very high proportion of education takes place within the framework of the school system, to a degree that (as we pointed out in the first chapters) "education" and "schooling" tend to be seen as synonymous (– even in the national monographs on which this report is based). It is easy to lose sight of the fact that there also exists a fundamental in-family education which may be complementary or in opposition to a given type of school education. Here too the various national monographs demonstrate how widespread this ethnocentric view is: in the working questionnaire, under the heading "What pedagogic projects?" the answers were almost exclusively concerned with state policies, school policies, teachers' ideas. Parents' ideas were rarely mentioned. There are signs too of underestimating the fundamental, and negative, role that school may play in a policy of eliminating minorities: it can easily and effectively participate in assimilating the minority groups subjected to it, all the more so as attendance is often compulsory. Yes, school can "form" a child – but its role may be conforming, reforming, or deforming.

One must never forget that, for Gypsies, school is an alien institution, and an integral part of a universe which has for centuries been a threatening one.

"School runs a double risk of transforming acculturation into deculturation, because it plays a role of *'cutting off'* (the child finds himself within an alien world) and because it is inherently geared towards the *inculcation* of new values. School is after all one of the major instruments of socialisation and one with which the child is in contact throughout virtually all the most important years of his life. Faced with a strange, alien teacher, usually mixed in with children who are also of a different background, and expected to behave in a passive and receptive manner, the child is very vulnerable. And one could ponder indefinitely the implications of the following observation by the authors of *La Reproduction:* 'All pedagogic action is objectively a form of symbolic violence as well as an imposition, by an arbitrary power, of an arbitrary cultural content' [Bourdieu and Passeron, 1970, p.19]. This is not to say that nothing should be undertaken, but that one must take account of the consequences of what one does. Conflict between two antagonistic systems of socialisation can be grave for the individual caught between them, taking the forms of role-conflict, loss of identity, cultural schizophrenia. Nowadays, the number of legally stateless persons is diminishing, as they acquire nationality. Will acculturation (in which schooling will play an active role) result in a growing number of 'culturally stateless persons' who will not know where to fit in?" [Liégeois, 1980b].

There is no point in cluttering this report with a detailed analysis of the historical conditions in which the schooling of Gypsy children has taken place. We have already, in part 1, gone into the policies followed over the centuries; then, under the heading "The History of School Provision" we pointed out that "In every state, school policy has been coherent with overall policy as regards Gypsies/Travellers." This policy of negation (whatever its forms) pursued over the centuries; the constant presence of negative, erroneous images and prejudices; the arbitrary and violent measures taken against Gypsies and Travellers; the fact that school is an institution uniquely – totally – part of the environment perceived by Gypsies as coercive: all imply that school can only be experienced as yet another imposition, as a tentacle grasping at the children to ensnare and assimilate them. An institution all the more disconcerting in that, although the child is obliged to attend, he is often not permitted to do so, or, having got in, must fight in order to remain, because his relations with other children are still tainted with the mark of centuries of conflict between nomads and the Settled. While present he has, moreover, the impression of representing a way of life that is somehow illegitimate, when his culture and language are marginalised or even stigmatised in word and deed. The layout of tables and chairs, the layout of ideas required from him, cannot be separated from, for example, the imposed layout of caravans on official sites. All are products of the same – alien – order.

Whatever the present efforts to make Gypsy and Traveller children feel at home in school, and to adapt teaching to suit them, such efforts cannot be separated from the broad spectrum of "Gypsy policy" of which they are a part. It will take more than a few months or even years to cleanse actions and minds of the mistrust which has characterised relations between the two communities for so long. It is thus all the more important for more and more Traveller children to have a positive experience of school, and equally important to discover, to understand, and to take into account, the generally misunderstood or ignored reasons which make Gypsy parents wary of sending their children there.

The following analysis pertaining to compulsory schooling at secondary level, may well be valid for other – most? – cases: "For the Gypsies, school, with its demand for attendance and the corresponding conditions of that attendance, is a constant source of anxiety and conflict... it is clear that the children do not see themselves as a problem. For them it is undeniable that school is the problem. The Gypsies' attitudes to their so called 'devious' behaviour is illuminating. For each of the instances of misconduct as described by the staff, they have their own rationalisation and justification... It is observable that their behaviour is a response to their dislike of school arising from their feelings of being victims of prejudice and discrimination. It is the sense of injustice which influences their behavioural responses more than anything else" [Ivatts, 1975, p.16].

"On his first day of school the Gypsy child must confront a totally new, and considerably different, world from that which he has known up to now: his parents, his lifestyle, their rules. Since this situation repeats itself throughout his school career, we perceive that the rapidity of his adaptation is astonishing. But if his first experience of school has been negative (difficult relations with teachers or with other children – Gypsy or not), the child will form an impression of school as enemy territory and it will be a hard job for the parents to persuade him to return: I regularly meet children who have stopped attending school altogether for these reasons... What is more, the Gypsy child will base his ideas of our society on his experiences in the classroom, and this is where his preconceptions will become more and more rooted the longer he attends" [Grimaud, 1984, p.46].

In addition to the fact that school has, up to now, been perceived as a threatening, forbidding institution, is the objective fact of its non-adaptation to the Gypsy child's needs. On the one hand the Gypsy has always perceived the risk he runs in submitting his children to a value-system which is not his and which he does not want them to pick up. On the other – and there is copious evidence on this point – up to now, "There has been no connection for Gypsies between scholastic success and economic success (since school provided no skills of relevance to Gypsy work-patterns) nor between scholastic success and social success (schooling being an alien concept, success at it brought no status increase in the eyes of the child's own community). In fact one could say truthfully that in both respects schooling was – still is – regarded as a handicap, since the time wasted at it has kept the child from picking up economic skills and loosened his sense of integration in the group" [Liégeois, 1983b].

Success, flexibility, social status – all are still totally unconnected to anything school has to offer. Indeed the submission of the child to the school system, and his success by that system's criteria, entails a degree of distancing from his family (sometimes with drastic results) due to the consequent weakening of the group's social coherence – which, as we explained earlier, is a paramount priority.

"This year six of our old girls got married. Not one of them wanted to marry a Gypsy. This girl has a balanced personality, but stressed to us that she had not wanted to marry a Gypsy" [report from the manager of a home economics training centre for adolescent girls, France, 1968]. "Two girls, both successful in school, had a very difficult adolescence: the first refused to live the Gypsy lifestyle and slashed her wrists to avoid getting married according to custom; the other did submit to the laws of the group, and she's better adjusted now than the first... Another Rom did well in school, and married a (non-Gypsy) schoolteacher. They had two children and he worked as a company 'rep' (a job which is quite similar to hawking, selling door-to-door). But in the end he couldn't bear being cut off from his own people; he deserted his wife and married a Gypsy girl" [in: *Journées d'Étude des Techniciens Sociaux*, France, CNIN, June 1972, p.18].

The concept of school failure is obviously just as subjective as that of success. For the Gypsies, school failure has up to now been the failure of the school, which has not been able to attract them, hold on to them, or equip them with the tools essential for adaptation to the modern world. There is even a (compensatory?) pride in emphasising that Gypsies get on just fine without school (that is, without the help of non-Gypsies). At present, Gypsies on the whole cope with their inability to read and write without feeling guilty for being "illiterate", despite being immersed in societies where there is continual bombardment from the written word. "We prefer to be Gypsies by first choice, than non-Gypsies by second choice" [a Gypsy speaking at an international seminar, cf. Liégeois, 1983b]. Likewise, in a complementary fashion, certain groups of Travellers do make use of their few members who can read and write: "This is particularly the case among the Belgikarja Roma, among whom a literate woman from a different ethnic group, an adult who learned to read and write outside the school system, or a young person who – unusually – attended boarding school, can provide the necessary link with the outside world" [Reyniers]. Yet we must be wary of generalising: "Other families have more school experience, be it because school has provided them with a means of affirming their identity in the 'world outside', or simply 'by accident'" [Reyniers]. If we wish to deepen our understanding of how the school is perceived, we should examine the uses of literacy – while bearing in mind that all generalisation is risky.

To this purpose we shall quote at length from the monograph compiled for this report focusing specifically on the question of education within the Gypsy milieu. Starting with a resumé: "Writing as a means of communicating one's own ideas is only relevant as regards strangers. As there are no strangers in a Gypsy community, it is writing itself which is the stranger, and the presence of semi-literate individuals suffices for those exceptional cases (letter-writing, official forms, etc.) where such skills are required. Since, for Gypsies, language is not an instrument of conceptual analysis, but their basic means of communication and interaction, it is seen as something personal to the group. They tend to be wary of how they use it with non-Gypsies, and avoid written communication, which they see as far less persuasive and expressive than person-to-person action" [Piasere].

To put it more concisely, but still being very wary of generalisations because "This could be quite meaningless in future situations unforeseeable at present. The use of the written code obviously implies the existence of transmitters and receptors... From the Rom Gypsy's point of view, the following four situations are possible:

Each of these situations will differ according to circumstances.

Transmitter (he who writes)	*Receptor* (he who reads)
1) Gadjo ---------------------------->	Gadjo
2) Gadjo ---------------------------->	Rom
3) Rom ---------------------------->	Gadjo
4) Rom ---------------------------->	Rom

1) *Gadjo-Gadjo*: For the Roma, this is the expected use of writing, whatever the circumstances. Writing was invented by Gadjé, for use by Gadjé. For Roma today, knowing how to read and write is seen as a Gadjo characteristic, an ethnic indicator, and all things written are seen as typically Gadjo and thus typically alien, be they books, newspapers, forms to be filled, or documents of whatever kind.

2) *Gadjo-Rom*: Living among the Gadjé, surrounded by the world of writing, the Roma recognise as 'useful' the ability to decipher this Gadjo code. Being able to read is seen, not as prestigious, but as advantageous. On the other hand, that it is not indispensable is clearly demonstrated by the number of literate Gadjé who behave stupidly. Knowing how to read may also be perceived as dangerous, since reading 'makes a person vulnerable to the "lies" of the Gadjé' [Dick-Zatta, MS.].

3) *Rom-Gadjo*: Since writing is an intrinsically Gadjo instrument, the Rom would never by choice use it in communicating with them. Even filling out a basic form or signing a document is considered a tricky business. If a Rom should master writing and become a writer himself, or if he takes to 'writing' through an intermediary (for example by dictating his life story to a Gadjo) he may often find himself mocked or criticised or ignored by the others. The fact of knowing how to write is not encouraged, and written composition which tells the Gadjo more than he ought to know is frowned upon.

4) *Rom-Rom*: In a very few cases we have come across Roma composing written texts expressly for other Roma: letters, postcards, and other brief messages. Apart from such situations, the Rom sees writing as a totally inadequate means of communicating with another Rom. Even when written communication does take place, it is the act itself which is significant, more than the actual information imparted. Without going into detailed analysis of the text, a letter such as the following is clearly communication for communication's sake:

'Dear Reja, we are well and hope that you are too. How is your wife? How are your children? I am well and so is Mama. I hope that you all are well. Mama says hello. Greetings to your wife and children. Hello from me. Stay well.'

(…) Today, as for decades past, most Gypsies only half-accept reading and writing; they prefer to be on the receiving end and let a few members of the group handle the informal and prestigeless task of knowing how to use a pen" [Piasere].

Evidence from various countries suggests that the situation described above is dominant – which is not to say that it is exclusive. Different groups have different attitudes, and within family groups there can be differences between generations or individuals.

To give an example from *England:* "Some (of the children) are eager to display the skills they have acquired. In a world where the all powerful adult has to bring them their forms and letters to decipher, literacy is seen as a powerful tool, it has given them considerable cachet, something which is not very common for them. One of the pupils entered a National Story Writing Competition for Gypsy children and won third prize; this aroused high glee amongst her family and friends and envy amongst the rest" [Joan Lockton, in *Traveller Education*, 1984, p.16].

Gypsy education

Several years ago in the course of a critical study of social work geared towards Gypsies, we made the observation that little (indeed at the time none whatsoever) attention has been given to the question of maladjustment or deviance *within the Gypsy context*. Gypsies as a whole were seen as maladjusted or deviant, to be "readjusted" or "reintegrated". This is yet another sign of rampant ethnocentrism and an evolutionism which is still alive and well, since only *one* society is taken as universal reference point, a model of "normality", and groups which do not conform are seen either as maladjusted or "backward", stuck in a primitive state from which they should be helped to emerge [Liégeois, 1977a]. The same observation also applies to the question of education *within the Gypsy context*: "Either it is mentioned, with the claim that it does not exist, or it is not mentioned in order not to have to admit that it does" [Piasere].

The report on education in the Gypsy environment cites a flagrant example of ignoring this facet of education while considering questions of schooling [Piasere]. In one of the countries covered by this study there exists a journal of high quality and with a wide readership. Those producing it have been involved in school provision for Gypsy children for decades, and the magazine reflects this. Over its twenty-year existence, it has published 796 articles totalling 5,760 pages. One hundred and forty of these articles are concerned with schooling, pedagogy, and didactics – to a total of 1,082 pages. If we add in a few more pages which deal with other aspects of school provision under other headings, at least 20% of the total material published deals with this subject. And – a single, three-page text, attesting to the importance of in-family education. That makes a total of 0.05% of the content on Gypsy education.

This is a clear illustration of a tendency which does not happen by chance but, as we have regularly emphasised, is linked with both history and politics. The periodical in question is far from alone in exhibiting it; indeed, as the author of the report points out, "We believe that if we were to subject other specialised periodicals to the same analysis, findings would probably be even more discouraging" [Piasere].

In-family education is not only alive and well, but continues to provide the perfect socialisation to enable the Gypsy child to adapt to his family circle and to the broader environment. We shall not repeat here the points raised in the section on "Education" – nor is this report the place to give a description/analysis of Traveller education methods. That is a task for ethnographers, though few such studies exist to date and those which do are rarely consulted by those involved in school provision. This lack is often lamented by teachers who would prefer to base their methods on existing dynamics rather than risk running into conflict with them. Just as we commented earlier on the potential benefits of linking training with information, a link between cultural anthropology and pedagogy would be similarly beneficial.

Generally speaking, teachers do recognise, even if only indirectly, the degree to which in-family education is responsible for producing a strong child who is well adapted to and integrated within a large and reassuring social body.

"Children and parents visualise the future in the same way: not as (hoped-for or dreaded) social change, but as a reproduction of the present: the children will live in trailers and continue in their parents' trades. This reproduction is not perceived as something to accept fatalistically, but as a desirable fact – as a value. In consequence, Gypsy children (at least, those in the group I deal with) do not exhibit the fragility linked with classes of immigrant children, and described as 'the second generation phenomenon': torn between family values and those of assimilation. On the contrary, they arrive in school armoured with strong values which permit them to experience it as a place of secondary values. They do not see school as providing anything connected with social status, future careers, or practical skill. To put it bluntly, scholastic failure does not exist for Gypsies; the concept makes no sense" [Cotonnec, 1983].

Evidence on this point is broadly in agreement. "Success, adaptation, and social promotion were outside any school curriculum. It must be borne in mind that even now, as far as Gypsies are concerned, 'scholastic failure' is nonsense. Or, when it does take on meaning, it is as the dramatic manifestation of yet another form of rejection" [synopsis of a Council of Europe seminar, cf. Liégeois, 1983b].

In most cases Gypsies find themselves, up to the present, *parallel to* the institution of school. This has the effect of "rendering futile all pedagogical practices linked to the institutional and psychological pressure on which a so-called normal school course is based" [Cotonnec, 1983]. Gypsy parents are, and remain, above all "parents of children" rather than "parents of pupils" [a distinction underlined by L. Guibert in correspondence with the author]. Many reports emphasise their frequent fear that school will submit their children to influences which will alienate them from their background, undermining parents' moral authority and weakening group cohesion. Parents do not see it as their role to reinforce the workings of the school institution on their children, for example by encouraging their studies. As far as they're concerned the important thing is their child, and it is up to the school to adapt to him – that is to say, above all, respectfully.

"The high concept that Gypsies have of the moral prestige and dignity of each person from the earliest childhood plays an important role in connection with school. Gypsy parents will not tolerate their children being humiliated, all the less so by strangers, and if this happens the children will be withdrawn from school. Moreover they will never force an unwilling child to attend, since he too has the right to make a free choice, and to have it respected" [Karpati/Massano].

Parents are proud of the education they provide and convinced of its quality, particularly in comparison with the education given by the non-Traveller society around them, and the results it brings.

In *Sweden* a child psychologist in close contact with families indicated that, when talking with parents, they were only interested in knowing what went on amongst the Swedes, since they felt they already knew about Gypsy families. "When, on a few occasions I wondered why they asked so few questions about the bringing-up of children, while their non-Gypsy counterparts asked so many, they answered: 'Swedes have problems, but we haven't.' On the basis of the analysis of Gypsy socialisation, this statement must be regarded as a true one. It is not a question of dissimulation. They may, of course, find their children troublesome, but generally speaking the means and aims of child rearing are no problem; they go without saying... They acknowledged me as an expert on child rearing, but not for Gypsy children. They were even rather interested to hear me tell what problems non-Gypsy parents had and what advice I gave in my professional capacity. On the other hand, I was clearly not regarded as an expert on Gypsy children. When, at times, I made suggestions on how to deal with upbringing situations they found irritating, the reply was usually: 'But that won't work with Gypsy children, you know'" [Gustafsson, 1973, p.94].

Moreover, parents are aware of the fact that schooling, as it generally exists, teaches their children far less than they do themselves:

"Even schooling in a proper school teaches us nothing. You learn stuff for Gadjé. It's a waste of time for Gypsy children. The staff think we have to adjust to settled life. They won't listen to us. They don't want to know what we need. We and only we are capable of teaching our children what they need to get on in real life: knowing about different metals, about repairing cane chair-bottoms... Gypsy children take an active interest in such things from a very early age. At six or seven they already want to go out with their father and mother. That's how they learn something worth knowing on the road" [a nomadic Manouche, aged thirty-eight, quoted by Reyniers].

"One commonly employed argument is that boys are better able to learn their future trade from their father than from the school (apart from which there is no formal vocational training in typical caravan-dweller occupations) and that girls can learn 'house' keeping just as well – or better – from their mothers. Another argument is that further education is 'simply training for unemployment' and that given the amount of available labour, employers are unlikely to recruit caravan-dwellers or Gypsies" [Hovens et al].

"Parents are not negative but often indifferent... they obviously prefer to keep them to their way of earning life, than to press them to waste their time in classrooms 'doing nothing'. They have so many problems to solve before they can see a probable prospective of a different way of life for their children. 'Gypsies were born to live free, running around the fields. Too much education is evil. It leads to wars. You can easily see it' (A. Sideris, President of the A. Varvara Association). 'Why be highly educated or qualified ? So many educated people are unemployed. Or should we exchange our trade for slavery in factories?'" [Korré/Marselos].

The relation between schooling and Traveller economic practices, which determine the individual's capacity to survive with independence, is direct and crucial, for three reasons:

First: as emphasised above, there is no correlation between presence in school/scholastic success, and economic success. So what's the point in undergoing – with difficulty – schooling, and getting nothing out of it, or even being penalised for it? Since the future cannot be foreseen, the best attitude is to live in the present, and (for the moment at any rate) the economic activities practised by Gypsies are the most appropriate for their situation.

Next: school fails to take into account the economic activities practised by parents, with two consequences. First, school is of no direct help in preparing for future work, and so can objectively be dismissed as useless. Secondly, it removes the child from his family for a considerable period each day, thereby depriving him of an opportunity to learn by working with his parents, and simultaneously depriving the family of the child's economic contribution. This two-way deprivation becomes particularly significant when the child reaches secondary school age. Almost all the national reports, and numerous other commentaries, strongly emphasise the negative short-term effect of the absence of the child from his family: by attending school, he doesn't learn to work, and he doesn't help the family. When he leaves school, he can't "get a job", but he doesn't know how to work like a Gypsy.

Finally, the above points take on particular significance when we see them within the socio-historical and socio-economic context outlined above. The actual economic situation of a certain number of families cries out for functional, useful, rapid schooling.

Even in the case of the immediate project of learning to read and write, and within the framework of adult training, "The grave economic problems of the participants pose a serious obstacle to their willingness to tackle the difficult task of learning to read and write. In this context, the fact that literacy will not bring an automatic and immediate improvement to their economic situation plays an important role. The experience of being able to read on the course, yet being unable to get any good out of it in the world outside, had a demoralising repercussion on the learning process" [Bremer Volkshochschule, 1983, p.30]

Two pedagogies

Traditional school methods do not "educate" the Gypsy or Traveller child. Gypsies are educated by traditional Gypsy methods – and there is a very significant gap between the methods and goals of the two systems. The conflicts which every child feels between his home and school environments are exacerbated in the case of the Gypsy child. He does not arrive in the school as a sort of empty jug to be filled; he brings with him his cultural baggage and psychological profile. In fact, there is no empty space within him – all of the space is already occupied, and it is a question of working with the existing elements, and building on them, rather than (as some still see their task) removing certain elements and replacing them with others. The child's entry into school represents a major break for both parents and children, as Gypsy society and socialisation in no way intermesh with it.

"School denies the Gypsy child. It denies his physical appearance, his mother tongue, his skills and his experiences. While the non-Gypsy child continues on his 'natural' path, the Gypsy child is being asked to 'start from scratch'" [Weiler, 1979, p.259, quoted by Reemtsma]. "Faced with the existing school system, with its focus on performance, teachers, and exams, many children, adolescents and parents feel threatened by school because its organisation, goals and teaching content have virtually no relation to Gypsy culture or to the child's experience" [Reemtsma]. "Gypsies and Travellers express a series of recriminations about school, which is accused of lack of respect for the essentials of their culture. The school institution is perceived essentially as a field of confrontation between their society and that of the Gadjé" [Reyniers].

School can be deeply upsetting for the child who attends it.

"Gypsy children would be motivated to attend Gadjo school if it gave them access to new and varied skills; instead, it tends to stifle eclecticism. While their society perceives childhood and adolescence as part of an uninterrupted continuum, children in school are pigeonholed by age. Just at the moment when the Gypsy community requires of the child that he form a coherent and richly symbolic vision of the Gadjo and his world, the Gadjé (by the method and content of their teaching) present him with a fragmented vision of themselves (analysing Gadjo words, different periods of history, different types of Gadjo: nations, states…) which tends to be entirely detached from the symbolic construction of the Gypsy. How can Gadjo school teach the child to be Gypsy?" [Piasere].

Gypsy children mature very early, yet school has a tendency to impose infantile behaviour on them, instead of developing their sense of responsibility and building on their capacities; teachers as well as parents frequently mention this. "A number of the parents said that Traveller children had skills and abilities that no 'country' children had – they could survive without adult help in situations that no 'country' child could cope with. They would not want them to lose these abilities or their strong family ties. Several parents stated that there was more to education than book knowledge and that many Settled people who considered themselves to be very educated were in fact very ignorant as their attitudes revealed" [McCarthy].

School can have a destructive influence on the society that entrusts it with its children. Particularly in the context of assimilationist policies, the automatic assumption is that Gypsies and their children are attracted by the lifestyle of the surrounding society. Yet their aspirations – be they in the realm of education, accommodation or work, are not necessarily the same as other people's, nor indeed are they necessarily the same from one Gypsy group, or even one Gypsy family, to the next. As we have already mentioned, at present in many societies school is charged with an enormous proportion of the child's overall education, responsibility for which has been transferred from the family. What is more, scholastic teaching – as a part of "education" in the broadest sense – is an adaptive, crucial, strategic vehicle reinforcing and maintaining – indeed reproducing – the profile of the society of which it is a part. Yet if the vehicle efficiently maintains the dominant society, it must be threatening to a minority society on which it is imposed from without, since it seeks educative hegemony.

It is within this context that Gypsy and Traveller parents' reservations must be considered. These are eloquently summed up in the words of a Greek Gypsy saying, "He who knows much, suffers much" [Marselos]. We must look deeper to understand their meaning.

"When one of the members of a group of parents once said, 'Children can die of knowing too much', it was perhaps not merely an expression of magical conceptions, but still more a symbolic way of saying that as a result of the knowledge imparted by the school the Gypsy child dies; it becomes a Swedish child instead" [Gustafsson, 1973, p.87].

"Perhaps we can begin to comprehend the impasse in which school provision for Gypsy children is still locked. A lot of time and thought have gone into investigating the school atmosphere, attendance, difficulty in relating to non-Gypsies; there are many didactic studies on things like the use of non-Gypsy language, the problem of culturally alien teaching materials and so on. Yet the fundamental (unconscious?) fear is of disturbing 'Gypsy thought', a possibility which up to now has effectively blocked the schooling process. 'Gypsy thought' baulks at the verbal autopsy of experience, social behaviour and belief. 'Gypsy thought' does not perceive language as having an existence independent of its practical everyday content. 'Gypsy thought' avoids distancing itself from particular experience and entering into the realm of the hypothetical and the deductive. 'Gypsy thought' fears Gadjo schooling precisely because it suspects that an intensive use of the written word would destroy it, thereby destroying community cohesion" [Piasere].

It would be easy to measure the breadth of the gap between the two education systems produced by the presence in school of Traveller children who are products and bearers of an educational system radically different from – and often opposed to – that of most schools. If we were to picture the systems as two circles, we would see that they hardly intersect at all. Or, if we were to represent the elements conveyed in the two systems (organisation of space and time, attitudes to various types of behaviour, degree of initiative, of independence, etc.) as two parallel columns, we would see that the parallels conform to their definition, that is, they do not meet – even less so, as most of the elements are in an opposition which is difficult to reduce. As school does attempt to reduce them, the child is disturbed and frustrated. Many studies and teachers' own observations have shown that the Traveller child cannot balance these contradictory relationships within the school context. Not only does the school actively seek to promote the values which it sees as its very function to transmit, but as a rule it also entirely negates the positive values upon which the

Gypsy child is so solidly based outside of school: his independence, initiative, mobility, creativity, solidarity... all become handicaps.

Quite apart from this point-by-point opposition, we are dealing here with "two different philosophies of education (reflecting two different conceptions of the world) the core principles of which seem to be the following:

Vision of others:
1) For the Rom, Sinti, etc., Gadjé are 'others' par excellence; they are considered to be the 'environment' in which one must live and survive both materially and symbolically.
2) For European non-Gypsies, Gypsies are 'others' among many 'others', an element of folklore among many other such elements, one problem among many, one marginal group among many.

Vision of self:
1) The Rom, Sinti., etc. do not see the world of children and the world of adults as separated by barriers. The Gypsy world is a whole, both vertically (inter-generationally) and horizontally (intra-generationally).
2) European non-Gypsies conceive and live their lives in stages: stages of status marked by 'rites de passage', stages in one's professional career, etc.

Restraints:
1) In order to live amongst Gadjé, the Rom, Sinti, etc. must cultivate eclecticism and a readiness to change, and even more importantly – a fundamental consideration – they must bequeath to their children a capacity for eclecticism and readiness to change.
2) The social division of work, like the work market, of European non-Gypsies is geared towards superspecialisations (of which 'Gypsiology' is but one) and the proliferation of school as a place of transmission privileged with selected knowledge, is a direct consequence.

Anthropologists and cognitive psychologists are in broad agreement as to the changes wrought by the introduction of written communication onto thinking patterns based on oral communication: decontextualisation of knowledge; materialisation of the linguistic act; rigidity of discourse; development of formalisation, type of memory, type of classification, development of individualism. It is clear, then, that a simple change of communication technique has enormous repercussions on thinking patterns. Writing changes a people's worldview totally: it modifies the structure of cognitive processes and perhaps even of perception itself. One must not, therefore, treat literacy and schooling as simple tools, untainted by cultural overtones, but instead conceive them as means with clearly defined and predictable consequences. The choice of 'No, but...' or of 'Yes, but...' of most of the Gypsy populations of Western Europe is no accident, but a strategy of adaptation to the non-Gypsy environment...

Understanding Gypsy thinking patterns is thus essential in order to comprehend the partiality – and thus to avoid the hypocrisy – of an 'intercultural' approach, since it is clear that the problem is no longer, for example, simply to introduce the teaching of 'Gypsy history', but how to teach history to Gypsies... The study of Gypsy thinking should have been the very first stage in the founding of a pedagogy for Gypsies, whereas most of the time Gypsy thinking has simply been denied and thrown into the rubbish bin to which is consigned all 'primitive thinking', all the thoughts that must be eradicated from the heads of 'backward' peoples, to be replaced by our, more 'civilised', ones" [Piasere].

Behaviour in conflict

Confrontational attitudes may develop partly as a response to the fact of having to attend school in the first place, and partly as a response to the school as it is. This consideration is important because each of these attitudes carries different implications for practice – and for policy. It is a good idea to sit down with parents and to examine carefully the reasons behind their attitudes. We repeat once again that no generalisations can be made, and that the range of attitudes and aspirations, of parents as well as children, is very broad. If all of them share the misgivings described above, and many oppose schooling because of them, there is nonetheless a growing number who do want schooling for their children – but not "at any price". "If we can't have them teached our way we don't want them teached at all" [an Irish Traveller parent quoted in Quirke, 1984].

"Many examples show that parents who are satisfied with a school will do everything they can to remain near it for as long as possible, and that members of the extended family group camped in the same area will follow their kin into attending the satisfactory school. Families may even move to the area expressly to send their children to school there." But, conversely, "the Gypsies will throw a spanner into the works to stop developments (at school) at the first suspicion of danger" [Ferté, 1984].

Though attitudes differ, opposition manifests itself in similar types of behaviour:

"The five children with whom I worked were called Valérie, Patricia, Roger, Christophe and Albert. In their own culture they became, respectively, Storia, Larma, Volki, Jessy, Humberto... The use of Gadjo names enabled them to avoid involving themselves 'wholly' when interacting with Gadjé... If someone calls me Roger instead of Volki, then the social (or scholastic) judgment he passes upon me concerns only my capacity to relate to the Gadjé (acculturation), but does not concern my socialisation within my own group (enculturation)" [M. Pragnère, MS.].

The child who does not wish to attend school utilises and manipulates the situation (whether consciously or not), explaining his absence to school personnel in terms of family or social reasons – or, to his parents, his refusal to go in terms of the bad treatment he receives there. Within the school itself there are other forms of resistance: "It is very common to come across children who are entirely or semi mute. When they speak you would think you were listening to a deaf-mute attempting to produce sound. Afterwards it is most surprising to hear these children, with totally 'normal' phrasing in well-pitched voices, talking nineteen to the dozen amongst themselves in the playground" [Ferté, 1984].

The reasons given for explaining absence from school are manifold. Here is a mixed bag of them, taken from various sources: "The distance from school, late bed-times, holidays and the need of help in the home (for girls). In this context, sickness can be an excuse for all sorts of other reasons." "The Gypsies exploit any flexibility and compromise shown in individual cases. Any leniency allowed to one child is used to apply to all the children, or is used as a guideline for future occasions." "All excuses are 'good', but in my experience, there is no real cause." "One mother said that her son was unable to go to school because he had no trousers. When asked what he was wearing at present she said that they were brown and not allowed in school. The grey ones had a big hole in the crotch." "The girls are helping their mothers (doing the washing)? The boys are helping their fathers with scrap?"

In an example from a secondary school in *England*, children habitually miss their bus; "Another facet of behaviour which identifies the Gypsies as a disruptive and uncooperative group is the persistent failure to wear school uniform... In the past, blatant breaches in the rule often resulted in the offender being sent home, but the more common breach nowadays is in regard to small items, such as shoe colour and design, no tie or irregular shirt colour and design, etc. The wearing of jewellery is also against school rules, and periodic purges usually hit the Gypsies hard with their liking for precious metal, rings and earrings... A more disturbing feature of their disruptive behaviour, as seen by the staff, is the common occurrence of the Gypsies operating a united power group within the school... they always sit together ... their social mixing with other children is peripheral and limited... Many senior members of staff are of the opinion that the school cannot offer them anything in the present situation. 'If you give them an inch they take a yard'; the children 'beat the system every time' and are 'out of tune with the school' in most ways.

It is, of course, not as simple as it seems. The children take with them to school attitudes which are anti-school and anti-authority. These, inevitably, elicit strong reactions and responses from the staff and other non-Gypsy children. The situation is thus compounded and results in a strengthened confirmation that the original definitions of each side were right" [Ivatts, 1975, pp.13, 14, 27].

"This refusal, conscious or not, is entirely functional; it is geared towards preserving culture and cultural identity, and thereby the social and psychological equilibrium of the group; all the more so since, in a society founded on oral tradition, without written archives, 'The perception of the new quickly merges with the old' [Mead, 1970, p. 52]. It is for this reason that, as one US Rom put it, 'The Rom avoid the school system like the plague! While most other American minority groups are organising to demand a better education for their children, the Rom are racking their brains for ways to keep them at home' [Dimas, 1975]. The author goes on to speak of 'collective truancy' giving the following factors to be taken into account:

'- reduction of time spent in school reduces proportionately the influence of the teachers' value system on the Rom child, and totally eliminates 'peer-pressure' from non-Rom children – two of the most powerful forces in the socialisation process;
- illiteracy blocks all socialisation through the written word, which in turn blocks identification with alien culture heroes in books and novels;
- illiteracy guarantees that Romani will remain the first language of every Rom;
- illiteracy tends to discourage mixed marriages...' [op. cit., pp.14-15].

Ways of rejecting school, or of utilising rejection, are manifold... Once again it is unwise to judge this attitude too quickly; broader analysis demonstrates that it is a question of the sometimes desperate measures taken by individuals to preserve their culture, who can succeed or fail in negotiating the acculturation process directed at them" [Liégeois, 1980b].

Even when it is no longer a question of children's schooling, but of literacy for adults, attitudes and behaviour are the same. Two examples:

First, an extract taken from notes made in the Paris area one March evening in 1971, during a meeting held by a voluntary organisation for teaching Gypsies. The author of the notes was brought along to the meeting by one of the Rom invited there. About a dozen Rom[6], half of them accompanied by their wives, were present. The question of when to hold the courses was under discussion; here are some reactions.

- "The Rom say that if it's on such-and-such an evening, it will clash with the 'Film of the Week' on telly, and no one will show up.
- Tuesday seems ideal: no film on the telly, and the local cinemas are closed. But it's the day the Pentecostalist families attend their meeting.
- The Rom argued very loudly, frightening the Gadjé present.
- Some try to corner the literacy teachers for themselves: 'You can come to my place, have dinner, teach me, my wife and my kids.'
- Some refuse to let their wives learn to read and write, laughing, 'Afterwards she'll be writing to lovers – My darling! My love!'
- Some emphasise that if there is an important meeting, for example if an important Rom happens to be passing through, or if there's a wedding on, no one will show up for class.
- The immediate wishes of the group: to be able to read posters and street signs" [Liégeois, MS.].

Next, a description of the workings of an adult class in *Sweden:* "Many students arrive at very irregular intervals during the school day. The lessons are not infrequently interrupted by the students walking in and out of the classroom, leaving the lessons to make telephone calls, talking to someone in a neighbouring classroom, and so on. Nor is it unusual for the students to leave the school before the end of the day's lessons. Much Romani is spoken during the lessons; this leaves the teachers outside the conversation and they sometimes seem to be forgotten completely...

When Gypsies were asked what they thought of the adult school, most of them answered that it was a good school, and that it did not need altering. Reading, writing and arithmetic were best. When asked to suggest improvements, they mentioned the length of the school day – which they would like shorter – and the size of their grants – which they would like greater...

One explanation, a convenient one in this situation, is that the Gypsies are really only interested in the money they get for attending school. For my part, I prefer to explain the conduct of the Gypsies in relation to the adult school as a meaningful, purposeful and logical expression of the Gypsies' effort *to preserve their cultural autonomy*. Such an explanation does not require us to see their reaction as an expression of a conscious intention, but rather as a result of these efforts" [Gustafsson, 1973, pp. 46-47].

In various questionnaires, the reasons most often mentioned by teachers for the absenteeism of Gypsy pupils are "lack of interest" or "parental opposition". As we have seen, such "disinterest" and "opposition" are only superficially true, a façade behind which we must always look for deeper causes. Disinterest is not simple negligence; it is conscious, aware, often well thought out. Opposition is not simple reaction, but occurs (in general if not in each individual case) as part of an overall strategy of refusal: "A long history of conflict between the school and their parents and elder brothers and sisters was reported (by the children) with some strength of feeling and even delight" [Ivatts, 1975, p.19]. We see once again that the schooling of Gypsy children is a question of society, which largely surpasses pedagogy, and a question of community, which largely surpasses the individual.

As some teachers commented on Traveller children's way of talking: "They are like the transmitters of a speech which they did not produce and which does not belong to them. Everything happens as if there existed an organisational frame of reference which permits Travellers to express their relation as Travellers (rather than as individuals) to schooling 'in general', in part independently of their individual experiences of schooling. The force of this attitude is such that it will always, at one time or another, be validated in the experience of each and that each child will thenceforth adopt it, thinking it his very own" [Cotonnec/Chartier, 1984, p.13].

The Gypsies have remained for the most part outside the school system which in addition to the threat it poses to their culture also seems to produce cumulative handicaps: unemployment, pauperisation, deviance, dependency... Can we say that they're wrong when we consider the harshness of school up to the present for a society such as theirs? As was once said of another minority: "One cannot speak of a future, since school as we know it is ethnocidal. Native resistance to the actual state of unimaginative and undignified schooling is evident proof of wisdom" [Malaurie, 1977]. Thus, "by far the most significant question to ask is why they attend school at all" [Ivatts, 1975, p.27].

Towards functional schooling

"The Gypsies' only means of defence against being absorbed by the dominant culture is to make use of school, without yielding to it" [Karpati/Massano]. It is a question of compromise between cultural values, which must continue to inspire and permeate lifestyle, and functional values which must allow for adaptation to the environment: compliance with laws obliging school attendance, fulfilling the school requirements without which licences to practise certain trades will not be issued, obtaining a driver's licence, ability to read ads in the press, etc.

"My children will continue to travel, and they'll have to make their own way. Schooling isn't going to help them to get on. As far as I'm concerned, they don't have to go; if they want to, they can. The main thing, if they do go, is reading and writing, and sums. The rest is useless" (a semi-nomadic Traveller, aged about forty). "The only thing we did at school was fight. All I learnt there was the letters and the numbers. Once you have the letters and the numbers you can do it all yourself. Me and my dad, we'd go out organ-grinding, for example to Malines. I'd copy out the letters from the roadsigns, then look them up in my book. That's it – Malines! You see? Me, I learnt two languages, I can read and write, but I did it all my own way, travelling. What do you want my kids to do with Gadjo schooling? That's not the way we live!" (nomadic Manouche, aged thirty-five) [Reyniers].

"Let's be honest: our kids are sent to school not so much out of free choice or because the parents think it's a good idea, but because the law says we have to, and if we don't it can cause trouble for us. Not all parents understand the importance of school; the proof is that once the children have finished primary very few parents send them on to secondary. They never stop to think that, without the cert. showing they've finished their legal minimum of schooling, those kids won't be able to get a licence to follow their chosen trade. The kids are finding it out for themselves, though. For the moment they can still use their parents' hawker's licence issued before this schooling requirement came into force. But they won't be able to get one of their own without their school cert. We've already lots of cases of kids going back to school" [Amilcar Debar, in Karpati/Massano].

All of the reports and most of the interviews emphasise that the parents wish above all – and sometimes exclusively – for their children to learn to read, write and count.

The rest is considered either a "plus" or useless, or even harmful (as explained in detail earlier, in the context of opposition to school).

"'We're all for instruction!' declares Jean Alciati (president of the *Centre Culturel Tzigane*). 'Teach us to read, write, and count. But leave your ancestors, the Gauls, outside the classroom. And as for education – we'll take care of that'" [*Ouest-France* (newspaper) 31/10/1985]. "Most important thing with us is reading… they learn all the other things outside of school" [in Quirke, 1984]. "Very few Travellers see school as a means towards earning a livelihood but rather as a place to pick up some useful skills. For a very small minority of children in houses state examinations are a real option and concern... From the point of view of the parents and children success is undoubtedly the achievement of literacy... They feel that once a child is literate they can teach themselves all they need to know about the world" [McCarthy]. "It is clear that for the vast majority of Traveller children and parents what is desired from the schools in the first place are certain basic skills, above all literacy, rather than certification to take part in non-Gypsy waged labour" [Acton/Kenrick].

This utilitarian "three Rs" approach to school, on the present wide scale, is a new phenomenon. Evidence from twenty or even ten years ago shows that up to that time adults felt they were managing perfectly well without literacy and didn't see why their children shouldn't do the same. Now, as a result of the various changes described throughout the preceding chapters, a new (and cautious) desire to acquire a few useful elements as quickly as possible, within well-defined parameters, is emerging.

"Everybody's suddenly so interested in our children! But then they write up little reports on them, labels that they burden us down with, or burden the kids with at any rate... Anyway, I see reasonable people, some saying this, some saying that – but what's the good of it in the end? No matter how many years you've put into educating them, into teaching our children to write, it doesn't look to me like you're making much progress. So I have to conclude that you're not trying too hard, and that the reports aren't altogether true. And as for us – there are little things that wound us: they make our kids do tests with cubes. That's what they do for abnormal children, for people who need some kind of adjusting. But all ours need, is to learn to read and write" [Mrs. Benoît, in Liégeois, 1980d].

In conjunction with these new "utilitarian" wishes, various reports emphasise that many families have a "traditional" concept of school: children are there to learn, not to play or walk about. The teacher is in charge, and his job is to provide the child with useful knowledge, with as little delay as possible.

At the same time the usefulness of school may include factors other than basic learning:

Certain parents "saw it primarily as a convenient crèche for their children" [Hovens et al]. "The children keep asking for broken chairs, scrap metal, and old clothes for their parents; during recreation periods they rummage through the rubbish bins to see if there's anything salvageable" [a schoolteacher, quoted by Reyniers]. "The result was that the school to a very high degree became a winter school. With the coming of spring most families went south. The Gypsies used the school as a place where all their children could stay (even toddlers of three years were 'smuggled' into school often hidden in their big sister's skirts). The reason for this was of course the poor housing conditions in the caravans in the camping place" [Gudmander/Rude].

Yet another use: children's school attendance can be a bargaining point in a hostile world: parents threaten to withdraw them if 'the powers that be' fail to meet certain demands (for halting space, supplementary social welfare such as clothing vouchers, transport for the children, etc.).

Convergence?

On the one hand Gypsy children, like other children, find themselves under legal obligation to attend school, and the authorities see no reason to exempt them: all children have the right, but also the duty, to attend school, unless the parents can guarantee to provide similar instruction and prove that they are so doing. On the other hand, within the European Community, more and more Gypsies are deciding that schooling their children, at least at primary level, will help them adapt to surrounding society. There is certainly no blurring of difference between Gypsies' wishes, and those of the school system – as we have demonstrated amply within this chapter. *We can, however, speak of a formal convergence between the desire to provide schooling and the desire to be schooled. The question is how to evolve a response to various demands while respecting the wishes of all.* Earlier chapters (notably "Structures" and "Teachers") have already put forward some possibilities. And, having noted the fundamental opposition of the two education systems in question, it is worth pausing to consider pedagogical practices in school.

Before tackling them, let us emphasise once again that the more efforts are made to meet each other half-way, the better are the chances that the present trend will grow, and that more and more Gypsy children will attend school. If we have seen Gypsies physically (or symbolically) tearing down their schools, we have also seen Gypsies building them, participating in their work, defending them and their teachers. We also see that "Parental motivation, more than their degree of schooling, directly influences children's success in acquiring literacy" [Reyniers, questionnaire for the present work]. We must also emphasise the role – generally ignored or underestimated – played by children in their parents' adaptation, in transforming their vision of school. If the parents feel that their children are happy and respected in school, their attitude changes profoundly – all the national reports give examples of this, many of them quite moving.

Parental confidence must be earned. To do so we must habilitate school in the eyes of Gypsies and Travellers; we cannot speak of re-habilitation since up to now school has deserved neither the trust nor interest of Gypsy families. *Now that many states seem to be discarding assimilationism, at least to some degree, and cultural diversity in general, and Gypsies in particular, are being seen in a new light, these theoretical changes must find practical expression.*

"The refusal to be assimilated, demonstrated over centuries and constantly reiterated by Gypsy participants, should lead educationists and the institutions within which they operate to conceive of school in terms other than as a means of assimilation. Programmes – and a state of mind – compatible with the dynamics of Traveller culture would avoid transforming the individual's very identity (his sense of security and individuality) into a source of conflict with the school" [synopsis of an international symposium, Liégeois, 1983b]. "Unless the schools recognise the differences in the positive sense of trying to identify and meet their differing needs, the schools are transformed into battlefields with both sides alienated from each other by the dichotomy of 'us' and 'them'. Such a relationship is not productive of true and profitable learning, it only helps to institutionalise the divisions thus perpetuating misunderstandings" [Ivatts, 1975, p.41].

Misunderstanding is perpetuated in part by the unquestioning use of inaccurate or misleading terms:

• The use may be *habitual*, and thus felt to be validated by experience; users lack perspective from which to critically examine and adapt such words. The prime example is (as noted earlier) the common all-encompassing connotation of the word "education" when in fact schooling is what is under discussion. Again, "education" can be used as a synonym for "teaching" or simply "instruction". If the distinction between these were made in spirit, word, and deed, parents would be much reassured. As frequently pointed out by Gypsy – and many other! – parents, one may be educated without undergoing formal instruction, and mere instruction can never replace education – particularly the type that they provide. Parents expect to find teachers – not "educators" – at school. They have no desire to delegate their educative duties in the way that most of the society around them does.

• Such terms may also be *technical*, yet simultaneously convey the ideology which inspires them, and which prevents their being clearly analysed; an example is the use of terminology such as "special classes", also referred to earlier. Parents object to this term (since it implies maladjustment and carries a risk of ghettoisation) – and school authorities are beginning to reject it too. One of the paradoxes of this erroneous name is that, now that there is general agreement to disband "special" classes or to avoid setting them up in the first place, many successfully adapted or specialised classes (as described under "Structures") are also in danger of disappearing, simply because they are called by the "wrong" name.

• *Fashion* plays a role too – certain words burst on the scene with a lovely innovative ring. There's no point in asking what they actually mean, since everybody's using them. A case in point at present is "integration" and related concepts. "Integration" with what? Into a framework of intercultural pedagogy (we shall return to this point) or into a single system to which all children are expected to conform? One can attempt precise definitions:

"Integration is interpreted as a dynamic process within which, and during the development of which, those involved must take an active part. We reject the interpretation of integration as a passive adaptation to changed social conditions" [Bremer Volkshochschule, 1983, p.11].

Yet case by case precision is insufficient when dealing with such widespread terms. Everyone assumes that he knows the precise meaning, and that this is also exactly what others have in mind. It's a practical set-up, and not conducive to sitting down and hammering out definitions. "Integration" is the "in thing". Yet if we stand back and observe, we see that even radically opposing factions all claim to be promoting "integration", "but the models of integration vary so much, from total assimilation to total autonomy with separate schools, that the common content of this integrationism amounts to little more than a preference that conflicts should be settled without resort to actual violence or coercion" [Acton/Kenrick].

It is thus preferable to avoid terms which mean "everything and nothing" and which in practice simply annoy those who use them as expressions of quite different concepts. If "integration" only means children using a common school, it is useless to use such an ambiguous phrase to describe it. Ambiguous because – although we won't go into the details of the debate here – sociologically speaking, integration is the first step towards assimilation. Ambiguous too because of the usual connotations of the word, such as listed in a dictionary: "assimilation, fusion, incorporation, unification"[7] – and it is in this sense, rather than the mathematical, economic, psychological or physiological, that it is commonly employed in pedagogical circles. Ambiguous too, because the very word integration implies that some children – be they immigrants or Gypsies – are being seen as "outsiders", "different", or even "maladjusted", and must therefore make an effort to fit into the school which is going to "integrate" them. Does anyone in France speak of the "integration" of "native French" children into school? What about in Britain? Ireland? Elsewhere? *The present "integrationist" movement in school circles is ethnocentric. It is developing within a context and with a state of mind contrary to those which postulate "intercultural education".*

An evaluation report from the Council of Europe on the subject of experimental classes emphasises their authoritarian and ethnocentric character: "We encountered no example of systematic effort to involve parents, even those handicapped by language barriers and social isolation, in the planning stages of experimental classes. As a rule, everything was pre-programmed, and proposed – not to mention imposed – in a pre-established situation" [Karagiorges, 1984, p.17].

The use of inaccurate, fuzzy terminology contributes to the perpetuation of misunderstandings and the general status quo between the two communities. Once school wants to be truly useful to all, and once parents want to benefit from the usefulness of the school, both sides must express their positions with clarity. This is why the use of the types of expression we have criticised here is harmful – all the more so since there is practically no consultation between the two principal partners (administration and parents) and thus little opportunity to clear up misunderstandings. *Convergence implies dialogue.*

Still on the subject of convergence, let us remind ourselves that, while it is well to be wary of the concept of "one school for all which (through 'integration') will quickly iron out differences in the name of equality", it is equally well to be wary of protectionism which, in the name of respecting difference, attempts to prevent any change at all. It is sobering to recall that this was the option favoured by some Nazis, notably Eva Justin, who based her conclusions on her own research and that of predecessors such as Weitershagen: "We must ask ourselves if this education, which for us and for our children has value, would not from the ethnographic point of view constitute a degeneration for them (the Gypsies)" [Eva Justin, quoted by Reemtsma].

"The populations among which Gypsies live should, in principle, neither impose upon them tools for which they feel no need, nor refuse them access to those they do decide on. But to avoid both pitfalls is a difficult task for anyone, and ambiguities are rife. For example, those who (in the name of 'respect' for a culture) seek to protect it from 'contamination' show little faith in its dynamics, its situation of ongoing contact with others, and the constant change which is the ongoing situation in every culture. And claiming to promote diversity and respect for identity without giving each – and particularly minorities – the possibility of acquiring the instruments for active adaptation, is hypocritical. Cultural plurality cannot become a situation of interculturalism unless the cultures involved can interact in an egalitarian fashion" [Liégeois, 1983b].

Teaching content

Teachers' reports on the material they have covered, and Gypsy children's success or failure with it, are in agreement on some points but widely diversified on others. The fact that they are diversified attests to the diversity of the children themselves, and that some succeed where others fail – also for a multiplicity of reasons. Yet it is also an indication of the subjectivity of the teacher, influenced by his or her own personal tastes and skills:

"Against the wisdom of many teachers, we would conclude that there is no real evidence of Gypsies having particular aptitudes or lack of aptitudes for any particular subject. Nor can we really see any reason to expect any. Of course the talents of particular children – and perhaps by statistical chance, small groups of children – may be specialised; but we are convinced that the generalised reports that Gypsies are 'good at this, bad at that' reflect on the whole the preferences and abilities of the teachers, rather than those of the pupils. Does the teacher fear the introduction of computing into schools? Then it will certainly turn out to be 'not the kind of thing Traveller children are good at'" [Acton/Kenrick].

Yet other conclusions, even under different forms, are similar. These concern fundamental skills such as learning how to hold a pencil or use a ruler, and an overall tendency of Traveller children to experience difficulty in the same areas: oral communication (as required by the school, that is), written communication, and mathematical abstraction, coupled with a tendency to do well in activities involving graphic and musical expression, practical activities requiring manual skills and concrete knowledge – particularly based upon direct observation and familiarity with nature and animals.

It would be wrong to form conclusions on the children's abilities even along these broadly agreed lines. The teacher would risk forming a rigid image of the type of pedagogy he should be providing, with harmful consequences (let us bear in mind the "Pygmalion Effect", described earlier). Instead, these indications ought to lead us to critically examine the content of what is being taught, and its relevance to the in-family education of the Gypsy child. It is important to begin by emphasising that learning about the school itself – which is already an important and difficult task – requires all the child's energy. Any other learning or intellectual progress will come as an extra, and that only when the child feels at ease in the school context. Perhaps this is why they are so reluctant to come, or do not come at all. Next, we must consider that the Gypsy child's socialisation occurs within a culturally determined context, and has as its aim the adaptation of the child to that context rather than to an alien and irrelevant context such as school. This is why it is worth reminding ourselves yet again that "the common ground uniting the teacher, the Settled children, and the Gypsy child, is very limited" [Kervadec, 1982, p.66]. *Since they are alien to his experience, all of the fundamental points of reference on which school is based have no meaning at all for the Traveller child.* He feels entirely disoriented, and unmotivated. Nowadays for example the new message is that learning to read is above all a search for meaning rather than a sterile exercise in deciphering, which in turn brings an emphasis on functional literacy, and this accords with parents' emphasis on utility.

The child, accustomed to handling both concrete and symbolic systems which are other than those of school, is not prepared to succeed in a school which does not accept and validate his familiar systems. It is thus indispensable to take into account the conditions of his existence and the qualities which he has had to develop within this context: constant invention of survival strategies, "a sharpened awareness of reality, a remarkable intuitive capacity" [Karpati/ Massano]. And some of these qualities may become disadvantages within the context of school:

"In order to be able, as illiterates, to live in a society where writing determines everything, they must develop compensating mechanisms. These become obstacles in learning to read, because they discourage it: for example the ability to memorise texts very quickly, to figure things out from a couple of pictures and guess what comes next, to pay attention to the movement of the teacher's lips instead of concentrating on making sense of the letters" [Bremer Volkshochschule, 1983, p.20].

It is thus a question of a meeting of several "codes" (family, school, outside world); sometimes they clash. The result, when school is rigid and monolithic, is conflict – be it externalised or interior. As many reports emphasise, one cannot therefore state that Gypsy children have, for example, particular language difficulties, or are incapable of abstraction, but that the teaching content and above all the method by which it is presented, are inappropriate.

Gypsy experience at school

These differences, which so easily become open conflicts creating difficulties for both child and teacher, have been perceived for a long time, and efforts to overcome them have been going on for a long time too. There are two general approaches. In the first, the child's characteristics are defined as handicaps to success in the existing programme, so the child – perceived as handicapped – becomes the object of intensive efforts to help him catch up on the delay he is judged to have, and to compensate for the deficiencies attributed to him. This is the broad route, still followed in a great many cases even at the level of governmental strategies of "integration by handicap" as criticised earlier on. Alternatively – and this is the preferred approach for many of those concerned, and that which accommodates cultural plurality – the cultural characteristics of all children regardless of origin can become active components of the dynamic of the school.

This approach implies first and foremost a *recognition* of all the learning both physical and intellectual which the child has already acquired within his own environment. This consideration is particularly important with regard to Gypsy children: "Gypsy culture is not, as we can say of other (immigrant) children, their 'heritage', euphemised into the past tense; it is an ongoing phenomenon, lived daily" [Liégeois 1983b]. There is a lot of talk nowadays about "learner-centred" pedagogy. Well, it is the child who is the learner – an observation so self-evident that it is sometimes lost sight of. The child cannot live two parallel social and cultural existences simultaneously, passing from one to the other every time he crosses the threshold of the school. It is therefore the child's characteristics which should serve as the basis of pedagogy, rather than being devalued and dismissed as a mere hindrance. As many of the reports remark, these characteristics are in no way intrinsically incompatible with the faculties the child needs to do well in school. Moreover, a significant number of the teachers most directly involved have a positive vision of their Gypsy and Traveller pupils' intellectual capabilities, finding them astute, and competent; teachers' criticisms tend to focus on these children's willingness to learn what they're presented with, and on matters of discipline.

Apart from recognition, this approach also implies *understanding*. Understanding of the fact that, for the school to accommodate Gypsy experience, and use it as a basis, it must also take into account what happens outside the school in various domains (economic, educational, living conditions and so on) which mould the child's personality and influence his behaviour. It also entails understanding that "certain behaviour perceived as determining should instead be perceived as determined (inattention for example)" [Balas, 1984, p.84].

It is to understand, for example, that children are reluctant to "talk about their homes and experiences, whether because they have been brought up to reveal nothing to outsiders, or because they're afraid of being criticised or ridiculed for their lifestyle which others will certainly disapprove of. Yet when communication switches from the verbal to the nonverbal plane, Gypsy children reveal remarkable expressive capacities" [Karpati/Massano]. "We have observed in certain (Gypsy) children a block on any form of verbalisation about their own environment" [interim report of a French pilot scheme, Ministry of National Education, 1984, p.31].

It is to take into account attitudes about teachers as well as work habits and group consensus:

"Haggling relationships, negotiation techniques. Attitudes of automatic distrust, vigilance, defensiveness. For the children, attitudes of flight and regrouping amongst themselves… These constants are generally perceived as obstacles or difficulties, yet if they can be appreciated in a positive sense they can be utilised as so many bases on which the teacher can lay his work. Thus the teacher can 'negotiate' in a much clearer way his relationships with parents and children, especially as regards administrative, financial, and school-related questions... Similarly, the teacher's expectations and input for the class must be thought out in the light of these elements. Thus, the often intense emotional bonds that may form between teacher and pupils cannot be expressed in the same ways one would use with Settled children. And come what may, they will always be delimited by this reality: that school is not a place where it is desirable for one to feel too good, and the teacher is not an acceptable role model" [Cotonnec, 1983].

"Individual cooperation with staff is seen by the Gypsy group as duplicity. The norm of the Gypsy group demands non-cooperation with the school. Any deviation or compromise produces a conflict within the individual and between the individual and the group. One is either for the school and against the group or vice versa. The personal and group conflict which is occasioned by ambivalent attitudes towards authority often results in troublesome and destructive behaviour. An individual who had been encouraged by his teacher to make a model waggon smashed it to pieces when it was completed... Personal survival within the Gypsy community is ultimately more important than success at school" [Ivatts, 1975, p.32]. These attitudes seem to emerge more strongly when – as in the above example – school attendance is enforced from without.

It is not enough to recognise and understand Gypsy experience; the school must also accord it full *respect*. Respect in particular for the wishes of parents who request that elements of their culture not be displayed in public without precautions. All parents hope for prudence, and to retain a modicum of intimacy for themselves. But apart from this general attitude, positions vary greatly. Some families oppose the use of Gypsy language – or any other cultural element – in the school. Others limit their objections to the language itself, wishing it to remain "secret", a tool in the struggle against assimilation; on the whole, these same families do support the teaching of Gypsy history. Yet other families favour the use of language and other cultural elements in school. This range of positions is based on a general underlay of shared belief that Gypsy culture cannot be taught in school, distrust of school as an alien institution, and the utilitarian attitude of parents to school, seeing it as a place to pick up extra skills rather than cultural elements – which they themselves are far more competent to transmit.

"There is no great pressure for innovatory methods, or for the utilisation of Gypsy culture and language from the majority of Gypsy parents – who do not really see school as a matter of culture at all but as an instrumental means to a particular skill, literacy... It is some of those Travellers who have more experience of non-Gypsy education, who have moved outside the safety of Traveller-dominated occupations, who perceive the cultural threat posed by the school and argue for bringing Gypsy culture and language into the school. Some Travellers, however, oppose this, fearing stigmatisation, and arguing that they want their children to be the same as all the other children (apparently believing that all non-Gypsy children are the same, more or less). And many parents are suspicious that their children may be made the subject of educational experiments at the expense of their own needs. One Traveller organisation in particular has identified itself with the backlash against 'progressive' education" [Acton/Kenrick].

Gypsy culture at school also means that non-Gypsy children will be exposed to it, and this may be useful in combating prejudice. If Gypsy culture is given a role in the school, it is validated by the fact, and all involved will be encouraged to view the Gypsies as a cultural minority, rather than as a social category. The pedagogic implications of such a shift of perspective are enormously important; so are the psychological ones.

"For parents to accept and be satisfied with the instruction their children are getting, it is absolutely imperative that they be taught – alongside non-Gypsy pupils – about their origins, starting in fourteenth century India and going right up to the present day in France, Europe and the world. Ninety per cent of parents know nothing of their origins or history, and would be happy for their children to discover these things, learn them, and talk about them with the rest of the family" [Pierre Yung, President of *l'Union des Tsiganes et Voyageurs de France*, 1980a, p.384].

In order to achieve the goals of recognising, understanding and respecting parents' wishes, and to enable Gypsy culture to fully express itself, the school must also develop *flexibility* in its structures and workings. Such flexibility must permit different cultures to express themselves in various ways, without those activities of particular relevance to them being treated as extras outside the normal curriculum or schedule, nor should such activities be artificially extracted from their cultural context. Flexibility would enable us to get away from the widespread dichotomy, both versions of which are incompatible with cultural plurality: assimilationist models, in which all children must learn the same things from the same programmes imposed by the politically dominant majority, versus the pitfalls of the new "patchwork multiculturalism" in which a supplementary programme of "heritage culture" is offered (usually outside school hours and normal school activities) in addition to the same old assimilationist curriculum. This practice disorients the child, overburdens him, and increases his likelihood of failure.

Such basic attitudes, essential if Gypsy/Traveller experience is to enter into the school, may seem simple and self-evident, yet are far indeed from being generally accepted and further still from wide implementation. Almost all the reports indicate that, insofar as Gypsy culture is taken into account at all, it is in a most fragmentary manner, with certain elements being extracted and either "folklorised" (to be used as occasional spice in a monotonous monocultural scholastic diet) or redefined as handicaps to be overcome. Even official national programmes concerning Gypsies and Travellers are still, in 1985, rife with such tendencies, mentioning such goals as "the necessity of instilling good habits of personal hygiene", "honesty and openness", etc., as well as sobriety and respect for representatives of majority society such as police officers. It seems that many teachers still are more inclined to push for change in Traveller culture and lifestyle, than towards respecting and building upon the dynamics of that culture and lifestyle.

Gypsy language in school

Whatever one's stance on the subject of use of mother tongue and/or bilingualism in school, the position of Gypsy language is a question demanding consideration: children may arrive at school with so little knowledge of the language of instruction that teachers end up appointing other Gypsy children as interpreters for them. Even more commonly, Gypsy children do have a fluent command of the teacher's language, yet their use of it is non-standard and almost impossible for the teacher to correct.

"The English spoken by Traveller children, however, is often non-standard, usually a regional vernacular. Often, however, because of nomadism, children attend school in a different region to that whose vernacular they speak. Irish Traveller children in particular are marked in British schools by their Irish English. But we are also told in Scotland that differences of regional accent could lead to difficulties of understanding in the schools" [Acton/Kenrick].

This is how a (French) schoolteacher put it: "It seems to me that, in the school context, there are three separate linguistic spheres:
1) the Traveller version, but not quite the same as that used at home; it's 'corrected' for use in the school. This is their mother tongue, modified for use with Settled people...
2) standard oral French, as spoken by the teacher
3) written French[8]
In theory, the teacher has a command of the last two, but not of the first; the children are in the opposite situation" [Cotonnec, 1983].

But if Gypsy linguistic practice cannot be ignored in school, pedagogy based on its dynamics, or even a simple recognition of its legitimacy, is still far from widespread. On the contrary, the children's use of language is still on the whole viewed as an obstacle to be overcome before even basic learning (reading and writing) can be accomplished – in the official national language. The few attempts made in various countries to recognise and make use of Romani in school, have come up against massive opposition (including from Gypsy parents themselves) and other difficulties (lack of teaching materials and trained personnel). This is yet another result of the history of the school institution, coupled with the history of the relations between Gypsies and their environment. Gypsies have a (minority) language, but without a territorial base; it has been suppressed and even banned repeatedly throughout the centuries. Since they have no "country of origin", they have neither consulate nor embassy. "Romani is the only international language which is not officially recognised in any country" [Calvet, 1985, p. 66]. It must be added that it is not (save as a very recent and still rare phenomenon) a written language. Romani thus faces even more obstacles than other minority languages as regards being introduced into the school. How much longer will we have to say, as in Greece, that "teaching Romanès in class is still a remote dream"? [Korré/Marselos].

However, the general trend at present is towards the use of the mother tongue in school:

"Language is now seen by educationists as a social practice, anchored and developed in the day-to-day realities of school and the broader social context, rather than as an entity in itself... To change from one language to another is to switch universes *in every sense*, so much so that we can take as 'concrete' the manner in which forms and colours are perceived, the way in which existence itself is conceived and lived. The acquisition of a language is the acquisition of a universe. Ethnolinguistics have brought us many examples, all the more striking in that the linguistic codes and cultural universes being compared are far removed from our own; the classic example of Whorf's [1956] analysis of Hopi Indian language is a case in point... This means that to teach a Gypsy child a language other than his own is to teach him a code which will mould his thinking, a code which is unfamiliar and in which he conducts himself awkwardly: he is thereby penalised on the psychological level as well as the scholastic.

It has been established, notably in UNESCO research, that the necessity of learning through a language other than the mother tongue causes a scholastic delay of about three years, and that it is essentially unfamiliarity with the language of instruction which lies at the root of poor scholastic performance [this fact is emphasised in connection with Gypsies, notably by Hübschmannova, note 22]. It has also been established that... the greatest progress in second languages is made by those who express themselves the most in the mother tongue: the fact is synonymous with validation of their cultural universe, freeing them from feelings of shame and inferiority which result from speaking badly a language which is being taught without regard for their roots... In fact, anomie or the loss of individual reference values occurs much more commonly in what one might call 'semi-linguistic' situations, than in bilingual ones. It follows from these considerations that teachers ought at the very least to have some knowledge of the structures of their pupils' mother tongue(s). This will both give teachers an insight into the children's thinking patterns, and help them to understand the interference of the first language on the second, and the types of mistake the children are likely to make as a result. Teaching French as a second language to children with a different mother tongue requires this type of in-depth preparation" [Liégeois, 1980b].

We could give many examples of reflections along these lines; we shall limit ourselves to a few recent overviews:

"Pupils with another first language than Swedish must receive significant portions of their instruction in their own first language for the following reasons, apart from the fact that the country has adopted an official policy of active bilingualism:

- pupils must be able to understand what their teachers are trying to teach them;
- pupils should feel secure with peers and teachers, in a familiar linguistic environment, in order to facilitate their continued learning;
- pupils' achievements should be judged according to the particulars of their own situation, i.e. conditions which characterise their particular linguistic and cultural groups, whether it be in the majority or the minority;
- requiring pupils to change languages (e.g. from home language to Swedish) during the time of their basic education in reading and writing imposes a serious strain upon them...
- instruction *about* a certain language is not sufficient. In order for pupils to be bilingual, instruction on a certain language must be combined with instruction *through the medium* of that language;

- at present, neither the amount of natural nor of regulated (through formal education) language stimulation in Sweden is sufficient with respect to minority languages.

Pupils with another first language than Swedish must also receive instruction in Swedish as a second language because:

- Swedish usually is the minority pupil's second language;
- minority pupils should receive Swedish instruction on their own conditions, which are not the same as those for pupils with Swedish as a first language. This should allow all pupils to feel secure and develop self confidence;
- Swedish instruction for immigrant pupils should not be regarded as remedial instruction which, among other things, causes them to miss part of the regular instruction given through the medium of Swedish;
- immigrant pupils' instruction in Swedish should be designed according to their particular learning requirements, taking into consideration their first language/home culture, their need for substantial oral and written skills, training in Swedish in natural communication situations, their need to read literature in order to build up vocabulary and concepts related to cultural and social relations in Sweden. One must also take into consideration that immigrant children do learn some Swedish naturally by virtue of their living environment" [Opper, 1985, pp.23-24].

The same report refers to observations made by Henning Johansson (of the University of Umeå) in the Torne Valley near the Finnish border. In this region the languages are Swedish, Finnish, and Saami (Lappish). Only Swedish is recognised, and multilingualism is looked down upon. Johansson introduced the following experimental approaches into a sample of classes: children studied their own history, visited workplaces of members of their own culture, and sang songs in their own languages. While Swedish remained the first language of instruction, children were allowed to express themselves in whatever language they wished, and a monitoring programme was set up. Moreover, parents showed an increased acceptance of bilingualism instead of discouraging it in the home.

After three years, the test group showed better results in mathematics than other children in the same region, and their results in Swedish were also better than those of other children in the same valley – in some cases better than the national average (the regional average being below the national level). Among the conclusions drawn was that it is the school which is "handicapped" if it fails to make use of the children's different cultural backgrounds, "and not the children who are handicapped by their cultural differences" [reported in Opper, 1985].

In Italy, near Padua, "An experiment in validating the Gypsy language (was carried out). The contrastive method employed not only enriched the Rom children's knowledge of their mother tongue, but also helped them to learn Italian" [Karpati/Massano].

It would seem then from every point of view to be pedagogically necessary and useful to utilise the mother tongue. Moreover it appears to be equally necessary and useful from the point of view of the child's formation: "Literacy which does not include literacy in one's mother tongue may result in an orphaned intellect" [Acton/Davies, 1979, p.92]. But, as we stressed earlier, school provision for Traveller children – of which the use of their language in school is but one aspect – is a social problem, not a pedagogical one. And quite apart from the purely policy-related considerations involved, it is important to emphasise the psychological consequences of this situation.

"The conflicts of bilingualism (in the strict sense) are located within a much broader – and unavoidable – conflict, that of contact between civilisations" [Bastide, undated MS., p.6]. "The conflict of bilingualism is merely a syndrome of a vaster conflictual ensemble: the lacerated individual, social and cultural laceration" [Memmi, 1951].

It is within this context that parents' misgivings must be understood and taken into account. As with the very idea of schooling itself, or the introduction of Gypsy culture into the school, opinions on the school use of Gypsy language are deeply divided. Some feel that the Gypsy language, used exclusively within the group, fulfils a protective function against outside influences: "We don't want it to be known, or taught; our children learn it and speak it fluently." Some parents complain that teachers and social workers, instead of getting on with teaching their children the majority language, try instead to learn Gypsy language themselves. The fact that Gypsy communities have regularly been subject to persecution reinforces both their mistrust of outsiders wishing to learn their language, and their caution as regards its use in situations which could be beyond their control. Nor does the universal use of the language as a form of opposition to the non-Gypsy world, and in dialect forms which serve as a reinforcement of the speaker's group identity and a demarcation between groups, favour scholastic use which implies loss of exclusivity, a written form utilisable by non-Gypsies, and a homogenisation to the detriment of the "exclusive" element of identity amongst various Gypsy groups.

Yet other parents are proud of their language, conscious of its importance and thus of the importance of supporting it and increasing its status; they want it to be recognised and validated by the school on a par with other minority languages. Still other parents are indifferent to the whole question: insofar as the acceptance of Gypsy children into school in the first place may still seem a distant possibility [see the statistics given above], it may seem premature indeed to develop a stance on the language. At the same time, however, we can continue to consider the question, and to evolve policies.

The first task is the advancement of the ideas and options outlined above, on the importance of the use of the mother tongue, and the development of theoretical knowledge and practice pertaining to it. Moreover the emphasis is now on language "experience": there is broad recognition that "The basis of a language is not its written form but the community which uses it in its daily life, within its social practices" [Verbunt, 1985, p.12]; on the other side of the coin, the question of the practice and relevance of school language in the home is also being looked into. There is agreement that the quality of the child's expression *within his own environment* must be taken into account. The fact that, to date, there exists no standardised version of Gypsy language is doubtless a disadvantage in the short term (no books, teaching programmes, trained instructors…). Yet it is also a strength: the language which will find its way into school will be a living one, identical with the child's daily linguistic experience. This will help to avoid some of the pitfalls faced by certain immigrant children, whose mother tongue instructors and teaching materials may – particularly if provided directly by the "homeland" – differ significantly from the usage of the children themselves.

In the light of certain classic studies concluding that members of different social groups express themselves differently (that, for example, working class speakers are better at argument and storytelling than intellectuals, etc. [cf. for example Labov, 1969]), some teachers have begun to examine Gypsy linguistic patterns: "Do Gypsies speak badly (do they have reduced linguistic capability) or do they speak differently (do they have a linguistic form particular to themselves)?" [Kervadec, 1982, p.37] and attempt to describe "Traveller talk" [see, among others, Kervadec, Cotonnec, and Acton/Kenrick]. Research has been undertaken, which should lead to further investigations, particularly as regards Gypsy children. Mention can be made of, for example, the work of the University of London Institute of Education (within the framework of their Linguistic Minorities Project), through an investigation of schoolchildren's linguistic resources (Schools Language Survey) using methodology evolved in cooperation with Language Information Network Co-ordination, a Europe-wide coordinating body. Let us go on to cite "the communicative approach to language teaching" developed by the Council of Europe since the late 1970s.

"The principles of this approach were adopted at the highest political level, in 1982, by the Committee of Ministers of Foreign Affairs of the Member States. It stipulates principally that:

- language-teaching must be founded on the needs, motivations, characteristics and resources of the learner;
- realistic and worthwhile objectives of language instruction must be clearly formulated;
- appropriate materials and methods must be developed;
- circumstances permitting, teaching programmes should be subject to evaluation.

The Advisor to the project... has called this evolution towards language learning based on communication 'a decisive step towards liberating the subject from the obsessive concentration on minor grammatical errors which has characterised it in the past'. The best-known aspect of this work has been the definition of the objectives of language-learning, as designated by the term *threshold levels*. Students who have attained this level will be able to cope with everyday situations in a foreign country, and get to know the people they meet there" [Council of Europe, 1984, p.34]. These principles, which have "served as a base for innovation in language-teaching in school and at adult level", could be applied to teaching Gypsy children the national language of their base country as a second language; they could also be used in the training of some of the teachers and other personnel who will be working with Gypsy children and their families.

Another element currently under discussion is the introduction of Gypsy language into the school. At present some efforts are being made in various countries, but the initiative is far from being widespread; the following observations from the *United Kingdom* apply to most of the European Community:

"Curiously the Swann Report (*Education for All*, HMSO, 1985) commissioned by the government to examine the disadvantages of ethnic minorities in education, concludes that bi-lingual education or even the teaching of languages other than English in primary schools would be bad for 'race relations'. Despite the efforts of educational reformers to the contrary, teachers often see bilingualism as a 'problem' rather than an asset" [Acton/Kenrick]. As a result the few instances of use of Gypsy language in school have been in connection with voluntary projects.

It may also happen that institutional and teaching conditions are fulfilled, yet efforts still come to naught:

In *Denmark*, the rules "presuppose that instruction is provided in every language for which at least twelve pupils have enrolled. However, in order to provide instruction in the language, it is a condition that it is written language, that teaching material is available and that it is possible to find a qualified teacher – normally educated in the homeland. If the above conditions have been fulfilled, the local authorities are under an obligation to offer instruction in the language concerned. The local authorities must see to it that the families who do not understand Danish are informed of the offer. It is for the parents to decide whether their children are to participate in the mother-tongue (national language) instruction provided." When there are less than twelve pupils, and local authorities thus decide against providing tuition in the children's language, they must establish an agreement with other municipalities (subject to the consent of the parents), because of the resulting protraction of the children's school careers. In 1983-84, thirty-three languages were employed in teaching in Folkeskoler (comprehensive schools) in Danish urban centres, in 280 classes in which 48% of all immigrant children were enrolled. It is up to parents to decide whether their child will attend this type of class, and in what language (if they themselves have several). Thus, among Yugoslav immigrants, Albanian, Turkish, Macedonian and Serbo-Croat are all spoken (and all available as languages of instruction in Denmark) but many parents opt for Serbo-Croat which is most widely spoken and ultimately the most useful for the children to have. We have given all these details [provided by Gudmander/Rude] as a concrete illustration of a school system which actively favours the use of children's first languages.

Romani is not, at present, among the languages taught, though two attempts in this direction have been made. The first, in Copenhagen, in collaboration with the vice-president of a Gypsy organisation, was all arranged, and then fell through: parents – including those who had participated in setting up the project – simply refused to send their children. The second venture is described as follows: "The municipality of Elsinore also tried to start mother-tongue instruction for the Gypsy group. Books were purchased and procured from Sweden and Norway. Arrangements were made with a Gypsy who was educated as a teacher in Sweden, to the effect that he was to travel to Denmark and give instruction once a week for three hours. The parents had mentioned this possibility several times and wanted it practised. The first three lessons were a great experience to everybody – mainly for the children who hung on the teacher's lips, while he talked and talked. The Danish teachers had never seen the children to be so much wrapped up in anything before. Everything seemed to be alright. On the same evening the storm broke – the telephones were glowing with abuses and curses. The following days the parents kept the children home from school. The teacher was sent round to some of the homes to try to ease the situation. He was well received everywhere – it turned out he was related to some of them – but it never came to any instruction again. It was simply refused. The spokesmen of the group never gave a reasonable explanation. Thus, it can be stated that in spite of many efforts no mother-tongue instruction for Gypsies living in Denmark is given" [Gudmander/Rude].

Sweden, too, has incorporated a recognition of the child's first language into its school system. Thus, in 1979-80, "mother tongue" teachers, covering fifty-two languages, comprised 3% of the total teaching force. Since the late '70s immigrant children in primary school can get instruction in and through their mother tongue, and some mothers – notably Spanish and Turkish – participate in the classes. The operative principle is that "All children must be able to feel that their language is adequate and that they can use their experiences and their own words while learning to read and write" [Skolöverstyrelsen, *Läroplan för Grundskolan*]. "Hitherto it has been practically impossible for Gypsy children having Romani as their home language to obtain instruction of this kind, but in recent years a number of books have been published in the language. One difficulty here is that Romani does not have a standard written language. Gypsy children have not been able to obtain books and newspapers, in their own language. Development work is now in progress with the aim of evolving a common written language. Another difficulty is the shortage of home language teachers. There is an urgent need for adult Gypsies to be trained for teaching duties of this kind" [Statens Invandrarverk, *Zigenare*, 1983].

It would certainly be worth taking into account the Swedish experience, which has not been without difficulties. Other countries, notably Norway and Yugoslavia, could also provide us with food for thought on teaching Romani and through Romani; this report has neither the time nor space to give them the consideration they deserve. In *Norway* two Gypsies attended teacher training college as mature students, and they are now actively involved in teaching Gypsy children. A first reader in Romani was published in 1979, followed by other titles. "In principle, the Gypsy children can learn to read in their own language, but this is dependent on a Romanès-speaking person in the class. Too often we do not have that and then our material in Romanès is useless" [Ragnhild Schlüter, MS., 1984]. In *Yugoslavia* some schools do seem to have developed teaching through Romani, but there are considerable difficulties here too despite the very significant number of Gypsies [cf. Puxon, 1979].

The conclusions one can draw from the above about school use of Gypsy language reflect the overall situation. Parents are divided in their reactions to the idea, while the authorities tend to react negatively (yet another confirmation of the fact that, when these same authorities speak of integration, they do so ethnocentrically: they want monolinguistic integration, through the use of a single national language). However in several countries – mostly outside the European Community – we can observe positive measures regarding the school use of Romani, with difficulties arising from lack of trained teachers, lack of teaching materials, and sometimes parents' rejection of the idea. Taking all of this into account, evolution is occurring both in pedagogical thinking[9] – which now tends to recognise the use of the mother tongue, at least in the earliest school years – and also in the expressed wishes of Gypsy parents and organisations, in the same direction.

The situation will change rapidly over the next few years, as the number of Gypsy children in school continues to grow despite difficulties and the inadequacy of most provision for them. This in turn will increase the demand for school usage of Romani, for analysis (e.g.grammar) of the language, and publications in and about it.

"All over Europe educational schemes have been started alongside the political movements of the last decade. The tiny Romani intelligentsia of today will be swelled a hundred-fold in the next generation; there will be a mass audience for the Romani literature which is beginning to emerge" [Acton/Davies, 1979, p.105].

"An essential condition for creating written language is the necessity of responding to concrete needs. Such need is scarcely felt, since the Gypsies have never practised reading and writing in any language. Things change when, having attained literacy, they begin to appreciate the advantages of written communication. Yet these advantages are limited in the case of very frequent international contacts with group members dispersed around the four corners of the world. In such a situation it is preferable to communicate directly in Romani than in any 'lingua franca'... This is where the need for a uniform written version is felt. And such a system exists" [Calvet, 1985, p.68].

There are more and more publications in the Gypsy language: transcriptions of songs and traditional or modern story-telling, translations of the Old Testament or the Gospels, dictionaries, grammars, children's books, readers and more. There are still grounds for complaint with regard to lack of materials, but – especially if exchange continues to intensify – this can be overcome. A common orthography could be developed and promoted, making possible exchange between countries and between dialects. The creation of a standard form [cf. for example Hancock, 1975] is certainly a daunting task, and will only become feasible when written versions of the various existing dialects have been successfully established – if indeed it still seems necessary at that point.

It is not a question of teaching Romani, if the teacher himself is not a Rom or if the class includes non-Gypsy children. Such as task is beyond his duty – and beyond his ability. What he must do, is respect the child's mother tongue, and incorporate it into his educational work.

"When you have a relationship of trust with the children and their parents, they will be prepared to share Romanès or Gammon with you; they may indeed find the idea of writing it down fascinating and novel. 'It'd be like having a third hand,' said one boy. The teacher will begin to find it natural to take part in conversations which inject Romani words into a still mostly English context, and to write those words down for the children, to write *'jukel'* and *'vardo'* as well as 'dog' and 'caravan' against their drawings. Gypsy children seem to feel that this makes the whole process peculiarly theirs.

Two warnings should be made at this stage. First, you must keep the special vocabulary of Anglo-Romanès or Gammon distinct from ordinary English. The children will come to you knowing full well what is Romani and what is not, and in what kind of situation it is proper to use Romanès. They know that Gaujos (non-Gypsies) will not generally understand Romani. You must take care not to confuse these categories, so that the child might introduce Romanès into a wholly English conversation with an ordinary English person. When working in a specifically educational context, therefore, you must compare the different vocabulary registers, i.e. translate: 'This is the Romanès... This is the English; copy out both!'

The second warning is, however, that the process of translation should *not* be used to extend a child's vocabulary, but only to reinforce its distinctiveness in use. Use only those Romani or Gammon words that the children themselves know. It is not your job, as an outsider, a Gaujo, who will never be a *native speaker* of Romani, to 'teach them Romanès'. Your aim is to draw out, to utilise and celebrate, the linguistic resources the children already have. If you are using Romani books, follow the pronunciation of the children. To 'teach Romanès', or to pose as any kind of authority on their secret language, is bound to provoke a hostile response" [Acton, 1984, pp.129-30]. "The important thing is to cross the psychological barrier about the problem of spelling and writing Romani words – to show that writing is not specifically a Gadjo art, but a universal human potential" [Acton/Kenrick].

The emergence of teachers from within the children's own community will change the situation and will make possible the teaching of and through Romani for children whose parents wish it. There are some countries (Sweden, Norway, and Finland) where Gypsies – like other members of minority cultures – are encouraged and facilitated to acquire professional teacher-training; a change of attitude and increased structural flexibility would enable other countries to adopt similar measures. Moreover, the present trend in many countries is to opt for teachers from within the immigrant community rather than importing them directly from the homeland (due to the aforementioned differences of experience, vocabulary, etc. between children in the homeland and immigrant children). The older policy of teacher exchange is generally founded on bilateral inter-state agreements; since Gypsies, having no home state, are not tied by any such agreements, this trend should be generally beneficial for them. (This is not to underestimate the general situation – rejection, assimilationism, stereotyping – and the overall level of schooling among Gypsy populations, both of which place them well outside the situation of most immigrant cultures.) The road towards improving the Gypsies' situation is particularly long and hazardous.

Even in, for example, *Sweden*, a country with a long-standing record for taking – and implementing – important decisions, a government commission on immigrant language teaching pointed out the particular difficulties associated with the Gypsy language: "Where Romany is concerned, teaching and linguistic development have been impeded by the lack of teaching materials in the language. The lack of trained teachers is an equally difficult obstacle... SKU recommends:

- that the Government regard the training of Gypsy home language teachers as a priority field for the allocation of home language teacher training grants;

- that the Immigration Board, acting in consultation with the NBE, the National Board of Health and Welfare and the National Board of University and Colleges, be commissioned to compile material on Gypsy culture in various countries" [SKU, 1984, pp. 59 and 61].

From the Gypsy point of view, and in the opinion of outside observers, the Swedish school situation and its results cannot be considered successful.

It would thus seem indispensable, if we are to avoid all discrimination, that Romani be recognised as one of the mother tongues for which provision is made in school, yet should also benefit from special measures (various teaching aids, consultation, etc.) so it can reach the status of those minority languages with official recognition or a home state/territory, and for the most part a long tradition of literary or scholastic usage. Romani shares many difficulties with other minority languages: dialectisation, lack of a standard version and standardised spellings, lack of qualified teaching personnel, etc. Yet Romani also has advantages – notably its resilience – which set it apart from other minority languages whose legitimacy, and appropriateness in the school setting, are accepted unproblematically:

"The traditional values of their cultures are being eroded. Their social environment is evolving too fast to leave room for adaptation. The critical mass of culture-bearers for the community, necessary for its survival, is vanishing so rapidly that we may soon see the point of no return; the birth rate is down, too. The intergenerational transmission of language is not taking place as it should" [Ó Murchú, 1985, p.70].

Another advantage of Romani is its supranational character: it is spoken in every country, yet belongs to none. *It has the widest geographic distribution of any language spoken in the European Community.* A poster of a comprehensive table[10] on display at the 1986 Expolangues exhibition in Paris, attracted the intrigued attention of visitors: what could this "Romani", present in every single country, be?

The art and method of teaching

Schooling is not, despite the protests of a few positivists, simply the practice of a technology. Method can be an overall approach, not a collection of tried-and-true recipes the following of which, in supposedly identical conditions, should give comparable results. Conditions are only rarely identical, especially when cultural criteria are taken into account; this is when we see that the use of supposedly polyvalent educational techniques renders them pedagogically inoperative, and at the same time stumbling-blocks for the children involved. The failure of so-called "compensatory education" is a well-known phenomenon, notably – and this is one of the major criticisms levelled at it – because it is not the children who should be subject to the intervention of educational psychology, but the methods (to render them more flexible) and the techniques (to ensure their adaptation). The context within which the schooling of Gypsy children occurs makes these considerations particularly urgent – as we have repeatedly emphasised throughout this report.

"One thing we must not forget is that for most of our history, only one in two hundred could spell his name. This is the problem when we try to educate Travelling children now. It's not like approaching a Settled community child. If we teach a Settled community child how to spell C-A-T, he can come home from school... and ask his parents to spell 'dog' for him... But with the Travelling child... if he asks his parents to spell dog, it is like asking a deaf and dumb person to say sound, because the Travelling child's parents do not know A from B, or should I say, A from a devil's foot" ["Pops" Johnny Connors (an Irish Traveller) quoted by Acton/Kenrick].

Now that the thrust is towards all schools welcoming all children equally, we must insist on flexibility of methods. In effect, if a number of Gypsy children are present in a classroom, forming a unified cultural "front", the pedagogical adaptations required will differ from those facing a teacher with a single Traveller child in the class. In the latter case, the easy way out is to try and get him into line with all the others. This tendency to realign the different, reduce diversity and homogenise variety under cover of teaching efficiency and "integration", is always ambiguous because it is very difficult to know where to draw the line. For example, the essential role of preschool is to "prepare" (that is, to adapt) the child for primary school. We must stop and ask ourselves the extent and nature of these school "prerequisites".

Is it not true that, by acquiring them, the very young child is effectively being assimilated into the dominant culture of the school? Isn't the function of the flexibility of preschool – the very aspect of it most appreciated by parents – in fact to prepare the child for the rigidity of primary school?

Many possibilities, both in theory and to a certain degree in practice, exist to permit a multicultural classroom in which every culture is respected. This European assessment report is neither the time nor the place for a detailed review of didactics or the teaching materials being developed here and there, but we can mention a few points.

Firstly, "functional education", based on the dynamics of the child's own experience, may also satisfy parents' desire for schooling which is first and foremost useful.

"It is in devising ways through which the children can reveal their strengths that the skills of teachers are demonstrated. One ten year old girl, for example, could not record the answer to 6 x 20 but knew immediately that six bunches of holly at 20p a bunch were worth £1.20. In written work teachers need to look beyond what is actually presented to them. Some pieces of work are apparently unworthy at first sight in terms of the knowledge of acceptable written and grammatical conventions but reveal both ideas and understanding on closer reading" [*A Survey of the Education of Traveller Children in West Sussex*, Report by HM Inspectors, DES, 1984, p.13].

In an example such as this we can appreciate that "The cultural aspect is no longer limited to the nature of the activity, but is more concerned with its purpose. The 'why' of the activity influences the 'how', transforming it into a cultural attribute" [Gilles Verbunt, speaking at a colloquium held in Toulouse, June 1985 – unpublished]. This is where we once again encounter the classical theory – but not necessarily the practice – of "functional education": "Functional education is that which takes the child's *need*, his interest in attaining goals, as a motivating force for the activity towards which we seek to inspire him... The structural point of view asks 'what?' The mechanical point of view asks 'how?' But the functional point of view asks 'why?' The functional approach is *dynamic*, in contrast to the other two which are relatively *static*" [Claparède, 1964, pp.7 and 37]. One of the basic principles of the theory is the value of the individual's actions "for his adaptation to his physical and social surroundings" [ibid. p.36].

This functional point of view permits us to postulate that "Reading, before it becomes a search for information, is a choice of what information one is looking for" [Balas, 1984, p.46], each child doing this in conjunction with his own personal experience. To this we may add the theories of Wygotsky and Jantzen [cf. Reemtsma] and many others. But the teacher must bear in mind that it is the *whole* of the situation which must be taken into account in pedagogical practice. "It is not sufficient to have a functional, or at least meaningful, basis (which would in itself imply a *degree* of functionality) for the activity undertaken to be functional and relevant. It is erroneous to distance oneself from a meaningful situation and hope that activity based upon it will remain significant; one must continue to practise the activity, seeking sense within its functionality" [Balas, 1984, p.47].

The functional approach implies respect by taking differences of experience into account. This in turn implies the use of methods which are varied and flexible in both form and content. *All the reports* agree on this point, and *link the quality of schooling with the degree of flexibility of practice, and with the degree of respect shown*: the use of games and free expression; role-playing; opening up the school to the outside world; inviting in Gypsy parents (in their capacity as artists, craftsmen and so on) to the school; giving pupils a choice between a specialised class and other, open, classes, for this or that subject; individualised backup teaching; the occasional usefulness of mixing all age-groups in the classroom, for mutual support (the older children don't feel stigmatised since they are there "to keep the little ones company", while the little ones feel reassured by the presence of the older children). These are only a few examples of ways of increasing flexibility, but we must follow them up by pointing out that, in practice, such flexibility is to be found almost exclusively in specialised all-Traveller classes. Is this because (for reasons pointed out earlier) most of the information available to us relates to classes of this type, or because "ordinary" classes are not, at present, adapted to the needs of Gypsy children? The two reasons are doubtless interrelated.

In every case, the way in which teaching is practised (for example, emphasis on this or that aspect of content, the teacher's approach) is of prime importance.

Let us give an example concerning the teaching of history: "Although some of the schools in Northern Ireland and England successfully incorporated Traveller history into lessons, other teachers told us that history and geography are seen as irrelevant by Gypsy children. But what history, what geography is taught in those schools? A history which has no mention of the persecution of Gypsies, a geography that makes no mention of nomadism – in short, a lying history and a lying geography which suppress the very existence of the Travelling people, a history and geography which underwrite the prejudice of the non-Gypsies against the Gypsies. If, as the English assert, it is proper that Japanese and German children be required to learn about the genocide in their national past, it is equally important that their children should do the same. In the experience of voluntary teaching of at least one of our researchers, history and geography which included, and set in general context, the situation of the Travellers, were amongst the most eagerly received of subjects" [Acton/Kenrick].

It is interesting to quote research carried out in a non-Gypsy community, which brings out many important points and which indicates that the above considerations regarding teachers' approach are neither recent nor specific: "Junior High School 43 on the periphery of Harlem, like most Harlem schools, was holding largely a custodial program for the 'culturally deprived'... Then the school became a pilot demonstration guidance program and what looked like a miracle occurred" – a sixfold increase in children going on to secondary level, a decrease in the drop-out rate, rapid progress. Yet "When one studies this pilot project, one does not find any revolutionary education methods... The 'miracle' seemed due primarily to an implementation of the belief that such children can learn. School personnel were told to adopt an affirmative view of their students and give up their earlier negative views. Therefore, certain educational methods previously considered questionable for lower-class children were now used... Most of the emphasis on discipline was toned down. Teacher responsibility for maintaining order was relaxed. Students felt that they were 'special' and that they were expected to achieve and learn. Teachers were evaluated more on their teaching skill than on their discipline. Because the school administration was eager for the success of the experiment, it opened many previously clogged channels of communication between itself and teachers, parents, and pupils... Teachers began to consider themselves competent and their students capable. Pupils were told that they were trustworthy and that their teachers were committed to helping them succeed... The cyclic relation between educational effectiveness and heightened morale is indicated by the fact that any program designed to increase educational effectiveness invariably heightens the morale of pupils, teachers, and supervisors; the heightened morale increases the chances of success of the educational program" [Clark, 1965, pp. 141-3].

The same process can be observed again in an all-Gypsy school, also in the USA. The Seattle Gypsy Alternative School consists of two prefab classrooms on the grounds of a larger school, where Gypsy children are accepted in consultation with their parents. The children "are highly motivated, responsible and quick to learn. Their teachers find them to be affectionate, spontaneous and rewarding. They are excited about having an opportunity to learn. When activities are well planned, they are extremely responsible. They have a strong sense of their own self-worth and have distinctive personalities" [Kaldi, 1981, p.8].

Teaching materials

Most teachers feel the need for basic materials onto which they can graft their own practices in accordance with changing circumstances: number of children, length of stay (if they are nomadic), cultural origins... This need is doubtless felt all the more strongly since the teacher has not had the benefit of specialised training for teaching Traveller children, and so has no core of tried and tested methods and materials to turn to. Parents too are beginning to demand adapted materials, seeking recognition and validation of their culture through its inclusion in school textbooks. Yet it must be admitted that, in general, the school establishment is not amenable to new curricula or approaches; indeed, it is often a vehicle for concepts long outdated for children in general, and particularly unsuitable for Gypsy and Traveller children. Some adapted material is being developed, but – with the exception of a few commercially published texts benefiting from careful presentation and marketing – this is so far only at an experimental stage and confined to specialised classes.

There are great disparities from one country to the next, whatever the type of text concerned. There are some countries with no basic teaching materials referring to Gypsy and Traveller culture, and others where quite a few such texts exist, but even in such countries the material is generally little known and even less widely distributed. Where such materials do exist, they are the result of initiatives from various sources, for example from the central school authorities.

In the *Netherlands* "The Ministries of Education and Science and of Welfare, Health and Cultural Affairs have provided funds to enable a teacher to produce an information pack containing background material on Gypsies. The pack is designed for both Dutch schoolchildren and teachers and aims to familiarise them with Gypsy culture and history so as to overcome prejudice and stereotyped thinking. The pack consists of a video-tape, booklets, information brochures, articles and a play. A separate handbook is being prepared for teachers with suggestions on how the material might be used in class. The same two ministries have provided funds for a group of teachers to put together adapted teaching material for the tuition of Gypsy children. This material will be an elaboration of that produced specifically for Gypsy children in the municipalities...

The National Educational Advisory Centres have drawn up a series of lessons entitled 'Around the Caravan', designed for the final year of primary school and early secondary school... The series concentrates on the themes of history of the caravan dwellers, and the way they live (including play, work and education)" [Hovens et al].

In *Ireland* in 1985 the Department of Education published a teachers' programme for work and progress: *Páisti an Lucht Taistil. Dréacht Curaclaim.* In the *United Kingdom* in 1983, the Department of Education and Science published a HMI Report, *The Education of Travellers' Children*, presenting different case studies as a basis for further discussion and initiatives. In *France* the Ministry of National Education commissioned the Gypsy Research Centre to produce a booklet entitled *Les Populations Tsiganes en France* (1981) aimed at the widest possible audience of school personnel. At least one Regional Centre for Pedagogical Documentation (Marseilles) has produced a teaching pack along the lines of the Dutch model.

Other examples do exist, and the authorities may also give financial support for the publication of textbooks or other teaching materials which they themselves have not produced. But, with a few exceptions, such measures have been one-off, outside of any holistic approach or continuity.

The initiative may also come from Gypsy/Traveller organisations.

In *Ireland*, "*Mincéir Misli* feel that it is extremely important that Traveller children learn to value their own traditions and their language and to this end they intend compiling a dictionary of Gammon from older Travellers. They also intend to become involved in the production of materials for school that are based on Travellers' own cultural background. *Mincéir Misli* operate a resource service to Travellers that offers advice and assistance to Travellers experiencing difficulties with statutory bodies including schools" [McCarthy]. In the *United Kingdom*, the National Gypsy Education Council is a meeting-ground for Gypsies and non-Gypsies, and has published (through Romanestan Publications) many works (poetry, songs, dictionaries, theoretical texts, an annual newsletter entitled *Traveller Education*) designed directly for school use.

In many countries, the most important role played by Gypsy/Traveller organisations is in conscientisation and contact: mediation between school and parents, providing information to schools or at meetings, and the like. It is certain, for reasons gone into above (the language is beginning to be written as the potential number of readers is growing apace) that Gypsy production of materials suitable for school use will increase from year to year: children's stories, novels, poetry, songs, dictionaries, specialised teachers' periodicals and more. "Literacy leads to literature, the publication of culture" [Acton, MS.].

Yet for the most part it is the teachers of Gypsy/Traveller children who produce their own material, which tends to remain in internal class use only; occasionally a few other teachers may use it or draw on it for inspiration. This classroom-generated material, especially as concerns basic learning, is often of very high quality, since it has evolved in direct response to real conditions. Yet the production, development and distribution of such material is hindered by all the obstacles mentioned earlier: lack of support for teachers, the difficulties they face in developing contact and information-exchange between themselves. The failure of school authorities to provide the necessary support – they could, for example, organise get-togethers for involved teachers, undertake publication, etc. – is also a major block to the potential distribution of adapted teaching materials. It is a familiar story of dissipated undertakings, repeated mistakes, growing complacency, capitulation. A waste of energy, often through the duplication of efforts that should have been complementary. Yet a very small investment by the school authorities in development and distribution within existing frameworks would – as with training and information – be amply and quickly repaid in both human and financial terms. These demands, coming from parents, Gypsy organisations and teachers, are legitimate: one cannot stipulate a division between valid cultures (with a right to recognition by the school) and other less valid ones which shouldn't be allowed in. Moreover, pedagogical thinking in a cultural context is often applicable to the field of education as a whole: "One could say that the schooling of Gypsy children, ignored up to now, is still at an experimental stage. This means that all directions are still possible for it, and *the Gypsy paradigm, the reflections to which it gives rise and the pedagogical practices which spring from it, may enrich school provision in general*" [Liégeois, 1983b].

On the subject of the development and use of teaching materials, it is important to draw attention to three more points. Firstly, that this development must occur in a pragmatic fashion, in direct collaboration with the children themselves.

For example, as the authors of a French reading primer, *Le Goût du Voyage* ("The Taste of Travel" – Nantes, 1983) put it, "We've always preferred to base our work on texts put together with the pupils... These classroom-tested texts, modified in accordance with our observations and the children's, constitute the framework of the book... The illustrations are a result of constant interaction with the children. We studied situations alongside our Travelling pupils, then the work was discussed in class and modified according to their suggestions" [from a press release about the book].

The second point, a corollary to the first, is that all material is merely a base from which teacher and pupils can work. There are no all-encompassing magic formulas.

"We have not attempted", write the authors of the above-mentioned primer, "to work out a programme for the teaching of literacy, but simply to present texts which can be used as a material workbase in conjunction with many methods. Each teacher can use these texts as he sees fit and integrate them into his own approach to teaching."

Part of a pilot scheme in Bremen (FRG) was the compilation of the *Bremer Sinti-Fibel*, a collection of texts and didactic material for teachers. Yet the manual "will only be applicable indirectly. Experience with the Sinti proves that they need very concrete educational content, which must be drawn directly from the practical experience of the group in question. In consequence this manual assumes the character of a descriptive example of a method for teaching basic literacy to Sinti. It is not therefore an altogether adapted reader, but rather a guide which can be adapted in the service of pedagogical practice" [Bremer Volkshochschule, p.33].

Given the diversity within the Travelling community, it is equally important to bear in mind how such works will be perceived by different groups of children: "Are there not sometimes mental blocks set up when a Manouche is given a reader intended for a Rom audience, and vice versa?" [Ferté, 1984].

Finally, in the majority of cases and particularly as regards books (audio-visual material is still a rarity), such works can also be used with non-Gypsy children, whether or not there are Gypsy children in the classroom with them. This possibility – or rather, this necessity, if every child is to be exposed to other cultures – is all the easier to implement when the material is either distributed by the school authorities, or commercially available – either way it becomes accessible to a wide public.

Teamwork

We have already repeatedly emphasised the need for teamwork. All the national reports insist on this point. But, though everyone wants the same thing, here too theory is taking a long time to find its way into practice. Teamwork becomes all the more vital as more school doors open to Travellers: a support system must be set up, as much for the children themselves as for their teachers. But the concept of "teamwork" must be broadly based, encompassing teachers, those involved in teacher training, pedagogical advisors, inspectors and so on. This approach makes it possible to split the workload and provide mutual support, while it prevents those who specialise from becoming isolated, ghettoisation (with its consequences for teachers and pupils), and a fragmented approach or inappropriate methods. Teamwork guarantees continuity in thinking, the accumulation of experience and insights which might be lost if they remained unshared. Consultation within a broad team affords the advantage of an outsider's clear perspective and encouragement in times of exhaustion or indecision. Gathering many partners around a common project allows for easier surmounting of administrative and ideological obstacles.

Implementation of the teamwork system would require no resources beyond those already in existence. And, as we have already said in connection with the distribution of teaching materials, any investment into improving working conditions (by providing support and consultation) will be quickly "repaid" in improved progress for the children, and above all in respect for their personalities.

The concept of teamwork must exist at various levels, but the principles and advantages remain the same: in the school, in the local community, in the district or region. This broader approach necessitates consultation between the various bodies involved (administration, voluntary organisations...) around the focal point of the school, which is after all inseparable from other elements of Gypsies' environment.

The team set-up also allows for the participation of a psychologist when necessary; his work is best suited to the group approach. At present psychologists in most countries are in a situation fraught with indecision and ambiguity. For years, up to the beginning of the 1980s, Gypsy families were (in connection with assimilationist policies) considered "handicapped", and their children enrolled in classes for the maladjusted (see "Integration by Handicap", above). The psychologist, with or without tests and IQ measurements, collaborated in the process. In the end, many came independently to realise that it was the system itself that was "maladjusted", and that Gypsy children's needs are not necessarily catered for with methods geared towards the handicapped. Thus, gradually, the psychologist's services came to be called on less and less. (This does not change the fact that, to this day, a very high proportion of Gypsy pupils are still – inappropriately – in "special" classes for problem children.)

A frequently voiced complaint from teachers, counsellors and others is the lack of information about Gypsies and Travellers, their situation, lifestyle, and economic activities. When seeking advice from outside experts, it used to be automatic to turn to psychologists, and nowadays social workers are a given; yet the idea of consulting an anthropologist or sociologist is still quite extraordinary. Occasionally, one might be invited to speak at a conference, but they are not routinely consulted, nor involved in setting up pedagogical projects.

Contact

With the training of teachers, adapting the school to the children attending it passes from theory to practice and becomes an ongoing process of developing new approaches.

"High priority must be given at all levels to the development of means and methods of teaching responding to the needs of immigrant children and a multicultural society" [Report of the Commission of the European Communities, (84), 244, p.37].

If this priority is to be met, contact, liaison, consultation and collective reflection must be facilitated as a matter of urgency; findings must be shared if innovation is not to be a synonym for endless gropings in the dark and repeated failure. This may be accomplished in various, complementary ways.

It is firstly a question of contact with *parents* and with *Gypsy/Traveller organisations* representing them. We have stressed the absolute necessity of such contacts over and over again; they are essential if different points of view are to be taken into account in the development of various pedagogical projects.

It is also a question of contact between *teachers* – at local, regional, national and international level – through personal contact and a system of liaison/support. All teachers working regularly with Gypsy children have been demanding such a system for years: they feel that it would help them to hone their methods, educate each other by pooling experience, coordinate their efforts (essential, given that teachers in different places deal with the same – nomadic – children), share their projects and achievements (much high-quality material, the fruit of long toil, never leaves the classroom in which it was engendered), keep up to date on developments outside the school (e.g. new legislation) which may affect their pupils, consult experts in any number of fields for their opinions on matters of relevance, to be aware of what is going on elsewhere in the country and further afield, etc., etc. We have dealt with the current situation as regards teachers' meetings in the preceding chapter. We take this opportunity to stress the need for a high-quality *liaison newsletter*, also much in demand, as a corollary to such meetings. Once again, the costs would be relatively low, given the large number of teachers involved and the usefulness of such an organ: in fact the costs of publishing a quarterly newsletter for hundreds are about the same as for holding a national meeting for a few dozen. The necessary structures for information and publication already exist in each country. All that is required is for the relevant authorities to be willing to create such a newsletter, which would benefit them as much as the teachers directly involved. While each individual country must take its own initiatives in this regard, organisations at international level – notably the European Community and Council of Europe – should set an example through the creation of a *European newsletter*. This would facilitate international exchange, keeping all concerned in touch with developments elsewhere, and complement the national newsletters – a combination of the two levels of publishing can be easily envisaged. It is up to the international organisations to tackle the question in conjunction with the various national bodies concerned. Moreover such international exchanges would favour the production of adapted teaching materials, particularly in the case of language groups which may be represented on a small scale in a number of states, and for whom local authorities may not have the resources to develop appropriate materials.

Contact must also take place between *classes*, within the country and between countries. Such an approach fires the children's enthusiasm in carrying out projects about their lives and their class, simultaneously expressing and affirming their identity. It might, for example, take the form of a children's story-writing contest, with the best entries being published (the UK's National Gypsy Education Council did this in 1983).

Contact also necessitates a *teachers' association* for those most directly involved. As already noted, such associations, usually national in scope, can play an essential role in liaison, information, even training; they free teachers from isolation and enable them to share their experience. However, lack of financial backup means that they are not fulfilling their potential even where they do exist; where they do not, it is important that they be created.

Contact may also come about through coordinated *action-research*, a demand voiced by many teachers. Such efforts give rise to a variety of results, already discernible in the few pilot projects to date on school provision for Gypsy children. Action-research gives teachers an opportunity to critically examine their own practices, to learn how to analyse and modify them, to become more actively involved in pedagogical innovation, to acquire research skills by engaging in research, and to increase their contacts with other involved persons.

As pointed out by the French Ministry of National Education in a report on pilot schemes (a joint French ministry/Commission of the European Communities project), "Generally speaking, teachers adopt a highly intuitional, subjective approach. Thus, as regards perceptions of 'immigrant' children, particularly in the role of learners, teachers' analyses are usually a jumble of vague preconceptions and generalisations based on the observation of random phenomena of indeterminate significance, uncorroborated personal interpretations, and reliable data. In other words, far-ranging conclusions are based on what may only be appearances" [Ministry of National Education (1984), p.40].

It is to be hoped that the ministry, having reached these conclusions, will take the necessary steps towards improving teacher training and enabling teachers to participate in research.

Action-research, by confronting the experiences which it provokes – particularly when we envisage a situation in which all children, regardless of cultural background, will be accommodated in every classroom – obliges us to take into account the transferability of the methods we adopt: insights, experience and approaches evolved in specialised structures must in principle be applicable in other classes too.

Contact in all its forms leads to innovation and adaptation. The more open the school system, the greater the number of local initiatives, and as a rule such initiatives increase in proportion with the degree of decentralisation. Decentralisation offers space for local innovations and, at its best, ensures that these are examined and disseminated by the central authorities; if, however, they fail to play this coordinating role, pedagogical progress is seriously impeded. Innovation is often impossible in centralised systems, where those who issue detailed instructions to be scrupulously adhered to by every element of the structure, are inclined to stick with the tried and true. In such a situation, the other types of contact mentioned earlier become all the more crucial if pluralism and innovation are to evolve.

Towards interculturalism

At the beginning of this chapter we emphasised the contradictions between the official functions of the school and its more covert workings, notably that of reproducing the society it represents. We also pointed out that "'Gypsy thought' fears Gadjo schooling precisely because it suspects that an intensive use of the written word would destroy it, thereby destroying community cohesion" [Piasere]. We also know – and at present most schools of thought are in agreement on this point – that any culture is an organised whole, a configuration rather than a loose collection of disparate elements; to touch one element is to modify the entire configuration. Any new element will have to fit into the existing whole, and it is impossible to foresee the effects of its introduction. This is true in every sphere, but particularly so in the case of schooling, which impacts on language, writing, history, personal development and more. It is imperative that we act cautiously.

Contemporary pedagogical thought advances the concept of individual liberation, the necessity of providing the means for self-realisation as an individual and as a member of the group. It is a lovely concept, provided everyone can benefit from its implications. It must be *broadened* to include those whose culture is radically different, and for whom "communal living" is a pervasive day-to-day reality, not a nostalgic past nor a future to aspire to. It is a concept which must postulate respect for pluralism, admitting that the means of access to liberation can be manifold, and that minority cultures require means of their own. Liberation of the individual cannot begin by negating him!

In the light of these considerations, and faced with the profound changes occurring in the host societies in which immigrant families find themselves, it is clear that a new approach to teaching is urgently needed. There are growing numbers of immigrant children in the classroom, and the various attempts at assimilation have generally had the opposite effect by pushing the child out of a school system inappropriate to his needs: the child thus marginalised finds himself, not integrated, but relegated, as we explained at the beginning of this report. Some immigrant families hope to adapt to their new environment whilst preserving their culture; others hope to return to the homeland and, to avoid the risk of this being a second experience of "immigration", with accompanying problems of adaptation, they hope to retain both their original worldview and language. Thus, in connection with new research findings (e.g. plurilingualism, taking the learner's socio-economic and cultural context into account) the Council of Europe and the European Community have both stressed the importance of intercultural pedagogy and education (the principles of which are widely known by now, so we will not repeat them here; viz. the numerous publications of the Council for Cultural Cooperation of the Council of Europe, and the Commission of the European Communities). Minority cultures – and thus Gypsies and Travellers – stand to benefit from these new ideas, and have an active role to play in their implementation. The next few years will be of crucial importance, for at this point ideas are well-developed and widely accepted, yet putting them into practice remains at an experimental stage and the political will for their implementation has yet to emerge. Intercultural education remains at the "project" level – let us analyse the preconditions for its realisation.

"In the light of acquired experience and from the European perspective, we must emphasise that interculturalism is not an abstract concept but a living social practice. Interculturalism is not merely a linguistic question, but to a far greater degree a sociological, psychological and economic encounter, in other words a social fact which can only be understood by an interdisciplinary approach... Interculturalism cannot attain its goals or establish itself in the long term without reference to the institutional context: it must become an integral component of the institution" [M.H. Neves, in Rey, 1982, p.4].

The fact that interculturalism is a "living social practice" rather than a simple method to be adopted, explains the difficulties which arise when we attempt to transfer it from the small-scale experimental stage to a broader context: it then becomes a social project rather than a purely pedagogical one. Lack of finance is a frequently quoted obstacle, yet as we have repeatedly pointed out this is a short-sighted approach. The necessary investment would quickly be recovered in terms of the children's better adjustment to their social and economic environment, and could be achieved as much through the redeployment of existing means – particularly in the field of teacher training, the sine qua non of classroom interculturalism – as through the creation of new ones. Once again it boils down to a lack of will; once again we are dealing with a problem of a social nature. Yet other obstacles are also mentioned: technical problems, timetable organisation, and a constant return to the dilemma of whether mother tongue and culture should be taught in addition to basic schoolwork – yet another burden on an already overburdened child; or inside normal school hours – but by taking this course, the child is missing out on others, and how many hours should he do? In fact this becomes a false dilemma when the intercultural approach is used, since this rejects the idea of juxtaposing or amalgamating cultural materials.

The goal to aim for is not the intellectual hybridisation of the pupils, but their enrichment and the cultivation of mutual comprehension through learning based on their individual cultural backgrounds. Additional arrangements, especially for mother tongue instruction or support teaching, can be made as required when overall structures become more flexible.

One of the principal difficulties is teachers' own attitudes. We have already described the negative reception the Traveller child usually gets in the classroom. Most of the national reports, based on questionnaires filled in by teachers themselves, show clearly that prejudice leads teachers – including "specialised" teachers – to believe that there is little or nothing of the children's own culture which could be utilised in the school; their contribution to the class is considered negligible; the majority of teachers show no interest in culturally-based teaching materials despite their recognition of the inappropriateness of the materials they are using. A recent official report on school provision for children from ethnic minorities emphasises the racism – latent and manifest – in teachers' practices, and above all as regards Travellers [The Swann Report, publ. 1985 in the United Kingdom, cf. Acton, 1985b].

To illustrate the difficulties involved in the implementation of intercultural pedagogy, we will quote a detailed example from a teacher in a *French* pilot scheme.

"Initial objective: to enable Gypsy children to improve their practical skills, and to help them to integrate into the French school system through the application of intercultural pedagogy. In the Gypsy children's support class, their culture was taken into account on an ongoing basis. From the moment that the class was set up in September 1980, the prime goal was to prevent the massive rejection to which pupils of Gypsy origin were subject from teachers as well as non-Gypsy pupils and their parents; to pull this group out of the scholastic rut in which it was stuck. In September 1980, two Gypsy pupils out of thirty learnt to read; pupils twelve years of age did not even know the basic sounds of the alphabet; relations between Gypsy and non-Gypsy pupils were often tinged with violence. One of the teachers determined to improve the situation, convinced that the key to better overall results was an improvement in literacy. During the first three years (1980-83) all teaching initiative came from the support class, which had no liaison with the children's ordinary classes.

Results within the framework of the European Project. 1982-83: teething troubles and going round in circles. Only two teachers get involved in the European Project, despite the support offered by the authorities and CEFISEM (Training and Information Centre on Schooling for Immigrant Children). Work on a preparatory course and interesting activities to help develop education about 'difference': reading autobiographical stories by Matéo Maximoff, a Gypsy author, and corresponding with him; putting together an audio-visual project and showing it to a large cross-section of pre-primary pupils. 1983-84: Storms. Still only two teachers involved in the pilot project. The same children (twenty-two non-Gypsies, six Gypsies), now in primary school, are taught Gypsy history, practise typical Gypsy crafts such as making canework chair-bottoms, read B. Solet's *The Gypsy Flute*. There were no hostile reactions from non-Gypsy parents. But, at the professional level, fellow-teachers' attitudes went from indifference to open hostility. Isolated, we informed the ministry's pilot team that we could continue only if we were joined by some of our colleagues. The ministry proposed a two-week training course which would bring the whole teaching staff together to discuss intercultural pedagogy.

1984-85: The training course is implemented and proceeds with satisfactory results. (…) It culminated in a school project... For the first time, the cultural specificity of the Gypsy children is recognised, and teaching methods are planned around their different learning rhythms. The support class ceased to be a ghetto... The entire teaching staff began to feel involved in our project... At the same time we also went out to the local community to try to explain what we were doing and to familiarise them with Gypsies: exhibitions, encounters with authors (including Matéo Maximoff) explaining Gypsy life, literary projects, school crafts exhibitions where the Gypsy children's skills were on display...

A provisional evaluation, compiled in 1985, revealed...
- the conclusion that the main obstacle to Gypsy children's pedagogical integration is failure in learning to read. Surmounting defeatist attitudes about children's learning abilities in this field must be given top priority...
- the necessity, if such an undertaking is to succeed, of first setting into motion human and institutional 'release mechanisms': the teacher faces a long stint as a 'pioneer' in getting others to recognise and respect cultural differences; from training course to school project (the idea of a common project still being a new one in our education system); the support of the school authorities and the CEFISEM (Training Centre).
- at the present stage of our project we cannot verify our initial hypothesis: to what extent is the children's progress a result of intercultural pedagogy, and to what extent is it due to the personal – sometimes 'militant' – involvement of highly motivated teachers? We note, however, that while recognition of identity does improve learning (by putting an end to physical and social isolation), classroom presence in itself does not appear – at least in the case of teachers without in-depth knowledge of Gypsy culture – sufficient to ensure cross-cultural exchange, but rather serves to confirm the overall status quo in a system where the reference points remain those of the dominant culture.

Will the ripples set in motion by our experiment have a more long-lasting effect than a momentary ruffling of the dormant surface of our education system?" [Christian Lacreu, personal communication with the author].

Reading such a statement – reproduced in detail because it is so representative of the current situation – it becomes clear that a profound change of heart is required, and that it must lead in turn to a profound change in practice. At the same time, the tendency towards interculturalism is gaining ground, among parents as well as the experts, even before the concept has been clearly defined:

"They (the children) should mix in with every other house-dwelling children. A house-dwelling child's going to learn the way of a Gypsy child, and the Gypsy child's going to learn the way of a house-dweller's child, and they're going to be friends. They're not going to be prejudiced against one another for the rest of their lives. When the house-dwelling child grows up and sees a load of Gypsies he's going to be friendly towards them... not condemn them and be prejudiced against them..." [Interview with Mrs. G. Taylor (an English Romani mother) in *Traveller Education*, no. 1, 1973, quoted by Acton/Kenrick].

For such aspirations to become reality, school must learn to welcome all children equally, and in the case of Gypsies and Travellers that will require fundamental change. School must also increase its structural flexibility: for example the "specialised" class with its supporting role need not be limited to Gypsy pupils. Its doors should remain open for children to come and go: some may need supplementary work in certain subjects, others the security of the smaller group, for a short or long period; group activities (arts, crafts, sports) give the children an opportunity to mix, particularly when these projects are run by parents (be they Gypsy or not: for example in Toulenne, France, the Traveller school provides three such groups, the community school with which it is linked offers six, so that children in either can choose from among all nine). Such contacts lead to collaboration and, bit by bit, to understanding: the existence of a specialised class or school for Traveller children allows for the provision of suitably adapted activities.

If all children, whatever their backgrounds, are to be accommodated in the mainstream classroom (the ultimate goal of interculturalism), the form and the content of teaching must be approached with the same degree of care as is structural flexibility. The point is to respect the culture of each, leading to mutual recognition, and to base teaching practice on cultural reality instead of confronting and attempting to restructure it. It is clearly impossible to demolish a culture in the hopes of reconstructing it with weakened materials on a shaky foundation – yet this truth is often forgotten. Each person arrives in the school with his own experiential background, which he must be able to employ as a referent, build upon, take for granted, present to others, validate. We must therefore examine our uses of school space, of time, evaluation systems (their usefulness and effects), the images conveyed in textbooks and by teachers, the usefulness of presenting elements from different cultures *side by side, in an egalitarian framework*. Such a presentation will in itself require research: different concepts of time, the value-systems embedded in each language, mobility vs. sedentarism, parents' work practices – any and all of these may be the subject of school projects in which each can participate, sharing his experience and growing in mutual comprehension as the concept of diversity becomes more widely accepted. Such an approach is entirely compatible even with the brief stay of a nomadic pupil; he can teach others while they teach him, with both sides learning how to examine their own experience. More and more documents are emerging with examples of such practices, underlining their pedagogical usefulness and their success in the eyes of all concerned.

Mention should be also be made of the role which can be played by parents in the process of mutual understanding, even if no Traveller children are present in the class. Thus in *France* the *Centre Culturel Tzigane* visits schools with a live show which leads children – and teachers – to find out more about Gypsies and Travellers. In *Ireland*, during a teachers' training session, a travelling showman explained that the Settled community needed to be educated to accept

Travellers better. Before the fair is set up he visits local schools, talks about fairs and circuses, and distributes leaflets for the children to work from. After he leaves, most teachers lead a discussion followed by a visit to the fair when it opens. Afterwards the children talk about their impressions. Perhaps some of the fairground children will join the class, and if someday Traveller children arrive they stand an improved chance of being accepted and of reciprocal exchange occurring [reported by Quirke, 1984]. Such practices have important consequences and should be encouraged by the school authorities; all too often they are hampered by administrational red tape.

During this process of mutual recognition there are many pitfalls to be avoided, and which we cannot describe in detail here. Suffice to mention the "folklorisation" that can occur when interculturalism is misunderstood as a promotion of quaint stereotypes: music, dance, food, etc. isolated from their context. Such an approach is all the more distorting in that it gives the impression of knowing, respecting and promoting the culture from which the elements are taken. Let us also mention the tendency to use the presence of short-term nomadic pupils solely as a springboard for projects of benefit to other children.

For example "Circus and fairground children, in school for two weeks at a time, complain that in every school their teachers take the opportunity of their presence to do a project on fairs and circuses" [Acton/Kenrick]. Similarly, "A reading lesson on the theme of life on the road... may well present the Traveller child with certain functional images, yet fail to convey them in context, the way they are lived, so as to give any child, regardless of his culture, a real 'feel' for the lifestyle" [Balas, 1984, p.42].

Let us also point out teachers' tendency to single out Gypsy children to perform tasks felt to "suit" them (such as manual labour or outdoor work), which in fact the children do not wish to do, and which effectively stigmatise them. "They are ambivalent about helping the school gardener. On the one hand they like being out of normal lessons... but on the other hand they feel that they are being discriminated against by not being treated like other pupils. They ask, 'Why is it always us who are singled out for dirty work?'" [Ivatts, 1975, p.18]. Finally, let us draw attention yet again to the tendency to use selected aspects of Gypsy culture as a teaching model for other children, without giving the Gypsy children the same opportunity to learn about their Settled peers. After all, Gypsy children and their parents do expect school to help them to understand their environment; they need "tools for negotiation" and "cross-cultural civics" [Liégeois, 1983b] which will help them to adapt. *It is thus insufficient – even with the best pedagogic intentions – to familiarise other pupils with elements of Gypsy culture, unilaterally: the same must be done for each culture represented in the school,* particularly as regards the dominant culture to which they must adapt, the institutions with which they will have to deal, the realities of non-Gypsy social life, etc.

"In this two-way movement, the Gypsy child sees himself recognised through his culture, and takes comfort from the fact. He feels validated: 'The teacher knows about our customs, our way of life.' On the other hand the teacher is also there to provide him with the key to his culture, the Gadjo world. The pupil is thus initiated into a different cultural model, which he will subsequently understand better, adapt to more successfully. This is not the same as adopting it!" [Ferté, 1984].

The practice of intercultural pedagogy implies a validation of the different cultures present in it. It should permit the child full exercise of all his capacities (although it is especially difficult for schools to allow Gypsy children to exercise their special characteristics of independence, maturity, adaptability, bilingualism…). The Traveller child should feel proud of his abilities and proud of his positive contribution to the class as a whole. The multicultural approach is particularly practical in the case of the Gypsy/Traveller, given the vitality of the culture, the fact that it is lived to the full on a daily basis, and the distance which most groups of Travellers have up to now kept between their own culture and the dominant surrounding one. Thus, what is sometimes said of members of other cultures, is rarely applicable to Gypsies:

"Interculturalism is not a viable option for most immigrants I know of. What these people need first and foremost is the opportunity to become the subjects of culture. Without this preliminary operation, the immigrant will continue to be lost among objects, behaviour, and words, all of which he fears may betray him at any moment" [Ducoli, 1982, p.20].

Education – notably school education – is the basis of changes in thinking. "And this is where I believe in pedagogy. Everything which helps people to think more clearly, more intelligently, is geared towards the acceptance of otherness" [Memmi, 1982, p.22]. The role of school, before we even begin to speak of interculturalism, is to participate in the validation and comprehension of differences; to transform antagonisms, even – particularly – long-standing ones, into accepted differences. It is therefore legitimate that we should expect school itself, in its structures and functioning, to be a model of openness and respect.

On the subject of extracurricular activities, we shall limit ourselves to a few brief observations. Firstly, that for children of primary school age, the school is the main source of activities and contacts outside the family circle. Even in relation to school, parents often have second thoughts about activities requiring children to share a means of transport, travel too far from the home base, or which carry a danger of infringing certain rules (of cleanliness and purity for example). Older, more independent children have a far greater degree of contact with their age-peers in youth clubs, sports halls and the like. This sometimes leads to a spontaneous form of interculturalism, since these youngsters are less confirmed in mutual negative stereotypes than their parents or older brothers and sisters. As for these older siblings, they face rejection every time they wish to go to the cinema, a dance, a café, solely on the grounds of being Gypsies or Travellers. There are countries in which this rejection is the norm, against which there is no point in complaining. The end result is a quasi-apartheid situation in which many officially public places are effectively off-limits to Travellers, while others are frequented exclusively by them. Yet despite such situations, cross-cultural contact between young adults is on the increase everywhere and will play an important role in a pluricultural society. Another change which will help bring pupils together in the school, is the introduction of new technology which in both form and content permits – even requires – new teaching methods. Learning new "languages" is a new experience for everybody, and may equalise the starting points of children from different cultural backgrounds.

In a certain report on school provision for immigrant children, a typographical error has given us the statement that "the meeting-pot theory has been abandoned in the US." The reference is of course to the melting-pot theory. In effect one can say that the pluriculturalism currently in evidence in a growing number of countries, and the unwillingness of various cultures to be dissolved into the dominant model, is preventing the stipulated fusion. The "intercultural pedagogy" approach opens up the possibility of transforming "melting-pot" to "meeting-pot". Yet interculturalism, for all its trendiness in certain circles, is still at an experimental stage even in the schools.

"Intercultural education implies an attitude simultaneously receptive and creative from the community at large; it requires administrators and teachers to have a good grasp of the cultures with which they deal, and to have access to appropriate teaching materials. These three requirements are often lacking or insufficient in practice" [Council of Europe, *Apprendre pour Vivre* (Learning for Living), 1984, p.27].

What is the actual situation in the various Member States?

"Nothing in the *Italian* scholastic establishment points towards an intercultural approach, even in the future" [Karpati/Massano].

"The 'pro-child' approach culminated in the abolition of corporal punishment in schools in 1980... The new curriculum makes reference to adapting to the differing environments of the children. However, this is the limit of its multicultural approach... The textbooks for young children deal with suburban well-off families, the colloquial language of the children is constantly corrected, arrogant circulars are sent to penniless families by the management demanding money for the upkeep of the school... Those teachers who would take a different approach are limited by the utilitarian prejudices of those in authority ... Traveller parents are seen as having no role in the education of their children. Multicultural education is a totally alien concept to the *Irish* educational system" [McCarthy].

"At present there is no concept of intercultural pedagogy for Sinti and Roma in the *FRG*" [Reemtsma].

"In many ways we would argue that official concepts of multiculturalism are very assimilationist, seeking to incorporate other cultures into a modified, but still unitary 'Britishness', of which English will remain the only language" [Acton/Kenrick, *United Kingdom*].

In *France* the Ministry of National Education emphasises in its report on a European pilot scheme that "The problem – an important one, considering the purpose of the project – persists: the apparent difficulty of integrating Teachers of Mother Tongue and Culture (ELCOs) into the school system... These studies seem to remain at the periphery of school activities, and the ELCOs themselves seem to integrate, or rather approach integration, solely within the practice of crosscultural activities" [Ministry of National Education, 1984, p.30].

"Since the early 1970s the view has prevailed in the *Netherlands* that the primary education system should provide adequately for the greatest possible number of children... A survey reveals that such an extension has so far made little headway throughout the Dutch education system, even though it has been much written about and discussed in recent years... Multi-cultural education also covers the training of teachers from minority groups and provides for education in the group's own language and culture. Little if anything has so far been achieved in this direction for Gypsies on account of the costs that would be involved and the smallness of their numbers" [Hovens et al].

Intercultural education is thus still at a theoretical stage, and we must ask ourselves if it can ever become reality while the minority groups which the children represent continue to be subject to inequality and rejection [cf. Liégeois 1983b, p.5]. Domination by a single culture remains an essential characteristic of the school. And it remains "a rule of political grammar, with nothing of the theoretical or irregular about it, that the plural is conjugated in the singular" [Liégeois, 1985b, p.209].

But, if school is a product of society, it is also a formative influence on that society, and it is perhaps in this way that, gradually, a transformation of content may bring about an equally gradual transformation of structures, mentality, and finally a general acceptance of new formulas. Nonetheless our approach would be too narrow if it were limited to seeking changes in the school system. It is imperative to bear in mind the entire socio-cultural situation, and this is why *we recommend adopting the politics of interculturalism as a first step.*

Gypsy children in school

We began this chapter by analysing the differences between the Gypsy and non-Gypsy education systems. We then went on to examine the presence of Gypsy language and culture in the classroom, before considering the importance of intercultural pedagogy – despite its limited application in practice to date. To finish off, we shall underline a few considerations which will influence our final recommendations.

What various groups expect from school can be radically different, or even in opposition. Amongst these discrepancies the gap between Gypsy expectations and those of the school authorities is perhaps the most extreme. The values and aspirations of Gypsy families, the scholastic institution, individual teachers, non-Gypsy institutions generally and the policies by which they are driven, are not the same, and confrontation gives rise to conflict (latent or violently explicit) within the school. Such conflict has its strongest impact on the most vulnerable party involved: the child. The school – that is, each body and individual involved in it – must carefully examine the situation and draw the necessary conclusions. If school wants the Gypsy child's presence (and all the more so when compulsory schooling forces him to attend) it must transform these conflicts into manageable differences. The best means of achieving this is not – as was long, and is still far too often, believed – to force the children into rigid uniformity. On the contrary, it is when the child's own capacities are welcomed and validated, and his experience drawn on in the classroom, that he has the best conditions for learning. Both theory and practice clearly demonstrate that it is when we insist that all children begin the scholastic marathon from a single starting point, that we maximise the disparity of the rate at which they cover the course:

"By treating all pupils, so unequal in fact, as equals… in practice, the school system sanctions initial inequality" [Bourdieu, 1966, p.336]. "The result is too often an incoherence in Travellers' schooling, an incoherence which seems to be founded on a misconception of equality: we fear that ignoring differences only succeeds in reinforcing them" [*Jeannette et l'École Obligatoire,* 1983, p.39].

If school wishes to be "liberating" rather than "reproductive" or "conservative" in the service of society-in-the-singular, there is no way round the taking into account of the children's diversity. To throw children into scholastic competition when conditions favour only some of them, is to put the rest into a conflict situation which will result either in their rejecting the institution (which in turn will aggravate their marginality), or else in a profound personality crisis in which the institution comes out on top [cf. Liégeois 1980b]. "It is as if the universal right to instruction, of which our civilisation was so prematurely boastful, were, by a perverse twist, denied more and more to the most underprivileged: they are the first to be denied it in the poor countries, and the only ones in the rich" [Faure, 1972]. The creation of categories and classes for the "handicapped" has, as we have seen, been an entirely inappropriate response to cultural questions. Gypsies and Travellers, as a group, are still outside the school, even when within its walls. Yet school may be in the process of changing, and the place it accords to Gypsy children will be indicative of just how profound – or superficial – the change has been.

Embryonic interculturalism may, if developed, allow for the "rehabilitation" of cultural differences which up to now have been interpreted as handicaps (even though nowadays they are termed "socio-cultural" handicaps). It will permit different individuals to live their differences without being reduced to them; if the school does its job correctly, they will learn to understand and accept each other as individuals. *It would doubtless be preferable to deal in terms of "singularities" or "uniquenesses" (with positive, validating overtones) than "differences" (implying stigmatisation).* And perhaps in the end such an approach will lead to the development of a "pedagogy of success" in which recognition is granted to the child and his skills, instead of penalising him for what he does badly because it is outside his experience. Recognition gives confidence which in turn leads to progress. "The impression of learning is a condition of learning. It gives the learner the measure and gratification of his progress" [Cotonnec, 1984, p.50]. This is one of the more practical, and profound, aspects of the learning process, which impact on the personality as a whole:

"I've always had a lot more authority over Gypsy children when helping them to dismantle a motor than when explaining how to get their grammar right" [M. Pragnières, MS., 1985]. From a Dutch study, "In the section dealing with the attitudes towards foreign Gypsies, whom Dutch Gypsies consider as belonging to a completely different category, a possibly very interesting paradox is found: foreign Gypsies are said to be more prepared to adjust, regarding externals, to 'civilian society', because they are more sure of their own identity. Dutch Gypsies are said to be less flexible in their attitude because they are afraid of losing (even more of) their identity" [ABGV, 1984, p.3].

The intercultural approach provides a way out of the eternal dichotomy between "Gypsy" classes and "ordinary" classes, since it satisfies the "adaptation" criterion stipulated at the end of the chapter on structures. It is equally acceptable to parents who refuse to see their children in "specialised" classes, and to those who want their children to "work together" in school. The intercultural approach, in its flexibility of form and content, can adapt to the child's own rhythms – to his personal level and the overall class profile. This is a pedagogical necessity but one which is rarely met in existing circumstances; many sources indicate that when the "scholastically successful" Gypsy child is transferred from specialised to ordinary class, his performance undergoes marked deterioration, since the intellectual content of teaching is but one of the elements involved.

The workings of the class do not necessarily have to follow the either/or model usually assumed for them: that if the scholastic menu is not predetermined then it will be a self-service free-for-all. In fact the findings of experiments along self-service lines are inconclusive, and not applicable as yet to the school system in general. Yet this is no reason for sticking to the menu. To continue in the same metaphor, we might provide a choice of menus, or better yet, for the purposes of intercultural pedagogy, a complete and balanced menu with various options for each course. Such a suggestion is compatible with existing school systems: "Harmonising programmes is not a question of unifying their content, but of harmonising their objectives" [J.-M. Sivirine, in Rey, 1982b, p.23]. If the objective – and this is generally agreed – is that children acquire basic skills to enable them to actively adapt to and participate fully in their environment, then the syllabus must remain open-ended. *Content need not be uniform – rather, it must be adequate to the task in hand.* This consideration unites Traveller parents' "utilitarian" view of the school, and the "functionality" stipulated by certain educationists:

"By 'functional' situation I mean a real situation, a life-situation which will lead to something other than abstract 'knowledge'. In consequence, learning to read, is reading. Reading is an activity which becomes meaningful because of its relation to a project, a goal. The only reason the child learns is because he's reading, and reading (rather than 'learning to read') is what he's doing... 'Reading' is always reading something: the activity and the goal must be integrated in the child's experience" [Balas, 1984, pp. 2 & 7].

Reaching agreement among the various parties involved as to what the school's basic objectives are, may give it the possibility to fulfil its mission in an unambiguous manner. As we have already stressed, the school's role is certainly not to "train Gypsies"; it has neither the means nor the duty to do so, nor do parents expect it. "In fact, what is expected of school is that it give children the means to validate their own culture – not to do it for them" [workshop report, in Liégeois, 1983b]. Teachers must be trained to welcome increased variety and flexibility without preconceived notions as to how the children ought to behave: indeed, it is the children's "behaviour" (in the broadest sense of the word) which should determine the teacher's approach. Teachers must be trained and informed in such a way that they are hampered neither by their ignorance (usually manifest in ill-concealed ethnocentrism) nor by their knowledge (having a basic understanding of Traveller culture doesn't qualify the teacher as an anthropologist).

School, particularly for the child from an ethnic minority, is, and will remain, an acculturising agent. Which is to say that, from the moment it becomes a factor in any child's education, it begins to have an impact on his formation in general. Yet at times – or perhaps always – there are certain forms of acculturation which are essential if one is to adapt successfully. And schooling can be conceived in such a way as to ensure that it is not at any rate an agent of deculturation. To put it another way, school can be seen as *complementary to* in-family education, rather than as supplanting it. If classes are successfully adapted, the two forms of education can *converge* rather than running as parallels (with no common points) or in opposition (in which case either the family feels threatened by school and rejects it, or the child's cultural and social roots are weakened as school gets the upper hand). In either of these cases, the child's identity – which ought to be his unshakeable core of reference – is transformed by the school into a source of conflict.

The acceptance of cultural variety in teaching content will allow the school to validate the children by validating their cultural experiences, while adapting to a wide range of situations.

"School has become, in European societies, the principal and sometimes the only force of cultural legitimation. All cultural practices deemed worthy of being taught in school, are legitimate (recognised, worthwhile, prestigious): for example a language studied in school, a culture taught or at least mentioned in the school. For this reason it is essential that immigrant children's homelands and cultures figure in textbooks, class projects, activities, class and school libraries, parent/teacher meetings, decisions by the school board, etc., etc.: prime factors in validating these cultures. By the same token the physical presence of mother tongue language teachers is further proof, to the children and their parents, of the 'worth' of these languages" [Mariet, 1980, p.15].

As for adaptability to varied situations, the nomadism of a significant proportion of Gypsy children puts it to a harsh test, all the more so considering the usual rigidity of the school establishment. Mobile structures, as we have already seen, are only a very partial answer: virtually all nomadic children who attend school do so in fixed structures (be they specialised or not). Two points are of critical importance to teachers. Firstly, they must learn to adjust their teaching approach to the unpredictable length of the child's stay: a day or several months, a single stay or periodic returns? Secondly, they must assess each child's level – a time-consuming and imprecise business. The child finds himself, from one school to the next, confronted by various teaching methods; he may even tackle the same material several times but with different approaches. Not surprisingly, he gets fed up and discouraged. In addition, repeated enrolments and the administrative difficulties they entail are disheartening to the parents, too. Various ideas have been put forward to enable the child's scholastic records to be transferred more accurately and smoothly, but so far are being implemented only on a very limited scale, and without great success. Existing propositions should be studied in detail as a first step in consultation between the various parties concerned, in order to evolve alternatives which would take full account of the realities of nomadism and of the legitimacy of parents' claim to schooling for their children without abandoning their lifestyle.

All of this requires a will and a flexibility, an openness which each citizen has a right to expect from the institutions of his state. The school systems of the European

Community are not, in theory, opposed to any of these suggestions. As concerns school provision for Gypsy children, centralised and decentralised systems each have their own advantages and drawbacks: what the centralised system lacks in flexibility and innovation, it makes up for in coordination (and vice versa). If we work at a pan-European level, we should be able to learn from the successes of each state.

There is need, therefore, for flexibility, in order that the necessary initiatives and subsequent innovations may arise. Unorthodox experiments may play an important role here, and they must be permitted to exist, before they can be judged. Teachers frequently complain that rigidity is the cause of non-adaptation and other obstacles that render their efforts useless. They must have leeway to operate with a flexibility which will allow their classes to satisfy the criterion of adaptability we have so often stressed. In this context, talk of "ordinary" or "specialised" classes becomes irrelevant; we also avoid labels, ghettoisation and rigidity. Instead, each class must constantly evolve in its adaptability, by responding to the needs of the children actually present within it.

"The child... has a right to pedagogy appropriate to his particular situation. His right to acceptance is a part of his fundamental right to schooling and vocational training" [Commission of the European Communities (84) 244, p.36]. The same synthesis document emphasises that "the methods of acceptance vary as much as the situations themselves" [p.36]. It insists on the importance of linguistic (mother tongue) backup for several years of primary school "even for those children with the benefit of preschooling" [p.11], on the introduction of flexible schedules, backup personnel (not just teachers), and on the necessity for small class size: "Effective numbers in 'reception classes' are around the ten to eighteen mark; this permits individual attention in the 'host' language" [p.12]. These practices are not seen as demeaning, nor the classes as being specialised, despite mention of "homogeneous reception classes" [p.12] where bilingualism may be practised.

It is a state of mind that must change, to enable us to pass from our present ethnocentric categorising to pedagogical pluralism, openness to parental participation, holistic assessment instead of interpretation from a one-sided structural or technical perspective, and participation in the implementation of an overall "intercultural policy" within which intercultural pedagogy will easily find its place.

Local authorities

"If we were pushed around less, we'd be more intelligent. For Gypsies there's nothing but persecution... You treat Travellers like dogs – except that dogs would get the protection of the SPCA! Don't fool yourselves that children can learn under such conditions. The more you put them down, the less they're going to study, and the less we're going to want them to. You know what education is? It's rejection, rejection everywhere. There's evictions, police, legal proceedings everywhere you turn. The kids are pulled out of school, they have no future, they have nothing at all, and they're treated as if it's all their own fault!" [Pierre Yung, President of *l'Union des Tsiganes et Voyageurs de France*, 1980a, pp. 291 and 53].

"I had [my children] for three years in the Harden school… and the Council [local authorities] and police came down one day to move us on, and I asked the policeman if he'd leave my caravan where it was for ten, twenty minutes till I went and fetched my children out of school, because they said they were going to move us out of the district, and the policeman said I've got no damn rights of having them in school. Well, my children need education like anybody else, they need to know the rights and wrongs of life, they'd like to read and write, I'd like them to read and write" [interview with Mrs. G. Taylor, an English Romani mother, in *Traveller Education*, no. 1, 1973, quoted by Acton/Kenrick].

In all the Member States of the European Community, the local authorities bear a direct responsibility for school provision. The degree of responsibility varies from country to country: it may be limited to providing school premises, or organising school lunches and transport, but it may extend as far as hiring teachers and elaborating the curriculum. These aspects have been covered in the preceding chapters, as has the question of the child's acceptance – or rejection – within the school. The present chapter deals briefly with local authorities' responsibilities with regard to general provision for Gypsy families – indirectly but crucially linked with the question of schooling.

The majority of the national reports compiled for this project stipulate a strong correlation between general attitudes to Gypsies – particularly nomads – and school attendance. Some sources go so far as to suggest that lack of provision of sites for Travellers is the only reason for their absence from school: "The single greatest reason for non-attendance, without any shadow of a doubt, is the lack of a settled place for Traveller families to live" [Dwyer, 1984, p.1]. Elsewhere it is generally emphasised that bad housing, notably the insanitary conditions which often characterise even official sites, are a source of general ill-health which affects the child's school attendance and exacerbates others' rejection of him: he is seen as living in dirt and, consequently, as being himself dirty and disease-ridden. Thus the effects, objective and subjective, of the situation in which families are placed regardless of their own wishes, are taken (consciously or not) as the causes of, and sometimes as justification for, the rejection to which they are subject. And this rejection is rarely considered, by those who practise it, as a fundamental cause of ill-health, non-attendance or academic failure.

In these conditions – already analysed at the beginning of this study, in connection with policies towards Gypsies and Travellers – schooling can only be considered in conjunction with factors essential to their physical, economic, and cultural survival.

It is significant that most conferences called to discuss questions of schooling end up devoting a great deal – sometimes all – of their attention to the wider issues of lack of provision, Gypsies' legal position, discrimination. Schooling can only be discussed within this context. It is not a question of lack of parental goodwill, but of a minimum degree of security.

Let us recall that intercultural pedagogy presupposes a certain degree of interculturalism in the general environment. Yet as regards attitudes towards Gypsies there seems to be little movement in this direction. "Local residents" remain as steadfastly convinced as ever, of stereotyped negative images; the arrival of nomads is in itself the signal for demands for their expulsion on any and all pretexts. It may go as far as demonstrations and protest marches demanding their eviction; roadside camps or even official sites may be violently attacked and once again the Traveller is without a dwelling-place. Buying or renting a piece of land or a flat is often difficult for Gypsies. The effective ban on Gypsies in public places is still very much the rule everywhere; only the degree of blatant visibility varies.

"It started to happen to me in Galway. I went to a dance. There was a friend with me and as we were going in the door we were stopped by a big man who said: 'You're not coming in.' I got a shock and said: 'What do you mean, I'm not coming in?' He said: 'No Travellers are coming in.' I turned and walked away. I felt real bad, so I went home. I sat there thinking about it, and I just couldn't get over it. I was saying why are we different from others? Why are Travellers treated like dirt?" "I know one Traveller girl who had never been to a dance in her life. She dressed up for it. Brendan Boyer was playing, he used to sing Elvis songs. She got refused. The doorman told her that the manager told them to keep out all Travellers" [quoted by McCarthy, in *Ireland*].

"The most violent reactions occur in lower middle class and working class districts, whereas in slum areas Gypsies find means of camouflaging themselves and coming to practical arrangements based on common interests. In 'posh' areas (where Gypsies are rarely seen) prejudice appears to be surpassed by curiosity and compassion. The curiosity fades quickly after a couple of encounters along the lines of 'a visit to the zoo'; the compassion cannot hold out in the face of lack of 'proper' expressions of gratitude, and is quickly transformed into contemptuous disapproval for such 'irresponsible parents who go on breeding children into such dreadful conditions'" [Silvia Fardella, *Italy*, 1983; MS.]. As a general rule, "All [social] classes are united in their opposition if not in their way of expressing it" [Paul Murray, *Irish Times*, 13/12/82].

Faced with such attitudes, local authorities carry a great responsibility. They use it in various ways; on rare occasions they may even oppose acts of rejection carried out by their constituents, on others they comply with public pressure for evictions and other punitive measures. They may opt for active neutrality (refusal to intervene without concrete and well-founded justification) or passive neutrality (by turning a blind eye to acts of discrimination). Up to now, with a few exceptions in recent years, local authorities' attitudes and policies have followed the same lines as those of the local population in general: rejecting [for a socio-historical analysis see Liégeois, 1983a]. This rejection can take various forms. *Simple rejection* as expressed in "no temporary dwellings" signs and being quickly moved on by the police (in the name of, for example, public order, preserving the peace, public health). *Violent rejection* by truncheon-wielding representatives of "law and order", by digging trenches around established camping spots, or surrounding them with boulders (in Ireland the authorities call these practices "landscaping" and "securing"), or the dumping of earth and even of refuse into campsites to force departure. *Indirect rejection* is on the rise at present; as overt violence becomes unacceptable, it is replaced by convoluted, petty regulations which have the same effect. For example a minuscule "official" site may be set up, and all camping elsewhere strictly forbidden. There may be an exorbitant parking fee, stopping officially limited to a couple of hours only, difficulties in getting children enrolled in school... Indirect rejection allows public authorities to retain a clear conscience, and is also compatible with assimilationist policies [since its purpose is to harass nomads into sedentarism – Sinéad ní Shuinéar].

The final quarter of the twentieth century is nonetheless marked by changes implemented by local authorities, and by new provisions for Travellers. The central authorities have tightened up urban bye-laws, thus reducing the margins (both physical and legal) where nomads formerly operated. At the same time however there has been a swing towards "humanitarian" attitudes which has had a moderating effect on rejection; this is reinforced by Gypsy, Gypsy-support, and human rights organisations which try to transform discriminatory practices into media events, thereby focusing public attention and pressure for a rethink of policy. State finance is now available to enable local authorities to make provision for Gypsies. Yet national directives calling for respect often remain purely theoretical, since their implementation depends on local initiative. It is at this level that long-standing antagonism is activated: local populations everywhere are vigorously opposed to having Gypsy neighbours imposed upon them, and if they cannot keep them out of the area altogether, the least they demand is that Gypsy be enclosed, segregated, and kept under control. Within this highly ambiguous context, local authorities are beginning to experiment with halting sites for nomads and group housing developments for the sedentary.

Finding a halting place is difficult for the nomad. The present tendency towards larger and larger agglomerations is due to the increasing rarity of suitable space and to complex, often discriminatory, legislation (ostensibly for the protection of "the environment", "public order", "public health", etc. – vague notions open to arbitrary interpretation) which is especially harsh on those whose permanent dwelling is a caravan. Even in those countries where local authorities have for years been under legal obligation to provide halting sites, a majority of caravans may still be stopping illegally, and precariously. Thus, in the *United Kingdom*, 35-40% of Travellers are on illegal sites [Acton/Kenrick]. In *France*, the Marseilles local authority proposed 171 pitches for 2,000 caravans [Marseilles, AREAT report, 1984]. In *Ireland* in 1960, 1,142 families had nowhere to halt but roadside verges; in 1980, 1,149 families were in the same situation: twenty years of provision have barely absorbed the increase in the Traveller population. Thus, those who travel, and those who have to halt (notably in order to work) are often on the look-out for somewhere to stop, even for a day or two. What they find is frequently highly unsuitable, even dangerous, and never secure: demolition areas, on footpaths, by railway lines, on industrial estates... Such stopping places are moreover quite illegal, since the same law which obliges local authorities to provide official halting sites simultaneously empowers them to prohibit the halting of caravans anywhere else. Legalised rejection is the end result: provision, inadequate in both quantity and quality, paves the way for the expulsion of all caravans parked elsewhere.

We will give but one example, from the *United Kingdom* [England and Wales]. "If a local authority can be 'designated' by the Secretary of State for the Environment as having fulfilled its duties under the Act (Local Government, Planning and Land Act – 1980) they receive substantial additional powers to move Gypsies on. In 'designated areas' the Local Authority can obtain from magistrates an order to Gypsies to quit any land (apart from official caravan sites or private caravan sites with planning permission) within twenty-four hours and resistance to eviction is made a criminal offence. A patchwork of no-go areas for nomadic Gypsies has thus been created, and 'designation' has thus become a key target of criticism by Gypsy groups as a form of 'apartheid'" [Acton/Kenrick]. Such practices, with or without ministerial backup, are widely applied in other states as well.

Due to lack of consultation and forethought, many official sites are quite unsuited to the needs of the families expected to use them. One of the most common major faults is bad location: usually an area deemed unsuitable for anything else (because of pollution, damp, noise, flood risk, or other danger) is seen as good enough for Gypsies. They also tend to be very badly planned: layout forces functional overcrowding, since what should be a residential site is in fact conceived as a supervised car-park, replete with on-site warden and intrusive social workers. Rightly or wrongly considered public space, such sites are moreover under constant police surveillance. The hugeness (eighty to a hundred or more caravans) of so many sites is yet another problem: neighbouring residents feel deeply threatened; ghettoisation, internal conflicts and economic difficulties arise from this dense concentration of so many people all competing for the same resources. Small sites have a great many advantages, but there are far too few of them, while megasites continue to be set up. And, once established, it is difficult indeed to reverse the trend – for example the "deconcentration policy" adopted in the Netherlands over a decade ago has made scarcely any headway. [For further details on these questions see the synopsis in Liégeois, 1985a; for Italy, Piasere, 1985b; for the UK, Acton, 1985b; for France, Liégeois 1981b, and the Reyniers reports of 1984, '85, and '86.]

Provision for the sedentary presents similar drawbacks, all the more so since it is imposed by "settlement" policies. The dwellings provided are often culturally inappropriate: too small for extended family groups, isolated by lifts and stairways, situated in areas where the residents have serious economic and social problems of their own, unsuitable for the practice of most economic activities, and generally guaranteeing conflict (particularly considering that coexistence is imposed on both communities). The bonds of solidarity are threatened by such a set-up – and this for families to whom life within and through the community is the foundation-stone and primary motivation of their very existence. Here again, experience has shown that consultation with the various parties concerned can, in conjunction with careful planning, result in much more suitable arrangements, particularly since in this as in all other fields Gypsies have an enormous variety of circumstances and aspirations.

Local authorities bear a particular responsibility through their intermediary role between regional/national institutions and local inhabitants (Gypsy and non-Gypsy), by their legal powers (particularly as regards site/housing and school provision) and by their direct personal contact with those affected. As a rule they also have broad discretionary powers of initiative and innovation, awaiting only the political will to override the prejudice of local populations. Such resolve is rarely forthcoming; in practice it is usually these very local authorities which make it difficult for Traveller children to get into school, and determined initiatives as regards halting sites, housing provision, adapted classes, etc. are still rare.

The key to resolving this impasse may lie at the regional level, where the authorities are relatively free of the need to appease the prejudices of local populations, and are well situated as regards consultation and coordination. But the role of central government remains crucial: to encourage or oblige local authorities to make adequate provision for both nomadic and sedentary Gypsies, and pending such provision to outlaw evictions; to provide practical backup in the form of research and pilot projects; to harmonise attitudes and legislation (which in practice are all too often contradictory) emanating from various ministries; to provide the finance for accommodation and schooling. This latter would provide yet another incentive for action from local authorities, because if they fail in this area it may pass into the direct control of central government; results in countries where such a stipulation operates – for example the UK with its "no-area pool" for school funds – are promising.

Other bodies

We have frequently drawn attention to the presence – and sometimes the importance – of various public and private bodies which may affect school provision for Gypsy children; for example, the role of religious missions in the first initiatives in this field. Various bodies – religious and humanitarian organisations, voluntary associations, social workers, etc. – still do play a role, the importance of which varies from country to country. The reasons for this vary too: in some countries the system is such that initiative must come from without; in others, those officially responsible for the schooling of Gypsy children are not fulfilling their obligations, and so supplementary efforts are made by various other bodies.

For example, in *Ireland*, "The educational system is based on the efforts of private bodies which are supported by the state. Because of the traditional role played in Irish society by the church, these 'private bodies' are nearly always the churches and given the primacy of Catholicism in Irish society, chiefly the Catholic church. The pattern then is for the church, in the form of the local parish priest, to initiate the establishment of a school. Once initiated, the building and running of a school is largely paid for by the state which contributes 90% of the capital and running costs and pays the teachers' salaries. However the state, while it is the chief financer of schools, does not run them" [McCarthy].

In *Belgium*: "In a country where public authorities do not fulfil their responsibilities towards a minority such as Gypsies and Travellers, private initiative springs up to fill the gap. Roman Catholic charities have a long association with persons of no fixed abode (a chaplaincy to travelling showmen, another chaplaincy to barge-dwellers, local committees for fairground operators, support committees for Travelling People). Some independent bodies (such as the Belgian League for the Defence of Human Rights) and quangos (such as the King Baudouin Foundation, linked with the Union of Belgian Cities and Villages) may also take action on behalf of Travellers." It is also worth noting that "in Belgium today, the number of volunteers and professionals actually involved in social/educational activities [with Travellers] is not more than a dozen, and all of them have evolved outside of ordinary school structures" [Reyniers].

In *Italy*, "It is significant that many teachers name *Opera Nomadi* (Nomads' Action – a private organisation) as the body responsible for the schooling of Gypsy children, instead of official organisations, an obvious sign of a lack of state involvement, and confirmed by the facts" [Karpati/Massano].

The reports from the various countries describe the efforts of these bodies in connection with school provision; taken into account with other sources, they permit us to form some generalisations. Firstly, significant breakthroughs in the field often originate from unofficial sources, since the authorities may be bogged down in inertia or simple lack of will. This consideration extends even to the financing of provision which may be essential, yet not seen as such by those with official responsibility. Within highly centralised systems, private initiatives and volunteer programmes provide the minimum flexibility essential for experimentation, the results of which may provide inspiration for adoption within the official system. In decentralised systems, they provide models which teachers can examine for their own needs, consolidate and in time reproduce. This is the case in the *United Kingdom*: "The areas where there is substantial provision for Traveller education today are the areas where there was a large amount of voluntary activity in 1973. It is true in fact that in the English and Welsh education system as a whole, local citizen initiatives are extremely important in determining the shape of provision" [Acton/Kenrick].

In the face of the difficulties surrounding schooling, private bodies and non-governmental organisations may play an essential supplementary – indeed, in some countries, the primary – role: providing backup outside class hours, reaching children who do not attend school at all, adult literacy programmes, etc. Such voluntary activities are usually carried out part-time, and may be peripheral to what the volunteers see as their main task within the Travelling community. There are often religious tones to the work: the goal may be, not reading as such, but reading the Gospels.

Since the 1960s, voluntary organisations in many countries have set up structural links (for example by forming themselves into an association) to enable them to operate more efficiently and obtain funds more easily. At the same time, in conjunction with assimilationist policies, the central authorities have set up a network of social services (not specifically aimed at Gypsies, but directly affecting them). These tendencies towards rationalisation and organisation of social action from various sources have often led to an amalgamation of forces, in which public authorities take over the running of private organisations which in this way become "para-public" social services. The end result is a homogenisation of practices and ideologies, in certain countries a proliferation of red tape, and a general transformation from voluntarism to professionalism, spontaneity to technicality, and activism to bureaucracy. Such organisations have a direct impact on the schooling of Gypsy and Traveller children, partly because they themselves play an important role in setting the socio-political tone surrounding the communities in question, and partly because it is their members (especially social workers) who are among the rare Settled individuals who wish to establish ongoing contact with Travellers – and they use their influence to encourage schooling. Weighing one thing against another, the influence of social work and its associate organisations veers towards the negative. [It is beyond the scope of this report to give a detailed analysis of social work; as a supplement to this very brief mention of the subject the reader may turn to detailed works published elsewhere. For further information on social work see for example Liégeois 1977a; for non-Gypsy organisations and associations, see Liégeois 1983a.]

"Social workers are now employed by all local authorities in the Irish Republic to work with Travellers. There are ten social workers in Dublin. Youth workers, child care workers and community workers are also employed, though on a much smaller scale. These are all Settled people. They are frequently working to a set of objectives that are very much in conflict with Travellers' own needs and objectives. For example, local authority social workers have integration and assimilation as their primary objective. Many Travellers do not want to be integrated and this is an obvious source of conflict... Few of the social workers involved would think that it is important to relate education to Traveller culture... most see their role as putting pressure on the families to send their children to school and sorting out any problems that arise in that process" [McCarthy].

Again in *Ireland,* the Committee for the Rights of Travellers has issued a postcard with a cartoon of two Travellers talking. "Gosh! Times are bad... Our campsite is infested with rats", says one. "Huh! You're lucky!" replies the other, "Ours is infested with social workers!" The flipside provides a few explanatory lines: "Social Workers to the Travelling people are employed by Local Authorities to implement a policy of Absorption, based on the 1963 Itinerancy Report. This policy is cultural genocide, directed against Travellers as a specific group, with the purpose of destroying them as a group. Other ethnocidal acts are denial of opportunity to use our language, preserve our traditions and maintain our basic social institutions."

In the *Federal Republic of Germany* "Caritas is the Catholic charitable organisation with the longest tradition of social work among the Sinti... it has blocked the emancipation of the Sinti people at the federal level... Instead of supporting the small Sinti associations which have been springing up since the 1950s, and offering them a forum for obtaining their civil rights, instead of backing them up in their social, educational, cultural and political demands, it has maintained a paternalist approach – geared towards integrating the Sinti into the parish" [Reemtsma].

In the *United Kingdom*: "Within the last few years since the end of the 1960s a Gypsy 'industry' peopled almost entirely by non-Gypsies has grown up, creating hitherto unknown structures in welfare, site provision and education. The traditional response of withdrawal in order to survive is becoming harder and harder for Gypsies. If, however, Gypsies organise, they can make their influence felt, by whatever means possible, as some are now doing. Then they can secure their right to live, to have a place to live and work on their own terms..." [Official policy statement of the National Gypsy Education Council, in *Towards Gypsy Power*, Romanestan Publications, 1977]. "Since 1968, an educational and welfare bureaucracy dealing with Travellers has begun to grow up, and will grow further. Nobody seriously bothered to ask the Gypsies what they thought of this, or whether this was what they wanted – but that, by now, is past history: too many people now have a career interest in its continuation and growth for much to be done about its expansion, which, eventually, could lead to the final bureaucratisation of the Gypsy way of life – as pointed out this could succeed where persecution over the centuries has failed" [Worrall 1979, p. 296].

The same applies to the *French* situation [cf. Liégeois 1977a] where moreover, since 1960, a centralising organism has been in existence – a sort of "Bureau of Gypsy Affairs" [thus dubbed in a critical analysis, alluding to the notorious Bureau of Indian Affairs in the United States – cf. Liégeois 1983a, pp. 257-76].

As a general rule, the role of organisations "concerned" with the "problems" of Gypsy communities is ambiguous and difficult to fulfil. "It is frequently claimed that they are intermediaries between public authorities and the Settled community, on the one hand, and Gypsies and Travellers on the other. Yet this 'linking' role often requires them to act as transforming agents, all the more so as they are in prolonged contact with small groups which may be in difficult circumstances... Next, their function as 'link' can be easily turned into 'buffer': while this sometimes plays a positive role in preventing violent confrontation, it also interposes where direct dialogue might be more fruitful. Finally, by dealing piecemeal with problems, retaining a local perspective, and subduing rifts and conflicts, such organisations may discourage the formulation of a broad overview. By this filtering and diluting effect, they play the opposite role to Gypsy organisations, which seek to condense grievances and make their voices heard while retaining all the intensity of their commitment...

Obliged as they are to negotiate with Gypsies, these associations have a difficult time in explaining what their role is, and a guilty conscience over their inability to do so. Obliged as they are to negotiate with public authorities, on whom they are financially dependent, they make compromises so that these will continue to listen to and fund them. Obliged as they are to negotiate with hostile local residents, if they are too openly pro-Gypsy then they too will be rejected. And so: can any association effectively defend a minority society from the very establishment with which it is itself so intimately linked? Even if theoretically independent, financial reality reinforces dependence, and, if the members' hearts are on the Gypsies' side, their administrative body is firmly linked to the other. In effect, such associations are torn between the reasons for their existence and what they must do in order to continue to exist" [Liégeois, 1985a, pp.170-1].

It would appear that there has been a gradual process of ossification overtaking what one British report called the social work "industry". Socio-educative projects, begun through a variety of private initiatives, have lost the flexibility that was their most precious asset, a synonym for potential innovation and adaptability to Travellers' changing needs. The careers which have sprung up from them have often been characterised by opportunity transformed to opportunism, constructive criticism to narrowminded conformism. Even within the system, voices have begun to question the purpose of its existence, and not only in relation to Travellers; as one social worker put it, it is time to ask "if the service has arisen in response to needs, or if it perpetuates the needs in order to justify its existence" [Barec 1976, p.60]. The proliferation of social services linked with assimilationism is part of the wider phenomenon analysed earlier under the heading "Integration by Handicap": cultural traits are redefined as social problems, Gypsies are classified en masse as "disadvantaged" and made the objects of charity. Such an approach discourages the social and economic dynamics which would permit families to retain their autonomy, redefining identity in purely negative terms and providing schooling geared towards goals other than the active attainment of independence.

The general trend, then, is for private initiative to lose its drive, and thus its potential for innovation. Yet there are still grounds for hope, in the form of numerous small local organisations. It is they who are best able to respond to the great variety of situations on the ground, and which have the closest contact both with Traveller families and with local residents and institutions. New tendencies are emerging which may lead in time to new practices. Primary among these is the increasingly important political role of Gypsy organisations – formed and run *by* Gypsies, not merely *for* them. They see their role as mediators, partners in consultation, and if necessary as pressure groups. There has been a rise – though to date on a very small scale – of meetings at local level, which may in time establish new patterns of direct cooperation. Local associations are inviting Gypsies to cooperate with them, and when they accept they are no longer content to play a passive, "token" role, as may have been expected of them in the past. Furthermore, a new approach to social services is also emerging, in which the social worker's role is redefined as collaboration, with the emphasis on practical rather than social assistance: those who ask for it should be provided with the instruments they require for successful adaptation, rather than having the means of assimilation imposed upon them. Such is the approach of *community workers* in the United Kingdom, *opbouwwerkers* in the Netherlands (at the service of various communities to help formulate action programmes, provide necessary skills, and support the community's claims), *Soziale Beratungsstellen* (advice bureaux on questions of a social nature) in the FRG. Another German project demonstrates the importance of a "linking organisation" in procuring practical and socio-political support.

If, on the one hand, social workers' concept of their role is changing (despite the immobility of the institutions which employ them), on the other, Gypsies themselves feel more and more involved in questions of aid for their own community: in the United Kingdom for example, Travellers who are active members of grassroots organisations have begun to call themselves "community workers" or "voluntary community workers". Will their numbers increase? Particularly in this field of practical and social aid, the effects of school education will make themselves felt, and will have a profound impact on the relations between Gypsies and their surroundings. Gypsy communities may, if they so wish, see more and more social workers arising from their own ranks, and who will in time be able to work within their own associations.

Vocational training

As we have seen in preceding chapters, the proportion of Gypsy children attending secondary school is very small indeed. Thus, the number of those who avail themselves of vocational training provided by the ordinary school system is minimal. Schooling culminating in preparedness for work is therefore virtually nonexistent in Gypsy experience – for all the reasons we have analysed throughout this report in relation to basic schooling. At the same time some of these reasons acquire a particular relevance when considered in the context of vocational training. We shall try to give a brief sketch of the overall situation, while emphasising that a separate report would be required to cover this subject, examining Gypsy economic practices, their in-family training methods, the relationship of Gypsy economic activities to the broader economic context, the potential of various training systems, detailed analysis of training programmes to date, etc.

An overview of training programmes so far indicates that many have been unsuitable, notably because they have failed to take account of the characteristics of Gypsy work patterns, the absence of basic "book-learning", and Gypsy commitment to self-employment (implying an unwillingness to be economically tied to people or places). Frequently, through *lack of forethought, lack of consultation, lack of training and information* for the teachers involved, and *lack of Gypsy involvement*, such programmes have failed to consider both trainees' capacities and aspirations, and market realities.

"Very many teachers see their role as preparing Traveller children for integration into the Settled community and they tend to measure success and failure in terms of this objective. This is almost sub-conscious with some of them but is reflected in certain statements: 'They have no models in their own community', 'Any culture they had disappeared with the dole' and so on. It is more graphically reflected by what is not said: teachers do not speak of success in terms of equipping a child to cope with his/her culture successfully. For example, they attach a negative value to Travellers' ability to outsmart and manipulate others in business dealings yet this same ability is very highly valued in the capitalist world generally. A great deal of the content of courses run for businessmen and salespeople consists of precisely this kind of aggressive and manipulative business dealing" [McCarthy].

Gypsy families have been much more unanimous in their negative reaction to such training than in their reaction to basic schooling; not without reason, they see it as limiting, useless and disruptive. Formulated without regard for Gypsy skills and aspirations, training programmes refuse to take cognizance of the discrimination which means that, no matter how qualified, a Gypsy is unlikely to "get a job". The result of such programmes is often "de-qualification" – the young person has failed to acquire in-family training, because he was busy attending a programme that in the end has trained him for nothing. Having seen what the school system has to offer, Gypsy consensus is that parents are far more effective in preparing children for work in the real world. A further problem is that, so far, there seems to be no middle ground in the curriculum followed by such programmes: either it's an unquestioning reproduction of "traditional" skills, or an equally mindless opting for anything "modern".

Anti-Gypsy *discrimination* is still the primary factor to be taken into account if useful training is to be provided. To illustrate, three examples, all from training projects financed by the European Social Fund. In Bray (*Ireland*) ten young Travellers and fourteen "Settled" young people underwent crafts training simultaneously. At the end of the course, only one Traveller found employment, while twelve of the Settled trainees did. Moreover, the "Settled" trainees who could not get work were in fact of Traveller origin. In the project report from Oldenzaal (the *Netherlands*), the refusal to hire qualified Gypsies is emphasised: ostensibly because no jobs are available, but in fact the reason is discrimination. The report from Bremen (*FRG*) draws attention to similar developments, and goes on to emphasise that any itinerant trade is automatically suspect and subject to attempts at being outlawed: the sharpening of scissors, knives, garden tools, etc., which the Bremen project had tried to promote, is mentioned in this context.

"In essence little has changed for the Sinti and Rom since their eviction from the Guilds in mediaeval times... Faced with such massive difficulties, foreseen from the beginning of the project, it proved impossible to succeed in our efforts to develop the grinding and sharpening trade by introducing modern technology and improved marketing. At the same time it became clear that, in addition to the subjective conditions which the Sinti must fulfil in order to be professionally independent, there are legal and other objective obstacles to be overcome if the Sinti are to live independently of social assistance and/or crime" [Bremer Volkshochschule, 1983, pp.39-40].

In other cases, when trainees have found employment, they are underpaid and thus have no motivation to stick with the job, particularly as they generally get only the jobs that no one else wants; *even when he is not rejected, the Gypsy is still exploited.* It is also pointed out that in some countries (e.g. the Netherlands: Oldenzaal) the earnings of an unskilled worker are virtually identical to what one would get from social welfare without working. The experience of most training programmes – conceived in the assimilationist mould – shows that, at the end of the day, trainees are not integrated but relegated, marginalised by society at large and by their own community. They are doubly penalised for the great efforts they have made to obtain vocational training, and doubly disillusioned in consequence: unable to find employment, they have lost a great deal of precious time that could have been spent in family apprenticeship. This does nothing to improve their confidence in the institutions of society at large.

The present economic situation, a difficult time for many as unemployment figures attest, is in danger of becoming critical for many Gypsy families, all the more so as many of their trades are being curtailed by legislation. Thus, a certain level of schooling is made prerequisite to the practice of any trade (e.g. travelling showman, roadside trader) yet no adequate provision to enable Gypsies to attain this level, exists; similarly, young people must bear the stigmatisation of being labelled "disadvantaged" in order to access training, if they have missed out on "ordinary" schooling. Nonetheless, the Gypsy economy remains well adapted to the surrounding environment and, characterised as it is by mobility, rapid adaptability, craftsmanship, etc. may become even more so in future. Its activities are enormously varied, some on the wane while others are being developed: all are based on the provision of goods or services to customers who are not Gypsies or Travellers. Each individual possesses a range of skills which render him very adaptable; from his earliest childhood he trains alongside his parents, an apprenticeship in diversity and change rather than the acquisition of a single profession. He will know how to exercise these economic skills according to time, place and fluctuating circumstances. Work is usually organised within the framework of the family group. When choosing an activity the priority consideration is that it leave the individual independent and free to determine his own work schedule. "This economic philosophy means that the choice of activities, be they consecutive or simultaneous, is a result of provisional compromise between the necessity of earning a living and the desire to maintain a lifestyle, within a changing socio-economic and cultural context" [Liégeois, 1985a, p.67]. Throughout his life the Gypsy is "prospecting", on the lookout for clientele and also new opportunities; he frequently demonstrates a flair for innovation despite the difficulties of his situation. The outsider's view of Gypsy work patterns generally fails to perceive their dynamics and potential; the trades which he sees being practised may well appear to be outdated and unremunerative, yet in reality there are probably other, less visible, irons in the fire, or in the offing. This is one of the reasons why training schemes evolved without consultation are so ill-adapted.

Quite apart from the questions of discrimination and of understanding Gypsy work patterns, any training must take account of other factors inseparable from the first two. Some of them are connected with the subjective experience of training:

"The Sinti involved felt that they were left behind by the speed with which the project developed, and all the more so as it represented (practically for the first time in Bremen) a vast range of programmes aimed at improving their situation… Many trainees developed serious mental blocks during the course of instruction, as they suddenly realised that up to now they had lived in near-total ignorance of 'the outside world' ... In certain cases it was an actual 'fear of knowing'. This is how one of the participants put it: 'Before, we were happy, we knew nothing; now, we're afraid.' Realisation of the necessity to learn and to find out, characterised the dilemma in which the participants found themselves" [*FRG*, Bremer Volkshochschule, pp.16-31].

"I worked in a factory for a while. But I'm sorry I did: it all goes way too fast in there! You don't have time to breathe. Why are the Gadjé so hot on schooling if that's all it leads to?" [a sedentary Traveller in *Belgium*, aged about forty; quoted by Reyniers].

"If a person knows a lot, he suffers a lot – just like you do." "We have enough troubles of our own. Leave us alone to make the best of them. We might be dead tomorrow." "It's good to learn letters. But why? To become labourers on the dole?" "The Gypsy doesn't want to be supervised by anybody." "Isn't it the educated people who are building all those bombs?" "Look at what they're doing. You call that development?" [comments from various Gypsies, collected in *Greece* by E. Marselos, MS., 1985].

"It is clear that any attempt to determine employment would fail because it is anathema to Travelling society, for that society thrives basically on its talent for discovering the host society's need for casual and mobile work. To interfere in vocational matters would be in direct conflict with the Travellers' ethos of making their own way by their wits and their strength" [*United Kingdom*, Ivatts, 1975, p.39].

"The Gypsies often had the idea that instructors were simply intent on putting them to work as quickly as possible in their own interests. This acted as a major brake on the confidence the Gypsies had in their instructors" [in the *Netherlands*, Teunissen, 1982, p.52].

Furthermore, it is important to bear in mind that, due to their associations with *prohibitions* (avoiding contact with the "unclean", for example), certain types of work are out of the running. Let us also consider the *change in social roles* implicit in breaking the parental monopoly on education, and subsequent behavioural changes likely to occur in young people trained outside the Gypsy system. We should also investigate the *subjective experience of failure* in the training situation, the more so as it takes place in a group, alongside other Gypsies. And we must never lose sight of the criterion of *functional usefulness*, felt even more urgently in the field of vocational training than in basic schooling.

"I've never been to school. I got married and started a family. I'm training my daughters very well in all the domestic skills. My son was in school until he was sixteen. What a waste of time! When I think of what he could have been learning if he'd been out and about with his dad! He ought to have been learning the scrap business. Now here he is at eighteen, starting from scratch" [a sedentary Traveller, aged about forty]. For travelling showmen who, like barge families, sometimes agree to be parted from their children to allow them to attend boarding school, "Two facts demonstrate that schooling still needs to be adapted. Despite the existence of special boarding schools and the fact that most showpeople do have a degree of schooling, the overwhelming majority of past pupils do not leave the world of the carnival. With the economic crisis, the emotional and economic bonds between parents and children are reactivated, and we cannot predict that, in future, parents will continue to accept separation from their school-age children" [Reyniers].

"*Great Britain* has drawn very few Gypsies into schemes of professional training. With the exception of the provision of funds for adult literacy classes, most National Gypsy Education Council members would prefer that Gypsies should not have to suffer the spatchcock remedies of unemployment that such policies as the Youth Training Schemes represent; if Gypsies were to enrol on them in any numbers it would be a clear sign of the collapse of the Gypsy economy" [Acton 1984, MS.].

In *Italy*, "Young Gypsies do not fulfil the preconditions for acceptance onto training programmes, since they don't have the required certificates. A few experimental courses for small groups who asked for them fizzled out as students lost interest. The young Rom of the Abruzzi region were the exception: many of them attended vocational courses and also secondary school. But employment difficulties forced them back into the traditional economy. The young Gypsy's first concern is to earn his living, rather than gain qualifications for work which he would only want to do occasionally and as a last resort" [Karpati/Massano].

"The Sinti showed great patience so long as they felt that what they were doing would be directly useful. They took an immediate interest in welding, as their own car needed repairs... for the same reasons, it is not surprising that the only interest they took in the garage set up as part of the project, was as a place to potter about on their own projects... It is abundantly clear that the traditional approach, consisting of orientation and training courses geared towards vocational training, is diametrically opposed to the Sinti way of learning and of earning their living. Apprenticeship, conceived as constructing models in the workshop only to knock them down afterwards, cannot be effective with people who require a direct, useful result of their actions as a stimulus" [*FRG*, Bremer Volkshochschule, 1983, pp. 25-26].

Finally, these considerations demonstrate that any attempts at training cannot be made in isolation from the general socio-cultural context in which they occur. The activities of different generations cannot be considered separately, nor can economic life be considered without reference to other social and political factors. This means, for example, that site provision is a priority insofar as it permits, or forbids, the practice of such and such a trade; that it is the family (rather than the individual, as in the non-Gypsy pattern) which must always be considered the basic economic unit; that a sixteen-year-old may easily be an adult, with responsibility for a spouse and children, and requires skills which can be put to immediate use, as part of training that can be paid, and considered as work rather than school (in *Ireland* for example, to avoid twelve- to fifteen-year-olds feeling they are still "at school", they attend what are called Junior Training Centres). Failing to respect existing dynamics and aspirations, many training schemes are doomed to failure. For example the report from the Oldenzaal pilot scheme (the *Netherlands*) points out difficulties besetting attempts at training and even employment (e.g. as mechanics, musicians, carpenters). Trainees complained that this left them with no time for their social life and visiting relatives, while other Gypsy families subjected them to considerable pressure (visits, phone calls, constant reproaches that they were not working "in the Gypsy way") – until the trainees gave in [cf. Teunissen, 1982, p.48]. *Without the agreement and goodwill of those concerned, and without the consensus of their social group, training is – understandably – unsuccessful.*

Within this context of general difficulty, training provision for young people and adults has increased enormously over the past few years, in projects that may be short- or long-term, independent or part of a local or national plan, under the most varied structures and offering a wide range of programmes, and many with direct Gypsy involvement in their planning or even day-to-day running. We shall only sketch a few of them here; critical analysis and conclusions remain to be formulated.

In *Ireland* a network of Traveller training centres covers the country. The first of these opened in Ennis in 1974; at present (April 1985) there are twenty-five operative with another two due to open before the end of the year. "In most cases the initiative in setting up these Centres was taken by the local committees working for Travellers but from 1976 onwards the Vocational Education Committees and the Industrial Training Authorities (AnCO) became involved. There has been substantial funding from the European Social Fund. These cater for the sixteen to twenty-five age group and trainees get paid an allowance. Young Travellers regard places in these training centres simply as jobs. The content of the training varies from Centre to Centre. Some Centres such as those in Ennis and in Galway provide a wide range of activities that include the traditional metalwork, woodwork, cooking, sewing, making soft toys, knitting and literacy with music and sporting activities and also have a strong emphasis on social activities. Others offer a much more restricted programme and less skills or culture. In one or two of these Centres, again in Ennis for example, there is a strong element of Traveller participation in the management and day to day decision making in the Centres. In most, however, there is no participation at all. The objective of these Centres is to provide vocational training so that Travellers can get work in the Settled community. The number who do is negligible given the very high rate of national unemployment (16%) and the discrimination against Travellers. Most of the training centre places offered last for twelve months. Occasionally trainees are allowed to do second courses. There is a lot of demand for places in these Centres which are seen as previously mentioned as jobs. A few of the training centres have developed small co-operative type businesses as a result of ex-trainees looking for more permanent work and realising the potential of the products they were producing. This has happened quite successfully in Galway and the Centre in Bray takes orders for particular products...

More recently the Government is operating a number of youth employment and community employment projects. 'Exchange House', a Travellers' Centre in Dublin, is using one of these schemes, which provide finance for some salaries, to operate a scrap collection business which employs five Traveller men. A number of other schemes are under consideration, particularly one where finance is given to community groups to employ young people to provide community services. ...The most significant event in adult education started in January of 1985 when twenty-four adult Travellers started a course in community development funded by AnCO – the Industrial Training Authorities. This course includes literacy among a wide variety of skills being taught with the objective of training Travellers to work on a community level with their own people" [McCarthy].

Despite the strength and long establishment of the infrastructures, it seems that the goal – learning trades which will enable trainees to "integrate" into their environment – is unattainable, for reasons already gone into: discrimination by employers and Travellers' own refusal to be alienated in their work; in the end the young "'graduates' have to revert to unemployment assistance. This causes them disillusionment and frustration. It is also a waste of the resources already used to develop their skills" [Keane, 1985, p.28]. Surely a change of perspective, breaking out of the assimilationist rut, and encouraging greater Traveller involvement, would give better results. Some undertakings, such as co-ops and small businesses (e.g. St. Kieran's Enterprise Centre in Bray) provide employment under improved work conditions in the meanwhile. As trainees visit each others' centres, they can exchange ideas and develop a greater group consciousness, and some are already emerging as future leaders. The same process is occurring within some of the centres, too: "The Training Centres also offer an excellent opportunity to young Travellers to develop leadership skills, and already in one Centre an ex-trainee is being prepared by the present Director to take over the direction of the Centre. In other Centres, Travellers sit on Management Committees, act as supervisors in the Centres, and in general are given opportunity to foster those skills which will, before too long, enable them to assume the leadership of their own community" [Keane, 1985, p.26].

The report from the Oldenzaal (the *Netherlands*) Gypsy pilot project [cf. Teunissen, 1982] clearly points out the many difficulties encountered and the impact they have had on final results. The original project was followed, in 1984, by the setting up of three Traveller training centres: in Breda (car demolition), Emmen (construction and repair of boats), and Sneek (welding); these were financed by the Ministry of Welfare, Health, and Cultural Affairs. In 1985, plans were under way for training projects in another five municipalities.

In fact, there are training schemes in operation in most of the Community Member States. They are on the increase in France, and firmly established in the FRG; the first pilot scheme is under way in Greece, plans are being made in Denmark and Italy… It would be well, at this juncture, for a general critique to be carried out, examining different approaches and their results. Important lessons may also be drawn from the experience of Sweden and Finland. In Sweden one of several projects worthy of examination is that set up by the National Board of Public Education, to train Gypsies as teachers at secondary level. Twenty candidates from different groups were given preparatory training, and twelve of them went on to university, where they receive a training allowance; the project has the backing of Gypsy organisations. Finland has been accumulating experience of training schemes since 1970; the areas covered include horses, clothing production, theatre, music, and applied arts (such as textiles, clothing, jewellery-making, ceramics, print layout, design).

When considering policy guidelines for training schemes, we find ourselves with the same checklist as applies to schooling in general: *flexibility, diversity of structures and programmes, functionality of activities,* and *teacher training. Family involvement* is particularly crucial at this stage, both in planning and through ongoing consultation; there is also great potential for employing trained Travellers as counsellors, experts, instructors, etc. "This is conducive to a dynamic working atmosphere; it requires very flexible attitudes which must be developed while retaining adaptability and with ongoing critical examination of activities to date. From the teaching point of view this means that educational programmes can only be offered on the 'open curriculum' principle" [Bremer Volkshochschule, 1983, p.15]. Within this necessity of forging a strong forum for consultation, Gypsy organisations also carry a responsibility both as regards Gypsy families and towards non-Gypsy institutions.

Preschooling and vocational training are – if the will for it exists – more amenable to adaptation in structure and teaching methods, and in choice of staff, than is mainstream schooling. It seems easier to break out of scholastic rigidity, to visualise training "modules" which can cover precisely specified ground in a reasonably short time-span. This will enable trainees to know exactly what they're getting; they would then choose what they find compatible with their family involvement and with their felt need for this skill or that. Some skills would bring immediate and tangible benefits – for example the Gypsy who is a skilled welder has increased his work potential and thus his independence.

Some of the training ideas mentioned earlier may be a source of practical, satisfying change: for example if the traditional parental role in vocational training were to be recognised. One could go on to build on this, in appropriate circumstances – e.g. by helping to organise markets and market research, drawing up contracts… Such an approach would lay a basis for improved relations between families and training centres: families would no longer be losing the economic participation of these young adults, who for their part would continue to benefit from traditional parental training. In some countries experimental steps have been taken towards providing part-time training, compatible with nomadism; but the most common stumbling-block remains general unwillingness to take Gypsy work patterns into account, particularly as regards nomads. There is also a lack of coordination between operations, and a need for reflection on questions of training. For example, one of the most complete studies of the subject, wide-ranging and innovative, and founded on the principle of community development, was done in Ireland, yet it is both ignored and unobtainable [ní Shuinéar, 1979].

The tradition, evolution and variety of Gypsy and Traveller trades demonstrates that there is potential in all of the fields with which they are traditionally associated. Time-honoured trades are still alive and well, craftsmanship is or can become art, showmanship and carnivals continue to find a ready market. At the same time every encouragement should be given to those willing to experiment with new ideas, as only time will tell whether these will take off or not – the experts predict that twenty years from now, one in four workers will be engaged in trades which do not exist today. Yet training programmes offered to young Travellers are more often modelled on the past than on the future, and are permeated with ethnocentric and outdated concepts of work patterns. The Gypsies themselves could give a few lessons in predicting future market trends, commercial know-how and buoyancy of economic organisation, to a great many of their would-be educators.

Some complementary considerations

The workplan for this study called for ascertaining the opinions of parents, Gypsy organisations and teachers, as well as summarising research on school provision for Gypsy and Traveller children. Each of the national monographs contains reflections on these different points, in varying degrees of detail. When compiling this synthesis report, I opted for inclusion of extracts from these and other sources throughout the text, to illustrate and complete the themes under discussion. This was in order to bring the text to life, while placing each of the opinions expressed within a precise context: compulsory schooling, curriculum... We shall not attempt to summarise, in this final chapter, the diverse opinions expressed, particularly as the authors themselves have not attempted to do so: on the whole, they supplied "gross" data, taken from interviews or written sources. The general picture, however, is of a wide variety and rapid evolution of opinions.

"We carried out some pilot structured interviews with interviewer-selected Traveller parents in Wales which often led on to conversations that confirmed our longstanding English experience that radically opposed opinions can be held within the same group, even within the same family, about the desirability of education to any particular level, about the organisation of schools, and the ability of particular teachers; on the other hand some individuals express different opinions in different company, the stronger minded pulling along more passive individuals in their wake; in short, Travellers are as diverse as non-Travellers. They do share, however, the common experience of discrimination, and persecution, which constrain their views of what is possible... but most Traveller parents have not been asked by us or anyone what they want for their children" [Acton/Kenrick].

"The times have changed and parents have to adapt to them. Today basic literacy is no longer enough, and the Sinti and Rom, having the same rights as any other citizens, should be demanding schooling, rather than seeing it as an obligation imposed from without." "There is no doubt that in future schooling will be a crucial factor in resolving the sensitive problems surrounding the Gypsies: today more than ever it is the best way of defending one's own ideas and values. An open mind, armed with these valuable tools, is better able to defend itself. Instruction is thus the most effective means of increasing awareness, and may provide the best mirror for our soul" [A. Debar, a Sinti, and B. Morelli, a Rom, quoted in Karpati/Massano].

The opinions of Gypsy/Traveller organisations appear in various contexts throughout this study. The experts compiling each of the national reports did so in connection with such organisations; indeed most of them had previous, often long-standing, experience of collaboration with them. By giving direct quotations from members of these organisations and from their policy statements in both the national reports and in this synthesis, a range of opinions has been expressed. Gypsy and Traveller representatives were also present at the initial meeting when the study was being set up, and again at the final meeting for summarising and recommendations.

The active presence of Gypsy/Traveller organisations in the political field is fundamental. We cannot go into the history and development of this phenomenon here, nor was this the object of the national reports [the interested reader can find further information in Acton, 1974; Liégeois, 1976a; Liégeois, 1985a]. Nor does space suffice for an analysis of the functions they fulfil – of crucial importance in the context of conflict we have described – as partners, spokespersons, pressure groups, information sources. This crucial importance will emerge clearly in the summarisation and recommendations which follow, notably as regards seeking the advice of those concerned, and observing the principle of consultation and cooperation. By the same token these organisations bear a great responsibility towards their own community as well as non-Gypsy institutions and the population in general. Up to now, their activities have been largely in connection with provision of halting sites for nomads and housing for sedentary families, and in the related field of discrimination: as we have stated earlier, these are priority questions, and schooling is directly dependent on their solution. Yet more and more Gypsy organisations are taking direct action in connection with schooling (with variations from country to country, depending on political context). Their activity introduces an essential dimension of participation and collectivism: "Only the collective dimension can guarantee cultural identity" [Perotti, 1981].

Each of the national monographs also points out the dearth of research material in relation to schooling and Gypsy children; we have given indications of this here and there throughout the report. This lack of research is apparent in every country; it appears that the question of school provision for Gypsy/Traveller children is a new one for researchers, too. The few studies that have been carried out to date have been of little direct usefulness to teachers: for example, the field of Gypsy in-family education is virtually unexplored. This is linked to the general context, determined by political and ideological factors. Policies of rejection or assimilation are hardly conducive to the respectful examination of the dynamics of Gypsy culture; this holds true for other minority and immigrant groups as well.

In this context, which still prevails to a certain extent, it is important to be wary of ambiguity in research: "The analysis carried out by 'experts' and the teacher's work of 'passing on knowledge' have always been, and still are, two sides of the same coin: to understand in a certain way, and to use the knowledge to 'domesticate' [Gypsies]" [Piasere]. Researchers bear an important responsibility, as regards their commitment, and those who make use of their findings bear a responsibility to stay within the realm of the facts: using research should entail neither manipulation nor extrapolation. As we have pointed out in this report, there are teachers who consider themselves (and who are considered by others) "experts" after a couple of weeks' work with Gypsy children; a similar situation exists with researchers who "start writing after camping for a week or two with a couple of Gypsy families, having studied anthropology through texts on Africa and Native Americans. Their generalisations are just as dangerous and distorted as those of teachers who only see Gypsies in the school environment" [Piasere, MS.]. The position of the researcher is not generally an easy one:

"The repetitiveness of studies without follow-up and often (through lack of consultation) without much point, coupled with the heavy weight of historical relations between Gypsies/Travellers and their environment, render legitimate Gypsies' negative reactions to research in which they are treated as passive objects... Researchers are – as a result of numerous pressures – too often bound into passive conformity. University classicism – necessary, but insufficient – is ill at ease with the commitment and critical stance of some researchers, and academic purists stigmatise those whom they consider unorthodox. The 'unorthodox', for their part, are handicapped by the fact that it is up to them, as isolated individuals or perhaps small groups, to convince those around them of the usefulness of their work. This is a losing battle in a vicious circle: since such studies are rarely accorded serious consideration, they remain, in fact, useless. And the researchers give the impression of begging funding for their own pursuits, whereas they ought to be recognised as providing a service" [Liégeois, 1985a, p.198; other reflections on this topic are carried in the same work].

"Very few academics have maintained a continuous research interest in Gypsies for more than a few years although some of those who once wrote a doctoral thesis on Gypsies have continued to mine their old notes to create academic papers without maintaining any ongoing involvement with Gypsies. It may well be, however, that some of the present crop of thesis-writers will yield some to whom contributions to the understanding and welfare of Gypsies come to be more important than the use of Gypsies to illustrate points within the disciplines of sociology, linguistics or anthropology. If they do become so involved they will have to face up to the fact that their specialisation will be seen as eccentric, self-indulgent and a diversion from more important topics by most of their academic colleagues, while many teachers and Gypsies, on the other hand, will accuse them of merely using Gypsies to build up a career" [Acton/Kenrick].

Our study of the state of research shows that it suffers from the same problems as most of the other fields we have analysed (teacher training, for example): lack of political will, lack of consultation, lack of coordination. And all too often, research findings never see the light of day: how many reports emphasise that "it's all gathering dust on the archive shelves" or "nothing has been done to date" – even when the research was commissioned by a government ministry? Policies and attitudes concerning Gypsies' schooling fit into three categories, and although we cannot analyse them in detail here, we can describe them briefly by analogy to animals, as: hedgehog policy, ostrich policy, and – in the best of cases – snail policy, which crawls along but pulls back into its shell at the first whiff of trouble. In addition to the lack of political will, lack of consultation is yet another problem:

"The present social climate towards educational problems no longer permits separation between the expression of social needs and the determination of research objectives. These needs must be evaluated, not only in principle, but by the creation of forums where researchers and their social partners (the local authorities, parents' associations, trade unions, adult education movements, teachers...) can meet to analyse together various educational practices and to suggest problem areas as suitable subjects for further research. Such forums would also permit, at the other end of the research process, the evaluation of results in the light of the initial questions, and measuring the impact of research findings on these questions." But "The function of research is not limited to adaptation and explanation; it must also establish a theoretical perspective, without which we cannot know reality in its complexity and diversity. Research gains nothing by ignoring its function of objectivising, which alone guarantees it the freedom in which to operate" [Carraz 1983, p.62].

Lack of coordination and liaison means that work is dissipated, many projects remain unknown, there is a repetitiveness of studies and educational experiments, and a lack of mutual criticism. We have already, in other contexts, emphasised the necessity of certain measures – for example, liaison; many of these would simultaneously benefit school-oriented research and thus improve the school situation generally. Similarly, institutional flexibility should allow those teachers who wish it, to gain perspective on their practices by subjecting them to research; they should be given the opportunity to be "participant-researchers" for a period [cf. Avanzini, 1985] which would help them, their colleagues, and other partners to adapt the school to the children who attend it.

An overall report on the role of research for the Gypsy and Traveller communities remains to be undertaken, and that is another day's work…

Footnotes

1. Almost all the national monographs were completed and submitted to the coordinator between the end of July and the beginning of November 1985, and represent the situation at that time.
2. NB that, although the author uses the term "nomad" as defined here, some of the quoted sources tend to use it as a synonym for "Gypsy/Traveller", regardless of lifestyle; viz. the titles of the German and French reports – Sinéad ní Shuinéar.
3. A very common attitude and one which permits authorities at all levels to wax poetic about their respect for "real" Gypsies while continuing to harass or ignore flesh and blood ones – S. ní S.
4. See Glossary.
5. That is, in the UK context, recent immigrants from Eastern Europe and Turkey; see glossary.
6. Here used in its gender-specific connotation, as "Gypsy" *man*. The term is also used collectively; see Glossary.
7. This is a direct translation of the author's quotation from a French dictionary. I have retained it rather than substitute an English dictionary equivalent because this is a concise summary of the tone of the word, as employed in the context referred to – S. ní S.
8. The contrast between spoken language and the more formal written version is more marked in French than in English – S. ní S.
9. As crystallised in the policies of the Council of Europe and other institutions of the European Community.
10. Compiled and presented by the Commission of the European Communities.

Summary and recommendations

The following summary and recommendations are presented in a brief format, to facilitate rapid reading and in order to present conclusions clearly. Due to the brevity of presentation, however, two points must be emphasised:

1 • These final considerations are merely the tip of a very broadly-based information pyramid. This study presents information of outstanding quantity and quality, unprecedented in its geographic scope and comparative format. National monographs were compiled in each Member State, utilising data from a broad range of sources: existing studies, research undertaken expressly for this project, consultation with various concerned parties. These monographs provided the base for the synthesis report in which the data they present have been compared, supplemented and analysed – particularly as regards schooling practice affecting Gypsy and Traveller children, general policy towards Gypsies and Travellers, and current trends in pedagogy.

The project has also had the benefit, at its inception and again at the concluding stages, of meetings bringing together those directly involved: Gypsy/Traveller representatives, the experts who compiled the national monographs, the author of this synthesis report, and representatives of the Commission of the European Communities. Consultation on these occasions led in the first instance to the formulation of a common outline for research, and in the second to the evolution of these conclusions and recommendations.

2 • These final considerations are the fruit of painstaking and detailed analysis. Each of the following Points – even those whose brevity may make them appear unduly harsh or simplistic – is in fact based on considerations presented, often at length, in the synthesis report. They are discussed there in great detail precisely because we feel that such a cautious and painstaking approach is indispensable. If one is to understand the background of these concluding recommendations, it is therefore

essential to *read the synthesis report in full*. The reader who finds these recommendations too superficial, too crude or overly theoretical, is likewise urged to consult the chapters from which they are drawn. The same goes for the reader who may think them too general, or trite: he will find that, when it comes to school provision for Gypsy and Traveller children, certain considerations which may appear to be self-evident (for example the child's right to attend school in the first place) are to a large extent still unattained goals.

At the close of this report, we do not presume to propose political or pedagogical formulas: we have demonstrated, and repeat yet again, that the required approach is above all one of flexibility; there can be no formulas, no blanket solutions. Throughout the report we have indicated tendencies, preventative measures, precautions, and – we hope – clarifications. These are supplemented here by political and pedagogical guidelines which we feel to be both practical and practicable – as indeed has been our intention throughout the report.

The proposals presented here are intended as a basis for further reflections, marking out the beginnings of a path which remains open to various approaches. Within the conflict-laden situation we have analysed, we could have sought out openings for compromise to facilitate co-existence. This, however, would have been at best a short-term approach: compromise is never more than a provisional and unstable half-measure. We have thus, throughout the report, attempted to go beyond immediate considerations, to propose basic measures in as broad a context as possible, without separating the specific from the general, the pedagogical from the political, or small-scale daily practice from the broader ideology whence it springs. What we have recommended is neither discriminatory nor "special", and is deliberately presented within the broader framework of current trends in educational theory. This seems to us the best way of respecting parents' wishes that their children not be confined to a scholastic ghetto, the best way to avoid ignoring (in vain) existing socio-political dynamics while attempting to set up parallel structures, and indeed the strongest position from which to criticise and modify such structures, postulating instead a fundamental respect of the individual and the group.

The situation of Gypsies and Travellers in general, and in particular in the realm of schooling, is bad, for reasons and in ways discussed at length in the text. This report and its conclusions are not alarmist: they are realistic. This is why we have recommended prudence even as we have stressed urgency, pointed out the need for reflection as much as that for action, and drawn attention to subtle variations without minimising the importance of the general picture.

This summary is now at the disposition of Gypsies and Travellers, their organisations, international bodies, national governments and all other concerned parties. The process of reflection on the points raised, remains for them to complete. The course of action also remains to be determined, since, after nearly six centuries in Western Europe, the Gypsies are still waiting for a coherent and respectful policy towards them to be evolved and put into practice. Schooling policy is an integral element of this question, and should also act as a driving force.

Following the presentation of the various analyses, the national reports, the final report, and the discussions which took place during plenary meetings, and

Bearing in mind

- that the Gypsy and Traveller populations of the Member States comprise a total of *nearly two million persons*, the majority of whom are citizens of the state in which they reside;

- that *half* the Gypsy and Traveller population is *under sixteen*, and that *the number of school-age children is at least 800,000;*

- and that *these figures must be regularly revised upwards* due to high natural population growth;

Considering

As regards schooling

1 • that about 30-40% of Gypsy and Traveller children attend school with a degree of regularity;

2 • that half of them never attend school at all;

3 • that a very small percentage get as far as, or enter into, secondary level;

4 • that results, particularly as regards the attainment of functional literacy, are not in keeping with the amount of time spent in school – that is, that school is not doing its job, even at a basic level;

5 • that adult illiteracy is generally above 50%, and in some places is as high as 80% or even 100%;

6 • that up to now, the schooling of Gypsy children has been a failure for all concerned, and that in this situation it is not a question of "re-forming" school, but of establishing it in the first place;

7 • that a school which suits some is not necessarily suited to others, despite widespread belief to the contrary – in itself a source of many failures. Divergence between what Gypsy/Traveller communities expect of the school, and what the school itself aims to provide, is (in comparison to the difference of expectation of other populations) maximal. The aspirations and values of Gypsy families and those of teachers, the school, non-Gypsy institutions in general and their underlying policies, are not the same; their confrontation produces conflict (be it covert or violently externalised) within the school;

8 • that school is all the more disconcerting to the Gypsy child and his parents in that he is legally obliged to attend, yet is frequently neither expected nor welcomed, and that, having arrived, he must often fight to be let stay on, since his relations with the other children are tinged by centuries of conflict between the two communities. Moreover, within the school environment the child is made to feel that his way of life is less than valid, since his culture and language, far from being taken into account educationally, are treated as marginal, stigmatised in word and deed;

9 • that in these circumstances parents find it difficult to obtain schooling for their children even when they wish to. It is also understandable that they often hesitate, or even refuse outright, to send their children to school, in view of the rejection they encounter there and the divergence between their expectations and those of an institution which remains, for them, ill-adapted, alien and intrinsically coercive, since it is an integral part of the environment which for centuries has been – and remains to this day – threatening and contemptuous. Gypsies in general find themselves in opposition to school even when their children are within its walls. As things stand, Gypsies and Travellers do not accept school any more than school accepts them, nor respect it any more than it respects them;

10 • that parents, under these conditions, remain distrustful of school, given the educational (and not merely instructional) function which it exists to fulfil, and thereby the importance of the influence which it exerts: a threatening influence, and one which may have a profoundly destructive impact on Gypsy culture. Faced with this, parents adopt a defensive attitude towards school, all the more so as they are not consulted by nor involved in it. Their position is thus reduced to submission to compulsory schooling;

11 • that resistance to schooling is, in the light of the above considerations, a sign of the resilience of Gypsy culture, and of parents' continuing ability to bring up their children into a lifestyle which is alive and well. Their legitimate demand is for a school which would be respectful of their aspirations, culture and future;

12 • that schooling is an important factor in determining the cultural, social and economic future of Gypsies and Travellers, particularly with regard to the tools which it may provide for adaptation to a changing environment. These tools may also serve to promote the cultural values of the communities in question, and to defend them when necessary;

13 • that each state, without exception, offers an ambiguous medley of projects, some successful, others characterised by failure. Almost everywhere, we come across repeated experiments and repeated mistakes, growing weariness and justified resignations – on the part of parents and children as well as teachers and administrators. Inappropriate methods are tried over and over again due to lack of consultation and coordination; the overall result is wasted time,

money and energy, a dissipation of the goodwill of those involved and exhaustion of parents' adaptive mechanisms. Parents respond to this pedagogical "lucky dip" with justified disinterest;

14 • that teachers are called upon to exercise their profession in conditions which are often difficult: even those in charge of all-Gypsy classes are not always there by choice; they are almost always deprived of materials, support, guidance, and the opportunity to exchange ideas with others in the field. Their initial training has not prepared them for the task, and in-service training as it stands is not sufficiently organised to do so. Many have little access to information. The production, revision and distribution of adapted teaching materials is hampered by difficult work conditions and, in general, by lack of official support. The overall picture is thus one of shortage and disorganisation, directly linked to a lack of political will to provide coordinated teaching;

15 • that, under these circumstances, we find a sense of exhaustion among teachers who, having themselves pursued innovations to adapt the school to the children in it, often without official support, isolated from each other and marginalised by the rest of the teaching staff, have nonetheless persevered in their work over a period of many years;

16 • that their demands for training and information, liaison and support, are well-founded when we examine the overall situation in which they are required to teach, and the qualities (pedagogical and otherwise) required to produce teaching which is both adapted and respectful;

17 • that the present debate contrasting the merits of "specialised" or "special" classes with those of "normalised" or "ordinary" ones, is irrelevant, as the synthesis report amply demonstrates. This debate dichotomises the situation, stirring up unnecessary acrimony between participants. The only really relevant criterion is the degree to which a class is suited to the children attending it, so that parents do not feel compelled to refuse to send their children, or to withdraw them from it because of rejection, irrelevant or culturally disruptive teaching, or lack of scholastic results.

With regard to the general situation

18 • that the scholastic situation of any given cultural group must be seen within its long-term historical context, as well as the political context of the moment; the schooling of Gypsy and Traveller children must thus be seen as much in the light of non-Gypsy policies, as the policies of the Gypsies themselves. No factor is isolated, nor understandable in isolation, be it in analysing the situation or in drawing practical conclusions from such analysis. Conclusions of a pedagogical nature are thus – unavoidably – political as well;

19 • in consequence, it is erroneous to interpret the *effects* of the overall situation (such as conflict, inhibitions, aggressiveness, disinterest, absenteeism, refusal) as the *causes* of scholastic failure. Insofar as relations between the Gypsy and non-Gypsy communities remain antagonistic, the relations of Gypsy parents and children with the school will be largely determined by this negative attitude. In this respect, the number of literate persons seems to be directly related to the quality of literacy teaching, that is, to the conditions which determine it;

20 • that Gypsy and Traveller society, after centuries of persecution and decades of assimilationist policies, is sometimes weary and demoralised. Assimilationist policies have not led, as foreseen, to integration, nor to adaptation and harmonious coexistence, but, on the contrary, to intensified marginalisation and rejection. The desire to assimilate Gypsies and Travellers into the wider society has never reduced the contradictory urge to exclude them from it;

21 • that rejection, in various forms, is the dominant attitude of society at large vis-à-vis Gypsies: difficulties in obtaining accommodation, evictions of nomads, refusal of admission to public places, etc. The resulting tension between the two communities has always been acute, and moreover tends to develop rapidly into full-blown conflict, particularly during periods (such as the present) of general economic difficulty: Gypsies and Travellers are readily available scapegoats, and as a result they are frequently mistreated and permanently insecure. School policy cannot be dissociated from these tendencies; indeed it is merely one form in which they manifest themselves;

22 • that schooling must take third place to the more urgent (and prerequisite) considerations of the economic activities by which those concerned earn their living, and the provision of accommodation (be it houses for the sedentary or halting sites for nomads) which would allow the practice of such activities. Instead, non-Gypsy society in general rarely takes positive account of Gypsy and Traveller economic practices, despite their time-honoured flexibility and resilience. As for the provision of accommodation, particularly as regards nomads: this is certainly one of the most disheartening aspects of the situation of Gypsies and Travellers in Europe today, and some of the most flagrant legislative contradictions affecting them arise between the legal obligation of children to attend school and the illegality of their halting to do so. In many countries there now exist mobile schools, in a lorry or caravan, which follow families as they are evicted from one illegal site to another. Difficulties connected with halting and accommodation also have a major – negative – impact on Gypsies' health, and this too affects their schooling. Pressure to "settle down", exerted in connection with assimilationist policies, has in fact led only to a deterioration of Gypsies' economy and health;

23 • that Gypsies and Travellers, particularly nomadic ones, are subject to intense surveillance and to measures – eviction in particular – which affect the group as a whole, rather than selected individuals in connection with specific allegations. Such practices, however common in the majority of Member States, are in fact in many cases in violation of international law concerning freedom of movement, freedom to exercise a trade and freedom to establish residence. Moreover, local legislation for the preservation of public order, public safety, etc. (usually the ostensible justification for such practices) is applicable in fact only to the personal behaviour of a given individual. Certain regulations are applied selectively and discriminatively, to the group as a whole: for example, tourists on holiday in their caravan will be treated quite differently from nomads in theirs;

24 • that prejudice and stereotypes give rise to, and are then cited as justification for, discriminatory attitudes and behaviour. Reality is effectively obscured by the imaginary, and when we examine the treatment to which Gypsies are subjected, we see that they are never defined as they are, but as they "must" be in order to justify socio-political policies towards them. The almost total lack of dialogue between Gypsies and Travellers on the one hand, and those responsible for formulating policies towards them on the other, makes it impossible to replace these false images with more realistic ones;

25 • that in this overall context, and in the light of the fact that school is exclusively and totally a part of this environment perceived by Gypsies and Travellers as coercive, school cannot but be experienced by them as yet another imposition, a sort of tentacle grasping their children towards assimilation. Parents are aware of the fact that the school's impact on the child can be formative – yet this may be towards conformity, reform, or deformation.

As concerns current trends

26 • considering that new formulas for teaching materials are beginning to emerge in response to the growing multi-ethnic nature of schools in many Member States;

27 • considering that these measures, developed in response to the need for intercultural education, open the way for new practices based on a validation of cultural differences and drawing upon the capabilities and experience of each child;

28 • considering that the postulates, practices and methods of this intercultural approach to education may serve to adapt school to the needs of Gypsy and Traveller pupils, and that these children may not only benefit from such a programme but may also contribute greatly towards its successful development for others, because of their unique characteristics: the vitality of their culture as experienced in day-to-day life wherever they find themselves, their dispersion among the surrounding society, their presence in all the Member States of the Community, and the fact that their presence in the classroom provokes a critical examination of the suitability of established teaching practices. The unique characteristics of Gypsy children force teachers to look beyond their habitual methods, to examine pedagogical questions from a new angle and try to evolve suitable responses. In this way, the presence of Gypsy and Traveller children can contribute much to the general debate, leading to new initiatives in the multicultural approach and challenging the school's capacity for flexibility and innovation;

29 • considering that practice has confirmed the usefulness and value of such a learner-centred approach based on the pupil's experience, lifestyle and linguistic practice, and developing a pedagogy with objectives similar to those of Gypsy and Traveller parents;

30 • considering at the same time that we must take pains to ensure, firstly that multicultural pedagogy develops in ways compatible with the fundamental premise of respect for cultural difference; and secondly, that its implementation, to date largely limited to immigrant children, should also apply to Gypsy and Traveller pupils. It would be paradoxical indeed if, under the pretext of their being citizens of the state in question, or that they have been resident for too many generations to be considered "immigrants", or that they have no territory of their own, and no formal diplomatic channels (such as consulates) to protect their interests, Gypsies and Travellers should be deprived of suitably adapted schooling just when it is finally being provided for other – newer – minorities;

31 • considering that the international European community, through its representative organisations (the European Economic Community and the Council of Europe) is in a position to treat these questions holistically, from a perspective sufficiently detached from the perpetual socio-political squabblings which threaten to block all progress in the individual Member States, and that it is in a better position to treat the question in terms of cultural groups rather than individual terms;

32 • considering that the aforementioned European organisations have already produced various documents (legislation, directives, conventions, resolutions, recommendations, reports…) which may serve as a springboard for future reflection and for concrete action, including legal intervention if required;

33 • considering that existing policies concerning immigrants on the one hand (particularly as regards school provision for their children) and regional and minority languages/cultures on the other, are equally applicable (in both the practical and the legal sense) to Gypsies and Travellers, as a means of improving their situation, with particular regard to their right to appropriate schooling, and the provision of resources towards this end;

34 • considering, finally, that change in the endemically conflict-laden general situation described above is essential if the school is to become genuinely responsive to Gypsy/Traveller needs, and thereby also a place of welcome. Often the main requirement for the realisation of such a goal is not financial at all, but a question of will, of imagination, and of flexibility, particularly on the part of institutions, and of a few principles which will be discussed in the Points which follow.

Emphasising

That it is essential that all measures be firmly founded on the dynamics of Gypsy culture

35 • Gypsies and Travellers have for centuries demonstrated their ability – despite the difficulties of their situation – to actively adapt to changing circumstances while maintaining a continuity of culture and a profound sense of identity. Gypsies and Travellers have a legitimate aspiration to retain their identity, language, and a lifestyle embodying certain tendencies (such as geographic and professional mobility and adaptability) which are at present becoming characteristic of the surrounding society as well, yet also embodying further characteristics such as communal living, economic autonomy, etc. which for the majority of members of today's industrialised societies will remain unattainable dreams;

36 • taking internal dynamics as a foundation implies a respect for nomadism, which is socially and culturally functional, and an integral factor in social organisation, conducive to adaptability and flexibility and essential to the exercise of certain trades. The dynamism of the nomad is reflected in his school performance, and the national reports stress that it is as false to postulate a correlation between sedentarisation and school attendance or scholastic success, as it is to assume that sedentarisation and improved living conditions are synonymous. For the school, taking nomadism into account is a technical question of how to receive and place the nomadic child; how to adapt teaching to his special needs and provide scholastic follow-up when he moves on. The only hindrance to implementing these changes, is simple lack of will;

37 • the importance and validity of in-family education is one of the priority "internal dynamics" which must be taken into account by the school. As we have seen, there is a very significant divergence – both in methods and goals – between education in the Gypsy home, and that provided by the school. Conflict between home and school value-systems, experienced to some degree by virtually every pupil, is greatly exacerbated in the case of Gypsy and Traveller children. It is essential to take account of the child's own aspirations, and those of his parents: these are the driving forces behind scholastic motivation. No child can be expected to live two separate social and cultural existences, passing from one to the other each time he crosses the threshold of the school. In the end, it is the child's own characteristics which must serve as the basis for teaching, instead of (as is all too often the case) ignoring or actively rejecting – and thereby devaluing – them. The postulates of intercultural pedagogy demonstrate once again that truism of sociology: that all social facts are interconnected, and that the child's school experience cannot be separated from his experience as a whole. Any further attempts – primarily by the school – to suppress existing internal dynamics, are to be avoided, as are corollary – difficult, and usually fruitless – attempts to replace these with new ones, devoid of resilience or hope;

38 • taking the dynamics of Gypsy communities as a foundation entails recognition of their capacity for, and inalienable right to, self-determination and the respect of the surrounding society. Gypsies must be treated as responsible partners, instead of as the passive objects of policy.

The necessity for consultation

39 • Understanding of and respect for cultural dynamics can be achieved through consultation. It is essential that, at the very least, Gypsies actively participate in the formulation of measures which will affect them, rather than being ignored or consulted only superficially before the implementation of policies based on misinterpretation of their reality, lifestyle and aspirations;

40 • when various bodies all declare their desire to provide schooling for Gypsy and Traveller children, it is imperative that this desire be a shared one, and that both sides, together, examine the implications. In this way, perhaps, school may cease to be regarded by Gypsy parents and children, as "somebody else's" – an alien institution. Priorities must be jointly determined. It is paradoxical (to put it mildly) to claim to be nurturing autonomy through the imposition of means evolved without consulting those concerned, and without provision for feedback. By contrast, schooling which is undertaken as a free choice builds the confidence of the participants, resulting in increased enrolment and improved attendance: observations from many sources demonstrate that when schooling is not compulsory it is both of higher quality and better attended;

41 • consultation promotes mutual comprehension, affording each side a better understanding of the other's priorities. It provides a basis for meeting the demands of each while respecting the interests of all. In the conflict-ridden context described above, getting the two sides round the table provides an opportunity for bridge-building, a chance to bring the two parallel courses into closer proximity or perhaps, in time, even convergence; to calm the passions which often arise from misunderstanding, and to transform conflicts into reconcilable differences. The first steps towards solidarity are consultation and a willingness to listen – in the absence of which (the present situation) antagonisms remain and fester;

42 • consultation greatly increases the possibility that the measures evolved will be adapted to those towards whom they are aimed, thus minimising the danger of their backfiring or never being put into practice at all. The end result is a reduction of costs – a consideration which decision-makers should easily appreciate.

The necessity for coordination

43 • It is piecemeal measures which most often fail; a holistic and comparative approach is thus required, with its implications of consultation between all

concerned, particularly parents and Gypsy organisations at both local and national level. Coordination will foster the expression and mutual complementarity of ideas, methods and authority, towards the attainment of agreed goals. Consultation would help to avoid repetition of failed experiments and perpetual starting over from scratch, with all the accompanying disillusionment. At present, coordination in the field of policy formation and implementation is virtually non-existent;

44 • as concerns teaching content and materials, coordination implies liaison right across the board: teachers, inspectors, educational advisors and all the rest. This would permit both a fairer distribution of the workload and mutual support, while avoiding the isolation which often accompanies specialisation (that is, the "ghettoisation" of specialised teachers and their pupils) and save them from working in the dark. Teamwork assures a continuity of thought, accumulation and sharing of experience, an exterior perspective which can offer valuable criticism, and encouragement in times of uncertainty. The coordinated involvement of several partners in a common project makes it easier to overcome administrational and ideological obstacles.

The necessity for flexibility

45 • Flexibility is essential in order to respond to the wide diversity of Gypsy and Traveller groups and the variety of their circumstances, lifestyles, and aspirations; it is essential if we are to avoid the indiscriminate lumping together of people who may have little in common, or assuming that what is appropriate for one group is therefore a panacea for all; it will help us to avoid the coerciveness which has characterised such measures in the past;

46 • the national reports frequently link the quality of schooling with its flexibility. Readiness to modify practices is generally correlated with degree of respect, since it is methods which adapt to the child and not vice versa. The reports also show that the course of a child's career may be characterised by stages, each of which will require a different response – that is, that various structures and approaches may be appropriate, either consecutively or simultaneously;

47 • flexibility allows for innovation through a variety of initiatives. Pragmatic, sometimes even unorthodox, alternatives play a vital role in innovation, and flexibility should at the very least be sufficient to allow for such approaches rather than rejecting them out of hand. Teachers themselves stress that inflexibility leads to inappropriate methods, frustration, and wasted effort, whereas when they are allowed to function flexibly they can adopt the suitably adapted approach outlined above. In this light, it becomes irrelevant to speak of "specialised" vs. "ordinary" classes; we also avoid labelling, ghettoisation, and general rigidity. Each class should instead be sufficiently flexible to evolve on an ongoing basis, in direct response to the needs of the children in it;

48 • as regards structures, the key words should be complementarity, openness, progressiveness. Any structure can lead to success – or to failure. This is simply another way of saying that there are no magic formulas, no panaceas, and that the exclusive promotion of any single type of class is an option dictated more by ideological and political than by pedagogical considerations;

49 • in other fields, the term "homeopathic approach" has recently come into use; it seems a useful expression for describing not merely flexibility within diversity, but also the necessity for prudence and progressiveness.

The necessity for precision and realism

50 • Precision and realism are essential if our actions, and the reasoning behind them, are to make sense. From the instant in which the decision is made to accept (on equal terms) the existence of a cultural minority, it becomes necessary to provide that group with the means to maintain, develop and validate its existence, notably by a careful study of the ways in which these may be achieved;

51 • being precise and realistic means that problems must be approached carefully and cautiously, armed with a degree of scepticism: a problem concisely formulated is halfway to being solved. When difficulties can be laid out in an impartial, "technical" manner, it is easier to avoid the acrimony that often springs from ideological passion (of whatever hue!);

52 • it is essential that the terms we use should have precise meanings. Fuzzy terminology is all the more insidious in that up to the present there is virtually no consultation between the various concerned bodies (notably parents and school administration) which might prevent or clear up misunderstandings;

53 • precision is also required when it comes to defining our objectives, and in reaching agreement on what they are to be, before we even try to decide on the means for achieving them. And, having defined the objectives, it is as well for each of the participants to know precisely what role they are meant to play, and to have a definite plan of action, the implementation and results of which can be monitored. Such an approach permits strict accuracy, evaluation, comparison, discussion of concisely defined points, and means that those involved can operate within the clear guidelines of a contract; it also facilitates consultation, coordination and mutual understanding;

54 • clearly defined goals provide the added benefit of enabling work to proceed in gradual stages, since it would be unrealistic to expect attitudes (be they the authorities' or the general public's) towards Gypsies and Travellers, to be transformed overnight. At the same time, such an approach avoids the equally unrealistic opposite extreme of simply waiting for these attitudes to improve before attempting any action.

The necessity for study and reflection

55 • Before any decisions are reached it is necessary to have a thorough grasp of the overall situation; this means that decision-making must be preceded and then supplemented on an ongoing basis by consultation with Gypsies, with the additional backup of in-depth coordinated research;

56• this need is particularly urgent in the field of school provision, since it is here that we so frequently observe the tendency to evolve methodology without an understanding of the realities which will determine how it functions;

57 • an increase in action-research projects would enable teachers to critically evaluate their own performance, training them to analyse and to transform it. It would help them to participate more fully in pedagogical innovation, to learn research techniques by practising them, and to increase their contacts with colleagues (teachers and others) in the field.

****

In the light of the considerations and conclusions presented above, postulating flexibility, precision, taking the dynamics of Gypsy culture as the foundation for all action, consultation with Gypsies, coordination of approach, research, and reflection,

We recommend

58 • *The adoption of a general policy of interculturalism* as a precondition for the development of intercultural pedagogy. In effect, school can accomplish nothing in the absence of an overall political climate favourable to the initiatives it seeks to implement. It would be unreasonable – indeed futile – to expect the school and its staff to shoulder the entire burden of change. Intercultural pedagogy must go hand in hand with increased interculturalism in the environment at large. We are painfully aware of the wide gap separating the present state of affairs from such a goal.

As regards the general situation

59 • *Gypsies should be securely guaranteed their basic legal rights.* At present, the authorities de facto sanction the discriminatory attitudes and practices which affect Gypsies on a daily basis. The situation of stateless Gypsies will also have to be regularised. Vigilance is also necessary to ensure that international conventions, and Community law in particular, are observed with regard to Gypsies.

60 • *Human rights must be understood as indivisible.* International organisations are laying more and more emphasis on this point, i.e., linguistic and cultural rights cannot be considered separate from other, "more basic" rights (such as health and adequate nutrition). This implies that Gypsies and Travellers should be granted formal recognition as a cultural and linguistic minority, all the more so in that they have no "homeland" to protect their interests and validate their identity.

61 • *That Gypsies and Travellers be given ample opportunity to learn what their rights are* – as a rule, they are informed only about their obligations. The proliferation of legislation directly affecting them (in connection with halting caravans, commerce, schooling, social welfare, freedom of movement, discrimination, etc.) and frequent misunderstanding of the law, lead us to recommend that each state should formulate a concise and practical legal guide, illustrated with concrete case histories and presented in a handy, easy to update format (for example as a file of loose cards).

62 • *Nomadism must be officially recognised, and provision made for nomads.* The usual attitude is to assume that nomads ought to settle down for good, and policies are geared – be it explicitly or implicitly – towards this goal. This on the one hand deprives the nomad of the fundamental right to choose his own lifestyle, and on the other hampers the dynamics and adaptive possibilities which are linked with nomadism, particularly as regards the exercise of certain trades and various aspects of social life. In every country where there are nomadic Gypsies and Travellers, their situation is precarious, marked by rejection and difficulties in finding halting places. Yet the school's reception of nomadic children is predetermined by the conditions of the parents' stay – e.g. the likelihood of eviction – just as the school's attitude to sedentary Gypsies and Travellers is predetermined by their living conditions. Likewise, the physical health of both parents and children is also dependent upon the reception (e.g. provision of halting sites) they get from surrounding society.

63 • *Whatever steps are necessary must be taken to protect and develop Gypsies' and Travellers' economic base*, which in turn will guarantee their dynamism and autonomy: providing adapted training courses, granting nomadic tradesmen the same legal status as sedentary ones, etc.

64 • *Detailed, accurate information must be produced with Gypsy collaboration:* the erroneous images which dominate at present give rise to inappropriate policies and attitudes of rejection. Information is the foundation-stone of tolerance, a precondition for the understanding and acceptance of the community at large. Information-flow between the two communities should be bilateral – an important element in the prevention of unfounded conflict.

65 • *That expertise be developed, and provision made, to promote consultation and coordination.* The desire to avoid specialised structures (with their inherent risk of segregation) requires, in various fields but particularly in that of school provision, that skilled persons (trained for and mandated to the task) be given the opportunity to assist, to inform, to coordinate. It is equally important that the authorities at every level (local, regional, national) fulfil the indispensable functions of consultation and coordination noted above, as well as mediation, coordination, practical assistance, information, encouragement and decision-making. It is not a question of setting up structures which will quickly become rigid, stifling the very initiatives they are meant to be promoting, but rather of making provision for meetings and information exchange within a system rendered flexible enough to ensure the participation of all concerned, and the coordination and continuity of efforts from various sources. In this way we can prevent the Gypsies' being "forgotten" by a political machine in which they find it difficult to make themselves heard, and which tends (through structures set up without Gypsy input) to describe them indiscriminately as impoverished, maladjusted, marginal, delinquent... We shall return to this issue in Point 84.

With regard to schooling

66 • *That regulations concerning compulsory schooling be applied flexibly, and with caution.* How can nomads deprived of the right to halt send their children to school? (It would be useful indeed if local authorities were to provide families they have evicted with a certificate to this effect, which could then be presented to the relevant authorities as an explanation of the children's absence from school.) And how can parents be obliged to send their children to school, if the school refuses – as it often does – to accept them, or rejects them more covertly by ignoring or humiliating them? How can parents be obliged to send their children to a school which patently fails to meet their needs, and which indeed does more harm than good? As we have noted earlier, school attendance goes down as pressure to attend increases, while conversely the highest attendance occurs in those places where compulsory attendance is not enforced.

The obligation to attend school is by no means synonymous with the right to be taught; indeed compulsory schooling is often a sterile exercise aimed solely at increasing the head-count, without any provision being made for adapted methods or structures, or for meeting the wishes of parents. Parents are acutely aware of the potential advantages to be gained by schooling, and do not need to be forced into sending their children. They do, however, seek to maximise their control over the influences to which the child will be subjected; this is why they are more likely to send their children when they can do so by free choice rather than as a result of coercion. They are also sensitive to the degree to which a given school is respectful towards the children, and useful to them; when such a school is found, nomads may come from great distances to enable their children to attend it, and sedentary Gypsies will happily send their children too.

The degree to which attendance is voluntary, and regular, is a good criterion by which to judge how well a class or school has adapted to the diversity which the children represent. We find that such adaptation is as frequently to be found among "ordinary" structures as among "specialised" ones. For parents, the essential consideration is how their children are treated, the degree to which they are respected, and to what extent the material being covered is of direct practical use to them.

67 • *That a wide variety of scholastic structures be retained.* It would be misguided indeed to reduce the present range of options; the criteria for doing so would be politico-ideological, rather than pedagogical. School provision for Gypsy children is still at an experimental stage in many respects, and if no panacea has as yet emerged (nor will any be found in the future) then no approach can be dismissed out of hand. Indeed, innovation can only increase the options at the school's disposal, for adaptation to the children who attend it.

The interculturalism stipulated within the classroom must also be implemented throughout the school: pluralism must permeate the entire system. One precondition for this is a variety of structures, geared towards the different needs of various cultural groups. When these diverse structures are also complementary, enabling the pupil to pass from one to another or to participate in several simultaneously, pluralism is assured. Each class must be a discrete element within an interlocking educative *whole*, in which each remains open to ebb and flow within the system. Within such a context, "specialised" classes (so called because they cater for Gypsies only) are neither ghettos nor an imposition, but can provide – with parental blessing – a long-term solution, or perhaps a means of transition to other (ordinary) classes. In any case, they should be conceived, not as self-contained, but as complementary to the rest of the system: neither more, nor less. It is not the existence of specialised classes as such which must be questioned, but the role which they are given, and which so often in practice entails their teachers and pupils being left to their own devices, in isolation from the flow of school life.

68 • *That flexibility of class structures should be accompanied by flexibility of teaching.* The range of teaching content must remain open-ended: it is not, after all, a question of every pupil getting the same, but rather of providing an appropriate response to pupils' own – varied – needs. Gypsy and Traveller parents, with their demand that the school's approach be directly utilitarian, are echoed by certain educational theorists, who stipulate that education should above all be functional. These goals are met by a learner-centred pedagogy geared towards specific objectives.

69 • *That teaching materials based on/incorporating elements of Gypsy and Traveller culture, language, and history, be developed.*

70 • *That the teaching programmes of* (all or predominantly) *Gypsy classes be subject to critical examination and evaluation.* The insights gained from such an exercise could also benefit teachers who have occasion to work with Gypsy/Traveller pupils only sporadically.

71 • *That teaching of and through Romani and other Gypsy/Traveller languages be systematically researched, then followed through.* This should be done on a foundation of existing findings in connection with other minority, regional and immigrant languages, since the official language of the school is so often, for the Gypsy child, a second language rather than his mother tongue.

72 • *That school provision for nomadic children, and the pedagogical follow-up which it implies, be systematically researched, then followed through.* The steps to be taken must be studied in detail, in consultation with all concerned parties, and action taken as quickly as possible towards recognising the reality of nomadism and the legitimacy of parents' demand for school provision for their children without renouncing their way of life. Among the possibilities to be explored is distance learning, combining correspondence with scholastic broadcasting and the personalised support of a visiting teacher. Such methods could be employed to reach vast numbers of Gypsy children – even beyond national frontiers, particularly in connection with teaching of and through Romani. It is probable that in the immediate future nomadism need no longer be an impediment to good quality schooling: new technology, especially videos which can provide personal tuition at any level, will give access to à la carte instruction, and it is likely that Gypsy children will adapt to it very quickly. Quite apart from the fact that (as mentioned earlier) nomadism is often correlated with scholastic success, this ongoing evolution of instruction media means that schooling can no longer be cited as a pretext for enforced sedentarisation of nomads, nor can nomadism be blamed for lack of provision.

73 • *That in classes of whatever type, the way in which the child is received and treated should take top priority,* notably by not rejecting him either physically or administratively. The school's first duty towards the child's culture is to respect it; only afterwards can pedagogical use be made of it.

74 • *That school provision for Gypsy children be dissociated,* both administrationally and pedagogically, *from definition as, and methods geared towards, "deprivation", "delinquency", etc.*

75 • *That provision be made for vocational training compatible with Gypsies' existing internal dynamics, based on careful consideration of economic viability, and examining both traditional occupations and those which may have future potential.* Although detailed coverage of vocational training is outside the scope of the present study, the basic analyses contained within it are of direct relevance, as are the present summary and recommendations. Vocational training must be approached with flexibility and imagination, in conjunction with training within the family itself and basic schooling, and with the goal of providing young people with solid means for economic development and adaptation to the surrounding environment. All activity in this field requires intense, direct consultation with parents, in order to ascertain their aspirations and benefit from their advice and capacity for innovation. In connection with this training-related consultation and development, Gypsy and Traveller organisations bear a unique responsibility both towards the families they represent and towards those who seek to provide the training: such organisations must be consulted, and assisted, in order to ensure the development of suitable training for young Gypsies. Since the present trend is towards legislation stipulating a minimum level of schooling as prerequisite for authorisation to practise certain trades, it is essential to respond with training programmes which will enable Gypsies to attain these levels.

76 • That the *criteria for engaging teachers* who will be dealing with significant numbers of Gypsy children in their classes include free choice, experience, and training. Supplementary specialist training – for example in intercultural pedagogy – should be recognised on equal terms with specialisation in other areas of teaching when assigning teaching posts (on a basis of competence to do a given job) and remunerated accordingly. Teachers' special skills must be recognised and validated; this would also have the effect of validating the classes in which they teach (at present, both tend to be treated dismissively) and of increasing job satisfaction – thereby decreasing the turnover of personnel.

77 • That teachers' *working conditions* be appropriate for the difficult job they are called upon to do, and the varied tasks they must take on. This is of particular importance in relation to class size. Many countries have introduced an "adjusted" method for counting immigrant pupils: in some, for example, when the number of immigrant children in a class exceeds 30%, it is counted as double when calculating required staff numbers; in others, regardless of what proportion of the class they comprise, each immigrant pupil is counted as 1.5 or two children. These considerations are entirely applicable in the case of Gypsy and Traveller children, and as a general rule, in any class where there is a significant proportion of Gypsies/Travellers, the total class size should not – at least in the early stages, or when the class is multi-ethnic – exceed twelve or at most fifteen. This is the officially agreed maximum in a number of countries, but to teachers in others may seem like the impossible dream.

78 • That *support provision* be made. This can take many forms: for example three teachers between two classes, or a "mobile" teacher who can be called in as required, or a teacher dividing his worktime among various activities. Support – as the present report has amply shown – is indispensable in a variety of ways: to welcome children into the school and give them the individual attention they need; to facilitate contact with parents; to coordinate classes and the material they cover; to promote teamwork; to free personnel to attend meetings, training sessions, etc.

79 • *That Gypsies be employed* in connection with the schooling of their children, as teachers and/or in other capacities. New methods of training and recruitment will have to be evolved as a first step, bearing in mind the entirely unprecedented nature of such employment, and the fact that Gypsies, unlike immigrants, have no diplomatic channels offering backup for such initiatives.

80 • *That improvement of teacher training be undertaken as an urgent priority.* Teachers face the task of teaching Gypsy and Traveller children without any preparation whatsoever. Regardless of what type of class the Gypsy child enters, the teacher cannot do his job properly without the necessary training – particularly now, as the "intercultural" model (with its vision of the multi-ethnic class as the norm) is gaining ground. When a "specialised" class is run by a teacher who is not specialised, it loses both its justification and its viability. *Initial teacher training* should be geared towards preparing teachers to work with children of different backgrounds, by familiarising them with the cultures they are likely to encounter in the classroom. They should also be trained in the principles of teaching the national language as a second language, which it is for many children of minority cultures.

In-service training is, due to its particular characteristics (notably flexibility, adaptability, availability through short courses and a variety of training modules) particularly suited to the needs of teachers involved with Gypsy children. It should be brought into immediate and intensive use as a means of preparing teachers who (in every country) generally enter the field without any training for the special demands of the job: training provision to date has been quite inadequate. Provision must also be made for *in-depth complementary training*, leading to higher qualifications and subsequent expansion of career opportunities as education advisors, teacher-trainers and so on. Both in-service and higher degree training would comprise a variety of modules geared towards a better understanding of Gypsies.

81 • *Teacher-training pilot schemes must be implemented throughout the European Community*, in order to initiate or accelerate the type of teacher training which is an indispensable prerequisite for the schooling of Gypsy and Traveller children. Such projects should be largely geared towards training Gypsies and Travellers themselves as teachers, and must be linked, and evaluated, at international level, so that findings can immediately be fed back and put to practical use.

82 • That in the near-virgin territory of teacher training, consideration should be given to redeployment of existing resources, the creation of new ones, and innovation in teaching content. As an immediate first step, a *small-scale provisional body at national level* (for example as described in Point 88) could set up mechanisms for organisation, multilateral consultation, proposing new measures, and the implementation and monitoring of teaching programmes.

83 • *That coordinated, high-quality information campaigns be undertaken.* Prejudice and stereotypes are often the source of attitudes – and subsequent behaviour – characterised by hostility and rejection; they may also lie at the root of inappropriate pedagogy. A study of the genesis of stereotypes, and an ongoing (but discreet) information campaign, are essential if the present situation is to improve. Both Gypsies and teachers will need fundamental backup to improve the conditions in which schooling takes place, through modification of the surrounding society's perception of Gypsies. What is needed in effect is no less than a general change of heart, enabling us to transform teaching from its present ethnocentrism into pedagogical pluralism. Teachers are the vital "middlemen" in this process. On the one hand, they must be capable of seeking out, and taking on board, relevant information; on the other, they must incorporate this information into their own teaching practice, and relay it to their pupils.

Information may be conveyed by various means: we are as concerned about the presence of quality information in school libraries as we are about school-oriented radio and television broadcasting. Moreover it is legitimate – indeed essential – that reference to Gypsies be included where appropriate in school textbooks (history, human geography, social science, literature) and that existing works be revised in order to purge them of stereotypes and false images, sources of misunderstanding and rejection. The necessity for quality, coordination and organisation leads us to recommend that in each state there should be a national coordinating body comprising representatives of the school authorities, teachers, and Gypsies, to take responsibility for developing improved means of collecting accurate information and making it available to, and through, teachers, training institutions, Gypsy and non-Gypsy organisations, parents' associations, local authorities and so on. It is easy to visualise written and audio-visual materials being produced on a European scale: complementary projects can be undertaken in different countries, and it is certain that, when it comes to getting to know about Gypsies abroad, the most interested parties of all will be Gypsy pupils themselves.

84 • *That potential for liaison, organisation, coordination and mutual and inter-institutional support in the realm of school provision, be acted upon and developed.* Most initiatives to date have been dead ends due to their isolation, lack of continuity, and parental non-involvement.

Intercultural pedagogy is not spontaneous pedagogy: much effort is required to put it into practice, and more effort still if the practice is to become widespread. Falterings, failures, weariness – these combine to produce pseudo-intercultural pedagogy, with an endemic risk of ideological quibbling. The necessity for organisation (emphasised in the reports and studies) and the absence of coordination (very specifically identified as the main cause of failure) lead us to recommend the implementation of new structures and the development of skills in the field.

It is firstly a question of *assigning personnel* to the task of ensuring this coordination, some of the possibilities for which have been outlined above. Locally it may be a teacher or education advisor (who would probably handle such questions on a part-time basis); at regional level, an inspector could do the job. Central education authorities must take charge of the training and appointment of such personnel and provide them with a system for liaison amongst themselves, e.g. by arranging meetings. This function can, if necessary, be carried out by a named education officer or liaison worker providing mediation, practical assistance and liaison. This role, and its importance, must be clearly recognised and supported by the different parties involved: the mediator's role is never an easy one, caught as he is between the interests and aspirations of those with whom he works, and the interests and aspirations of those who employ him, be they the local community or a central ministry.

Next, it is a question of *setting up liaison and consultation bodies* linking representatives of parents, teachers and local authorities. Such bodies would facilitate and complement the work of coordination personnel, by allowing direct contact between those concerned, defining measures to be taken, monitoring their progress and analysing results. A shared willingness to get together is all that is needed for such groups to be formed. Participants will have to take time out from already busy schedules, but will find their effort quickly and amply rewarded in the positive results of such meetings.

Finally, in pursuit of the dual goal of information and liaison, we urge the setting up of *liaison newsletters* dealing with school-related issues, as well as more *technical pedagogical and analytical publications* describing new approaches, their concrete workings and any difficulties they may have encountered. This opens up possibilities for sharing knowledge and information, evaluation, updating, and identifying available resources (see Point 88 below).

85 • *That the relevant authorities take on their full responsibilities*, firstly, by providing themselves with the means for concerted, ongoing reflection on the question of school provision for Gypsy and Traveller children and, secondly, by the practical implementation of conclusions reached through such reflection. Public authorities are responsible for decision-making, and for providing incentives: if they fail to fulfil this role, or do so only superficially, the result in practice is either "laissez faire" (in which negative attitudes operate unchecked), or that Gypsies and Travellers are simply ignored administrationally, or that they are mistakenly lumped into categories where they do not belong, and treated accordingly. *Every point of the present summary is of direct concern to the public authorities. It is equally important that they clearly state their position on each of the recommended measures, as it is for them to participate in their implementation*, since practical goodwill, understanding, and the setting of example can accomplish more than simply changing the regulations. If we want to adapt the schools, it is better to set a good example to negatively disposed communities, than to start by trying to force them to change their behaviour. Indeed, such change cannot be accomplished "by decree"; one must play an active role in it by providing administrational support, coordination, financial aid – investments which pay quick dividends in the scholastic domain. Even in states with highly decentralised systems one can see the potential usefulness of central authorities having the means (above all financial) to intervene and to respond to appeals from local authorities, instead of (as at present) citing the lack of such means as a justification for rejecting the nomad.

86 • *That in conjunction with the necessity for coordination which we have repeatedly emphasised, Gypsy/Traveller organisations must be consulted, and directly involved in the implementation of projects, on an ongoing basis.* It would be

equally desirable that some of these organisations be made responsible (having first been provided with the necessary means) for organising various actions in connection with schooling: taking part in teacher training, compiling information and teaching material, etc.

87 • *That research be intensified* in all areas pertinent to school provision for Gypsy/Traveller children: educational sciences, sociology of education, linguistics, etc. Such research would furnish the insights needed if provision is to be properly adapted; by comparative analysis of different projects it would put a stop to the endless repetition of experiments doomed to failure; it would enable projects (past or present) to be evaluated according to standard criteria; it would allow many of the concerned parties to collaborate actively – notably through action research. Research activities must, like all other activities, be well-coordinated: research will only begin to make sense to those involved when it is seen to have a real impact on the collaborators' own specialist areas of concern, such as teacher-training, production of high-quality information, development of teaching materials, etc. As Gypsies themselves become active in research and in teaching, and as the number of authors and available written material in the Gypsy language continues to grow, these developments will doubtless have far-reaching effects on school provision for Gypsy children.

88 • *That in every country with a significant Gypsy/Traveller population, a national centre be set up with specific responsibility for monitoring every aspect of school provision for Gypsy and Traveller children.* Throughout the synthesis report, analyses of enrolment procedures, teacher training, existing pedagogical practices and intercultural pedagogy, demonstrate the necessity of a national coordinating and advisory body. It would fulfil a range of functions: as a centre where information, advice and documentary resources would be available not only to teachers but to administrators in various fields; a centre for the coordination and dissemination of various ideas and projects, for producing teaching materials, curriculum development, teacher-training programmes and the like; for keeping everyone up-to-date by publishing a newsletter, etc.

The centre must be completely flexible: it should be conceived as a focal point, a meeting-place for those (teachers, Gypsy organisations, administrators and so on) who make use of it through access to the information it distributes and the insights and expertise it can supply. The actual structure of such a centre will depend largely on how much it is expected to do: it may be able to perform adequately even if it comprises only a handful of individuals already active as teachers, counsellors or inspectors, and given the necessary remission of other duties for their involvement in this project. This would be a minimal approach, at an insignificant cost yet already capable of exerting considerable impact, and would need to be implemented as a matter of urgency if we are to break out of the present impasse. If, however, the centre itself is to undertake teacher training (particularly of a supplementary nature, for those already employed in the field); if it is to publish and distribute teaching materials, or the newsletter it compiles; if it is to undertake any of the necessary research – then obviously it will require a larger staff.

The administrative structure of such a centre must be compatible with the system and practices of the state in which it is located, and with broad developments concerning cultural minorities. It may be attached to a centre for educational research; to a teacher-training institute (as is already the case with many existing centres concerned with minority or immigrant cultures); to one of the "multicultural resource centres" recognised by international organisations and by the relevant ministries; to a university department (e.g. of social sciences, educational sciences); to a Gypsy/Traveller cultural centre (such as are currently being set up in several countries) – yet retaining both its operative independence and its focus on school provision.

Finally, we recommend

89 • *That the Commission fully play the roles which are its duty, and for which it already possesses the means: coordination, mediation, moderation, encouragement and, should the need arise, arbitration between the various involved parties*, in a context which will remain conflict-laden for the foreseeable future. The institutions of the European Community can and must play an important role with regard to Gypsy and Traveller populations, notably by encouraging Member States to take positive, appropriate measures; by coordinating policies of particular relevance to Gypsies and Travellers; by assisting liaison between projects and those involved in them, and disseminating the insights arising; by providing direct aid to such projects as may be of urgent priority and/or of high symbolic value. For a cost which is insignificant in comparison to the positive effects produced, Community-wide coordination, impetus and mediation can be realised, thus enabling the Community, its individual Member States and the various authorities concerned to finally consider Gypsy/Traveller-related questions with all the care and understanding which these populations have a right to expect.

90 • *That the Commission monitor – as it has the authority to do – the implementation of various directives*, to prevent their being applied without reference to or consultation with Gypsies themselves. The Commission has both the means and the scope for innovation, to implement its own plans for action and to allocate resources. This should play a major role in creating a climate favourable to Gypsies, and encourage individual governments to take positive action on their behalf.

91 • *That the Commission study with particular attention the question of mobile dwellings, freedom to exercise trades requiring mobility, and freedom of movement for Gypsies and Travellers* (particularly as covered by Regulation 1612/68). Within the context of overall policy regarding mobile/migratory workers, it would be useful if the booklet setting out the relevant Community regulations were also to cover the special situation of Gypsies and Travellers, and that their specific problems as seasonal workers or small independent businessmen, be taken into account.

92 • *That the Commission study ways and means* of utilising existing financial resources towards the *provision of housing* for sedentary and semi-nomadic Gypsies, as well as the improvement of *halting sites* for the nomadic.

93 • *That the Commission examine its potential for active involvement in school-related issues, in accordance with the principles and necessities developed above.* The Commission has been playing a significant role in this field for several years now: for example the Resolution of the Council and of the Ministers for Education, dated 9th February 1976, comprising a general educational action plan, and Directive 77/486/EEC relating to school provision for migrant children. These texts, and many others, offer a solid base for school policy and provision, and the Commission must study their applicability to Gypsies and Travellers as a matter of urgency. For example, Directive 77/486/EEC obliges the host country to provide schooling adapted to the specific needs of immigrant children (who are citizens of other Member States). The host country is also responsible for both the initial and in-service training of teachers for this task. What is more, "Mother tongue shall henceforward be considered an important component of the child's personality, an indispensable factor in his well-being". It is hard to see on what grounds Gypsy children, whose forefathers immigrated centuries ago, could be denied the benefits of all that these statements imply. And the fact that they have no "homeland" to stand up for them, nor any diplomatic representation; the fact that they are present in all the Member States, and in a difficult socio-political situation, only reinforces the responsibility of the Commission, European Parliament, and Education Committee towards them.

Within the framework of its educational programme of 9th February 1976, stipulating equal opportunity for all the children of the Community, the Commission should undertake an inventory of existing teaching materials and the production of new ones for use in the classroom, teacher-training programmes, and in relation to the teaching of Gypsy languages. Producing these materials at international level would maximise cost effectiveness, while Community involvement coordinating the efforts of various national institutions would broaden reflection and its application.

Recently, the Commission has been actively promoting lesser-used languages, and its activities promoting regional languages and cultures and ethnic minorities demonstrate its responsibility towards, its interest in, and the beginnings of its response to such minorities. These measures should be quickly and fully extended to Gypsies.

94 • *That the European Social Fund should quickly examine the scope for large-scale intervention on behalf of Gypsy and Traveller communities.* It bears responsibility for such action (and indeed has exercised it on several occasions in short-term Gypsy related projects); priority consideration should be given to the development of training programmes. The European Social Fund also bears a responsibility in relation to school provision: since 1974 the Commission has been authorised to call upon it to assist Member States in their efforts to provide schooling adapted to the needs of immigrant children, and it can also finance training courses aimed at teachers and others involved in school provision for these children. Such courses could provide young Gypsies and Travellers with an opportunity to become trained for participation in school provision for children from their own community.

95 • In order to instigate and facilitate the development of positive, adapted measures along the lines detailed above, it is recommended *that the Commission study, in conjunction with the Member States, the possibility of increasing the number of pilot schemes, and of setting up a network linking such projects*, with the aim of promoting cooperation and information exchange at international level (of particular importance in Gypsy/Traveller affairs) and carrying out broad comparative analysis. By providing continuity, such a linking system would also permit the development of "longitudinal" reflection, which is lacking at present. It is equally necessary to emphasise that the development of pilot schemes involving Gypsies has enormous symbolic value whatever the country, and plays an important role in inspiring reflection among the various bodies concerned, even before operating as a driving force in more extensive accomplishments – often all the more so when the project is linked with similar schemes abroad.

96 • *That the Commission arrange regular gatherings of an ad hoc group of independent* Gypsy and non-Gypsy *experts,* in a spirit of information and coordination, in order to obtain their advice on measures to be taken and to evaluate projects in progress.

97 • *That the Commission play a mediating and coordinating role, by assembling,* whenever the necessity arises, *Gypsy representatives, independent experts and government officials,* to enable them to discuss specific topics as well as general policies.

98 • *That the Commission encourage dialogue and cooperation between Gypsy organisations* in the different Member States.

99 • *That the European Parliament take account of Gypsy presence within the Community,* and set up – as it has already done for regional languages – an intergroup.

100• *That,* particularly in this field of school provision for Gypsy children, *cooperative relations be developed between the Commission, the Council of Europe, and UNESCO.*

Cover of the book carrying the conference proceedings of the "Summer University" of 5-12 July 1989, organised by the Gypsy Research Centre with the support of the French Ministry of National Education and of the European Commission.

This was the first major European conference following — indeed, held within a few weeks of — the adoption by the Ministers of Education of the Resolution of 22 May 1989, on school provision for Gypsy and Traveller children. Sixty-five delegates from ten Member States spent eight days exchanging information and, using their own experience as a springboard, collaborated in defining priorities for their work. The book, published in English, French and Spanish, remains an important reference document.

Afterword

Arthur R. Ivatt
HMS Inspector of Schools
Great Britain

An HMI colleague once said that if we got the education of Gypsy (*Roma*) and Traveller children right, then we would have got it right for all children. The profound nature of this assessment is daily brought home to me when I see the progress that has been made since the first synthesis report by Jean-Pierre Liégeois and the obvious and increasingly appreciated benefits which these developments promise for all children in schools. A good example of this is the interest generated in the promotion of effective independent learning which has emanated from work on distance learning materials in County Durham in the United Kingdom (UK) under the European Commission's Socrates Programme. Under the same programme, the National Association of Teachers of Travellers (NATT) (UK), has been developing quality reading materials with a story based on the cultural reality of Gypsies and Travellers. This book, together with the associated learning materials, demonstrates the importance of knowledge having cultural relevance and being affirmative of identity; again making a valuable contribution more generally to the practice of inter-cultural education.

I should perhaps hasten to say that because of my professional involvement in the last few years with the education of Gypsy and Traveller children, I am more acutely aware of developments and progress in England than elsewhere in Europe. However, my attendance at international meetings, and the knowledge gained from association with UK Socrates project partners, has provided ample evidence of widespread and encouraging progress in many Member States of the European Union. For example, innovative projects to promote the attendance at school of secondary aged Gypsy and Traveller pupils have linked Cleveland (UK) with Helsingor (Denmark) and Cork (Ireland), and Bradford (UK) with colleagues and schools in Italy and Ireland. Imaginative work has also taken place in Scotland at the Murray House Institute of Education-Heriot Watt University, that has established productive links with many Member States. My rather fragmented knowledge, however, of the many advances which have been made in so many parts of Europe, has been helped by the excellent *Interface*[1] news journal which so many of us receive appreciatively. This regular testimony of growth in interest and concern and, indeed, action at all levels across Europe as a whole, is heartening to those who wish to see all children and young people successfully receiving their educational entitlements with dignity and respect. I labour the particular point of pan-European developments to avoid any offence which might inadvertently be implied by my frequent reference to the situation and progress in the United Kingdom.

In 1985 I was fortunate enough to join the European Commission's expert group which met frequently in Brussels, and so was able to witness the vital developments surrounding the decisions on the commissioning of the research which resulted in the publication of Jean-Pierre Liégeois' report *School Provision for Gypsy and Traveller Children.*[2] As a member of this group I had a privileged vantage point to see first hand the exciting developments which followed the publication of the report. In 1986 the Ad Hoc Group of experts and representatives of national Ministries of Education was set up to advise the Commission. It was clear at this early stage that the report would act as an important catalyst to developments across all Member States. Later, the motion for a Resolution was submitted to the Council and the Ministers of Education. On the May 22nd 1989 the *Resolution on School Provision for Gypsy and Traveller Children* was issued. The Resolution, among other things, required Member States to stimulate developments and to report on their progress and effectiveness within three years. Needless to say, the Resolution had a significant impact because for the first time the issue of Gypsy and Traveller education was automatically added to the agenda of governments. In the United Kingdom, for example, the report and anticipated Resolution was partly instrumental in securing central government funding for the education of Gypsy and Traveller children. Thus in 1990, a new specific grant was introduced as Section 210 of the 1988 Education Reform Act. This grant programme contributed an additional £10 million to foster the development of education for Gypsy and Traveller children. The programme, which applied to England and Wales only, was also to include fairground and circus children, since mobility was seen as the main structural hindrance to accessing schools.

The report by Jean-Pierre Liégeois was a synthesis of commissioned studies within each Member State. In 1988 the research was extended to include two new Member States, Portugal and Spain. The domestic report on the United Kingdom was produced amid some controversy. The quality and range of educational policy and practice at the time was not fully reflected in the report. However, since the general approach was more sociological than pedagogical, the contribution to the synthesis report was generally sound and academically secure, if failing to do adequate justice to the professional commitment and level of provision in many areas.

The sociological focus of the synthesis report is the key factor which ensures the maintenance of its relevance and importance despite the passing of the years. In reading the text again, I was struck how time has not eroded the skilled and informed contextual analysis of the condition and situation of Gypsies and Travellers in Europe. The analysis and description is important at another level. Placing the analysis firmly within the historical and cultural spheres, has ensured that policy initiatives have, to a greater or lesser extent, been cognisant of the legitimate status of the communities themselves in terms of culture, linguistics and ethnicity. This has had a positive influence on aims and objectives in Gypsy education. Although, no doubt, a variable picture still exists across Europe, the general thrust of policy and provision has been within the context of inter-cultural education and is not about the rehabilitation of an under-class of deprived and disadvantaged communities. The previous deficit model which, under the guise of humanitarian intentions, masked such pain and humiliation, has in an encouraging and growing number of cases, given way to enlightened policy initiatives. These are reflective of tolerance and understanding instead of persecution and prejudice, inclusion instead of exclusion, and acceptance of diversity instead of assimilation. For this fundamental change in perception and understanding we will always be indebted to the inspired work to which so many contribute, and which was manifested in the synthesis report and is here re-published. This new edition must be considered as essential reading for all those involved in the education of Gypsies and Travellers, whether it is at classroom level or at the level of administrators and policy makers.

Before considering the extent to which the canvas has been painted, it is perhaps illustrative to review the progress which has stemmed from the report and other work, in England. Independent and international evaluation suggests that there has been significant progress achieved in the last ten or more years. In April 1996 the Office for Standards in Education (OFSTED) produced a report on *The Education of Travelling Children*.[3] This document provides ample evidence to demonstrate that the levels of access and attendance, together with achievement, have shown a marked improvement over the last decade. The seventy-three annual reports written for central government by Local Education Authorities (LEAs) with special Gypsy and Traveller education projects, revealed in 1994/5 that a total of 351 additional teachers were employed and that most of these worked peripatetically by supporting a number of different schools. Other specific and specialised posts included 170 classroom assistants and fifty-four Educational Welfare Officers. All of these professional employees work within Traveller Education Services specifically established to secure unhindered access and full integration into mainstream education. Much of the work of these services is rightly focused on supporting individual Gypsy and Traveller pupils who may have had a late start in formal education or a disrupted experience and spasmodic attendance at many schools. The report comments that the best practice also concentrates on changing attitudes and structures within the sphere of education and the wider world as far as possible. Good practice is also characterised by an attempt to permeate the curriculum with accurate and positive images of Gypsies and Travellers, and to establish their legitimacy as a people, together with a recognition of their enormous cultural, social and economic contribution to the world. Such approaches are also in the interests of improving the quality and accuracy of knowledge for all children. Much of this work has been facilitated by culturally orientated books and other learning materials produced both by the commercial market and by the many professionals working in this field. *A Horse for Joe*[4], produced by the Wiltshire Traveller Education Service is a good example, as too, is the series of counting and other books developed by the Norfolk (UK) Traveller Education Service.[5] In Devon (UK) a series of lovely oral history books have been produced detailing the life histories of Gypsies and Travellers.[6] Added to these invaluable resources have been the notable and important publications as part of the *Interface Collection*.[7] Academic and action research has also played an important part in positive developments. It is exciting that the first British professorship in Romani studies has recently been established at the University of Greenwich (UK).

These developments are increasingly seen as crucial to successful and happy learning at school for Gypsy and Traveller children. It clearly links to an earlier point about the importance of the cultural relevance of knowledge and that levels of achievements will continue to be depressed unless this pedagogical reality is more generally appreciated. The OFSTED report[8] commented on this aspect of provision in England.

"The response to school of Gypsy and Traveller children is crucially influenced by the children's awareness of the level of their acceptance by teachers and other pupils. Where the presence of Gypsy and Traveller children is openly acknowledged, and where accurate and positive images of the different nomadic communities are featured within both the resources of the school and the curriculum, then the response is lively and there is a genuine openness to learning. In contrast, where the ethos of the school implicitly or explicitly suggests that the Gypsy and Traveller pupils are best served by an incognito status, …the response lacks confidence, is tentative and reserved."

If educational institutions are to facilitate real curriculum access and successful and happy learning, then these aspects of provision need to be given the highest priority. Within this context the place of the Romani language in the curriculum also needs to be given careful consideration and a higher profile. The views of parents are vital on this particular issue, but language and culture are important especially if Gypsy and Traveller pupils are to feel happy in school and truly accepted for themselves.

There is little doubt that the progress made in Gypsy and Traveller education in the last ten years in England has been outstanding. The significant and constructive contributions made at international gatherings by Gypsies and Travellers, and by the many professional people involved, is indicative of the advances made. There has been a multitude of structural changes in the education system to facilitate better access, regular attendance and improved levels of achievement. At government level several policies have been developed to bring about important changes in structures and practice at local authority level. A number of examples will, perhaps, be illustrative of these changes. In January 1998 a system of dual registration was introduced which allows Gypsy and Traveller children to be placed on the register of more than one school. This allows attendance at school during the travelling season without the loss of the school place at the school where the child would attend when more settled and not travelling. The continuity of support has also been fostered by the introduction of a national system for educational/school record transfer. All Gypsy and Traveller parents are issued with a 'Green Card' which is used by the families to record the schools visited. This allows for the more rapid transfer of individual pupil records between schools. The Department for Education and Employment (DfEE) has also provided advice to schools in relation to the attendance regulations and the special circumstances which should apply in relation to nomadic Gypsy and Traveller pupils. These positive and helpful changes recognise the legitimate mobility of some families which may temporarily interfere with school attendance. All of these developments have been significant in that they represent an intention to secure equal opportunities in education for Gypsy and Traveller pupils despite a nomadic lifestyle.

Perhaps the greatest progress has been made in terms of the re-jigging of professional perspectives. These changes have not, in the main, been in consequence of family mobility but motivated more by an attempt to secure access and regular attendance for semi-settled Gypsies and Travellers. Notwithstanding this, the record is impressive. Most Traveller Education Services help schools to identify the pupils' needs and then to organise a programme of support with clearly defined objectives and date-related targets. There is a process of review and further negotiated support depending on assessed needs, in the form of a contract or service level agreement. The main focuses for support include settling pupils into school; intensive remedial tutoring (to compensate for lost schooling or late entry to formal education); supporting pupils in transfer between primary and secondary school and curriculum development. Most Services also provide in-service training (INSET) for schools and other agencies to encourage an enlightened and realistic understanding of the cultural background of Gypsies and Travellers. This is aimed rightly at ensuring that professional and institutional responses are appropriate and unconditioned by negative stereotypes that have traditionally prevented or hindered access for Gypsy and Traveller pupils.

The good practice which has been developed is further characterised by an approach which encourages independence, both of parents and pupils, to access their children to schools, and to become independent learners respectively. The work is also aimed to help schools to become self-sufficient in catering for the particular needs of Gypsies and Travellers. Specialist Education Welfare Workers are also part of this process. They support parents in accessing education but are also intent on extending the professional skills of "mainstream" welfare service providers. Although the long term objective of Traveller Education Services is to work themselves out of a job, this cannot be achieved only by a change in professional practice. It also needs the lasting structural changes to ensure that families with nomadic lifestyles are provided with a satisfactory education.

Structural changes have been achieved at both local and central levels. At local level, the development of good quality distance learning materials has done much to improve the continuity of education for those families who are still nomadic. With the application of new technologies it may be possible to make open and distance learning a viable alternative to actual school attendance. Some recent changes and planned developments at government level are also very positive steps in the right direction. There is likely to be enhanced flexibility at Key Stage 4 (for fourteen- to sixteen-year-olds) so that the curriculum can be more responsive to pupils' needs and facilitate vocational and work experience opportunities which may be seen as relevant to occupational ambitions. In response to the disappointing number of Gypsy and Traveller pupils who fail to transfer to, or succeed in, secondary education, the DfEE is making a video film for parents. This film will exercise the issues in the light of actual experiences portrayed within four case studies. In response to an OFSTED report on the achievement of minority ethnic pupils the Government has established an Advisory Group to help in the implementation of a ten point action plan.[9] The group has one member who is a Gypsy, and another who is a coordinator of a Traveller Education Service. It is also encouraging that the Government has established a Social Exclusion Unit to address the issue of social exclusion in society. Gypsy and professional organisations have been invited to provide evidence to the Unit and it is hoped that Gypsy and Traveller issues will be a central consideration of the Unit's actions. The Government's commitment to the education of Gypsies and Travellers is perhaps best illustrated by a recent ministerial comment.

"The problems of racism, social exclusion and educational failure are particularly acute for Gypsy and Traveller children… However, we are making good progress, particularly at primary level, through targeted support to schools with particular numbers of Traveller children. But much remains to be done to tackle problems which for too long have been brushed under the carpet, among a community of up to 150,000 children."[10]

OFSTED is also engaged in inspecting the quality of Traveller service delivery in relation to raising standards of achievement for all pupils.

I have devoted some time to describing the essential details of good practice as observed in England. The work in Gypsy and Traveller education has been based on sound educational principles. These are the foundations of all good education and need to be central to both policy and pedagogy and not marginalised to the realms of "special measures". In these bold and unashamedly confident statements, I have tried to set the stage for a further comment on the importance of the book, *School Provision for Ethnic Minorities: The Gypsy Paradigm*. It is because of the inherent philosophy underpinning the pan-European analysis of the situation of Gypsies and Travellers that it has been possible to bring to institutional and professional practice the correct principles and perspectives that have led to the development of such good and successful practice. This is now the hallmark of so much of the provision in Member States. Such progress has not always been easy and there are too many examples of where advances have been modest and only achieved as a result of a battle with vested interests in the form of out-dated professional attitudes, hidden prejudices and stereotypical images from the past. It is praise indeed that after ten years we are able to say that the catalyst impact of the report when first published, resulted in successful and effective actions because they were on the right track from the start. This is not to say, of course, that there was no good and enlightened practice to be found ten years ago. Well prior to this report, there was in many different pockets all over Europe, positive activity which, in its own helpful way, contributed to the composite final report. But what the report did do was to provide a unifying structure to good practice and to lodge it within the hierarchy of decision making both at institutional and governmental levels.

The re-publishing of this report is thus timely. So many of those involved across Member States in the field of Gypsy and Traveller education will know that there has been a great deal of innovative work and that much of this has been adopted and institutionalized as regular practice by schools and colleges, local and regional education authorities and Ministries of Education. It may be that it is right now for there to be an audit of what has been achieved and what still needs to be accomplished. Such an audit, conducted, say, by the European Commission, would have the benefit of a vast body of expertise to draw from, and not least, the increasing numbers of Gypsies and Travellers who are actively engaged at one level or another, either as parents and/or teachers, social workers and mediators. They, in particular, would undoubtedly be able to place a firm steer on the future direction of policy which would be more reliable and realistic than has hitherto been available. A review might reflect on the areas where progress has been less marked.

This report rightly emphasises the need for a multi-dimensional analysis of the total environment of the Gypsy and Traveller populations across Europe. In many countries the issues of health and accommodation are but two areas which should continue to merit attention because of a lack of progress. In some Member States commentators have indicated that the situation has worsened rather than improved. Hawes and Perez in their book *The Gypsy and the State*[11] liken some UK legislation, and particularly the 1994 Criminal Justice and Public Order Act, which deals with citizens' rights and accommodation for Gypsies and Travellers, as a form of ethnic cleansing. Political and economic spheres also require close scrutiny as these are not always secure and have far-reaching implications for the rights of citizenship including legal places to live, access to vocational training and fair work opportunities. The unwelcome reception in 1997 given by many to the Czech Roma arriving in Dover (UK) is a stark reminder of the strength of racist prejudice which still exists towards these communities. Similar reactions are to be noted in different Member States and no one country has the monopoly of racism and xenophobia. The European Commission's own document *Legal instruments to combat racism and xenophobia* draws our attention to this endemic condition.[12] "Nearly all countries report increased numbers of racist incidents and attacks on foreigners and individuals belonging to ethnic, racial or linguistic minorities." This is a European-wide phenomena that has been highlighted and dented by the European year against the evils of racism and xenophobia.

The situation in Eastern and Central Europe must continue to be monitored. The evidence suggests that discrimination and racist attitudes are widespread and manifest in policies at all levels including local and central government. We are indebted to those who are monitoring human rights issues in these parts of Europe. The Council of Europe and the Organisation for Security and Co-operation in Europe, together with a number of voluntary foundations, have made a valuable contribution in publicising the issues. In the countries of Eastern and Central Europe there are significant Roma populations and their treatment needs to be radically improved. The European Union is fully aware of what standards are achievable and required in terms of human rights and any decisions surrounding enlarged membership of the Community should be cognisant of the state of progress in relation to the situation and treatment of Gypsy peoples.

In drawing attention to these areas of concern and inaction it has not been my intention to suggest that all is rosy in the education garden and that there has been little, if any, progress made in other areas of provision and human rights. Within education there is still an enormous task facing us. There are too few Gypsy and Traveller children participating freely and fully in the public education systems in Member States. The level of literacy within the community is still significantly below that for the "Settled" populations. School attendance is generally unsatisfactory. In the OFSTED report[13] it is stated that as many as 10,000 Gypsy and Traveller children at the secondary stage are not even registered at any school in England. A further cause for concern is that Gypsy and Traveller pupils feature disproportionately in the statistics on exclusions from school. When figures are available, the levels are frequently masked by unrecorded exclusions. These exclusions can take a number of forms. For example, there is what might be called a "blind" exclusion where a family seeking admission for their child(ren) is illegally turned away from a school. However, the categorisation of exclusions is not important. What is important is that the exclusions from schools are too frequently the result of misunderstandings and a professional misjudgment about pupil behaviour. This book usefully reminds us that the life of the school cannot be other than a reflection of the wider society. We know, of course, that many schools do attempt, and indeed achieve, an enlightened approach based on a positive vision and ethos. This is what schools ought to be about, but too frequently many fail to reach the standard and continue to be the mirror images of the prejudiced communities they serve.

An honest audit of progress to date would no doubt present a healthy credit balance in relation to the wide range of wonderful books and other learning materials, including those fostering the use of the Romani language. Much of this has been produced by special projects in many Member States. Some of these have been referred to above. In nearly all situations these books and resources have been put to good use and have been instrumental in embellishing the curriculum for all children. But if we are to be really truthful, then it has to be admitted that progress in curriculum development has been only modest. With the political and logistical pressure on the school curriculum in most Member States, and the legitimate concerns about competency levels in basic numeracy and literacy, it is perhaps not surprising that schools, left to their own devices, fail to have the time, or more importantly, see the need, to develop the curriculum in a way which addresses the issues of cultural and ethnic diversity. The culling of books with negative stereotypes about Gypsies and Travellers is another area which has sometimes been neglected. A further negative aspect of response to the educational needs of these communities, is that of post-school education and vocational training. Developments in this area have been patchy although considerable progress has been made in many Member States to train the young people of the communities to be teachers, mediators and social workers.

Perhaps the balance sheets of any audit of progress would implicitly suggest that the proof of the pudding in regard to the total worth of all the efforts across Europe, would be a measured assessment of what actual achievements individual pupils have made. While there are significant and notable successes, and this is particularly true at a generalised level in primary education, there must still be concern at the disappointing levels of achievement overall. This is especially true at the secondary and post-secondary stages. The reasons are frequently practical and cultural in nature, but there is an increasing concern by many teachers and educationalists, that even when some Gypsy and Traveller pupils attend school regularly and, indeed, start school during the nursery years, performance levels remain stubbornly depressed. Serious academic research at an international level now needs to be conducted in this area of education.

There is perhaps one further issue which is worthy of mention in the context of an audit of the education of Gypsy and Traveller children. This is the issue of ethnic monitoring. Because of the marginalised status of Gypsies and Travellers, and their frequent occupation of twilight citizenship, they are not always included as a specific and legitimate group when it comes to monitoring and measuring the outcomes of the education system for other minority ethnic communities. It seems an obvious point but, unless their progress as a group can be monitored and compared with the average scores for all children, then it continues to be easy to ignore their gross under-achievement.

It is not the aim of this suggested audit to put a damper on actions which have been taken or, indeed, to underestimate the importance and value of all the laudable and noteworthy advances described above. The debit side of the accounts mentioned for two main purposes. Firstly, we need to note that the real successes in the work have come from actions which have been rooted in the general philosophy which underpinned the original analysis of the plight of Gypsy and Traveller communities across Europe. The report's contemporary relevance is unnervingly apposite. Secondly, it is important to remember that although we have witnessed over a decade of constructive progress in the realm of education, there is still much to be done and many barriers to be breached. The challenges do not stand alone. If they did it would instill a false sense of easily achievable goals. The reality is more daunting but not insurmountable.

As this book frequently reminds us, education is an integral part of the whole and it is as well to keep at the front of our thinking that further progress will continue to require actions which embrace not just education but also the wider issues affecting the lives of Gypsy and Traveller communities. This is pertinent to all Member States and wider afield in Eastern and Central Europe. Stress has already been placed on the importance of changing attitudes and structures in order to secure lasting change. This approach is perhaps also shrewdly cognisant of the fact that additional support and well-intentioned funding programmes might not always be present. This reality must place an urgency on our actions. I am unrepentant in repeating the assertion that this process is secured more firmly when there is a greater degree of involvement of Gypsies and Travellers in the process. Successful actions in education depend on a collaborative partnership of all those involved. This has to be true in regard to actions which affect the total environment of these communities. Effective inter-agency structures, at both governmental and other levels, need to be strengthened and formalised within Member States. This is needed to ensure coordinated actions which are uniform and compatible with the principles and practices of the European Union and the Commission in relation to its many polices and Directives.

The history of Gypsy and Traveller education will make more comfortable reading when it focuses on the decade 1987 to 1997. Readers will be interested but disturbed to scan earlier chapters detailing the chronicle of failures and mistakes. However difficult this reading may be, it is important that we are aware of it. Some history is strategically and helpfully provided in this book. Its importance is made clear in the text and is still of relevance if we wish in the future to avoid the ingredients of past mistakes which have been rooted in prejudice and ignorance. Observers and researchers would be correct to describe the model of development in this area of public education provision as a 'bottom-up' model. This has certainly been the case in the United Kingdom. Over the last thirty or so years we have seen the first initiatives taking place at grassroots level. Such actions were not always the most enlightened but they did have the advantage of being more action-research orientated. This made them more open to the necessary refinements — a process facilitated by sympathetic professionals and other helpers who, in the main, were thoughtful and sensitive to the needs and reactions of the communities with whom they worked. The philosophy behind much of this early work was the same as that which underpinned the synthesis report. The subsequent success and continued progress was instrumental in slowly involving, or if you like ensnaring, first, school institutions, then local education authorities, and finally, Ministries of Education. The determinants of good practice were influenced mutually by the informed actions in the field and the evaluations which recorded progress and provided signposts for the future. At a time in most Member States when informed policy and provision were receiving serious attention by Ministries of Education, the Commission's report *School Provision for Gypsy and Traveller Children*[14] provided an essential marker and prescriber for further well-informed actions at all levels.

The Commission's influence, both in terms of its commissioned research and its various funding programmes, such as Socrates, is vital to the continued progress of work and innovative actions in the field of education and related areas of social policy. It is also important that the Commission establish routines for the rigorous and independent monitoring and evaluation of its programmes. The feedback from these will not only make their own contribution to meeting the demands for public accountability, but will also provide the necessary pointers to future work and the enhancement of the repertoire of good and excellent practice.

The book *School Provision for Ethnic Minorities: The Gypsy Paradigm*, rightly notes that progress across Member States in the field of education has been at the cutting edge of general policy developments towards Gypsy and Traveller communities. This is perhaps one area where there are concerted and serious efforts being made to secure basic human rights. However, human rights are, of course, much broader than just education and it is critical that we remind ourselves of the adage that if we get the education of Gypsy and Travellers right, then we will be getting it right for all children. This is also true of human rights. If human rights were secure for these communities in Europe then they would more than likely be secure for us all. As Margaret Brearley said in her recent report,[15] "The treatment of Roma and Gypsies has become a litmus test for a humane society. Their widespread suffering is now one of Europe's most pressing, but most neglected, human rights issues."

The re-publishing of this report will be another step towards keeping the issues on the agenda and to ensuring that actions to address the obvious needs are based on an accurate and humanitarian analysis of the situation of the Gypsy and Traveller peoples in Europe.

Editorial note: Arthur Ivatts has been involved in the education of Gypsies, Roma and Travellers in the United Kingdom for the past thirty years. His academic background is in anthropology and education. Since 1976 he has been one of Her Majesty's Inspectors of Schools, and from 1982, he has held the national responsibility within Her Majesty's Inspectorate.

1. *Interface.* Information newsletter published by the Gypsy Research Centre at the Université René Descartes, Paris, with the assistance of the European Commission, DG XXII-Education, Training, Youth.

2. Jean-Pierre Liégeois, *School provision for Gypsy and Traveller children*, Commission of the European Communities, Luxembourg, 1987.

3. *The Education of Travelling Children*. A report published by the Office of Her Majesty's Chief Inspector of Schools. London: March 1996 Ref:HMR/12/96/NS.

4. *A Horse for Joe*. A children's story book published by the Wiltshire Traveller Education Service and Wiltshire County Council. ISBN 0 86080 285 X. Trowbridge (UK) 1993.

5. Two *1-10 Counting Books* and other titles. Published by the Norfolk Traveller Education Service. Norwich (UK) 1993. Bk. ISBN 1 873505 167. Bk.2 ISBN 1 873505 18 3

6. Two examples include: *Moving with the Times* by Goody Reilly. Published by Devon County Council. Exeter 1995. ISBN 1 85522 473 9. and *The Life and Story of May Orchard* by Dorothy Orchard. Published by Devon County Council. Exeter 1994. ISBN 1 85522 453 4.

7. The *Interface Collection,* developed by the Gypsy Research Centre at the Université René Descartes, Paris, is published with the support of the Commission of the European Communities. The distribution of certain titles from the Collection in Central and Eastern Europe takes place with the assistance of the Council of Europe.

8. op. cit. See footnote 3.

9. *Recent Research on the Achievements of Ethnic Minority Pupils,* by David Gillborn and Caroline Gipps. Published by HMSO for OFSTED, London 1996. ISBN 0 11 350084 X .

10. *Equality and the sum of its parts*, article by Estelle Morris MP (Minister in the Department for Education and Employment), Published *The Times Educational Supplement*, 26 September 1997.

11. *The Gypsy and the State — The Ethnic Cleansing of British Society,* By Derrick Hawes and Barbara Perez. Published by the School for Advanced Urban Studies, University of Bristol. Bristol 1995. ISBN 1 873575 769.

12. *Legal Instruments to Combat Racism and Xenophobia.* Published by the Commission of the European Communities. Luxembourg 1993. ISBN 92 826 5423 0

13. op.cit. See footnote 3.

14. op.cit. See footnote 2.

15. *The Roma/Gypsies of Europe: A Persecuted People,* by Margaret Brearley. Published by the Institute for Jewish Policy Research. London 1996. ISSN 1363 1314.

Bibliography

(NB: This gives data for English language versions wherever they exist. However, where the author has quoted from the French version – titles preceded by an * – in-text page references may differ.)

ABGV (Associatie Bastiaenen Geerts Vriesema). – *The Dutch Gypsies. A Preliminary Study of their Social Position. Summary and Possibilities for Further Research.* – Nijmegen, unpublished manuscript, 1984.

Acton, Thomas. – "The Functions of the Avoidance of Moxadi Kovels (Amongst Gypsies in South Essex)" in *Journal of the Gypsy Lore Society*, vol. L, parts 3-4. Liverpool, 1971.

Acton, Thomas. – *Gypsy Politics and Social Change.* – London: Routledge and Kegan Paul, 1974.

Acton, Thomas / Davies, Gerwyn. – "Educational Policy and Language Use Among English Romanies and Irish Travellers (Tinkers) in England and Wales" in Hancock, Ian F. (ed.), *Romani Sociolinguistics, International Journal of the Sociology of Language* no. 19. – The Hague / Paris/ New York: Mouton, 1979.

Acton, Thomas. – "New Weapons in the Struggle for Gypsy Education" in *Traveller Education*, no. 17. – London: Romanestan Publications, 1982.

Acton, Thomas. – "The Romani Language in Educational Work" in Acton, Thomas and Kenrick, Donald (eds.), *Romani Rokkeripen To-Divvus.* – London: Romanestan Publications, 1984.

Acton, Thomas. – "Gypsy Education: At the Crossroads" in *British Journal of Special Education*, vol.12, no. 1, London: National Association for Special Education, 1985a.

Acton, Thomas. – "Multiculturalism in One Country, A Review of the Swann Report" in *Traveller Education*, no. 20. – Warley, Brentwood: Romanestan Publications, 1985b.

Acton, Thomas. – "Practice Concerning Travelling and Camping by Nomads in Great Britain" in A. Reyniers, *Les pratiques de déplacement, de halte, de stationnement des populations tsiganes et nomades en France*, tome 3.- Paris: Centre de recherches tsiganes, 1985c.

Asséo, Henriette. – "L'histoire" in Liégeois, Jean-Pierre (ed.), *Les populations tsiganes en France* – Paris: Ministère de l'Education nationale / Centre de recherches tsiganes, 1981.

Avanzini, Guy. – "Débat Recherche: la relation Praticien-Chercheur" in *Praticiens-chercheurs*, ICEM, no. 3. – Cannes: La Bocca, 1985.

Balas, Bernard. – *L'enfant tsigane et la langue écrite. Réflexion sur les fondements d'une pédagogie interculturelle*. – Toulouse: DESS, Université de Toulouse, 1984.

Barec, Nicole. – "Etre travailleur social et vivre son idéologie" in *Rencontre, Cahiers du Travailleur social*, no. 17. – Paris, 1976.

Bastenier, A. / Dassetto, F. / Schever, B. – *Mômes d'immigrés en maternelle: fréquentation, impact et enjeux institutionnels*. – Louvain-la-Neuve: CIACO, 1985.

Bastide, Roger. – *Réflexions sur le bilinguisme*. – Unpublished manuscript, n.d.

Beckers, Paulus. – *Enkele maatschappelijke aspekten van hat Woonwagenleven*. – Ghent, 1969.

Belloni, Kali. – "Témoignages" in Liégeois, Jean-Pierre (ed.), *Les populations tsiganes en France* – Paris: Ministère de l'Education nationale / Centre de recherches tsiganes, 1981.

*Berthier, Jean-Charles. – "The Socialisation of the Gypsy Child" in *International Social Science Review*, vol. XXXI, no. 3. – Paris: UNESCO, 1979.

Beugen, M. van / Burgmans, A. / en Schaijk, H. van. – *Wonen op Wielen; Woonwagenbeleid als toetssteen van Welzijnsbeleid*. – Nijmegen: Link, 1975.

Binns, Dennis. – *Children's Literature and the Role of the Gypsy*. – Manchester: Manchester Travellers' School, 1984.

Blot, Bernard. – "La scolarisation des enfants de travailleurs migrants: orientations actuelles", in "Réunion nationale d'études pour la scolarisation des enfants de travailleurs migrants", Orléans, 24-28 April 1978, in *Le non-verbal et le soutien*. – CREDIF, no. 512, 1978.

Bourdieu, Pierre. – "L'école conservatrice" in *Revue française de sociologie*. – Paris, 1966.

Bourdieu, Pierre / Passeron, Jean-Claude. – *La reproduction, éléments pour une théorie du système d'enseignement*. – Paris: Editions de Minuit, 1970.

Bremer Volkshochschule / Sinti-Haus Bremen. – *L'élaboration et la mise en oeuvre d'un curriculum adaptable relatif à l'alphabétisation des Sinti ainsi que l'élaboration et la réalisation d'un programme de formation professionnelle spécifiquement adapté aux Sinti*. – Final report to European Social Fund by Project EP 200/80, 1983.

Carraz, Roland. – *Recherche en éducation et en socialisation de l'enfant*, Rapport de Mission au ministre de l'Industrie et de la Recherche. – Paris: La Documentation Française, 1983.

Castanié, J.-C. – "Orientations générales pour la scolarisation des enfants de travailleurs immigrés", in *Enfants étrangers et soutien*, Douai, 6-10 March 1978. – CREDIF, 1978.

CEDEFOP — *Systèmes de formation professionnelle dans les pays membres de la Communauté européenne*. – Berlin: CEDEFOP, Etudes comparatives, 1983.

Charbit, Yves. – *Les enfants de migrants et les pays d'origine*. International colloquium. – Ankara: Centre international de l'Enfance, 1977.

Claparède, Edouard. – *L'éducation fonctionnelle*. – Neuchâtel: Delachaux et Niestlé, 1964.

Clark, Kenneth. – *Dark Ghetto: Dilemmas of Social Power*. – London: Gollancz, 1965.

*Commission of the European Communities. – *Report from the Commission to the Council on the Implementation of Directive 77/486 on the Education of the Children of Migrant Workers* – COM(84)54. Brussels, 10 February 1984.

Conquy, Leslie. – "Les études réalisées en France en matière de scolarisation des enfants tsiganes" in Liégeois, Jean-Pierre (ed.), *La scolarisation des enfants tsiganes et nomades*. – Paris: Ministère de l'Education nationale / Centre de recherches tsiganes, 1981.

Cotonnec, Alain. – "Groupe scolaire de Clayes-sous-Bois", in *Journées d'études sur la scolarisation des enfants tsiganes*, Ministère de l'Education nationale. – Caen: Ecole normale du Calvados, 1983.

Cotonnec, Alain / Chartier, Anne-Marie. – "Ils nous mettent au fond des classes: parole préliminaire sur l'école" in *Etudes tsiganes*, no. 4. – Paris, 1984.

Couillaud, Xavier. – *De la "Culture d'origine" et de la "Pédagogie interculturelle". Eléments de réflexion*. – Paris: CIEMM, 1981.

*Council of Europe. – *The Training of Teachers of Gypsy Children*. – Strasbourg: Council of Europe, Council for Cultural Co-operation, Doc. DECS/EGT (83)63.1984.

Dégrange, Michel / Liégeois, Jean-Pierre. – "Le Tsigane et son double" in *Hommes et Migrations*, no. 807. – Paris, 1971.

Dégrange, Michel. – "Stéréotypes et dictionnaires" in *Etudes tsiganes*, no. 1. – Paris, 1974.

Dégrange, Michel. – "Effets d'une information sur un racisme" in *Hommes et Migrations*, no. 956. – Paris, 1978.

Dégrange, Michel. – "L'apprentissage d'un stéréotype: le 'Tzigane' " in *Pluriel-Débat*, no. 23. – Paris, 1980.

Dégrange, Michel / Liégeois, Jean-Pierre / Michon, Jean-Claude (with the collaboration of Rita Cauli and Jean-Pierre Duteuil). – *Nomades et sédentaires: images réciproques*. Report for the Commission of the European Communities. – Paris: Centre de recherches tsiganes, 1980.

Dégrange, Michel. – "Ce qu'on dit des Tsiganes, quelques mécanismes de rejet" in *Tsiganes et Gens du Voyage*, Paris: Cahiers Droit et Liberté, 1981.

Deligné, François / Miscoria, Marinelle. – "A Trappes, une école sur un terrain" in *Etudes tsiganes*, no. 4. – Paris, 1984.

Dick-Zatta, Jane. – "La tradizione orale dei Rom sloveni" in *Lacio Drom*, n° 3-4, 1986.

Dimas, Thomas. – "L'analphabétisme des Tsiganes américains: un facteur de conservation de leur culture" in *Etudes tsiganes*, no. 4. – Paris, 1975.

*Ducoli, Bruno. – "Education and Cultural Development of Migrants", in Alaluf, Matéo. – *Migrant Culture and Culture of Origin*. DECS/EGT (82)4. – Strasbourg: Council of Europe, Council for Cultural Co-operation, 1982.

Dwyer, Sister Colette. – *Education and Training for Travellers*, Fourth Triennial Report Submitted by the National Coordinator for the Education of Travelling People, unpublished manuscript, Dublin, 1984.

*Faure, Edgar: *Learning to Be: The World of Education Today and Tomorrow.* Education on the Move Series, UNESCO. Paris: UNESCO and London: Harrap, 1972.

Ferté, Patricia. – *La scolarisation des enfants tsiganes.* Report submitted to the Direction des Ecoles du Ministère de l'Education nationale as part of a pilot project, 1984.

Ferté, Patricia. – "Les livres pour enfants et les bandes dessinées ayant pour thème les Tsiganes et les nomades" in *Tsiganes, qui êtes-vous?* Brochure de l'Ecole normale du Val-d'Oise, 1985.

*Foucault, Michel. – *Madness and Civilization. A History of Insanity in the Age of Reason.* London: Routledge, 1971.

Freese, C. / Murko, M. / Wurzbacher, G. – *Hilfen für Zigeuner und Landfahrer, Forschungsbericht.* – Stuttgart / Berlin / Köln / Mainz: Schriftenreihe des Bundesministers für Jugend, Familie und Gesundheit, Bd.86, 1980.

Fresco, Luigi. – *La visione degli zingari dataci dai tesi narrativi e documentari per ragazzi, adolescenti, giovani.* Master's thesis, Università di Verona, 1986.

Gille, Marguerite. – "Les antennes scolaires mobiles" in *Etudes tsiganes,* no. 4. – Paris, 1984.

Grau, Richard. – "Réflexions sur les identités culturelles et linguistiques en France" in *Pourquoi?*, no. 193. – Paris, March 1984.

Grimaud, Joël. – "Les apprentissages fondamentaux, la maîtrise de la lecture et de l'écrit" in *Etudes tsiganes*, no. 4. – Paris, 1984.

*Gudmander, Bendt Gudmand. – "Report on the Experimental Class organised at Lindegade School, Helsingør (Denmark)" (Addendum VI to CDMG (84)1) in *Council of Europe's Experimental Classes* – Strasbourg, 1983.

Gustafsson, Inga. – *Studies of a Minority Group's Efforts to Preserve its Cultural Autonomy.* – Stockholm: University of Stockholm / IMFO-Group, 1973.

Hancock, Ian F. – "Problems in the Creation of a Standard Dialect of Romanès" in *Working Papers in Sociolinguistics*, no. 25. – Austin, Texas: Southwest Educational Development Laboratory, 1975.

Hermans, A. / Lierde, K. van. – *Nomadisme et pauvreté (analyse comparative des problèmes des nomades aux Pays-Bas, en RFA et en Belgique).* Report for the Commission of the European Communities. – Louvain: Université Catholique de Louvain, 1980.

Hohmann, Joachim S. – *Zigeuner und Zigeunerwissenschaft.* – Marburg / Lahn: Metro Bd. 6, 1980.

Hübschmannová, Milena. – *Notes about the Position of Gypsies-Rom in Czechoslovakia.* – Prague: Sociological Institute of Czechoslovak Academy of Science, n.d.

Hundsalz, Andreas. – *Soziale Situation der Sinti in der Bundesrepublik Deutschland.* – Schriftenreihe des Bundesministers für Jugend, Familie und Gesundheit, Bd. 129, 1982.

Iniesta, Alfonso. – "La compleja escolarización gitana" in *La Comunidad gitana.* – Madrid: Cuadernos Inas, no. 8, 1982.

Instituto de Sociología aplicada de Madrid. – *La escuela "puente" para niños gitanos.* – Madrid: Secretariado Nacional gitano, 1982.

Istituto della Enciclopedia Italiana. – *Le minoranze linguistiche nei Paesi della Comunità Europea.* Synthesis report for the Commission of the European Communities. – Rome, 1984.

Ivatts, Arthur R. – *"Catch 22 Gypsies", A Report on Secondary Education.* – London: Advisory Committee for the Education of Romany and other Travellers, 1975.

Jazouli, Abdil. – *La nouvelle génération de l'immigration maghrébine.* – Paris: CIEMM, 1982.

Jeannette et l'école obligatoire. – Collective work, unpublished manuscript, 1983.

Kaldi, Leita. – "A School for Gypsies" in *Innovation*, Newsletter of the International Educational Reporting Service, no. 29-30. – New York: UNESCO, 1981.

*Karagiorges, Andréas G. – *Evaluation of the Educational Aspects of the Council of Europe's Experimental Classes for the Academic Years 1981-1982 and 1982-1983.* DECS/EGT, (84)51. – Strasbourg: Council of Europe, Council for Cultural Co-operation, 1984.

Keane, Hawley. – *National Council for Travelling People 1969-1985. A Short History.* – Ennis Committee for the Travelling People, 1985.

Kemény, István. – "Sur les Tsiganes de Hongrie" in *Les Tsiganes.* Problèmes politiques et Sociaux, no. 503. – Paris: La Documentation Française, 1985.

Kenrick, Donald. – "The Portrayal of the Gypsy in English Schoolbooks" in *Internationale Schulbuchforschung*, Zeitschrift des Georg-Eckert Instituts, no. 1. – Westermann, 1984.

Kenrick, Donald / Puxon, Grattan. – *The Destiny of Europe's Gypsies.* – London: Chatto-Heinemann, 1972. [A revised and updated version of this book was published by the Interface Collection in 1995 under the title *Gypsies Under the Swastika.*]

Kervadec, Anita. – *Apprendre à lire à des enfants tsiganes.* Paper given at the Université de Haute-Bretagne. – 1982.

Labov, William. – *The Logic of Nonstandard English, Language and Social Context.* – Harmondsworth: Penguin Books, 1969.

Lafaurie, Nicole. – "L'école des Cailloux Gris d'Herblay" in *Etudes tsiganes*, no. 4. – Paris, 1984.

Lallemand, Suzanne / Delaisi de Perceval, Geneviève. – "Les joies du maternage de 1950 à 1978 ou les vicissitudes des brochures officielles de puériculture" in *Les Temps modernes*. – Paris, October 1978.

Leblon, Bernard. – *Les Gitans dans la littérature espagnole.* – Toulouse: Institut d'Etudes hispaniques et hispano-américaines, Université de Toulouse le Mirail, 1982.

Leblon, Bernard. – *Les Gitans d'Espagne.* – Paris: Presses Universitaires de France, 1985.

Liégeois, Jean-Pierre. *Mutation tsigane.* – Bruxelles: Editions Complexe, 1976.

Liégeois, Jean-Pierre. – "Travailleurs sociaux et minorités culturelles" in Liégeois, Jean-Pierre (ed.) – *Idéologie et pratique du travail social de prévention*, Toulouse: Privat, 1977.

Liégeois, Jean-Pierre. – "Gitans et pouvoirs publics en Espagne" in *Ethno-psychologie*, no. 1. – Le Havre, 1980a.

Liégeois, Jean-Pierre. – "Pédagogie et acculturation" in *La scolarisation des enfants tsiganes et nomades* – Paris: Ministère de l'Education nationale / Centre de recherches tsiganes, 1980b.

Liégeois, Jean-Pierre. – "Economie et assimilation" in *Esprit*. – Paris, May 1980c.

Liégeois, Jean-Pierre (ed.). – *La scolarisation des enfants tsiganes et nomades.* Journées nationales d'étude de Dijon. – Paris: Ministère de l'Education nationale / Centre de recherches tsiganes, 1980d.

Liégeois, Jean-Pierre. – "Réglementation et scolarisation" in *La scolarisation des enfants tsiganes et nomades*. – Paris: Ministère de l'Education nationale / Centre de recherches tsiganes, 1980e.

Liégeois, Jean-Pierre (ed.). – *Les populations tsiganes en France.* – Paris: Ministère de l'Education nationale / Centre de recherches tsiganes, 1981a.

Liégeois, Jean-Pierre. – "Rejets éternels, les collectivités locales face aux Tsiganes et aux nomades" in *Pluriel-débat*, no. 28. – Paris, 1981b.

*Liégeois, Jean-Pierre. – "The Schooling of Gypsy Children" and "Summary by the Rapporteur" in *The Training of Teachers of Gypsy Children*. – Strasbourg: Council of Europe, Council for Cultural Co-operation, DECS/EGT (83) 63. 1984.

*Liégeois, Jean-Pierre. – *Gypsies and Travellers*. – Strasbourg: Council of Europe, 1985. [A revised and updated version of this book was published by the Council of Europe Press in 1994 under the title *Roma, Gypsies, Travellers*.]

Liégeois, Jean-Pierre. – "Tsiganes: l'émergence d'une minorité" in *Les minorités à l'âge de l'Etat-nation* (collective work). – Paris: Fayard, 1985.

*Liégeois, Jean-Pierre. – *Gypsies. An Illustrated History*. – London: Al-Saaqi, 1986. [in-text reference to French version, Liégeois 1983.]

Lorenzo, Annie. – *Profession? Forain*. – Paris: Editions Charles Massin, 1985.

Louis, A. – "Forum on Recent Innovations in Gaujo Methods of Education Organizational Problems of a Gypsy-School: The Romany School of Richmond" in Acton, Thomas (ed.) *Current Changes Amongst British Gypsies and Their Place in International Patterns of Development*, unpublished manuscript. – Oxford: National Gypsy Education Council, 1971.

Malaurie, Jean. – "Autonomie et progrès des peuples arctiques" in *Canal*. – Paris, 1977.

*Mariet, François. – *Maintaining migrants' links with the culture of their country of origin*. DECS/EGT (79)77. – Strasbourg: Council of Europe, 1980.

Martin-Heuss, Kirsten. – *Zur mythischen Figur des Zigeuners in der deutschen Zigeunerforschung*. Frankfurt: Haag & Herchen Verlag (Forum für Sinti und Roma, Band 1), 1983.

*Mead, Margaret. – *Culture and Commitment – A Study of the Generation Gap*. London: Bodley Head, 1970.

Memmi, Albert. – *La psychologie du bilinguisme*. Extrait du 70ème Congrès de l'AFAS, fasc.III. – Tunis (n.d.).

Memmi, Albert. – "Différence, racisme et dominance" in *Pour: Vers une société interculturelle?* no. 86 (special issue). – Toulouse: Privat, 1982.

Michaud, Gilles. – "Angoulême, Les Molines 'fermées pour cause d'insécurité'" in *Etudes tsiganes*, no. 4. – Paris, 1984.

Ministère de l'Education nationale, Direction des Ecoles. – *Approches interculturelles et réussite scolaire des enfants de migrants*. Commission of the European Communities pilot project activity report 1983/84. – Bruxelles: Commission des Communautés européennes, 1984.

Muel, Francine. – "L'école obligatoire et l'invention de l'enfance anormale" in *Actes de la recherche en Sciences Sociales*, no. 1. – Paris, 1975.

Nikkinen, Reima. – "The Future of Gypsies and Gypsy Culture in Finland". Lecture given at University of Tampere summer school, in Huttunen, Kari – *Roma of Finland (Gypsies in Changes and in Quest of Equality)*. – Unpublished manuscript, 1976.

ní Shuinéar, Sinéad. – *The Training Centre as a Nucleus for Traveller Community Development.* – Unpublished manuscript, 1979.

*Ó Murchú, Helen. – *Overview and Synthesis of Dossiers Established on Some Forms of Current Pre-Primary Provision in Lesser Used Languages in the EEC Member States.* Brussels: Commission of the European Communities, for the European Bureau of Lesser Used Languages, 1985.

Opper, Susan. – *The Function of Home and Parents in an Intercultural Society.* Report on a pilot project sponsored by the Council of Europe and the Swedish National Parent-School Association. DECS/EGT (85)25. – Council of Europe, Council for Cultural Co-operation, 1985.

Perotti, Antonio, with an introduction by Xavier Couillaud. – *De la "Culture d'origine" et de la "Pédagogie interculturelle". Eléments de réflexion.* – Paris: CIEMM, 1981.

Piasere, Leonardo. – "Les pratiques de voyage et de halte des populations nomades en Italie" in Reyniers, A. (ed.), *Les pratiques de déplacement, de halte, de stationnement des populations tsiganes et nomades en France,* tome 3. – Paris: Centre de recherches tsiganes, 1985.

Piasere, Leonardo. – "A scuola dai Gagè. Ovvero quando l'educatore diventa disadattato" in Zatta, Paolo (ed.), *Scuola di Stato e Nomadi*, Padova: Francisci / Università verde, 1986.

*Porcher, Louis. – *The education of migrant workers' children: interculturalism and teacher training.* DECS/EGT (79)82. – Strasbourg: Council of Europe, 1979.

Puxon, Grattan. – "Romanès and Language Policy in Yugoslavia" in Hancock, Ian F. (ed.), *Romani Sociolinguistics, International Journal of the Sociology of Language* no. 19. – The Hague / Paris/ New York: Mouton, 1979.

Quirke, Margaret. – *Planning and Providing Education for Gypsy, Fairground and Circus Children*, unpublished manuscript. – Dublin: 1984.

*Rey von Allmen, Micheline. – *Course on "The intercultural training of teachers"* (Lisbon). DECS/EGT (82)11. – Strasbourg: Council of Europe, Council for Cultural Co-operation, 1982a.

*Rey von Allmen, Micheline. – *Symposium on "The intercultural training of teachers"* (L'Aquila). DECS/EGT (82)61. – Strasbourg: Council of Europe, Council for Cultural Co-operation, 1982b.

Reyniers, Alain. – *Les pratiques de déplacement, de halte, de stationnement des populations nomades et tsiganes en France,* tomes 1 - 2 - 3. Report submitted to the Ministère des Affaires Sociales. Paris: Centre de recherches tsiganes, 1984 / 1985 / 1986.

Rosenthal, Robert A. / Jacobson, Lenore. – *Pygmalion in the Classroom.* – London: Holt, Rinehart and Winston, 1968.

Sánchez Ortega, María Helena. – *Documentación selecta sobre la situación de los gitanos españoles en el siglo XVIII.* – Madrid: Editora Nacional, 1976.

Sayad, Abdelmalek. – "Culture dominante, cultures dominées" in *Projet*, no. 171. – Paris, 1983.

Schlüter, Ragnhild. – *Les Tsiganes dans le système scolaire norvégien.* DECS/EGT (83) Misc.23. – Strasbourg: Council of Europe, Council for Cultural Co-operation, 1983a.

Schlüter, Ragnhild. – *Le projet "Les Tsiganes – Une minorité en danger" à l'Ecole normale de Levanger* (Norvège). DECS/EGT (83) Misc.28. – Strasbourg: Council of Europe, Council for Cultural Co-operation, 1983b.

SKU (Språk- och kulturarvsutredningen). – *Different Origins – Partnership in Sweden, Education for Linguistic and Cultural Diversity* (English summary) Published by the Commission on Migrants' Languages and Culture in School and Adult Education in Sweden. – Stockholm: Utbildnings Departementet, 1984.

Tallaght Branch Sub-Committee (Irish National Teachers' Organisation). – *The Education of Travellers' Children – Report.* – 1984.

Teunissen, Tijmen Ir. – *From Vilified Minority to Fellow Citizens.* European Social Fund / Municipality of Oldenzaal. – Unpublished manuscript, 1982.

Travelling People Review Body. – *Report of the Travelling People Review Body.* – Dublin: The Stationery Office, 1983.

Vaux de Foletier, François de. – *Mille ans d'histoire des Tsiganes.* – Paris: Fayard, 1970.

Verbunt, Gilles. – "Pour une politique de l'intégration" in *Projet* no. 171. – Paris, January 1983.

Verbunt, Gilles. – "Des langues qui se délient" in Verbunt, Gilles (ed.), *Par les langues de France, 2.* – Paris: Editions du Centre Georges Pompidou, 1985.

Weiler, Margaret. – *Zur Frage der Integration der Zigeuner in der Bundesrepublik Deutschland.* – Köln, 1979.

*Whorf, Benjamin Lee. – *Language, Thought and Reality.* – New York: Cambridge MIT Press, 1956.

Williams, Patrick. – "La société" in Liégeois, Jean-Pierre (ed.), *Les populations tsiganes en France* – Paris: Ministère de l'Education nationale / Centre de recherches tsiganes, 1981.

*Wittek, Fritz. – *The Education of Migrants' Children* (Vienna and Lower Austria). DECS/EGT (83)70. – Strasbourg: Council of Europe, Council for Cultural Co-operation, 1983.

Worrall, Dick. – *Gypsy Education. A Study of Provision in England and Wales.* – Walsall: Walsall Council for Community Relations, 1979.

Yung, Pierre. – "L'instruction des enfants" in Liégeois, Jean-Pierre (ed.), *La scolarisation des enfants tsiganes et nomades* – Paris: Ministère de l'Education nationale / Centre de recherches tsiganes, 1980.

Glossary

Buffer: Term used by Irish Travellers, equivalent to Romani *Gadjo*.
caravan: As an adjective on its own, or in conjunction with -dweller, -dwelling etc., an anglicisation of *Woonwagenbewoner* (literally "caravan-dweller"), Dutch Travellers' name for themselves.
carnet anthropométrique*: Special identification papers for nomads, in use in France 1912-70. While all residents of France (and of most other European countries) must carry official identity papers, these differed from standard identification both in the amount of detailed physical information (full-face and profile police photographs, imprints of all ten fingers, length of neck, diameter of head, any distinguishing physical marks, etc.) and in obliging the holder to report to and obtain the signature of the mayor or head of police of each townland both on arrival and before departure.
country (adjective): "non-Traveller" (Ireland)
DES: Department (= ministry) of Education and Science (UK)
education**: Culture or development of powers, formation of character, as contrasted with the imparting of mere knowledge or skill.
FRG: Federal Republic of Germany: pre-reunification "West Germany"
Gadjo, pl. *Gadjé*: non-Gypsy (Romani)
galley (slavery): Until steam took over, ships were powered by a combination of wind and oars, with manpower for the latter frequently provided by convicts.
Gypsy***: Term used to denote ethnic groups formed by the dispersal of commercial nomadic and other groups from and within India from the tenth century, and their mixing with European and other groups during their diaspora.
Gypsy language(s)***: The varieties of Romani and other languages which have become the distinct mother tongues or ethnic speech of particular Gypsy groups.
halt, halting place, halting site: Anywhere that nomadic Gypsies/Travellers camp. It may be anything from an illegal, insecure overnight stopping-place on a motorway verge, to an authorised, serviced caravan park. The term has been used throughout precisely because it is neutral enough to cover both these extremes and everything in between.
Hauptschule: An intermediate-level school, accepting pupils between the ages of ten to fifteen (FRG).
HMI: Her Majesty's (schools) Inspector (UK)
HMSI: Her Majesty's Schools Inspectorate (UK)
home: In the Belgian context, a special boarding school for children of nomadic parents.
intergroup*: An ad hoc group formed by Members of the European Parliament drawn together by their common interest in a given question; see Recommendation 99.
INTO: Irish National Teachers' Organisation, a primary teachers' trade union (Ireland)
itinerant: Adjective describing a profession, etc., requiring mobility. The term has also been

used, administratively, in Ireland, as a (non-ethnic) noun denoting "Traveller".
Land, pl. **Länder**: Germany is a federation of *Länder*, each having a degree of internal autonomy; cf. the states of the U.S.A.
LEA: Local Education Authority (UK)
NGEC: National Gypsy Education Council, a mixed Gypsy/Gadjo voluntary association (UK)
pedagogical counsellor: A liaison officer employed to keep teachers up to date with developments in pedagogical thinking, help them improve their own teaching, etc.
pedagogy**: The art or science of teaching.
Rom (pl. **Rom, Roma**) ***: A broad term used in various ways:
a) The totality of those ethnic groups of Gypsies (e.g. Kalderash, Lovari, etc.) who speak the "Vlach" or "Xoraxané" (or "Rom") varieties of Romani;
b) Any Gypsy in Eastern Europe and Turkey, plus those outside the region of East European extraction;
c) (following the usage of the World Romani Congress) Any Gypsy.
Depending on context, the word is both an umbrella ethnonym and a gender-specific term denoting adult male.
Romani, Romanès***: A North Indian language, related to Hindi and Punjabi, used by the majority of Gypsy groups; today it exists in many varieties, some very heavily influenced by the languages of host countries past and present.
schooling**: The action of teaching, or the state or fact of being taught, in a school; scholastic education.
sedentary: Living in one place. Used of Gypsies/Travellers who are not – for the moment at any rate – nomadic.
Settled: Neutral adjective describing non-Gypsies/Travellers. Capitalised because it denotes ethnicity.
Traveller: A member of any of the (predominantly) indigenous European ethnic groups (e.g. Woonwagenbewoners, Mincéiri, Jenische, Quinquis, Resende and so on) whose culture is characterised, inter alia, by self-employment, occupational fluidity and nomadism. These groups have been influenced to a greater or lesser degree by ethnic groups of (predominantly) Indian origin with a similar cultural base (see *Gypsies*). There is no rigid dividing line between the two; indeed, the term *Traveller* would cover the multitude of ethnic groups in both categories, but it has been used in conjunction with *Gypsy* in deference to the self-differentiation of those concerned. It is worth pointing out that, while all Travellers (including those of Indian origin) see non-Traveller society as an essentially undifferentiated whole, and label it accordingly (e.g. "Gadjo", "Payo", "Buffer"), they themselves have no single term covering all "non-Gadjé".
VEC: Vocational Education Committee, local policy-making body for vocational training (Ireland)

* definition provided by Jean-Pierre Liégeois
**definition taken from the *Oxford English Dictionary*, 1989 edition
*** definition provided by Thomas Acton and/or Donald Kenrick

****

Resolution of the Council and the Ministers of Education meeting within the Council

of 22 May 1989

on school provision for gypsy and traveller children

(89/C 153/02)

THE COUNCIL AND THE MINISTERS FOR EDUCATION, MEETING WITHIN THE COUNCIL

Having regard to the resolution of the Council and of the Ministers for Education, meeting within the Council, of 9 February 1976[1] comprising an action programme in the field of education,

Considering that on 24 May 1984 the European Parliament adopted a resolution on the situation of gypsies in the Community[2] in which it recommended in particular that the governments of the Member States coordinate their approach and called on the Commission to draw up programmes to be subsidized from Community funds aimed at improving the situation of gypsies without destroying their separate identity,

Considering that gypsies and travellers currently form a population group of over one million persons in the Community and that their culture and language have formed part of the Community's cultural and linguistic heritage for over 500 years,

Considering that the present situation is disturbing in general, and in particular with regard to schooling, that only 30 to 40% of gypsy or traveller children attend school with any regularity, that half of them have never been to school, that a very small percentage attend secondary school and beyond, that the level of educational skills, especially reading and writing, bears little relationship to the presumed length of schooling, and that the illiteracy rate among adults is frequently over 50% and in some places 80% or more,

Considering that over 500,000 children are involved and that this number must constantly be revised upwards on account of the high proportion of young people in gypsy and traveller communities, half of whom are under 16 years of age,

Considering that schooling, in particular by providing the means of adapting to a changing environment and achieving personal and professional autonomy, is a key factor in the cultural, social and economic future of gypsy and traveller communities, that parents are aware of this fact and their desire for schooling for their children is increasing,

Noting the results and recommendations of studies carried out on behalf of the Commission on the schooling of gypsy and traveller children in the 12 Member States of the Community and the guidelines emerging from the summary report, consultations of gypsy and traveller representatives and discussions between experts and representatives of the Ministries of Education,

HEREBY ADOPT THIS RESOLUTION:

The Council and the Ministers for Education, meeting within the Council, will strive to promote a set of measures concerning school provision for gypsy and traveller children aimed, without prejudice to any steps already taken by Member States to cope with specific situations which they face in this area, at developing a global structural approach helping to overcome the major obstacles to the access of gypsy and traveller children to schooling.

These measures will aim at:

– promoting innovatory initiatives,

– proposing and supporting positive and appropriate measures,

– ensuring that achievements are interrelated,

– widely disseminating the lessons learned,

– promoting exchanges of experience.

1. At Member State level

Within their constitutional and financial limits and the limits of their own specific national policies and structures, the Member States will make every effort to promote:

(a) structures:

– support for educational establishments, providing them with the necessary facilities for catering for gypsy and traveller children,

– support for teachers, pupils and parents;

(b) teaching methods and teaching materials:

– experiments with distance teaching, which is better adapted to the reality of nomadic life,

– the development of forms of educational follow up,

– measures to facilitate transition between schooling and continuing educational training,

– consideration for the history, culture and language of gypsies and travellers,

– use of new electronic and video methods,

– teaching materials for educational establishments involved in the schooling of gypsy and traveller children ;

(c) recruitment and initial and continuing training of teachers:

– adequate continuing and additional training for teachers working with gypsy and traveller children,

– the training and employment of teachers of gypsy or traveller origin wherever possible;

(d) information and research:

– increased provision of documentation and information to schools, teachers and parents,

– encouragement of research on the culture, history and language of gypsies and travellers ;

(e) consultation and coordination: promotion of social-mindedness among the population:

– appointment of trained staff to carry out coordination tasks,

– the encouragement of liaison groups bringing together parents, teachers, representatives of local authorities and school administrations,

– designation, where necessary, of a State authority or authorities involved in the schooling of gypsy and traveller children in States with a large number of gypsies and travellers to assist in coordination of the necessary measures including, where appropriate, those relating to the training of teachers, documentation and the production of teaching material.

2. At Community level

2.1. Community involvement in this field is useful for encouraging national initiatives concerning the exchange of experience and for promoting innovatory pilot schemes.

2.2. Organization of exchanges of views and experience by means of meetings at Community level of the various partners concerned and more particularly of representatives of gypsies and travellers, young gypsies and teachers.

2.3. The Commission will continuously document, promote, coordinate and assess all the measures at Community level with the assistance of an outside body if necessary.

2.4. The Commission will ensure that these measures fit in with the other Community measures already planned in the field of education. It will ensure in particular that these activities are compatible with other Community activities such as those of the European Social Fund and with those of other international organizations, especially the Council of Europe.

2.5. A report on the implementation of the measures provided for in this resolution will be submitted to the Council, the European Parliament and the Education Committee by the Commission before 31 December 1993.

---

1 - OJ n° C 38, 19.2.1976, p. 1
2 - OJ n° C 172, 2.7. 1984, p. 153

The Interface Collection

Interface: a programme

The Gypsy Research Centre at the Université René Descartes, Paris, has been developing cooperation with the European Commission and the Council of Europe since the early 1980s. The Centre's task is to undertake studies and expert work at European level; a significant proportion of its work consists in ensuring the systematic implementation of measures geared towards improving the living conditions of Gypsy communities, especially through the types of action with which it is particularly involved, such as research, training, information, documentation, publication, coordination etc., and in fields which are also areas of research for its own teams: sociology, history, linguistics, social and cultural anthropology...

In order to effectively pursue this work of reflection and of action we have developed a strategy to facilitate the pooling of ideas and initiatives from individuals representing a range of different approaches, to enable all of us to cooperate in an organised, consistent fashion. The working framework we have developed over the years is characterised both by a solidity which lends effective support to activities, and by a flexibility conferring openness and adaptability. This approach, driven by an underlying philosophy outlined in a number of publications, notably the ***Interface*** newsletter, has become the foundation of our programme of reference.

Interface: a set of teams

A number of international teams play a key role within the programme framework, namely through their work in developing documentation, information, coordination, study and research. With the support of the European Commission, and in connection with the implementation of the Resolution on School Provision for Gypsy and Traveller Children adopted in 1989 by the Ministers of Education of the European Union, working groups on history, language and culture - *the Research Group on European Gypsy History, the Research and Action Group on Romani Linguistics,* and *the European Working Group on Gypsy and Traveller Education* – have already been established, as has a working group developing a Gypsy encyclopaedia. Additional support provided by the Council of Europe enables us to extend some of our work to cover the whole of Europe.

Interface: a network

- these Groups, comprising experienced specialists, are tackling a number of tasks: establishing contact networks linking persons involved in research, developing documentary databases relevant to their fields of interest, working as expert groups advising/collaborating with other teams, organising the production and distribution of teaching materials relevant to their fields;

- these productions, prepared by teams representing a number of different States, are the result of truly international collaboration; the composition of these teams means that they are in a position to be well acquainted with the needs and sensitivities of very different places and to have access to national, and local, achievements of quality which it is important to publicise;

- in order to decentralise activities and to allocate them more equitably, a network of publishers in different States has been formed, to ensure both local input and international distribution.

Interface: a Collection

A Collection was seen as the best response to the pressing demand for teaching materials, recognised and approved by the Ministers of Education in the above-mentioned Resolution adopted at European level, and also in the hope of rectifying the overall dearth of quality materials and in so doing to validate and affirm Gypsy history, language and culture.

Published texts carry the *Interface* label of the Gypsy Research Centre.

- they are conceived in complementarity with each other and with action being undertaken at European level, so as to produce a structured information base: such coherence is important for the general reader, and essential in the pedagogical context;

- they are, for the most part, previously unpublished works, both because they address essential themes which have been insufficiently explored to date, and because they do so in an original fashion;

- their quality is assured by the fact that all are written by, or in close consultation with, experienced specialists;

- although contributions come from specialists, the Collection is not aimed at specialists: it must be accessible/comprehensible for direct consultation by secondary level students, and by teachers of primary level pupils for classroom use. The authors write clear, well-structured texts, with bibliographical references given as an appendix for readers wishing to undertake a more in-depth study;

- although contributions come from specialists, the Collection is not aimed at any particular target group: in an intercultural approach to education, and given the content of each contribution, every student, and every teacher, should have access to Gypsy/Traveller-related information, and may have occasion to use it in the classroom. The texts on offer, being the work of extremely competent contributors, may embody new approaches to the topics covered (history, linguistics etc.) and as such will be of relevance not only to teachers, teacher trainers, pupils, students and researchers, but also social workers, administrators and policy makers;

- contributions may be accompanied by practical teaching aids or other didactic tools; these tools and materials are prepared by teams in the field, experienced teachers and participants in pilot projects. Their output is very illustrative of *Interface* programme dynamics : an association of diverse partners in a context of action-research, producing coordinated, complementary work, with a scope as broad as Europe, yet adapted to the local cultural and linguistic context;

- format is standardised for maximum reader-friendliness and ease of handling;

- the *Interface* collection is international in scope: most titles are published in a number of languages, to render them accessible to the broadest possible public.

A number of topics have been proposed, of which the following are currently being pursued:

- *European Gypsy history*
- *Romani linguistics*
- *Rukun*
- *Reference works*

Jean-Pierre Liégeois
Director, Interface Collection

The Interface Collection publishers' network as of October 97 : Alternative (Romania) — Anicia (with the Centro Studi Zingari - Italy) — Centre régional de Documentation pédagogique Midi-Pyrénées (France) — Kastaniotis (Greece) — Litavra (Bulgaria) — Parabolis (Germany) — Presencia Gitana (Spain) — Rromani Baxt (the Cultural Foundation of the International Romani Union, for some language-related works) — University of Hertfordshire Press (United Kingdom).

Titles in the *Interface* Collection: a reminder

The Collection is published with the **support of the European Commission**. Some Collection titles may receive Council of Europe support for distribution in Central and Eastern Europe. All orders, whether direct or through a bookshop, must be addressed to the relevant publisher. A reduced unit price is available to bulk purchasers (schools, associations etc.). Inter-publisher agreements should make all titles easily obtainable: for example the English version of *From India to the Mediterranean* can be ordered from UHP, customers in Spain should contact their local supplier, PG, for copies of *Śirpustik amare ćhibăqiri,* etc.

1. • *Śirpustik amare ćhibăqiri*, Marcel Kurtiàde, CRDP. Pupil's book — ISBN: 2-86565-074-X
   • Teacher's manual available in Albanian, English, French, Hungarian, Polish, Romanian, Slovak and Spanish, each with its own ISBN.

2. • *La Gran redada de Gitanos*, Antonio Gómez Alfaro — PG - ISBN: 84-87347-09-6
   • *The Great Gypsy Round-up*, Antonio Gómez Alfaro — PG - ISBN: 84-87347-12-6
   • *La Grande rafle des Gitans*, Antonio Gómez Alfaro — CRDP - ISBN: 2-86565-083-9
   • *La grande retata dei Gitani*, Antonio Gómez Alfaro — ANICIA/CSZ - ISBN: 88-900078-2-6
   • *Marea prigonire a Rromilor*, Antonio Gómez Alfaro — EA - ISBN: 973-9216-35-8

3. • *Gypsies: from India to the Mediterranean*, Donald Kenrick — CRDP - ISBN: 2-86565-082-0
   • *Los Gitanos: de la India al Mediterráneo*, Donald Kenrick — PG - ISBN: 84-87347-13-4
   • *Les Tsiganes de l'Inde à la Méditerranée*, Donald Kenrick — CRDP - ISBN: 2-86565-081-2
   • *Zingari: dall'India al Mediterraneo*, Donald Kenrick — ANICIA/CSZ - ISBN: 88-900078-1-8
   • *Τσιγγάνοι: από τις Ινδίες στη Μεσόγειο*, Donald Kenrick — EK - ISBN: 960-03-1834-4
   • *Циганите: от Индия до Средиземно море*, Donald Kenrick — LIT - ISBN: 954-8537-56-7

4. • *Os Ciganos : Fontes bibliográficas em Portugal*, Elisa Mª Lopes da Costa — PG - ISBN: 84-87347-11-8

5. • *Textes des institutions internationales concernant les Tsiganes*, Marielle Danbakli — CRDP - ISBN: 2-86565-098-7
   • *On Gypsies: Texts issued by International Institutions*, Marielle Danbakli — CRDP - ISBN: 2-86565-099-5
   • *Текстове на международните институции за циганите*, Marielle Danbakli — LIT - ISBN: 954-8537-53-2

6. • *Gitans et flamenco*, Bernard Leblon — CRDP - ISBN: 2-86565-107-X
   • *Gypsies and Flamenco*, Bernard Leblon — UHP - ISBN: 0-900-45859-3
   • *Gitani e flamenco*, Bernard Leblon — ANICIA/CSZ - ISBN: 88-900078-8-5
   • *Gitanos und Flamenco*, Bernard Leblon — PA - ISBN: 3-88402-198-2

7. • *English Gypsies and State Policies*, David Mayall — UHP - ISBN: 0 0900458 64 X

8. • *Gypsies under the Swastika*, Donald Kenrick, Grattan Puxon — UHP - ISBN: 0 0900458 658
   • *Los Gitanos bajo la Cruz Gamada*, Donald Kenrick, Gratan Puxon — PG - ISBN: 84-87347-16-9
   • *Les Tsiganes sous l'oppression nazie*, Donald Kenrick, Grattan Puxon — CRDP - ISBN: 2-86565-172-X

9. • *Storia degli Zingari in Italia*, Giorgio Viaggio — ANICIA/CSZ - ISBN: 88-900078-9-3

10. • *Bibaxtale Berśa*, Donald Kenrick, Grattan Puxon — PG - ISBN: 84-87347-15-0

11. • *Minorité et scolarité : le parcours tsigane*, Jean-Pierre Liégeois — CRDP - ISBN: 2-86565-192-4
    • *School Provision for Ethnic Minorities : The Gypsy Paradigm*, J.-P. Liégeois — UHP - ISBN: 0 0900458 88 7

12. • *Sinti und Roma unter dem Nazi-Regime - 1 - Von der "Rassenforschung" zu den Lagern*, K. Fings, H. Heuß, F. Sparing, Einleitung H. Asséo — PA - ISBN: 3-88402-188-5
    • *De la "science raciale" aux camps - Les Tsiganes dans la Seconde Guerre mondiale 1*, K. Fings, H. Heuss, F. Sparing, préface H. Asséo — CRDP - ISBN: 2-86565-186-X
    • *From "Race Science" to the Camps, The Gypsies during the Second World War 1*, K. Fings, H. Heuss, F. Sparing, foreword by H. Asséo — UHP - ISBN: 0-900-458 78 X

14 • *Un ragazzo zingaro nella mia classe*, G. Donzello, B. M. Karpati — ANICIA/CSZ - ISBN: 88-900078-4-2

Rukun :
- *O Rukun ʒal and-i skòla*, Research and Action Group on Romani Linguistics — RB - ISBN: 2-9507850-1-8
- *Kaj si o Rukun amaro ?* Research and Action Group on Romani Linguistics — RB - ISBN: 2-9507850-2-6
- *I bari lavenqi pustik e Rukunesqiri*, Research and Action Group on Romani Linguistics — RB - ISBN: 2-9507850-3-4

Publishers' addresses :

- **ANICIA**   Via San Francesco a Ripa, 62
  I - 00153 - Roma

- **CRDP**   Centre Régional
  de Documentation Pédagogique Midi-Pyrénées
  3 rue Roquelaine
  F - 31069 - Toulouse Cedex

- **CSZ**   Centro Studi Zingari / Laćo Drom
  Via dei Barbieri, 22
  I - 00186 - Roma

- **EA**   Editura Alternative
  Casa Presei, Corp. B, Et. 4
  Piaţa Presei Libere, 1
  RO - 71341 - Bucureşti 1

- **EK**   Editions Kastaniotis / ΕΚΔΟΣΕΙΣ ΚΑΣΤΑΝΙΩΤΗ
  11, Zalogou
  GR - 106 78 - Athènes

- **LIT**   Editions Litavra / за ИК »ДИТАВРА«
  Gurguliat 6
  BG - 1000 - Sofia

- **PA**   Edition Parabolis
  Schliemannstraße 23
  D - 10437 Berlin

- **PG**   Editorial Presencia Gitana
  Valderrodrigo, 76 y 78
  E - 28039 Madrid

- **RB**   Rromani Baxt
  22, rue du Port
  F - 63000 - Clermont-Ferrand

- **UHP**   University of Hertfordshire Press
  College Lane Hatfield
  UK - Hertfordshire AL10 9AB

- *Irish distributor:* Pavee Point Travellers Centre
  46 North Great Charles Street
  IRL - Dublin 1